About the editors

Susan Parnell is an urban geogra⸏⸏⸏ in the Department of Environmental and Geographical Sciences at the University of Cape Town (UCT). She is centrally involved in the African Centre for Cities, serving on its executive. Prior to her appointment at UCT she taught in the Wits University Geography Department (Johannesburg) and the School of Oriental and African Studies (London). She has held academic fellowships at Oxford, the London School of Economics and Political Science (LSE), Durham and University College London. Other recent books include: *A Routledge Handbook on Cities of the Global South* (co-edited with S. Oldfield; Routledge, 2014); *Urbanization, Biodiversity and Ecosystem Services: Challenges and opportunities. A global assessment* (co-edited with T. Elmqvist, M. Fragkias, J. Goodness, B. Güneralp, P. Marcotullio, R. McDonald, M. Schewenius, M. Sendstad, K. Seto and C. Wilkinson; Springer, 2013); *Climate Change at the City Scale: Impacts, mitigation and adaptation in Cape Town* (co-edited with A. Cartwright, G. Oelofse and S. Ward; Earthscan, 2012); and the four-volume *Key Issues in the 21st Century. Urban Studies: Society* (co-edited with R. Paddison, D. McNeill, W. Ostendorf and S. Teisdell; Sage, 2010).

Edgar Pieterse is holder of the South African Research Chair in Urban Policy. He is director of the African Centre for Cities and professor in the School of Architecture, Planning and Geomatics, both at the University of Cape Town. Recent books include: *Rogue Urbanism: Emergent African cities* (Jacana, 2013); *African Cities Reader I & II* (Chimurenga, 2010 and 2011); *City Futures: Confronting the crisis of urban development* (Zed Books, 2008); and *Counter-Currents: Experiments in sustainability in the Cape Town region* (Jacana, 2010). In 2010 he co-founded an international biannual magazine, *Cityscapes*. At present, Pieterse is leading a national policy process to craft the Integrated Urban Development Framework for the South African government.

Africa's urban revolution

edited by Susan Parnell and Edgar Pieterse

AFRICAN CENTRE FOR CITIES

Zed Books

LONDON | NEW YORK

Africa's Urban Revolution was first published in 2014 by Zed Books Ltd, 7 Cynthia Street, London N1 9JF, UK and Room 400, 175 Fifth Avenue, New York, NY 10010, USA

www.zedbooks.co.uk

Set in OurType Arnhem, Monotype Gill Sans Heavy
by Ewan Smith, London
Index: ed.emery@thefreeuniversity.net
Cover designed by Rawshock Design
Cover photo © Leon Krige
Printed and bound by TJ International Ltd, Padstow, Cornwall

Distributed in the USA exclusively by Palgrave Macmillan, a division of St Martin's Press, LLC, 175 Fifth Avenue, New York, NY 10010, USA

A catalogue record for this book is available from the British Library
Library of Congress Cataloging in Publication Data available

ISBN 978 1 78032 521 7 hb
ISBN 978 1 78032 520 0 pb

Contents

Figures, tables and box

Figures

Tables

Box

Acknowledgements

This volume is the culmination of a series of dialogues and research exchanges that the African Centre for Cities (ACC) has facilitated since its founding at the University of Cape Town (UCT) in 2008. With the establishment of ACC we were determined to create Africa-wide platforms that would allow scholars, practitioners, policy managers and activists to convene on a regular basis to interrogate the urban development *problematique*, in order to foster an endogenous reading of 'the urban' that was both theoretically robust and connected to fields of practice. The first of these was the African Urban Innovations Workshop that we convened in Cape Town on 1–5 September 2008. It was a fascinating week of exchange and deep learning that was made possible through funding from the Rockefeller Foundation. The synthesis of this workshop is captured in Chapter 11 of this volume, but at the time it formed the basis for an African input into the World Urban Forum in Nanjing, China. Since then, ACC has convened various sessions focusing on urban development policy imperatives in Africa at every World Urban Forum gathering, slowly but surely seeding many of the perspectives collected in this volume.

The Innovations Workshop put ACC in a good position to host the launch of the African chapter of the Sustainable Urban Development Network (SUD-Net), an initiative of UN-Habitat aimed at nurturing a network of actors and existing networks to promote a multilateral and interdisciplinary approach to sustainable urban development. The launch happened in February 2009 and was supported by UN-Habitat and the Swedish International Development Cooperation Agency (SIDA). In fact, this volume is in print in large measure due to SIDA's commitment to promote critical, independent scholarship on the policy implications of African urban transition. Their support is deeply appreciated.

Inevitably, the intellectual currents that emerged from these processes drew on and infected numerous other of ACC's continental initiatives, such as the Association of African Planning Schools, the State of African Cities programme, and the African Food Security Urban Network. Some of the chapters in this volume explicitly reflect this cross-pollination. Also included are two articles originally published in *Global Environmental Change* and *Population and Development Review*. Thanks to Elsevier and Wiley for permission to republish. An extended version of Chapter 8 appeared in *Urbanisation and Socio-economic Development in Africa: Challenges and opportunities*, edited by Steve Kayizzi-Mugerwa, Abebe Shimeles and Nadège Désirée Yaméogo (Routledge, 2013). We are grateful to all our colleagues in ACC, our associates and friends and the various networks that we anchor for the intellectual generosity that has been important for the credibility of this volume. Thanks to Ken Barlow, Judith Forshaw, Ewan Smith and the rest of the Zed team, who are an absolute pleasure to work with.

The most important person responsible for the realisation of this volume is our highly valued research assistant, Saskia Greyling. She always goes well beyond the call of duty to get things done and her fingerprints are all over this book. In fact, we dedicate this volume to the new crop of African urban scholars and students who are happy to explore a world beyond binaries and certainty and who are conscious of the imperative of being ethically grounded. We hope that our contribution to the ceaseless work of meaning making will aid their journey and bring much needed new insights into the world.

Finally, we need to acknowledge the generous and consistent support of SIDA, the Rockefeller Foundation, Mistra Urban Futures, the National Research Foundation, Stellenbosch Institute for Advanced Study, UCT Signature Theme and the African Centre on this journey.

Susan Parnell and Edgar Pieterse
Cape Town, July 2013

1 | Africa's urban revolution in context

Edgar Pieterse and Susan Parnell

'Revolution: ... *any fundamental change or reversal of conditions*'
(*The Concise Oxford Dictionary*, 9th edition, 1995)

Africa's dramatic demographic transition is a profoundly spatial story. Not only will the continent give birth to thousands of new towns and cities as it crosses the 'magical' 50 per cent urban threshold shortly after 2030 (UN DESA 2011), the absolute growth of population and the increasing concentration of Africa's people in cities will transform the landscape of the urban hinterlands as demand for building material, food, energy and water escalates. This is not a future transition; the African urban revolution is already firmly under way. The continent is 40 per cent urbanised at present, which means that there are 414 million African urbanites (2011 figures), and Africa already has more city dwellers than Europe, Australasia, North or South America. Only Asia has more people living in cities. The overarching argument of this book is that Africa's urban transition, which manifests across sectors as diverse as transport, education and religion, is not afforded the serious attention that it needs or deserves. Impacts from the rise of an urban Africa are formative locally, but will reverberate globally (see Chapter 11). Our main concern is to sharpen the awareness of world policy makers (from those in local government to the global institutions that wield power at the city scale), but we are hopeful that scholars, civil society activists and business leaders will also find value in the chapters and that collectively we can debate competing visions to ensure a positive outcome for Africa's inevitable urban revolution.

The purpose of this introductory chapter is to set the scene for the chapters that follow by presenting trend data on the speed, scope and dynamics of the urban transition. Of course, the revolution that is occurring is not just about numbers; it is also about Africa's urban leadership, institutions and technical domains, such as design, technology and finance. Mindful of the importance of the general lack of capacity to manage the rupture that is taking place all across Africa because of the shift to cities and the absolute growth in population (UNCHS 1996; Stren and White 1989), we look back over the postcolonial era to identify the historical forces framing the policy context for Africa's present and its urban future. We have included a chapter on war and conflict (by Beall and Goodfellow) in the opening section of the book as a sobering reminder that violence, while not necessarily centred on cities or taking place throughout the continent, is disproportionally influential in shaping the contemporary African landscape. Many of the chapters take as their central concern the persistence of widespread urban poverty; the depth of chronic poverty is another distinguishing feature of African cities compared with those elsewhere in the world. Notwithstanding the very low levels of average income on which urban Africans survive, taken together the chapters present an optimistic outlook on the changes that are likely to be ushered in by the urban revolution and offer new ways of imagining African urbanism.

One word of caution is imperative. The scope of this book is continental, and this scale brings with it problems of generalisation. Africa incorporates over 50 countries, thousands of cities and millions of people. Africa is a vast territory (larger than China, India, the USA or all of Europe), with many different climate zones and a complex web of cultures, religions and languages: there is no one Africa. The African urban revolution cannot be seen through a solitary prism, just as responses to the dilemmas and opportunities raised in the book's chapters must, of necessity, be numerous. The volume has no coherent or singular argument or position, other than to assert the absolute importance of cities. We are hopeful that we will provoke a realisation of the need to build a larger policy and intellectual project to understand, contest and shape Africa's urban futures. In this sense, our book stands alongside a companion volume that dwells more on the phenomenological, cultural and aesthetic dimensions of African urbanism (Pieterse and Simone 2013).

So what if Africa is urban?

Time and numbers do matter. Location matters too. Under conditions of rapid and large-scale change, simple questions such as how many people there are and where exactly they plan to live over their lifespans become critical, especially if you are disbursing scarce resources or making long-term decisions that will fix the infrastructure on which tens of millions of people's livelihoods and prosperity depend. The purpose of this section is to draw attention to the scale, rate and dynamics of urbanisation in Africa in order to contextualise the policy imperatives faced by those tasked with managing the building and maintenance of African cities, the stimulus of their economies and the protection of the most vulnerable of their residents or natural systems. The bigger picture also puts the struggles of ordinary people, to access food (see Chapter 6) or to find affordable transport (see Chapter 7) into perspective. In other words, our objective is to get a sense of the nature of the shift in the size of the population and the associated changes in settlement patterns to assess what urban growth and higher levels of urbanisation mean for policy and politics in Africa. Fox's account (Chapter 14) probes in much greater detail the specificity of Africa's path towards urbanisation and the relationship between

1.1a Roman Catholic Cathedral at Kampala (*source*: Light 1941, plates 224)

urbanisation and industrialisation, where the African record is one that defies traditional expectations. Underlying his account, and indeed the book as a whole, is the question of African urban exceptionalism. Closer scrutiny of particular places and issues will negate a generalisation of the African city, but we would suggest that there are at least some common themes regarding drivers of change on the continent that relate to the time frame and form of the urban revolution in Africa.

Africa is at least unusual in that its urban transition has, compared with that of other world regions (except parts of Asia), been delayed. At the point of colonial independence, most of Africa was predominantly rural, with less than one in eight people living in a town (Freund 2007). Not only that, as captured by some of the first aerial photography of Africa, undertaken by Mary Light and published in a text authored by Richard Upjohn Light in 1941, most urban centres that did exist were either small colonial towns (Figures 1.1a, b and c) or traditional villages (Figure 1.1d). As the post-World War Two population expanded – a result of, among other things, the introduction of antibiotics – three factors transformed Africa's settlement experience. First, the number of new towns and cities increased; second, at the same time the proportion of people living in cities rather than in the countryside grew; and

1.1b Dar es Salaam port (*source*: Light 1941, plates 149)

finally there was a significant rise in the number of very large cities, some of which, such as Lagos and greater Kinshasa, are predicted soon to be among the world's largest metropolitan centres (UNCHS 1996; McKinsey Global Institute 2012). Today, Africa's 50 largest cities all have populations of over a million people (Figure 1.2), roughly the size of Birmingham in the United Kingdom or Amsterdam, Holland's largest city. Africa is no longer a continent of villages and towns; it encompasses the full spectrum of scale in urban settlement.

1.1c 'Nairobi, metropolis of East Africa' (*source*: Light 1941, plates 226)

Although the antecedents of Africa's urban revolution can be traced to the second half of the twentieth century (Simon 1992; O'Conner 1983; Iliffe 1995), it is only now that the size and importance of urban Africa are becoming widely apparent. Along with the belated acknowledgement of the increasingly dominant urban reality has come the imperative to radically reconfigure professional and policy responses to Africa's human settlements (see Chapter 10; Parnell et al. 2009; Myers 2011; Pieterse 2008). The last formal cross-national collation of population figures from across the continent is for 2011, over 50 years into the postcolonial era, by which time Africa's population was already almost 40 per cent urban (Figure 1.3). The United Nations Department of Economic and Social Affairs (UN DESA) forecasts that Africa will be 50 per cent urban by the early 2030s and 60 per cent urban by 2050. What these percentages imply for those managing cities on the ground is more revealing

1.1d Bari village (*source*: Light 1941, plates 284)

if we consider the numerical scale of urban growth as reflected in Figure 1.3. Everybody accepts that the data are problematic. Nevertheless, several scholars are at pains to show that Africa's rate of natural population growth, which is the highest in the world, is a more significant factor in understanding the urban transition than migration from rural areas (see Chapter 3; Potts 2012; McGranahan et al. 2009). This point about the relative importance of natural urban growth and migration, which are both driving Africa's urban expansion, is significant because it reveals why, no matter what governments try to do to keep development and people in rural areas, increasing levels of urbanisation are probably inevitable and must be confronted.

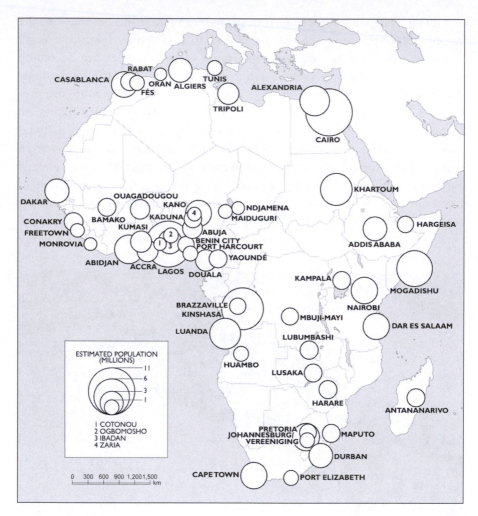

1.2 Africa's largest urban centres

As a number of the chapters in this book reveal (see especially Chapter 4), in the economic revival of the continent, decades of experience have shown that urbanisation is a central characteristic of Africa's recent past, and that it has also had largely desirable developmental outcomes. Across this volume, the authors take the position that the anti-urban bias of previous generations, most infamously articulated by Lipton (1977), is outmoded, and that Africa's future is, opportunely, urban. However, there is also consensus that the rapidity of the urban transition (as shown in Figure 1.3) has put great stress on the ability of Africa's urban leaders to manage change.

The overarching point to be taken from the data in Figure 1.3 is that both urban and rural populations are expanding, but that cities are growing faster. Africa's urbanisation trend line is most like that of Asia (even though the absolute numbers of people are vastly different), but completely different to

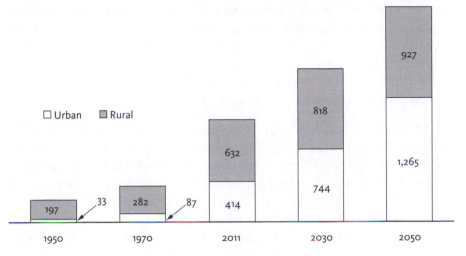

1.3 Africa's rural and urban population, 1950–2050 (millions) (*source*: UN DESA 2012)

the pattern in Latin America and most Organisation for Economic Co-operation and Development (OECD) countries (see Figure 1.4). This is very important because it ties in with Africa's unique place in the global economy and how its position impacts on the policy landscape that shapes how 'the urban' is perceived and addressed by African policy makers. We return to this point later on. This comparison is also important because it reminds us that Africa and Asia have had to manage their respective urban transitions in vastly different conditions to those faced by other world regions when they confronted the rapid expansion of cities and the shift of national population distribution through urbanisation. For instance, Africa must deal with the foundations of urban management, including the supply of basic services and supporting network infrastructure, but it must do this in a manner that ensures a highly efficient urban form and metabolism because of the new imperatives for low-carbon economies and settlements (UNEP 2012). The fiscal arrangements of urban construction have, in the late twentieth and early twenty-first centuries, also become much more international, removing or reducing the power of local elites over the big infrastructure investments.

How Africans manage their urban revolution is not a matter solely of domestic importance. The United Nations Population Fund usefully summarises the longitudinal dynamics that sit behind the global demographic shifts illustrated in Figure 1.4 and sets out the wider ramifications where demographic change is taking place:

At the world level, the 20th century saw an increase from 220 million urbanites in 1900 to 2.84 billion in 2000. The present century will match this absolute increase in about four decades. Developing regions as a whole will account for 93 per cent of this growth – Asia and Africa for over 80 per cent.

7

Between 2000 and 2030, Asia's urban population will increase from 1.36 billion to 2.64 billion, Africa's from 294 million to 742 million, and that of Latin America and the Caribbean (LAC) from 394 million to 609 million. As a result of these shifts, developing countries will have 80 per cent of the world's urban population in 2030. By then, Africa and Asia will include almost seven out of every ten urban inhabitants in the world.[1] (UNFPA 2007: 7–8)

The time frames in which the escalation of the number of people in the world and the shift in their geographical location have taken place are staggering. However, they mask the fact that, once we establish the broad quantum of how many people are classified as living in urban settlements, we need, immediately, to move down in scale and consider the immense diversity of settlement size and the internal capacity of urban places. Like most other regions in the world, the vast majority of urban Africans live in cities or towns of fewer than 0.5 million people, and will probably continue to do so. It is projected that by 2015, 54 per cent of the urban population will live in settlements with fewer than 0.5 million people; this compares with 9.9 per cent in cities of between 0.5 and 1 million; 26.1 per cent in cities of 1–5 million; 2.4 per cent in cities of 5–10 million; and only 7.5 per cent in cities with

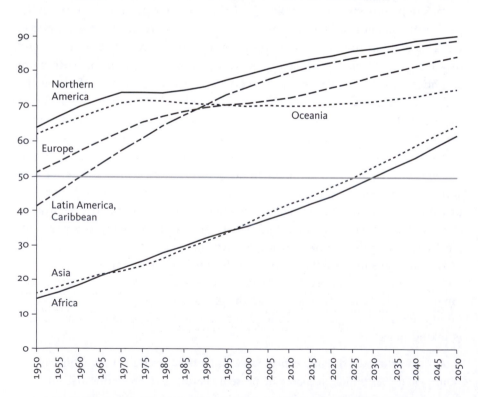

1.4 Percentage of the population that is urban by geographic area, 1950–2050 (*source*: UN DESA 2012)

more than 10 million people (UN DESA 2012: 282). This distribution of the urban population differs profoundly from the populist image of megacities exploding all over Africa and Asia. The institutional reality, however, is that small cities and towns are not immune from crisis. While large cities in the global South present specific management challenges precisely because of their scale, the concentration of poverty and the paucity of municipal capacity (UN-Habitat 2009), few small urban settlements, especially in Africa, have a viable local government or a tax base capable of supporting a more equitable and just pattern of investment (see Chapter 8). Making the requisite fiscal and governance reforms to accommodate the new realities of African settlements requires both political will and administrative reform. As Parnell and Simon discuss in Chapter 13, to date African governments have been slow to respond to the urban revolution that is transforming their nations by reprioritising their expenditure and policy focus.

Just as important as the size of any one city is the system of cities of which it is a part. African cities have several distinctive features. First, they are integrally connected to rural areas through the practice of circular migration, a strategy for maintaining multiple bases so as to optimise livelihoods and mitigate the risks of settling permanently in economically, environmentally, socially or politically precarious African towns (Potts 2012; Chapter 12). Second, there is the sponge of the urban fringe or peri-urban edge; this is often a porous settlement boundary which is neither urban nor rural in its character or governance (Gough and Yankson 2000). What is also distinctive in Africa is the phenomenon of urban primacy, which in many African countries is a direct hangover from the colonial era (Myers 2011; O'Conner 1983). Urban primacy refers to the dynamic whereby one large capital city serves as the centre point of the national settlement system and is typically three to four times larger than the second largest city in the country. Maputo in Mozambique is a typical example. This dynamic makes the governance of these large primate cities highly contentious, especially as newer political opposition parties tend to make their biggest inroads in these cities (Resnick 2012; see also Chapters 2 and 13). In other words, primate cities can overshadow other settlements in political importance and centrality, challenging national power and on occasion making governments reticent about embracing urban issues such as land use, planning reform and professional training (see Chapters 9 and 10) or about dealing with specifically urban problems that require complex governance at the city scale, such as transport (see Chapter 7).

Another distinctive feature of urban Africa is the predominance of informal modes of urbanisation in terms of both social and economic reproduction. In Chapter 12, Simone gives some indication of the complex adjustments urban slum residents have to embrace in order to navigate the dysfunctionalities imposed on their everyday existence. Rakodi, in Chapter 5, reminds us that nowadays residents rarely depend wholly on the state or on traditional leaders for social assistance or community organisation, since there is a range of faith-based structures acting as critical institutional intermediaries to navigate power in African cities. The problem for residents and their organisations is that it is not always clear with whom they should be interacting in their efforts to improve urban livelihoods, especially of the poor. African cities, more than most others, are characterised by overlapping and even competing systems of power. Learning where power lies in the city can be as challenging as persuading those in power of the need for change.

Poverty, informality and the absence of a strong local state with a clear and unchallenged mandate to manage the city are arguably the leitmotifs of African urbanism today. The most telling illustration of this is the extremely high level of 'slum' living conditions in Africa, even compared with other regions in the global South. Table 1.1 compares the percentage of urban dwellers living in areas formally designated as slums and breaks down those statistics further to demonstrate the depth of deprivation by showing the number of deficiencies to which slum dwellers are subjected (UN-Habitat 2008). It should be noted that both the reintroduction of the use of the pejorative word 'slum' and its formal definition are widely contested (Gilbert 2007). Perhaps for this reason, the first UN-Habitat *State of African Cities* report nuanced the rather crude original definition of a slum by tabulating whether slums are moderately deficient (one or two deficiencies of the five listed in endnote 2) or severely deficient (three or four deficiencies). Data in Table 1.1 are based on the UN-Habitat classification of slum dwellers.[2] What is significant here is the regional variation, rather than the conceptual or measured integrity of any particular variable.

TABLE 1.1 Percentage of urban dwellers living in slums in three developing regions, 2005

Region	In slums	With moderate (1–2) deficiencies	With severe (3–4) deficiencies
Sub-Saharan Africa	62	63	27
Latin America and the Caribbean	27	82	18
Southern Asia	43	95	5

Source: UN-Habitat 2008: 90.

The manifestations of slum life – severe overcrowding, lack of sanitation, constant threat of bodily harm and abuse, and so on – are linked to the structural poverty and systemic exclusion experienced by a large proportion of the urban population in most African cities, even those that have high average incomes and service standards, such as Accra, Gaborone or Johannesburg. These depressing conditions are made more intractable because of the extremely high levels of income inequality that exist. Urban inequality in Africa, measured in terms of the Gini coefficient, is already among the highest in the world, rivalling Latin America (Africa Progress Panel 2012). In the larger African economies such as South Africa, income inequality is far more severely skewed, with Gini ratios of over 0.7 for many of the largest cities (UN-Habitat 2008). The Gini coefficient depends on income data, and so is a notoriously inaccurate measure, especially in Africa where data are not generally robust. But as Crush and Frayne show in Chapter 6 on food security, in Africa, where measures of social protection are all but absent for most urbanites, the amount of money a household can lay its hands on is a key determinant of survival. Food security, they argue, is more than just affordability; it is also the outcome of availability and distribution or access. In African cities, these aspects are precarious, and so millions of urbanites go hungry – one of the most tangible expressions of poverty.

It is also surprisingly difficult to secure accurate data about the levels of access to basic services in rural and urban areas in African countries. Most of the data are aggregated at a national level, and service delivery standards are not factored to reflect the differential costs between urban and rural areas (Mitlin and Satterthwaite 2013). Figure 1.5 provides a snapshot of how much Africa lags behind other world regions with regard to basic services.

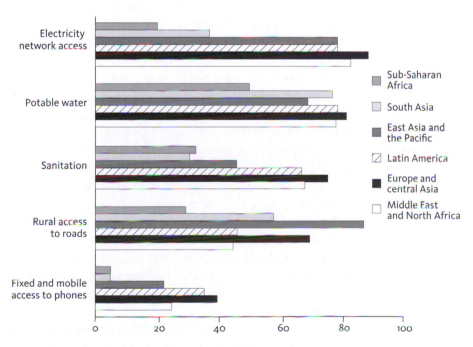

1.5 Percentage of people with access to selected basic services (*source*: Ajulu and Motsamai 2008: 3)

The scale of slum conditions in most African cities and towns can be linked to a variety of factors. Most importantly, it stems from the contradictions in the urban land management system and a general outmoded code of practice for land use control (see Chapter 9). Cities in Africa typically have the worst of two inappropriate regulatory systems. It is not uncommon for there to be areas of the town (often on the edge) where there are traditional land use controls that were intended for subsistence-based settlements. Overlaying these traditional practices are laws administered by municipalities that date from the colonial era (Mamdani 1996). Modernist legislation and urban standards, a system of urban management that was intended to protect elite colonial interests rather than provide for universal application in postcolonial African cities, continued to serve as a template for urban planning, land use regulation and public housing provision during the post-independence era. Postcolonial governments hardly changed either of the earlier urban management schemes, and the result is one of planning ambiguity, confusion and even chaos. Taken together, the complex urban governance regimes, diffuse fiscal interests, rapid growth of the population and pent-up poverty create a volatile cocktail that should make the African urban revolution a key global issue. The collective response, however, is complacency.

The lack of transparency in urban management law and practice has not, until recently, been challenged or reformed, possibly because of lack of demand for effective or transparent urban government from developers. It is also possible that what happened, or failed to happen, in cities was not seen as especially important politically. The ruling party in national governments also typically fixated on national political ambitions and displayed a deep ambivalence towards the importance of decentralised government (Myers 2010). Initially this emphasis on the national interest was understandable as these were vulnerable governments, often espousing radical ideologies during the Cold War era and also stuck in dependency relationships with former metropole economies. Cities were small and rural development was prioritised because it fitted neatly with nationalist ideologies that equated a return to 'the land' with postcolonial freedom. When the lean years of structural adjustment rolled in (roughly the 1980s to the mid-2000s) and social investments were severely cut, urban areas, which were already profoundly deficient in terms of infrastructure and associated services, were badly hit. Under structural adjustment, cuts in public sector funding and the shrinking of the civil service depleted already weak local government. As a result, at exactly the time when urbanisation across Africa was increasing, there was inadequate local government to address the related challenges (Rakodi 1997).

African economies had also stagnated for most of this period (from 1960 to the 2000s) as a result of active mismanagement, highly disadvantaged connections with the global economy, rent-seeking and profligate elites and limited fixed investments manifesting as systemic dysfunctionality (Chabal 2009; Mbembe 2001; Chapter 4). One, albeit limited, indicator that captures the impact of this situation is the lack of improvement in gross domestic product (GDP) per capita values between 1960 and 2010. The report *African Futures 2050*, published by the Pardee Center for International Futures and the Institute for Security Studies, explains that over the entire half-century (1960–2010), 'Eastern Africa gained only about $150 per capita and Western Africa about $130 per capita, while GDP per capita in Central Africa has remained almost unchanged since 1960' (Cilliers et al. 2011: 30). This is an unfathomable accomplishment of economic, political and social failure. In practical terms, it means that the formal economy remained very small and provided secure employment for only a fraction of the labour force. Consequently, by 2012, despite more than a decade of robust GDP growth, it was reported by the Economic Commission for Africa (ECA) and the African Union (AU) that '[m]ore than 70 per cent of Africans earn their living from vulnerable employment as African economies continue to depend heavily on the production and export of primary commodities' (ECA et al. 2012: 13). This impact of this dynamic is most pernicious on the youth. The same report finds that:

> only 17 per cent of working youth have full-time wage employment in the low-income countries. The proportion is 39 per cent in the lower middle-income countries and 52 per cent in the upper middle-income countries. (ibid.: 14)

The dearth of urban work and the inadequate incomes of urban youth make the confluence of Africa's demographic and urbanisation transitions painful. The urban youth of Africa are disadvantaged both relative to older African populations already living in cities and in comparison to the same age cohort in cities in other world regions. Africa's share of the global population was just under 15 per cent in 2010 and it is expected to reach 23 per cent by 2050 (Africa Progress Panel 2012: 34). This reflects in part the fact that Africa has the fastest growth rate of the 0–14 years cohort, and as a proportion of its total population this youth bulge has not yet peaked. It also points to a substantial youthful population that will require education, healthcare services, housing and, of course, and most importantly, stable employment (see Figure 1.6). If stable employment, with regular income, even if low, is not achievable, it is impossible to solve the problem of slum formation.

Relatively mainstream multilateral institutions in Africa have come to a very similar conclusion about the implications of the exponential growth of urban youth:

> Strong growth across the continent has not been translated into the broad-based economic and social development needed to lift millions of Africans out of poverty and reduce the high levels of inequality experienced in most

countries. On the contrary, the continent continues to suffer from high levels of unemployment, particularly for the young and female population, with limited opportunities to absorb new labour market entrants. (ECA et al. 2012: 12)

It is against this alternative account of Africa's urban population growth that the unbridled optimism of reports by private sector think tanks such as McKinsey Global Institute (2012), Monitor (2009), Hatch et al. (2011) and others needs to be considered. The reports basically tell a story that assumes that GDP growth will remain the primary development goal and political priority. The logic is that economic growth will enlarge a middle class of consumers who can contribute, through investments and demand, to a sectoral diversification of African economies. Within this, cities are the linchpin to drive increased consumer demand and ensure greater economic productivity. If governments can get their acts together to invest in the 'right' kinds of basic and connective infrastructures – roads, ports, airports, information and communications technology (ICT), energy, water and so on – then they will also be able to make doing business easier. Despite the crude development policy thinking that shapes many of these glossy reports (with some notable exceptions), it seems that the new private sector actors have a real impact on the policy landscape, outstripping the influence of scholars, civil society pressure groups and the old-style development industry. It is not immediately clear why there has been such a noticeable shift with regards to who sets the intellectual agenda on African development, but it may be related to the growing volumes

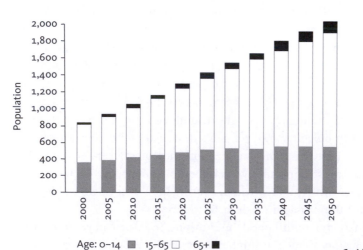

Age: 0–14 ■   15–65 □   65+ ■

Age	2010	%	2050	%
0–14	416m	40	546m	27
15–65	582m	56	1,320m	66
65+	35m	4	142m	7
Total	1,033m	100	2,008m	100

1.6 Africa's demographic structure by age cohort, 2000–50 (population in millions) (*source*: UN DESA 2011)

of highly targeted and partial foreign direct investment (FDI) flowing into African countries, investment that is contributing to the further distortion of African urban landscapes (Van Synghel and de Boeck 2013).

In summary, Africa displays the fastest rate of urban growth in the world, albeit from a low base level. However, at the moment most African countries are not able to capitalise on this demographic shift, because urban residents are structurally trapped in profoundly unhealthy conditions that impact negatively on productivity, economic efficiencies and market expansion. As a consequence of sluggish economic performance, the tax base in African cities remains limited and fragile, making it difficult for governments to raise the revenues necessary to address the litany of urban ills referred to here. Yet the global economy is shifting its axis to the emerging powers, at the same time there is a broader shift towards a fundamentally different, much more resource-efficient economy, and technological opportunities are emerging to fuse citizenship and urban living; within this context the African urban transition could be truly revolutionary. However, this demands a different scholarly agenda to what has been the norm for some time. The rise of Africa's cities will not be ignored. How the revolution is navigated will depend on how well the forces of change are understood and taken up. In this regard the role of the continent's intellectuals in framing the debate about cities must be underscored.

The chapters that follow focus on key aspects of the urban revolution that are currently taking place in Africa. They were all written by scholars and/ or practitioners who, as staff, students, associates or funders, have a close association with the African Centre for Cities (ACC). Restricting authorship in this way was intentional. ACC is an interdisciplinary research hub based at the University of Cape Town, one of the very few African institutions able to draw on the critical intellectual mass necessary to produce a volume that can address a continental urban agenda. This volume highlights specific aspects of the urban transition that has been experienced most acutely in Africa, compared with the process in other parts of the world, but further study will need detailed sectoral and city-specific work from across the continent. In order to get to grips with what exactly Africa's urban revolution implies for specific cities, particular countries and the rest of the world, careful research, critical reflection and sound leadership are vital. As the continent that will be disproportionately shaped by the way in which society thinks about cities, Africa must assume an increasingly central position in the urban imaginary of theorists and practitioners. With this challenge in mind, the contributors to this book have set out substantive areas of academic and policy concern in which the urban revolution is driving change across the continent.

Notes

1 It is important to heed the warning that urban projections that go too far into the future, e.g. 2030, must be treated with great circumspection because the underlying data sets for many developing countries remain extremely problematic (Satterthwaite 2007).

2 A slum household is defined as a group of individuals living under the same roof and lacking one or more of the following conditions: access to improved water; access to improved sanitation facilities; sufficient living area (not more than three people sharing the same room); structural quality and durability of dwellings; and security of tenure. Four out of five of the slum definition indicators measure physical expressions of slum conditions. These indicators focus attention on the circumstances that surround slum life, showing deficiencies and poverty as attributes of the environments in which slum dwellers live. The fifth indicator – security of tenure – has to do with legality, which is not as easy to measure or monitor, as the tenure status of slum dwellers often depends on de facto or de jure rights – or lack of them. This indicator has special relevance for measuring the denial and violation of housing rights, as well as the progressive fulfilment of those rights (UN-Habitat 2008: 92).

References

Africa Progress Panel (2012) *Africa Progress Report 2012. Jobs, justice and equity: Seizing opportunities in times of global change*. Geneva: Africa Progress Panel.

Ajulu, C. and D. Motsamai (2008) *The Pan-African Infrastructure Development Fund (PAIDF): Towards an African agenda*. Global Insight 76. Johannesburg: Institute for Global Dialogue.

Chabal, P. (2009) *Africa: The politics of suffering and smiling*. London: Zed Books.

Cilliers, J., B. Hughes and J. Moyer (2011) *African Futures 2050: The next forty years*. ISS Monograph 175. Pretoria: Institute for Security Studies.

ECA, AU and ADB (2009) *Assessing Progress in Africa toward the Millennium Development Goals. MDG Report 2009*. Addis Ababa: Economic Commission for Africa (ECA), African Union (AU) and African Development Bank (ADB).

— (2012) *Assessing Progress in Africa toward the Millennium Development Goals. MDG Report 2012: Emerging perspectives from Africa on the post-2015 development agenda*. Addis Ababa: Economic Commission for Africa (ECA), African Union (AU) and African Development Bank (ADB).

Freund, B. (2007) *The African City: A history*. Cambridge: Cambridge University Press.

Gilbert, A. (2007) 'The return of the slum: does language matter?'. *International Journal of Urban and Regional Research* 31(4): 697–713.

Gough, K. V. and P. W. Yankson (2000) 'Land markets in African cities: the case of peri-urban Accra, Ghana'. *Urban Studies* 37(13): 2485–500.

Hatch, G., P. Becker and M. van Zyl (2011) *The Dynamic African Consumer Market: Exploring growth opportunities in sub-Saharan Africa*. Pretoria: Accenture.

Iliffe, J. (1995) *Africans: The history of a continent*. Cambridge: Cambridge University Press.

Light, M. (1941) 'Plate photographs'. In R. Light, *Focus on Africa*. Special Publication No. 25. New York, NY: American Geographical Society.

Lipton, M. (1977) *Why Poor People Stay Poor: A study of urban bias in world development*. London: Temple-Smith.

Mamdani, M. (1996) *Citizen and Subject: Contemporary Africa and the legacy of late colonialism*. Princeton, NJ: Princeton University Press.

Mbembe, A. (2001) *On the Postcolony*. Berkeley and Los Angeles, CA: University of California Press.

McGranahan, G., D. Mitlin, D. Satterthwaite, C. Tacoli and I. Turok (2009) *Africa's Urban Transition and the Role of Regional Collaboration*. Human Settlements Working Paper Series. Theme:

Urban Change No. 5. London: International Institute for Environment and Development.

McKinsey Global Institute (2012) *Africa at Work: Job creation and inclusive growth*. Washington, DC: McKinsey Global Institute.

Mitlin, D. and D. Satterthwaite (2013) *Urban Poverty in the Global South: Scale and nature*. Abingdon: Routledge.

Monitor (2009) *Africa from the Bottom Up: Cities, economic growth, and prosperity in sub-Saharan Africa*. Houghton, South Africa: Monitor Group.

Myers, G. A. (2010) *Seven Themes in African Urban Dynamics*. Discussion Paper No. 50. Uppsala: Nordiska Afrikainstitutet.

— (2011) *African Cities: Alternative visions of urban theory and practice*. London: Zed Books.

O'Conner, A. (1983) *The African City*. London: Hutchinson.

Parnell, S., E. Pieterse and V. Watson (2009) 'Planning for cities in the global south: a research agenda for sustainable human settlements'. *Progress in Planning* 72(2): 233–41.

Pieterse, E. (2008) *City Futures: Confronting the crisis of urban development*. London: Zed Books.

Pieterse, E. and A. Simone (eds) (2013) *Rogue Urbanism: Emergent African cities*. Johannesburg: Jacana.

Potts, D. (2012) 'Viewpoint: what do we know about urbanisation in sub-Saharan Africa and does it matter?'. *International Development Planning Review* 34(1): v–xxii.

Rakodi, C. (ed.) (1997) *The Urban Challenge in Africa: Growth and management of its large cities*. Tokyo: United Nations University Press.

Resnick, D. (2012) 'Opposition parties and the urban poor in African democracies'. *Comparative Political Studies* 45(11): 1351–78.

Satterthwaite, D. (2007) *The Transition to a Predominantly Urban World and Its Underpinnings*. Human Settlements Discussion Paper. Theme: Urban Change No. 4. London: International Institute for Environment and Development.

Simon, D. (1992) *Cities, Capital and Development: African cities in the world economy*. London: Belhaven Press.

Stren, R. E. and R. R. White (eds) (1989) *African Cities in Crisis: Managing rapid urban growth*. Boulder, CO: Westview Press.

UNCHS (1996) *An Urbanizing World: Global report on human settlements 1996*. Oxford: Oxford University Press for United Nations Centre for Human Settlements (UNCHS).

UN DESA (2011) *World Population Prospects: The 2010 revision*. New York, NY: Population Division of the Department of Economic and Social Affairs of the United Nations Secretariat (UN DESA).

— (2012) *World Urbanization Prospects: The 2011 revision*. New York, NY: Population Division of the Department of Economic and Social Affairs of the United Nations Secretariat (UN DESA).

UNEP (2011) *Towards a Green Economy: Pathways to sustainable development and poverty eradication*. Paris: United Nations Environmental Programme (UNEP).

— (2012) *Sustainable, Resource Efficient Cities: Making it happen!* Paris: United Nations Environment Programme (UNEP).

UNFPA (2007) *State of the World Population 2007*. New York, NY: United Nations Population Fund (UNFPA).

UN-Habitat (2008) *State of the World's Cities 2008/2009: Harmonious cities*. London: Earthscan and United Nations Human Settlements Programme (UN-Habitat).

— (2009) *Planning Sustainable Cities: Global report on human settlements 2009*. London: Earthscan and United Nations Human Settlements Programme (UN-Habitat).

Van Synghel, K. and F. de Boeck (2013) 'Bylex's tourist city: a reflection on utopia in the post-political city'. In E. Pieterse and A. Simone (eds) *Rogue Urbanism: Emergent African cities*. Johannesburg: Jacana.

2 | Conflict and post-war transition in African cities

Jo Beall and Tom Goodfellow

Introduction

Cities in the developing world have often been viewed as sites of both contemporary misery and future dystopia (Hall and Pfeiffer 2000; Davis 2006). Part and parcel of this vision of apocalypse is the notion of cities as inevitable hubs of violent conflict; Safier wrote in 1996 of the 'frightening prospect' of 'chronic civic disorder brought about by the build-up of tension spilling over into explosive violence that is produced by conflict between groups ... sharing or invading the same urban space' (Safier 1996: 12). Meanwhile, until very recently at least, the whole African continent has likewise been subject to overwhelming pessimism: in a 1994 article entitled 'The coming anarchy', Kaplan termed Africa a 'dying region' (Kaplan 1994), and *The Economist* followed suit in 2000 with its cover page lamenting 'The hopeless continent'. The association of Africa with war and crisis thus combines with a more ubiquitous tendency of many urbanists towards 'noir' visions of the city (Judd 2005; Beall et al. 2010) to reinforce perceptions of African cities as the epitome of urban hell: 'the unsafest places in the world' (Kaplan 1994).

Yet it is far from clear that, even in the most war-torn or pervasively conflictual African states, cities have been the primary sites of violent conflict. Indeed, the position and role of urban areas in the myriad forms of conflict affecting the continent are still little understood. A countertendency in Western urban studies is to see cities in more utopian terms as vibrant, creative and convivial spaces (Glaeser 2011). This has percolated somewhat into discourses on African cities (see Nuttall and Mbembe 2008; Simone 2004) and, together with a more general optimism emerging with regard to the continent's future prospects (see Beall 2011), provides a lens through which to explore the potential of urban areas to play a positive role in relation to conflict management and reconstruction. However, the ability of cities to become sources of security and hope rather than of instability and violence depends heavily on the political and institutional environment. This chapter provides a broad-brush analysis of the relationship between cities and conflict in Africa in recent decades. With a particular focus on the challenges of governing cities after the cessation of violent conflict, it draws out lessons about the conditions under which

18

urban spaces can contribute to generating a more peaceful African future. Notwithstanding the tumultuous events north of the Sahara since 2011, the discussion is largely confined to sub-Saharan Africa, in line with much of this book and with the usual regional geographic categorisation (although this is not to say that the conflict dynamics we identify do not apply elsewhere).

The chapter begins by suggesting a heuristic categorisation of forms of violent conflict in order to make sense of the diversity of conflicts on the continent. It then proceeds to examine the position and roles that cities have played during wartime in recent large-scale conflicts on the continent, exploring the conditions under which they have been sites of particular violence or, in other cases, islands of relative stability. The next two sections examine a range of cases to discuss the – often overlooked – effects that the cessation of war can have on cities. The first of these sections examines the more negative impacts that give reason for pessimism, while the second reviews some more positive experiences and potential grounds for optimism. The conclusion briefly reflects on how best to navigate the opportunities and challenges generated in cities emerging from armed conflict, in order to avert the proliferation of other forms of everyday violence or 'civic conflict' in urban areas.

Three forms of conflict and their implications for urban areas

The recent literature on cities in contemporary warfare (Graham 2004; 2010; Herold 2004; Abrahamsen et al. 2009; Coward 2009) has paid relatively little attention to Africa.[1] Enduring perceptions of the continent see it as being overwhelmingly rural, despite the fact that it is now almost 40 per cent urban and due to be 60.5 per cent urban by 2050 (Kunkeler and Peters 2011: 278). These perceptions are reinforced by the fact that many of the conflicts ravaging the continent since independence have been understood as rural-based rebellions, thus rendering cities marginal or irrelevant to prevailing analyses. In fact, as we demonstrate below, cities have played important roles in war on a number of levels and are critical sites for determining the durability of peace in the post-war period. This issue deserves much more attention, especially now, given that in recent years some of the continent's most devastating conflicts have drawn tentatively to a close.

The distinctions we draw below between three forms of conflict – sovereign, civil and civic – goes beyond two more common sets of distinctions: the first between interstate war and civil war, and the second between political and criminal violence. The analytical framework we provide aims to capture the fact that all violent conflict has a political dimension, and that conflicts can evolve and transform over time. Moreover, it provides a spatial perspective that enables us to explore the role of cities and urban governance in different forms of conflict and in their mitigation.

Sovereign conflict refers to situations where there is explicit and direct intervention in warfare by international actors. This may either mean interstate war of the kind that is relatively rare in Africa, such as the conflict between Ethiopia and Eritrea in the late 1990s, or the direct intervention of other sovereign states into an existing civil war, as in the US intervention in Somalia in 1993. Cities are affected by sovereign conflicts insofar as such conflicts often involve attempts to capture and control capital cities, which (along with non-capital primate cities) are important centres of sovereignty and wealth. After major sovereign conflicts, the capital city can also play a fundamental role as a point of international engagement in reconstruction efforts.

Civil conflict refers to violent conflict between two or more relatively organised groups within sovereign boundaries. In civil conflicts, parties to the conflict are politically and militarily organised internally (although there is often external support) and have publicly stated political objectives (as well as often unstated economic objectives) (Cramer 2002; Keen 1998). In such conflicts, one or more of these groupings represents (or claims to represent) part of the state, while at least one of the parties in revolt must exercise some de facto authority over a part of the national territory and its population. In other words, in civil conflict the monopoly of violence formerly held by the state is partially taken over by rebels, local warlords, organised criminal groups or private militias (Sambanis 2004). Traditionally, civil conflicts have been closely associated with terrain, for example the proximity of ethnic groups to homeland territories or the social and military attributes of rural areas where military organisation can more easily take place beyond the reach of the state (Kalyvas 2006). The relationship between civil conflict and urban areas is complex, as will be explored further below. Cities are often economic hubs in war economies, but, depending on circumstances, they can either become sites of insurgency and combat or serve as places of refuge or relative security during conflict, such as Kinshasa in the Democratic Republic of Congo (DRC) or Luanda during Angola's protracted civil war.

Both civil and sovereign conflict can be considered forms of war, and in relation to them we use the words 'conflict' and 'war' interchangeably. Indeed, some conflicts are at some times civil and at other times sovereign wars. The third form of conflict we identify – *civic conflict* – refers to forms of violent conflict that are distinct from warfare. Civic conflict involves the violent expression of grievances vis-à-vis the state or other actors. It refers to diverse but recurrent forms of violence between individuals and groups and can include organised violent crime, gang warfare, terrorism, religious and sectarian rebellions, and spontaneous riots or violent protest over state failures such as poor or absent service delivery. Civic conflict can sometimes overlap with civil conflict; however, it differs from it in that civic conflict is ultimately a demonstrative or reactive process, demanding participation and response but rarely seeking to take control of formal structures of power. The other critical defining feature of civic conflict is that it generally takes place in cities, which provide the physical and social infrastructure for significant mobilisation on a large scale, against marginalisation or state neglect. In many cases it can be closely linked to the state's failure to cope with the demands and challenges of urbanisation.For the same reason, the state itself may be the aggressor in cases of civic conflict: indeed, violent acts against urban dwellers, such as forced slum clearances, can also be thought of as civic conflicts. These violent acts also ultimately result from the state's failure to cope in the face of specifically urban issues such as the provision of adequate housing, employment and services for the urban poor.[2]

The tripartite construct of sovereign, civil and civic conflict is not intended to be a rigid typology or an 'absolute' classificatory system; rather, it is designed as a heuristic framework for analysing the ways in which cities and conflict intersect over time. It provides a lens for exploring the fact that, while both sovereign and civil war have been in decline since the late twentieth century (Gurr et al. 2000; Kaldor 2006; Newman 2009), many forms of low-level instability and violence persist (Fox and Hoelscher 2010; Harbom and Wallensteen 2009), and these tend to centre on urban areas. It also highlights the political nature of many forms of urban violence, which are often written off as merely 'criminal' or 'social' violence. Research has shown that when sovereign and civil wars come to an end, urban-based violence in the form of civic conflict often increases. This has been explicitly discussed with respect to contexts such as Guatemala, El Salvador and Nicaragua (Pearce 1998; Rodgers 2009), but also applies to many African cases, as we demonstrate below. Moreover, given the pace of urbanisation and especially urban growth across much of sub-Saharan Africa, which itself is often accelerated by sovereign and civil conflicts and then their cessation, the prospect of civic conflict looks likely to increase. Before turning to some of the challenges associated with post-war transition in cities, we look now at the role cities have played – as both arenas of warfare and islands of relative peace – in some of Africa's most significant conflicts.

African cities in the midst of sovereign and civil conflict

The literature on cities and modern warfare has highlighted how, as sites of critical networked infrastructure, cities are pre-eminent strategic targets (Coward 2009; Graham 2010), while as sites of social interaction and political mobilisation they can be subject to attempted 'urbicide': a deliberate effort to destroy urban social fabric (Graham 2004; Weizman 2004). However, in relation to sovereign conflicts, the increased focus on cities – sometimes referred to as the 'urbanization of security' (Coward 2009) – is not a shift that has come easily to international security actors. Cities have generally been thought of as 'places where battles should not be fought', with urban conflict being 'regarded as an unfortunate aberration' (Ashworth 1991: 112). Nevertheless, by the late twentieth century the very fact of urbanisation was acknowledged as making urban warfare more likely:

> for two reasons; (1) the amount of open space is decreasing, thus increasing the odds that land forces will have to fight in urban areas; and (2) cities themselves will generate social, political and economic conflict. (Rosenau 1997: 372)

By the early twentieth century, international actors (especially the United States) were only too aware of the challenges of – and the necessity of – urban warfare, given their protracted engagements in Iraq and Afghanistan (Herold 2004; Graham 2010). With respect to Africa, however, a critical moment in terms of the recognition of the realities of urban warfare came in Somalia in 1993. This arguably had very significant and long-term repercussions for international intervention in Africa and, therefore, for experience of war in sub-Saharan Africa more generally. On their attempted invasion, US forces found 'a dense warren of poorly constructed, unreinforced-concrete buildings that was difficult for outsiders to operate in' (Rosenau 1997: 380). US confidence, which was based on the relative ease of victory in the 1991 Gulf War, was shattered as 'it became apparent that the firepower which had demolished the Iraqi Republican Guards was ill-suited to the streets of Mogadishu' (Bacevich 1993: 32). American forces were alarmed that many buildings struck were reoccupied within minutes by Somali guerrillas skilled in the use of rocket-propelled grenades, and found their assumed technological advantages seriously limited in this urban environment and against an opponent expert in asymmetric warfare (Rosenau 1997: 380–1).

When international forces withdrew after the death of 18 American soldiers and hundreds of Somalis (Lindley 2010), there was a major shift in perspective regarding the kinds of military engagement in which they were willing to engage in Africa. This had important implications, not least for the genocide that unfolded in Rwanda the following year. Kigali became a major battleground as the rebel Rwandan Patriotic Front (RPF) marched to the capital to end the genocide. Moreover, some RPF battalions were already embedded in the parliament building under the terms of a peace agreement that had collapsed; missiles and gunfire tore across the capital, devastating its infrastructure and at the same time making it look all too much like another potential Mogadishu (Dallaire 2003). As a consequence, the extent of international engagement in Rwanda to avert genocide was minimal (ibid.; Melvern 2000). Although there had been a number of major sovereign interventions in conflicts from Angola to Mozambique prior to the events in Mogadishu in 1993, since then most civil conflicts on the sub-continent have attracted no serious international military intervention, making sovereign conflict a relative rarity in sub-Saharan Africa. The remainder of this section therefore explores some of the ways in which cities have been implicated in civil wars with little or no explicit international intervention.

There is no simple relationship between civil war and cities in Africa, or indeed anywhere else. However, important analytical insights can be gained from attempting to understand how certain civil conflicts have been affected by, and have impacted on, the rural–urban divide: a distinction that remains relevant despite the problems associated with it (Corbridge and Jones 2006; Tacoli 1998). As suggested by Wolf's (1969) *Peasant Wars of the Twentieth Century*, and indeed by images of Mao Zedong, Ho Chi Minh and Che Guevara, most long-term and large-scale civil conflicts worldwide have been fought in rural areas (Auvinen 1997). In this respect, Africa is not very different, as rural struggles orchestrated by guerrilla leaders from Amilcar Cabral to Yoweri Museveni would attest. However, Mkandawire has argued that in Africa, despite the fact that civil wars were mostly fought on rural terrain, they ought to be seen as fundamentally urban in origin, rooted in significant 'urban malaise' (Mkandawire 2002). Most African rebellions, he argues, are led by urban-based elites, even though the vast majority of foot soldiers are rural dwellers. The two most prominent forms of civil conflict in Africa are those in which excluded urban elites shift their struggle to the countryside after being defeated in urban confrontations, and those where externally supported rebel movements in exile advance towards the capital, fighting their way through the countryside. In both cases, he argues, 'the locus of discontent is urban' rather than being based on any agrarian crisis (ibid.: 191).

This is an important argument with implications for the future, given the pace of urban growth and the likely amplification of 'urban malaise' if the crucial problems besetting African cities are not addressed. It does not, however, change the fact that the theatre of African civil war is generally the countryside. This is not to say that conflicts have been exclusively rural: many civil wars in Africa have involved considerable urban combat. As well as the aforementioned cases of Mogadishu and Kigali, West African cities such as Brazzaville, Monrovia and Freetown were the sites of devastating violence in the context of civil wars in the 1990s (Ellis 2003). Sometimes the population of cities has actually shrunk in wartime due to the impact of bombardment and insecurity; indeed, this was the case in Kampala in the 1980s, when many people retreated into subsistence in the hinterlands (Bryceson 2006). Major attacks on Juba in 1992 during the second Sudanese civil war also led to a period of population flight from the city (Martin and Mosel 2011), and during a particularly violent episode in Mogadishu in 2007–08 a remarkable two-thirds of the urban population temporarily abandoned the city (Lindley 2010: 2).

Nevertheless, in some of Africa's deadliest and most long-running wars, major cities remained relatively unscathed most of the time. Kinshasa, for example, remained a place of relative security and calm throughout the DRC's years of turmoil since 1996 (Ellis 2003; Freund 2009). So too, for long periods of time, did Goma in eastern DRC, which in many respects is more surprising given its location in the Kivu region, the site of some of the worst violence in the protracted Congo wars (Vlassenroot and Büscher 2013). Even more notable as an island of relative peace, however, has been the town of Gulu in northern Uganda which, for over two decades, was located at the epicentre of the conflict between the Ugandan government and the Lord's Resistance Army (LRA) (Branch 2013). Juba was also for the most part considered a place of refuge during the protracted conflicts in southern Sudan, despite the aforementioned attacks on the city at certain times. Refugees fleeing both the LRA after it spilled over the Sudanese border and the conflict between the Sudanese government and the Sudan People's Liberation Army (SPLA) headed to Juba for protection (Martin and Mosel 2011).

There are various reasons why cities remain sites of security for such long periods in this way, rather than becoming major arenas of conflict. In some cases it is because the government forces in the civil war still hold firm control of urban areas and they remain relatively impenetrable to rebels; this was arguably what happened in Kinshasa, Gulu and Juba (Mkandawire 2002; Branch 2013; Martin and Mosel 2011). Juba was considered the only secure town in the region during Sudan's second civil war from 1983 to 2005. In other cases, where the grip of central government is much less firm – such as in Goma – it is more likely to be because local power brokers and warlords find it in their interests to keep a city relatively secure due to its important role in the local or regional economy (Vlassenroot and Büscher 2013). This has also been observed in relation to cities in other relatively 'stateless' zones such as Quetta on the Afghanistan–Pakistan border (Gazdar et al. 2010). In fact, controlling such cities and maintaining a degree of urban peace can be central to the legitimacy of rebel movements.

When cities become havens in this way, one clear consequence is rapid urban growth. During the course of Angola's civil/sovereign war, the capital city Luanda grew approximately five times in size (UN DESA 2012), and cities such as Goma, Gulu and Juba have likewise experienced extraordinary rates of growth. Gulu, for example, went from being a small provincial town to Uganda's second largest city by 2007 (Branch 2013) and Juba doubled in size between 1993 and 2005, before doubling again from 2005 to 2010 (Martin and Mosel 2011). While conflict should certainly not be mistaken as the ultimate cause of Africa's urban transition, which has much deeper causes (see Chapter 14), it has clearly shaped the character of urbanisation and especially urban growth in many parts of the continent. Moreover, it is not only war itself that leads to soaring rates of urban growth in hitherto 'safe' cities. When civil conflict is largely over and the mobility of populations is easier, the pull of safe cities becomes even greater; indeed, the most rapid periods of growth for the cities discussed above were after the main hostilities had ended.

Post-war urbanism

The challenges of rapid urban growth and the risk of violent civic conflict Some of the most spectacular rates of urban growth worldwide in recent times have come in the wake of civil war. After the civil war and 1994 genocide in Rwanda, Kigali grew at an astonishing 18 per cent annually from 1995 to 2000 due to massive refugee return and people's desire to head to the city for both economic opportunity and relative anonymity (Goodfellow and Smith 2013). As noted above, Juba's growth rate in the five years after Sudan's comprehensive peace agreement (CPA) was around twice that of the late 1990s and early 2000s and much higher than in the first decade of the war (1983–93), when the city grew only slowly. Since 2005, large numbers of young unskilled or semi-skilled males in particular have headed to the city in search of better jobs and an urban lifestyle (Martin and Mosel 2011: 4). In West Africa, too, urban populations have mushroomed in the wake of war; Liberia saw significant urbanisation (Butman 2009) and Freetown has witnessed a 'continuing stream of rural to urban migration' (Maconachie et al. 2012: 194); from a pre-war population of around half a million, Freetown had increased to around 2 million people by 2010 (Kunkeler and Peters 2011: 282).

This demographic pressure obviously puts cities under renewed strain. Among other things, issues pertaining to the ownership and use of urban land can become acutely problematic (Martin and Mosel 2011; Goodfellow and Smith 2013) and basic needs such as food security and water supply are more likely to go unmet (Kapagama and Waterhouse 2009; Maconachie et al. 2012). Moreover, the systems that previously established a degree of wartime stability and elite rent sharing in 'haven' cities can collapse if the end of the war means that new organisations take control, whether they be victorious former rebel groups or branches of the central state reasserting their dominance. All these factors can combine to augment the potential for urban tensions to increase. This raises a question with regard to Mkandawire's (2002) point about the urban roots of rural insurgency: if the ending of rural-based wars leads cities to be put under ever greater pressure, exacerbating 'urban malaise', could this lead to further rural insurgencies led by disgruntled urbanites? The conditions would certainly suggest that the risk of repeat conflict is high. Goldstone (2002) links the risk of violent political conflict to urbanisation and to differential population growth rates between ethnic groups, both of which are often a feature of post-war situations in Africa. Indeed, the risk of political crisis is almost double in countries with above average levels of urbanisation but below average levels of gross domestic product per capita (ibid.: 10).

However, while renewed rural insurgency can and does occur in some places, recent history shows that in many instances this is not the case. In fact, increased urban malaise in the twenty-first century seems to be leading not to renewed political violence in the form of rural-based civil war but more commonly to urban-based violent *civic* conflict. This may partly be due to 'war fatigue': populations weary of war but aggravated by the renewed tensions of urban life may turn to forms of violence other than war to vent their frustrations or to meet their economic ends. Following deadly urban riots in September 2009, a Ugandan politician observed that when war has devastated people's lives in the past and important grievances persist in the present, there is a deep reluctance to contemplate war – but not necessarily other forms of violent conflict. People 'don't want a war but they want something else they are unable to explain', something 'starting in the city', which is a great concern because 'nobody will command it ... and it is worse than a war that has a commander ... you don't know who to call responsible'.[3] This sentiment expresses many of the reasons why a concern with civic conflict is so important in contemporary Africa. There is ample evidence of increases in what we have termed civic conflict *after* war ends. In Freetown, for example, crime rates have increased annually since the war ended, with drug trafficking now a major issue. In addition, youth gangs have emerged that, far from being 'criminal' as opposed to 'political', demonstrate 'more similarities than differences with what is subsumed under the banner of "armed conflict"' (Kunkeler and Peters 2011: 282).

Juba has also been a site of increasing civic violence. It has been noted that, while it was relatively peaceful during the war, the end of fighting has actually increased urban insecurity. One resident of Juba noted that 'before the CPA there was security within. Now there is no security; is this the meaning of freedom?' Another commented: 'Before the peace the enemy was definite. Now, in comparison, the enemies are many and unknown' (Martin and Mosel 2011: 30). The handing over of Juba's policing duties to the South Sudan Police Force by the SPLA in 2008 has seemingly worsened the situation (ibid.: 30). The possibility of a similar outcome of increased urban conflict after the end of war has also been noted in relation to Gulu (Branch 2013).

The phenomenon of rising levels of civic conflict after the end of civil war, sometimes to the extent that people feel considerably less secure in peacetime, clearly reflects a problem with the governance of post-conflict urban spaces across Africa – and in other parts of the world, judging by experiences in cities such as Managua, Nicaragua (Rodgers 2009) and Dili, Timor-Leste (Moxham and Carapic2013). At the root of this problem is something that might be termed the 'myth of the temporary city'. Again and again, governments and international development actors fail to realise that the urban growth that occurs in wartime is extremely difficult to reverse and is likely to be permanent, instead treating their swollen cities as a temporary aberration. In Monrovia, state rhetoric has framed rural return as 'essential for national development' (Butman 2009: 1), but the fact is that many people have rationally chosen urban self-settlement over refugee camps or a return to their villages (ibid.: 5).

Equally, in Juba the SPLA's policy of 'taking towns to the people' has basically been an attempt to prevent rural–urban migration; however, South Sudan's president Salva Kiir admitted in 2010 that 'achievement in this regard was, if at all, minimal' (quoted in Martin and Mosel 2011: 7).

Furthermore, civic conflict can arise quite some time after the formal cessation of civil war. This is well illustrated by the failure of Mugabe's regime in Zimbabwe to expand formal employment or income-earning opportunities, which inevitably led urban dwellers in Harare to engage in irregular economic activities. This in turn became a central motive behind the targeting of the urban poor alongside political opponents in the largely urban-based Movement for Democratic Change (MDC) during the so-called 'urban cleansing' undertaken in 2005. Operation Murambatsvina resulted in around 700,000 people losing their homes, livelihoods or both (UN-Habitat 2005). The residents of the Harare settlements that were bulldozed fell into two main groups. On the one hand were elderly homeowners, unemployed and subsisting through the rents received from subletting rooms, outbuildings and houses to low-income urban tenants. On the other were the tenants themselves, much younger, with few prospects, and who had been largely ignored by government policies (Brett 2005; Potts 2006). The example of 'urban cleansing' in Zimbabwe offers an important reminder that social differentiation is an intrinsic element of urbanism and that state failure or neglect is a key factor in civic conflict. The Zimbabwe case also reminds us that the long view is important. The war of independence ended in 1980 and Mugabe came to power with overwhelming political support and democratic dividend, something his regime has sought to sustain through support for and from ex-combatants in relation to land redistribution in the countryside. It remains to be seen whether the conditions will prevail to enable the civic conflict that erupts periodically in Zimbabwe's large cities to evolve into sustainable urban governance solutions.

New urban identities and opportunities for peace The end of civil war does not always result in an entirely negative trajectory in cities. There are some positive dimensions of post-war urbanism to learn from, and sometimes cities can offer great advantages for those who live in them during and after episodes of civil conflict. An interesting example of the economic advantages that derive from conflict can be seen in the city of Goma in eastern DRC, which in certain periods has thrived, even in a context of devastating violence and protracted regional warfare (between 1996 and 2003). Geographically distant from a central state, which was largely based in Kinshasa almost 2,000 kilometres to the west and was in any case largely incapacitated, Goma benefited from becoming the centre of cross-border trade between the densely populated and mineral-rich eastern DRC and the regional markets of Uganda and Rwanda. It has been argued that Goma not only became a place of immense opportunity but also developed its own distinct 'transboundary' identity associated with its economic dynamism and political autonomy and as a regional centre of gravity for conflict intervention, including on the part of international agencies. Goma is widely considered a 'rebel city' that shuns the shackles of the central state of both the DRC and neighbouring Rwanda, but its inhabitants have at times turned this negative force of rebellion into more positive forces of autonomy and independence, carving a space of relative order out of the chaos of the Congo wars and their aftermath (Vlassenroot and Büscher 2013).

Cities can provide an opportunity for, and enable the demonstration of, not only economic success but social and political upward mobility, particularly on the part of those who come out of the conflict as victors. In Mozambique the liberation struggle that was waged between 1964 and 1975 was fought largely in the rural areas, where a disaffected peasantry was mobilised initially against the Portuguese colonists and subsequently by both Frelimo (the Mozambique Liberation Front) and Renamo (Mozambican National Resistance) in the post-independence civil war between 1977 and 1992. Frelimo's longer-term nation building project, by contrast, was very much forged in the cities, particularly the capital Maputo, home to those who benefited from and became bastions of the regime and where party political power and personnel were concentrated (Sumich 2010). In the words of one of the Maputo elite interviewed by Sumich, the commitment to a nationalist project rooted in the capital 'created a situation where something that would normally take generations happened in just a decade or so' (ibid.: 3). The nexus between nation building and the city meant that the population of Maputo 'internalised nationalist values, identity and systems of meaning more concretely than many other parts of the nation' (ibid.: 11).

Goma is a city free of any significant relationship with national government that has managed to thrive in certain respects, while Maputo represents an attempt by the national government to create an urban-generated national identity. The post-conflict experience in Kigali is rather different again, representing not so much an effort to create an urban-based identity as an attempt by the state to develop a sort of 'model' city for Africa in terms of orderliness, low crime and investment potential (Goodfellow and Smith 2013). It constitutes perhaps the most striking recent example of a post-war urban spatial and socioeconomic transformation that has managed to avert the onset of widespread civic conflict. Despite the aforementioned urban growth after 1994, which was largely fuelled by the return of successive waves of both Tutsi and Hutu refugees, the city was stabilised remarkably quickly and has been applauded by the UN for its low levels of crime, its cleanliness and its protection of the environment. Far from becoming a site of rising violence, the city is an unusually secure space by regional and even global standards, bucking the trend in terms of post-conflict urban change (ibid.).

However, none of these somewhat more encouraging narratives of post-conflict urbanism are without their darker undersides. Goma is a space of continuing insecurity, despite the opportunities it offers, and a place in which the mutual suspicion between Rwandese and Congolese communities festers (Vlassenroot and Büscher 2013). In Maputo, meanwhile, Frelimo's nationalist project had resonance for some urbanites but not others, and, in recent years, growing frustration on the part of urban residents who have not benefited from the peace and growth dividends has resulted in incidents of unrest and rioting (Sumich 2010). These new manifestations of open critique also show that efforts to create a national identity are unable to mask the everyday short-comings of the Frelimo government and its failure to deliver for the poor in the nation's capital city. As for Kigali, the impressive outcome in terms of public security is built to a considerable degree on the closure of political space and a state-driven development agenda that is not always well equipped to accommodate the needs and voices of the poorest and most vulnerable in the city. As such, it represents a model of effective post-war urban transformation but with exclusionary overtones that cast doubt on its sustainability, particularly given rates of urban growth that are likely to generate increased demand for both jobs and political voice in urban areas (Goodfellow and Smith 2013).

All these examples represent partially successful attempts by both states and urban populations to capitalise on the potential that cities offer as spaces in which to overcome conflict, accompanied by governmental failures to fully accommodate urban populations politically. The case of Durban, meanwhile, provides evidence of more concerted efforts to transform the city as a political space. It offers an example of peace building in a conflict-affected city that linked urban challenges and opportunities to the priorities of national reconstruction. In the province of KwaZulu-Natal, the transition from apartheid to a non-racial liberal democracy was accompanied by political violence that assumed the proportions of a civil war, leading to the loss of thousands of lives. Calm was facilitated by a number of political compromises by both city and national government that involved accommodating the *amakhosi* (chiefs) and their supporters who had fought against the African National Congress (ANC) during the final years before the latter came to power. The ANC-dominated metropolitan government in greater Durban turned a tight and effective political coalition into a broader and more inclusive developmental coalition that embraced the largely suspicious and hostile *amakhosi*. This was made possible by the leadership of a small group of committed leaders who had a shared political history and who had the support of the ANC and government structures, while at the same time retaining a degree of autonomy that allowed them to respond to city-level imperatives (Beall and Ngonyama 2009).

It remains to be seen whether this developmental coalition in Durban will remain inclusive and adaptive to change and to the demands generated by new forms of exclusion. Nevertheless, it provides an example of a relatively encouraging post-conflict urban outcome that clearly highlights the importance of political institutions and institutional flexibility when accommodating competing interests in a volatile post-conflict environment. It serves as an important reminder that fairly radical adaptation on the part of state organisations may be critical for avoiding civic conflict in post-war contexts.

Conclusions

While understanding the causes of civil conflict is vital for a continent that has experienced a disproportionate amount of war in the past half-century, it is equally crucial to understand the demographic and socio-spatial consequences of past civil war in both the short and long term. In this chapter we have argued that cities are spaces that, while often relative havens of security during wartime, are particularly vulnerable to the emergence of new forms of violence that we collectively term 'civic conflict' in the wake of civil and sovereign wars. This vulnerability to continued instability occurs not so much because cities are intrinsically violent places but because of the pressures of rapid urban growth, the misguided assumption by policy makers that this growth will be temporary, and the attendant failure to integrate burgeoning urban populations into institutionalised politics.

In order to manage urbanisation and urban growth in ways that minimise civic conflict, city governments need both a degree of local autonomy from the central government and sustained support from it. In contexts where local autonomy is high but support from the centre low, such as in Goma, the prospects of meeting urban service delivery challenges are obviously limited. On the other hand, in cases such as Kigali where support for the city government from the centre is strong but the autonomy element somewhat lacking, the capacity of the city government to be locally responsive is diminished. This is problematic as there is arguably a limit to how long demands can be left unmet and latent conflicts deferred or suppressed in dense and diverse urban spaces, especially when exacerbated by tensions relating to prior civil wars (Goodfellow and Smith, forthcoming; Beall et al. 2011). To some degree, both local autonomy and central support were present in Durban; this has also been observed in some other successful cases of urban conflict reduction outside Africa, for example in Colombia, where new roles for city mayors (facilitated by a new national constitution) played a critical role (Gutiérrez Sanín et al. 2009).

The socioeconomic and demographic changes wrought by civil war and post-war transition therefore require institutional innovation in cities, and the concerted coordination of national and city-level strategies to deal with urban challenges. As Parnell and Simon argue in Chapter 13, national urbanisation and urban policies are critical but often missing aspects of development planning. The need for such policies is especially pressing in the period following civil war, although, sadly, it is particularly likely that they will remain absent in post-conflict contexts due to the perception that this area is not a priority or that the urgency of urban challenges is temporary. Meanwhile, if policy coordination is one essential prerequisite of effective post-war urban stability, the other (even more problematic) side of the coin relates to politics itself. While it is extremely challenging to institutionalise political processes that are inclusive of a range of political, ethnic and socioeconomic interests in post-conflict urban spaces, this approach is critical for urban peace (Bollens 2007: 11). If African cities are to face a brighter future in the twenty-first century, national and local governments need to act in concert and take post-conflict urban growth seriously as representing part of a long-term historical shift, which means institutionalising channels for urban dwellers to make demands on the state.

Notes

1 This began to be addressed by the Cities and Fragile States programme of the Crisis States Research Programme, which this paper draws heavily on in parts. See Beall et al. (2011) for an overview.

2 See Beall et al. (2011) for a fuller discussion of the rationale for this tripartite categorisation.

3 Interview by Tom Goodfellow with Hussein Kyanjo MP, 13 October 2009.

References

Abrahamsen, R., D. Hubert and M. C. Williams (2009) 'Guest editors' introduction to special issue on urban insecurities'. *Security Dialogue* 40(4–5): 363–72.

Ashworth, G. J. (1991) *War and the City*. London: Routledge.

Auvinen, J. (1997) 'Political conflict in less developed countries 1981–89'. *Journal of Peace Research* 34(2): 177–95.

Bacevich, A. D. (1993) 'Learning from aid'. *Commentary*, December.

Beall, J. (2011) 'Invention and intervention in African cities'. 2010 Carl Schlettwein Lecture, Centre for African Studies, Basel.

— and M. Ngonyama (2009) *Indigenous Institutions, Traditional Leaders and Elite Coalitions for Development: The case of Greater Durban, South Afri*ca. Crisis States Research Centre Working Paper 55 (Series Two). London: London School of Economics and Political Science.

— T. Goodfellow and D. Rodgers (2011) *Cities, Conflict and State Fragility*. Crisis States Research Centre Working Paper 85 (Series Two). London: London School of Economics and Political Science.

— B. Guha-Khasnobis and R. Kanbur (eds) (2010) *Urbanization and Development: Multidisciplinary perspectives*. Oxford: Oxford University Press.

Bollens, S. (2007) *Comparative Research on Contested Cities: Lenses and scaffoldings*. Crisis States Research Centre Working Paper 17 (Series Two). London: London School of Economics and Political Science.

Branch, A. (2013) 'Gulu Town in war ... and peace? The town as camp in northern Uganda'. *Urban Studies* special issue on cities, conflict and state fragility in the developing world.

Brett, E. A. (2005) 'Authoritarian patrimonialism and economic disorder: the politics of crisis and breakdown in Uganda and Zimbabwe'. Unpublished mimeo. London: Crisis States Research Centre, London School of Economics and Political Science.

Bryceson, D. F. (2006) 'Introduction'. In D. F. Bryceson and D. Potts, *African Urban Economies: Viability, vitality or vitiation?* Basingstoke: Palgrave Macmillan, pp. 3–38.

Butman, M. (2009) 'Urbanization vs. rural return in post-conflict Liberia'. Unpublished MA thesis, George Washington University, Washington, DC.

Corbridge, S. and G. Jones (2006) *The Continuing Debate about Urban Bias: The thesis, its critics, its influence, and implications for poverty reduction.* London: Department of Geography and Environment, London School of Economics and Political Science.

Coward, M. (2009) 'Network-centric violence, critical infrastructure and the urbanization of security'. *Security Dialogue* 40(4–5): 399–418.

Cramer, C. (2002) 'Homo economicus goes to war: methodological individualism, rational choice and the political economy of war'. *World Development* 30(11): 1845–64.

Dallaire, R. (2003) *Shake Hands with the Devil: The failure of humanity in Rwanda.* Toronto: Random House.

Davis, M. (2006) *Planet of Slums.* London: Verso Books.

Ellis, S. (2003) 'Violence and history: a response to Thandika Mkandawire'. *Journal of Modern African Studies* 41(3): 457–75.

Fox, S. and K. Hoelscher (2010) *The Political Economy of Social Violence: Theory and evidence from a cross-country study.* Crisis States Research Centre Working Paper 72 (Series Two). London: London School of Economics and Political Science.

Freund, W. (2009) *The Congolese Elite and the Fragmented City: The struggle for the emergence of a dominant class in Kinshasa.* Crisis States Research Centre Working Paper 54 (Series Two). London: London School of Economics and Political Science.

Gazdar, H., S. Ahmad Kaker and I. Khan (2010) *Buffer Zone, Colonial Enclave or Urban Hub? Quetta: between four regions and two wars.* Crisis States Research Centre Working Paper 69 (Series Two). London: London School of Economics and Political Science.

Glaeser, E. (2011) *Triumph of the City: How our greatest invention makes us richer, smarter, greener, healthier, and happier.* London and New York, NY: Penguin Press.

Goldstone, J. (2002) 'Population and security: how demographic change can lead to violent conflict'. *Journal of International Affairs* (56)1: 3–23.

Goodfellow, T. and A. Smith (2013) 'From urban catastrophe to "model" city?: politics, security and development in post-conflict Kigali'. *Urban Studies* 50(5).

Graham S. (ed.) (2004) *Cities, War and Terrorism: Towards an urban geopolitics.* Oxford: Blackwell Publishing.

— (2010) *Cities Under Siege: The new military urbanism.* London: Verso Books.

Gurr, T. R., M. G. Marshall and D. Khosla (2000) *Peace and Conflict 2001: A global survey of armed conflicts, self-determination movements, and democracy.* College Park, MD: Center for International Development and Conflict Management, University of Maryland. Available at www.systemic peace.org/PC2001.pdf [accessed 13 August 2013].

Gutiérrez Sanín, F., M. T. Pinto, J. C. Arenas, T. Guzmán and M. T. Gutiérrez (2009) *Politics and Security in Three Colombian Cities.* Crisis States Research Centre Working Paper 44 (Series Two). London: London School of Economics and Political Science.

Hall, P., and U. Pfeiffer (2000) *Urban Future 21: A global agenda for twenty-first century cities.* London: E. & F. N. Spon.

Harbom, L. and P. Wallensteen (2009) 'Armed conflicts, 1946–2008'. *Journal of Peace Research* 46(4): 577–87.

Herold, M. (2004) 'Urban dimensions of the punishment of Afghanistan by US bombs'. In S. Graham (ed.) *Cities, War and Terrorism: Towards an urban geopolitics.* Oxford: Blackwell Publishing, pp. 312–29.

Judd, D. R. (2005) 'Everything is always going to hell'. *Urban Affairs Review* 41(2): 119–31.

Kaldor, M. (2006) *New and Old Wars: Organized violence in a global era*. Second edition. Oxford: Polity Press.

Kalyvas, S. (2006) *The Logic of Violence in Civil War*. Cambridge: Cambridge University Press.

Kapagama, P. and R. Waterhouse (2009) *Portrait of Kinshasa: A city on the edge*. Crisis States Research Centre Working Paper 53 (Series Two). London: London School of Economics and Political Science.

Kaplan, R. D. (1994) 'The coming anarchy'. *Atlantic Monthly*, February.

Keen, D. (1998) *The Economic Functions of Violence in Civil War*. Adelphi Papers No. 320. Oxford: Oxford University Press.

Kunkeler, J. and K. Peters (2011) 'The boys are coming to town: youth, armed conflict and urban violence in developing countries'. *International Journal of Conflict and Violence* 5(2): 277–91.

Lindley, A. (2010) 'Leaving Mogadishu: towards a sociology of conflict-related mobility'. *Journal of Refugee Studies* 23(1): 2–22.

Maconachie, R., T. Binns and P. Tengbe (2012) 'Urban farming associations: youth and food security in post-war Freetown, Sierra Leone'. *Cities* 29(3): 192–200.

Martin, E. and I. Mosel (2011) 'City limits: urbanisation and vulnerability in Sudan: Juba case study'. London: Overseas Development Institute.

Melvern, L. (2000) *A People Betrayed: The role of the West in Rwanda's genocide*. London: Zed Books.

Mkandawire, T. (2002) 'The terrible toll of post-colonial "rebel movements" in Africa: towards an explanation of the violence against the peasantry'. *Journal of Modern African Studies* 40(2): 181–215.

Moxham, B. and J. Carapic (2013) 'Unravelling Dili: The crisis of city and state in Timor-Leste'. *Urban Studies* 50(5).

Newman, E. (2009) 'Conflict research and the "decline" of civil war'. *Civil Wars* 11(3): 255–78.

Nuttall, S. and A. Mbembe (eds) (2008) *Johannesburg: The elusive metropolis*. Durham, NC and Johannesburg: Duke University Press and Wits University Press.

Pearce, J. (1998) 'From civil war to "civil society": has the end of the cold war brought peace to Central America?'. *International Affairs* 74(3): 589–90.

Potts, D. (2006) '"Restoring order"? Operation Murambatsvina and the urban crisis in Zimbabwe'. *Journal of Southern African Studies* 32(2): 273–91.

Rodgers, D. (2009) 'Slum wars of the 21st century: gangs, mano dura and the new urban geography of conflict in Central America'. *Development and Change* 40(5): 949–76.

Rosenau, W. (1997) 'Every room is a new battle: the lessons of modern urban warfare'. *Studies in Conflict and Terrorism* 20(4): 371–94.

Safier, M. (1996) 'The cosmopolitan challenge in cities on the edge of the millennium'. *City* 1(3–4): 12–29.

Sambanis, R. (2004) 'Poverty and the organisation of political violence'. In S. M. Collins and C. Graham (eds) *Brookings Trade Forum 2004: Globalization, poverty, and inequality*. Washington, DC: Brookings Institution, pp. 165–211.

Simone, A. (2004) *For the City Yet to Come: Changing African life in four cities*. Durham, NC: Duke University Press.

Sumich, J. (2010) *Nationalism, Urban Poverty and Identity in Maputo, Mozambique*. Crisis States Research Centre Working Paper 68 (Series Two). London: London School of Economics and Political Science.

Tacoli, C. (1998) 'Rural–urban interactions: a guide to the literature'. *Environment and Urbanization* 10(1): 147–66.

UN DESA (2012) *World Urbanization Prospects: The 2011 revision*. New York, NY: Population Division of the Department of Economic and Social Affairs of the United Nations Secretariat (UN DESA). Available at http://esa.un.org/unpd/wup/index.htm [accessed 13 August 2013].

UN-Habitat (2005) *Report of the Fact-finding Mission to Zimbabwe to Assess the Scope and Impact of Operation Murambatsvina by the UN Special Envoy on Human Settlements Issues in Zimbabwe*. Nairobi: UN-Habitat. Available at www.unhabitat.org/downloads/docs/297_96735_ZimbabweReport.pdf [accessed 4 September 2013].

Vlassenroot, K. and K. Büscher (2013) 'Borderlands, identity and urban development: the case of Goma (Democratic Republic of the Congo)'. *Urban Studies* 50(5).

Weizman, E. (2004) 'Strategic points, flexible lines, tense surfaces, and political volumes: Ariel Sharon and the geometry of occupation'. In S. Graham (ed.) *Cities, War and Terrorism: Towards an urban geopolitics*. Oxford: Blackwell Publishing, pp. 172–91.

Wolf, E. R. (1969) *Peasant Wars of the Twentieth Century*. New York, NY: Harper and Row.

3 | Sub-Saharan African urbanisation and global environmental change[1]

Susan Parnell and Ruwani Walawege

Scientific evidence for global environmental change (GEC) in Africa presents a *prima facie* case for increased human migration and displacement. Closer scrutiny of the evidence on demographic change, however, suggests that migration and displacement are less important variables in explaining the human dimensions of GEC on the continent than is commonly thought. Natural population growth in cities is a more important dynamic in the evolving system of human settlement in Africa, and this significant shift in where people live, both now and in the future, is overlooked because of the emphasis on the potential impact of environmentally induced migration. Even without any movement from the countryside, cities represent the fastest growing sector of the sub-Saharan African population. The existing vulnerability of African cities, with their rapidly growing populations and weak management, means that any environmental change is likely to have significant consequences for cities. Taking the sub-Saharan African demographic evidence seriously means that the scholarly and policy emphasis currently directed to GEC migration and displacement might be more effectively redirected to questions relating to the interface between GEC and urban areas.

Introduction

Simplistic notions of 'push and pull' models of migration and urbanisation belie the great complexity of human movement and settlement in Africa, especially under present and predicted conditions of GEC. If we are to understand the interface of African migration and urbanisation in relation to shifting regimes of ecosystem services and the increasing environmental hazards associated with climate change, we will need to unravel each of these dynamic processes and the interplay between them (Sánchez-Rodríguez et al. 2005). The task is complex because changes in urbanisation and environment are not linear, the data for Africa are poor (Potts and Bowyer-Bower 2003; Potts 2010; UN-Habitat 2009) and, in the case of urbanisation, the process is deeply politically charged (Jones and Corbridge 2010; McGranahan et al. 2009; Pieterse 2008). Already there has been a very public spat over Myers' (2005) predictions of up to 700,000 climate migrants, the majority from Africa

(Brown 2008; Dodson 2011; Parry et al. 2007). While there are weak indications of situations where the hypothesis of mass GEC-induced migration is likely to hold true, this assessment of African urbanisation suggests that there are other, often more salient, conclusions about the impact of GEC that put the focus on the natural expansion of African urban populations and not just on displacement and migration. This approach therefore shifts the emphasis on why, where and how GEC will have an effect in Africa, making migration a less substantive issue and cities more critical sites of significant GEC impact. The overall argument of this chapter thus concurs with that of Warner (2010), i.e. that the impacts of GEC in sub-Saharan Africa are likely to drive further migration, some circular in character, but much of it permanently to African cities. The view presented here goes further, suggesting that Africa's rapidly expanding and very fragile urban areas (many of them coastal) are likely to be a major locus of the impact of GEC over the next 30 to 50 years because of their rapid rate of population growth and weak state capacity to manage GEC-induced urbanisation and GEC at the city scale.

The chapter is structured in three parts: the first provides a brief summary of the patterns and forecasts for sub-Saharan Africa's biophysical experience of GEC. It establishes that there is indeed a *prima facie* case that predicted environmental change might precipitate new and different forms of human movement in Africa, but also highlights the gap in knowledge about locally downscaled or city regional climate predictions and the vulnerability of settlements. The next section reviews continental trends in urban growth, urbanisation and migration and the shifting urban system in Africa over the last century. Contrary to the view that suggests that GEC is a likely driver of migration, we show that there is little consensus on what drives (or draws) people into sub-Saharan African cities. In the final section, bearing in mind the inconclusive nature of the literature on urbanisation and migration, we set out a speculative assessment of the drivers and impacts of GEC-linked migration in Africa. In order to do this, we follow Black et al. (2011) in arguing that we need to understand the foundational drivers of urbanisation, exploring its links with GEC rather than seeing GEC as an isolated driver of urban growth and urbanisation.

Global environmental change: trends and predictions for Africa

Africa is a continent that experiences a variety of climates across a range of regions, from humid tropics to the very arid Sahara (Christensen et al. 2007). What is clear from the data is that climate changes are of sufficient magnitude, if not predictability, to trigger altered human responses; these include shifts in agricultural production and forced migrations in response to natural disasters (IOM 2009). However, there is insufficient detail to make local-scale predictions of how or where GEC might drive migratory movements. Studies of observed temperature show a warming trend that is consistent over the continent, but not uniform. Decadal warming rates in the tropical forests, for example, are 0.29°C (Malhi and Wright 2004), while in South Africa they are between 0.1°C and 0.3°C (Kruger and Shongwe 2004). New et al. (2006) show an increase in the number of warm spells over southern and western Africa between 1961 and 2000, and a decrease in the number of extremely cold days. Decreasing temperature trends have also been observed in eastern African weather stations located close to the coast and to major inland lakes (King'uyu et al. 2000). Local impacts of global sea level rises are only just beginning to be modelled for African locations (Brundrit 2008; 2009).

The precipitation pattern across the continent is not only complicated, with spatial and temporal variability, but inter-annual variability remains high in most areas. Recent region-specific precipitation studies show a number of trends, including decreases in West Africa (Chappell and Agnew 2004; Dai et al. 2004; Nicholson et al. 2000) and in the north and south of Congo (Malhi and Wright 2004). Increases have been noted in the annual rainfall along the Guinea coast during the last 30 years (Nicholson et al. 2000). Studies in southern Africa show no detectable, long-term trend but inter-annual variability has increased since 1970, with higher rainfall anomalies and more intense and widespread droughts (see, for example, Fauchereau et al. 2003). A change in seasonality and extremes has also been noted in this region (New et al. 2006; Tadross et al. 2005a).

As with other regions, there are complex mechanisms governing these patterns and their changes. Our understanding of these has increased over the years but more research is needed in order to improve our ability to assess the impact that climate change may have on the continent and at the city region scale. Africa remains one of the most vulnerable continents to climate change (Boko et al. 2007) and yet very few regional or sub-regional climate change scenarios have been constructed in Africa using regional climate models (RCMs) or empirical downscaling. A summary of key future vulnerabilities for the continent, as noted in the Fourth Assessment Report (ibid.), is provided in Tables 3.1 and 3.2 below, with more specific reading indicated in the last column.

The impacts that any of the changes listed in Tables 3.1 and 3.2 can have on cities are many and complex. Major cities sited along the coast, for example, as is the case with most of the major cities in sub-Saharan Africa, are likely to be affected by sea level rise through increased storm flooding and damage, inundation, coastal erosion, increased salinity in estuaries and coastal aquifers, rising coastal water tables and obstructed drainage. Displacement of people, destruction of property and loss of livelihoods are also impacts that may be associated with this. Similarly, cities are vulnerable to extreme heat events, flooding and landslides as a result of possible future climatic

TABLE 3.1 Future trends for GEC in Africa by climate variable

Climatic variable	Future projections	Specifications of relevant study	Source or further reading
Air temperature	An increase in the mean annual air temperature of between 3°C and 4°C is shown compared with the 1980–99 period	Medium high Special Report on Emissions Scenarios (SRES) A1B used with 20 general circulation models (GCMs)	Christensen et al. 2007
	Up to 9°C warming on the North African Mediterranean coast in June to August and up to 7°C for the southern African region in September to November	GCM scenario based on the A1F1 emission scenario, for the period 2070–99	Ruosteenoja et al. 2003
	A 3.7°C increase in summer and 4°C increase in winter in southern Africa in the 2080s	RCM HadRM3H (Hadley Centre Regional Climate Model version 3H) using the A2 emission scenario	Hudson and Jones 2002
	Cooling of 0.8°C per year in the global tropics, primarily due to an increase in vegetation density		Bounoua et al. 2000

Precipitation	Decreases along the Mediterranean coast by 20%, extending to the northern Sahara and along the west coast	SRES A1B and A2 emission scenarios for 2080–99	Christensen et al. 2007; Hudson and Jones 2002
	Likely increases of around 7% in tropical and eastern Africa, and a high probability that winter rainfall in southern Africa will decrease, especially in the extreme west, by between 30% and 40%		
	South Africa indicates an increase in summer rainfall over the convective region of the central and eastern plateau and the Drakensberg mountains	Empirically downscaled projections	Hewitson and Crane 2006
	Decrease in early summer rainfall and increase in late summer rainfall over eastern parts of southern Africa	RCM-based projections	Tadross et al. 2005b
	Number of extreme dry and wet years to increase in the Sahel	Using data from four GCMs simulations	Huntingford et al. 2005
	Drying for northern Africa and wetting in central Africa	Global drought simulation for the twenty-first century under the A2 scenario	Burke et al. 2006
Extreme events	Increase of between 10% and 20% in cyclone intensity with a 2–4°C sea-surface temperature rise		Lal 2001
Tropical storms	More frequent and intense storms over the Indian Ocean		McDonald et al. 2005

TABLE 3.2 Future trends for GEC in Africa by sector

Sector predictions	Future projections	Specifications of relevant study	Source or further reading
Water sector	The Quergha watershed in Morocco is likely to change between 2000 and 2020 A 1°C increase in temperature can change runoff in the order of 10%, assuming there is no change in precipitation The impact in the area is equivalent to the loss of one large dam per year		Agoumi 2003
Streamflow	Africa-wide, the range in 2050 is from a decrease of 15% to an increase of 5% from the 1961–90 baseline For 2100 the range is from a decrease of 19% to an increase of 14% For southern Africa, all countries except South Africa will experience a significant decrease For South Africa, increases under high emissions scenarios are under 10%	Using 10 scenarios by five GCM models – Commonwealth Scientific and Industrial Research Organisation Model (CSIRO2), Hadley Centre Coupled Model, version 3 (HadCM3), Coupled Global Climate Model 2 (CGCM2), the atmospheric general circulation model developed at the Max Planck Institute for Meteorology (ECHAM) and Parallel Climate Model (PCM)	Strzepek and McCluskey 2006
Ecosystems	Changes are expected in both species range and tree productivity, which may add stress on forest systems		UNEP 2004
	Grassland changes to be expected due to changes in CO2 levels and average temperature		Muriuki et al. 2005; Levy 2006
	Mangroves and coral reefs (one of the major ecosystems in Africa) are likely to be affected Some of the endangered species include manatees, marine turtles and migratory birds A rise in sea level may also allow mangroves to recolonize coastal lagoons		Boko et al. 2007

Ecosystems (continued)	Coral bleaching is likely due to ocean warming on reefs A loss of both low-lying corals and biodiversity is expected Proliferation of algae and dinoflagellates may affect more people due to the consumption of food sources In South Africa, changes in estuaries due to reductions in river runoff and inundation of salt marshes due to rising sea level are likely		Lough 2000; Muhando 2001; Obura 2001; Boko et al. 2007; Clark 2006
	Assuming no migration, a 10%–15% species fall is expected within the International Union for Conservation of Nature critically endangered or extinct category by 2050, increasing to 25%–40% by 2080 The change is less extreme when free migration is allowed – 10%–20% by 2080	Using SRES A2 and B2 scenarios in sub-Saharan Africa in 141 national parks, with HadCM3 GCM for 2050 and 2080	
	Within the mammal population, a westward range shift in the equatorial transitional zone in central Africa and an eastward shift in southern Africa are expected	Shift due to latitudinal aridity gradients	
Hot spots	A critical 'unstable' area has been identified for an east–west band from Senegal to Sudan, separating dry Sahara from wet central Africa The Okavango River basin could be negatively impacted by climate change (greater than human activity)	Based on six GCMs and a composite ensemble of African precipitation modelled for the period 2070–99 and derived from 21 coupled ocean–atmospheric GCMs	de Wit and Stankiewicz 2006 See, for example, Biggs et al. 2004; Anderssen et al. 2006
	Megacities along the coast will be vulnerable because of the potential sea level rise and the high risk of flooding		Nicholls and Tol 2006; Awuor et al. 2008

changes. As a consequence, cities may suffer from infrastructure damage, damage to transportation, water and sanitation systems, adverse economic and tourism impacts, among other effects (UN-Habitat 2011). It is therefore very important that, together with the growth of cities in sub-Saharan Africa, the potential impacts of and vulnerabilities to changes as a result of GEC need to be studied in greater detail.

Defining and deciphering African urbanisation and migration

Understanding the future impact of GEC (Tables 3.1 and 3.2) on migration presupposes that there is a consensus on the current drivers of human settlement. However, this is more than usually difficult to establish for Africa, where data are out of date, census figures are not always accurate and the important statistics are not always in the public domain. Despite the fact that there has recently been a number of high-profile international publications providing a synthesis of urbanisation trends in Africa (UN-Habitat 2009; World Bank 2009), no uniform official definition of 'urban' and 'rural' is used across the continent, and some countries do not even have definitions (Potts 2005; 2010). This lack or inadequacy of definitions helps explain some of the variation in estimates across sources and acts as a general warning to treat the data presented here with some caution. It also reflects real ambiguity among scholars over what is understood by 'migration' and by 'urban' life in Africa (see the contrasting accounts in IOM 2009; Myers 2003; Crankshaw et al. 1992; Simone 2004; and Potts 2010). The position adopted in this chapter is that it is critical to understand the sub-Saharan African experience of both urban growth and urban migration in order to reflect on possible GEC impacts, although of course growth, migration and climate are interlinked dynamics in what, in global terms, is a very late urban transition (Montgomery 2008) (see Figure 3.1). Sub-Saharan Africa's 'urban turn', which is widely understood to be distinctive because urbanisation and industrialisation have been uncoupled (O'Connor 1983; Rakodi 1997; Todaro and Smith 2009; World Bank 2009), may also prove uniquely destructive because of the temporal coincidence of inadequate urban management, rapid urbanisation and the escalation of those impacts of GEC, such as increased rainfall intensity, that could drive migration to cities (Annez et al. 2010) and/or adversely affect those cities (Bicknell et al. 2009).

The academic literature on sub-Saharan Africa has long highlighted the importance of fluid human movement across the continent, with circular, rural-to-rural and urban-to-urban migration as well as the urban absorption of traditionally peri-urban or traditional settlements by the physical expansion of cities (Freund 2007; McGregor et al. 2006; Potts 2010). Until recently, African cities were, with notable exceptions (Cairo, Lagos, Johannesburg) generally small, low density and without significant economic muscle (O'Connor 1983; Simon 2007). However, the fast growing character of African urban areas has

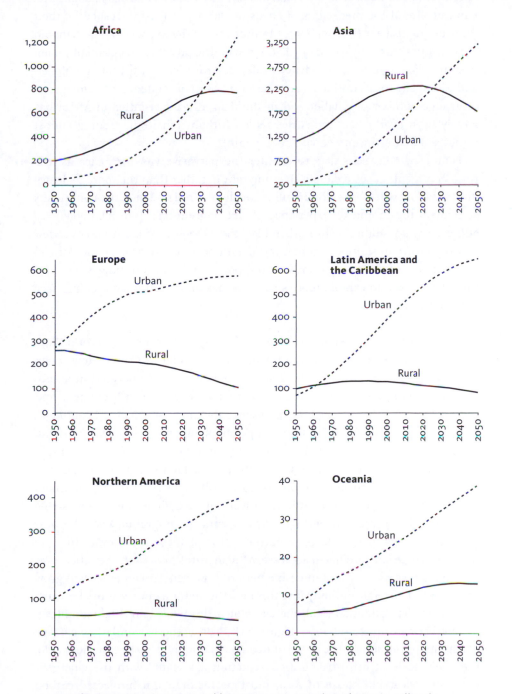

3.1 Urban transition in major world regions, 1950–2050 (population in millions)
(*source*: Commonwealth Secretariat 2010)

long been a source of concern (Rakodi 1997; Stren and White 1989), as has the looming size of the megacities of Lagos or Cairo, not least in respect of their exposure to disaster (Wisner 2003; Monitor 2009). The absence of sub-Saharan African cities from any world city listings, with the possible exception of Johannesburg, compounds the tendency to depict Africa as a vast, underdeveloped and essentially rural continent (Pieterse 2010). As a consequence, the emergence of a huge number of smaller and medium-sized urban centres in Africa has largely been overlooked and Africa's silent urban transition is going almost unnoticed (Satterthwaite 2009; Simone 2010).

Failure by GEC scientists to counter the pervasive view of Africa as 'the rural continent' poses a danger that 'migration' rather than the more inclusive 'urbanisation' will be the dominant or sole lens through which the continent's settlement future and its experience of GEC is examined (see IOM 2009). To address any possibility of anti-urban bias, the chapter begins with an overview of African urbanisation, highlighting the importance of taking the African city as a site of GEC as seriously as the prospect of rural outmigration, and then drills down to explore more specific issues of migration and its interface with GEC.

Urban growth Africa's population is large. At 965 million in 2007 (World Bank 2009), it is almost as large as the populations of India or China. How, when and why population shifts in Africa are important, not least because urbanisation is changing everything about twenty-first-century African livelihoods and settlement forms. Even though Africa is currently the least urbanised continent, by 2050 it will have a higher number of people living in cities (1.2 billion) than Europe, Latin America or North America (Commonwealth Secretariat 2010). Only Asia will have a greater number of urban residents (Figure 3.1). Despite its already large urban population, Africa is still more rural than it is urban, and so, even without the additional drivers of GEC, it is not unreasonable to predict that there will be high rates of rural outmigration over the next three to five decades. Indeed, at current rates of movement, more than 50 million people are predicted to leave African rural areas for the cities over the next ten years. In that same time period, however, African cities will grow twice as fast (by 100 million) just through the natural increase of the existing urban population. In total, the cities of Africa will expand by 150 million people between now and 2020 (Figure 3.1). Even if the currently low average consumption rates of African urbanites are maintained (Satterthwaite 2008), the sheer scale of infrastructure construction associated with the emerging cities of Africa, like those of Asia, must be factored into projected carbon emission escalations (World Bank 2010), and therefore this kind of increase in the urban population is itself identified as a driver of GEC.

The combination of exceptionally rapid urban growth with the weak urban management structures and the lack of local and national state capacity that are found across the global South, but especially in Africa (UN-Habitat 2009), sets up particular dynamics for GEC-induced urbanisation and urban growth (Kraas 2007; Simon and Leck 2010). The challenge is not to assert which will be the most serious issue – the governance, economic or environmental dimension of the urban crisis – but to understand each of the additional challenges GEC will pose for migrating populations and for growing cities. Before we return to a distillation of the differential impacts of GEC, it is essential to get some sense of the scale and pace of urban change in Africa; the very rapid, undermanaged and underfunded urban transformation is what really sets the sub-Saharan African experience of GEC apart from Asia, where the huge number of urban residents, land scarcity and density of cities in vulnerable ecological regions also makes GEC an intrinsically urban question (Sánchez-Rodríguez et al. 2005; Seto 2010).

Urbanisation in Africa There is an unambiguous trend of rural-to-urban migration and an associated increase in the proportion of the African population living in cities and towns (Figures 3.1 and 3.2). Confusingly, both processes are referred to as urbanisation, since the English term 'urbanisation' has at least two related meanings. First, urbanisation refers to the movement of people from the countryside to the town. Second, urbanisation measures the proportion of the national population who live in urban rather than rural areas. Some but not all countries have official definitions of these terms, although there is no uniform international classification (see World Bank 2009 for a full discussion on classification). Clearly, the proportion of people living in urban areas will rise not only due to migration but also due to the natural growth of the existing urban population (Potts 2005). In the African context, urbanisation levels will also increase because of the reclassification of settlements from rural to urban. In some cases this is merely a bureaucratic task but, especially in Africa, cities do expand through encroachment, as former peri-urban areas are incorporated into the town or urban jurisdiction (McGregor et al. 2006). Some estimates suggest that between 1950 and 1980 as much as 26 per cent of the increase in the overall rate of African urbanisation can be attributed to such definitional changes (McGranahan et al. 2009). The net effect of all these contributing factors (growth, migration, reclassification) is a very high average rate of urbanisation in Africa of 3.3 per cent per annum (Figure 3.2), although, of course, there are important regional differences (Potts 2009; World Bank 2009). As a result of the high growth rate and rapid in-migration to cities, Africa is forecast to go from having an urbanisation level of just 35 per cent in 1950 to 48 per cent in 2030 and 60 per cent in 2050 (UN-Habitat 2009).

Lest the impact of GEC-induced migration on cities be misinterpreted or overstated and/or all urbanisation be attributed to new environmental forces,

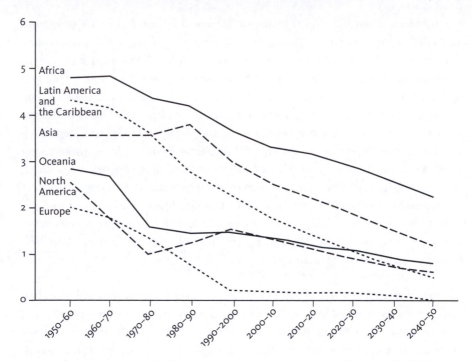

3.2 Comparative rates of urbanisation, 1950–2050 (percentage) (*source*: UN-Habitat 2009: 24)

it is important to single out which components of urbanisation (migration and/or natural growth) drive the expansion of towns and the changing pattern of African settlement. At the moment only one-third of Africa's city growth is caused by in-migration. All countries and regions have natural population shifts but in Africa, where the fertility rate is higher than average (3.3 per cent per annum compared with 2.2 per cent globally) (Demeny and McNicoll 2003; Montgomery 2008), natural growth is more important than on other continents (UN DESA 2010). The shifting distribution of people in a country or on a continent also stems from migration resulting from local economic, environmental or even political forces. As a result of these varied demographic trends, there are differences in the proportions of urban and rural people across Africa (Figure 3.3), reminding us that predicted GEC is just one of many factors driving the change in the sub-Saharan African settlement system.

Assessing the migration impact of GEC is made more complex by the fact that urbanisation is not linear and Africa has a long tradition of return migration, oscillating migration and circular migration, which makes it very difficult to detect or measure patterns of population settlement change over time (Potts 2005; 2010). Indeed, so important is this strategy of moving between places as a means of securing a viable livelihood that the literature on migration in Africa is far richer than that on urban settlement or on natural urban

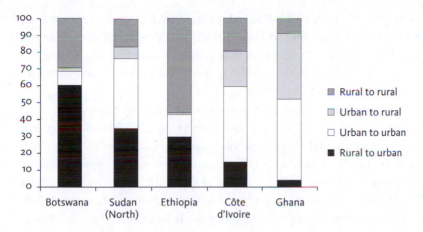

3.3 Comparative migration patterns in selected African countries (percentage) (*source*: Adapted from Todaro and Smith 2009: 344 using data prepared for *World Development Report 1999*)

growth. The relationship between migration and GEC in Africa has recently been reviewed fairly comprehensively (IOM 2009), while the link between GEC and the African city is only just beginning to be tackled substantively, even in primary academic publications (Bicknell et al. 2009; Simon and Leck 2010).

On a continental scale, McGranahan et al.'s (2009) work on urban transitions provides the most comprehensive assessment of the relative importance of migration versus natural population growth as a driver of population distribution. Their work, when set in context, is especially important because it highlights sub-Saharan Africa's unique demographic profile, based on high fertility rates, and demonstrates that natural population increase is a far bigger (and more enduring) contributor to overall growth than is the case in either Latin America or Asia. Moreover, they show that natural population growth is predicted to outstrip migration as a driver of urbanisation in sub-Saharan Africa throughout the period until 2050.

The data presented thus far reveal why it is unwise to look only at that proportion of the population that migrates when investigating the demographic and settlement impacts of GEC. To put it bluntly, even without the anticipated increase in droughts, floods, famines and other climate-induced rural-to-urban migrations, the bulk (60 per cent) of future population growth of cities will come from the offspring of current urban residents (Montgomery 2008). This is true even in Africa, a continent with low levels of urbanisation. The rapid growth of sub-Saharan African cities is caused less by rapid migration than by the high rates of natural urban population growth. Using UN-Habitat figures, McGranahan et al. (2009) suggest that Africa's urban population is the combined result of an overall natural urban population growth rate of 2.2 per cent a year and an in-migration rate of 1.1 per cent a year (making up a total growth rate of 3.3 per cent). Poor education, inadequate healthcare (lack of access to contraception and abortion) plus the dominance of patriarchal values are cited to explain the high fertility rates in Africa that are driving the above average rates of urban population growth (Beauchemin and Bocquier 2004; World Bank 2009; UN-Habitat 2009).

The growth of urban populations is important because cities place enormous demands on ecosystem services such as water, air, food, biodiversity and construction materials and there is such a paucity of capacity (institutional, human and financial) to deal with the pressures that urban growth implies (UN-Habitat 2009). In other words, urban settlements in Africa are fragile even before potentially increased migration associated with GEC is taken into account. That said, any GEC-linked migration would inevitably increase movement within and between African countries, further expanding cities and towns (IOM 2009). It seems reasonable to suggest that GEC will generate an increase in migration, leading to further urban population growth, and that this will possibly make in-migration rather than natural urban population growth the most important driver of city expansion. This would have important policy implications. The specific issue of rural-to-urban migration in Africa should therefore be considered independently, and it is to this issue that we now turn.

Migration and global environmental change in Africa Migration, forced and voluntary, is a well-established response to economic pressure (McDonald 2000) and environmental crises in Africa (IOM 2009). Relocation or movement (often temporary) has long been depicted as a positive adaptive reaction to economic livelihood insecurity (Rakodi and Lloyd-Jones 2002) and is now also cited as a positive response to exposure to climate change and disaster risks (Wisner 2003). But not all African migration is voluntary. The continent already has 20 per cent of all refugees globally and 45 per cent of all internally displaced people (IDP) are found in Africa (Internal Displacement Monitoring Centre 2008). There are millions of Africans displaced by war and conflict each year, a fact not unrelated to ecological crises, especially water shortages (IOM 2009). In other words, even without GEC, there is already a pattern of environmentally induced migration in Africa, some of it voluntary and some forced; some of it temporary, some permanent; some of it to towns and some between rural areas.

If, as seems inevitable based on climate scientists' predictions (Tables 3.1 and 3.2), GEC shifts the patterns and pace of migration streams that exist in Africa – possibly feeding urban in-migration and/or reinforcing circular migrations – it seems reasonable to judge the scale of future impacts against current migration patterns. Unfortunately, the academic literature offers a very confused view of the causes, dynamics and patterns of migration in Africa (Table 3.3) and thus it is unclear exactly what adding GEC into the mix might imply for sub-Saharan Africa's migration future. Working through the multiple drivers of African in- and outmigration as identified in Table 3.3 (push factors, pull factors, push–pull dynamics and other explanations for human movement), it is difficult to assess the trajectories of new (or intensified) GEC-induced migration streams. This problem of classification and overlapping causes should not lead to a rejection of the notion of GEC-induced migration. Rather, especially given the fragility of African rural and urban livelihoods, it is imperative to highlight the fact that GEC may be a catalyst for human movement or act as one of many drivers of settlement change (ibid.).

The diversity of academic explanations for population movement in Africa that is presented in Table 3.3 reflects not only varied intellectual positions, but also the complex migratory movements that are typical across Africa. One difficulty with using the recently published scholarship on migration to examine the dynamics of GEC-induced movement is that it is dominated by arguments propounding 'African exceptionalism' with respect to circular migration (Potts 2010). The argument for circular migration was first presented to counter earlier, simplistic modernisation narratives of the projected permanent urban migration that would accompany industrialisation (see Mabin 1990 for an African perspective on the literature). The most common view now put forward by migration scholars across Africa is that economic and/or environmental stress create an imperative for poor people to have a base in both town and the countryside (IOM 2009). In many respects, the migration literature implies an African preference for circular migration as a livelihood strategy, suggesting that life in town is undesirable and/or that people return to rural areas as soon as it is possible to do so, negating the evidence of extensive permanent movement to urban areas by rural people. There are remarkably few longitudinal studies tracking if and when migrants cease to move between town and countryside and settle permanently in urban areas in response to either increasingly environmentally hostile rural conditions or more favourable urban conditions. McGranahan et al. (2009) point out that the decision to cease circular migration hinges as much on what cities can offer as it does on the GEC-induced stressors of degraded and uncertain rural livelihoods:

> It is likely that as a consequence of climate change this movement will increase and intensify, and possibly become more permanent ... What transpires will depend largely on the capacity of local governments to provide basic infrastructure and services, with the support of national and regional government. (ibid.: 12)

Assuming, as McGranahan et al. (ibid.) and Annez et al. (2010) do, that GEC will put further pressure on Africa's rural areas (see the *italic* text in column 1 of Table 3.3) and that this will encourage more permanent urban migration,

TABLE 3.3 Explanations for migration in sub-Saharan Africa that might be amplified or muted by GEC

1. Push – the decline of rural areas	2. Pull – the attraction of urban areas	3. Push and pull – circular and oscillating migration	4. Other drivers of settlement change
Urban bias in subsidies privileges the built and social environment of cities but creates rural wastelands and causes people to migrate to cities (Lipton 1977).		Informal networks of migrants across city regions and country boundaries link migrants in an unsettled system of perpetual motion, precluding Africans assuming full urban citizenship of any one city (Simone 2010).	War causes urban outmigration, as in the case of Somalia, where Mogadishu has had huge population change with deaths in the city and massive levels of in- and outmigration (Marchad 2006).
Drought and famine, which have been pervasive across Africa, permanently push the poor off the land and into town (O'Connor 1983).	Although globalisation ignores African urban economies and creates a decline in agricultural labour, leaving poor cities but an even poorer countryside, so urbanisation is a product of relative contemporary advantage (Simon 1992).	Circular migration is a rational response to inadequate rural and urban livelihoods, especially under conditions of urban poverty associated with structural adjustment (Potts and Mutambirwa 1990) or state repression (Potts 2010).	Traditional land tenure supports a peasantry and enables people to avoid the shift to cities (Shackleton et al. 2001).
Land degradation and agricultural mechanisation destroy rural jobs and cause rural outmigration (Pieterse 2008).	Cities grow because they offer social and economic advantages (Commonwealth Secretariat 2010).	Food shortages and crop failures lead to temporary relocation to towns (Cross et al. 2006; Crush et al. 2011).	
Rural poverty and conflict drive people out of rural areas (Bryceson and Potts 2006).	Cities are the economic engines of countries and will attract people (Todaro and Smith 2009; World Bank 2009).	Unsustainable rural subsidies fail to offer safety nets, feed costly circular migration and only delay inevitable urbanisation (Parnell and Crankshaw 1996).	

High levels of dependence on agriculture that is not irrigated creates an African weakness to climate variability, causing people to move to towns (Barrios et al. 2006; Annez et al. 2010). Urbanisation has been associated with economic growth, even where this growth is not sufficient to absorb all labour (Kessides 2005).	Service delivery (such as subsidised housing) and some low-skilled jobs absorb some but not all migrants to the city, creating urban opportunities (c.f. Beall et al. 2006).	Forced migration creates temporary single migrants and splits households between town and (mining) settlements (Crush et al. 1991).
	Much cross-border migration is temporary and circular (Potts 2009; Cross et al. 2006).	The incorporation of peri-urban areas into African cities is a key driver of urbanisation (McGranahan et al. 2009).

GEC is likely to compound rates of urban growth – increasing pressure on already vulnerable African cities and towns. However, it is also possible that pressures in badly managed cities that are exposed to increasing GEC risk may encourage poor households to maintain their rural links. As yet there are no documented cases of urban-based GEC risk exposure driving urban outmigration or circular migration, but Bicknell et al. (2009) have begun to document the toll that climate change is taking on the poor of Africa's cities, many of whom are migrants. Unless a city is at major risk from GEC – as in the case of Cairo or Lagos (Seto 2010) – it is likely that Africa's urban areas, despite high unemployment and inadequately secure infrastructure, will be a better place for GEC refugees or migrants. Cities are where the very poorest may be able to access food and other aid, and, as many migrants know, this is where the economy is strongest.

Predictions of increasingly frequent droughts and floods have created understandable concerns that the numbers of IDP in Africa will escalate as the impacts of GEC become ever more visible (IOM 2009). The initial concern was that these IDP would leave Africa and seek refuge in the global North, raising fears about the cost of a legally binding refugee response and calling into question the definition of an environmental refugee (ibid.). In fact, it appears that the migratory responses to environmental disasters such as drought have been national or cross-border movements within Africa (Cross et al. 2006), from inland rural districts to cities and coastal regions, rather than transcontinental migrations to Europe or North America (Annez et al. 2010). The burden of climate-induced refugee absorption is thus, like the impact of climate change itself (IPCC 2001), almost certainly going to be felt most harshly in sub-Saharan African cities.

Conclusion: growth, mobility and displacement under conditions of environmental change

The fact that there has only very recently been any significant attention paid to the possible impacts of GEC on sub-Saharan African migration and urban change make it difficult to use peer-reviewed academic scholarship as a basis for predicting the impact of GEC on urbanisation and migration. In addition, the absence of detailed forecasts of GEC for Africa and its major city regions, the lack of consensus about the drivers of migration and urbanisation, and the reticence of politicians to put migration and urbanisation on to the developmental agenda make it very difficult to offer any robust views on how GEC might be interpreted at the continental level, let alone on a more local scale.

What the discussion thus far suggests is that predicted GEC adds a further variable into an already unstable context, and that, as a result, sub-Saharan African migration and urbanisation, already rapid, could well escalate. Black et al. (2011), in responding to the alarmist projections of the impact of environmental change on migration, develop a framework that links the direct and indirect effects of environmental change to the more traditional political, economic and demographic drivers of migration, rather than seeing migration as a response to GEC. Their embedding of the impacts of environmental change into the wider migration decision-making process provides a useful device for reflecting on whether people move voluntarily or are forcibly displaced. This, in turn, opens the way for more appropriate policy and political responses to GEC-induced migration. If, using the evidence presented in this chapter, we augment their findings on the interplay between GEC and the multiple drivers of migration by including the links between urban growth and urbanisation, we gain an insight into the city-scale dynamics of GEC.

When the GEC challenge is considered with respect to urban growth, very specific technical and management responses can be identified. The scale of natural population growth in cities creates a need for national and local capacity to ensure that urban ecological resilience is maintained and that basic environmental health and human rights are upheld across the city. Creating sound urban management practices in rapidly growing urban areas may require specialised interventions in coastal cities, megacities and city regions. However, not all responses to the impacts of GEC on cities can be reduced to technical and management requirements – there is a very real political element that must be taken into account. The growth of urban populations in locations that are either ecologically sensitive or subject to significant environmental change impacts could trigger political challenges. Especially in megacity regions, it is possible that any portion of the urban population exposed to environmental hazards will be internally displaced; the numbers of such people could be sufficiently large in national terms, or the affected population could have sufficient political power, that the intra-urban migration associated with environmental change will need to be considered as a driver of political change.

The thrust of this chapter has been to show that the scholarly literature relevant to informing GEC impacts has hitherto focused on mobility and displacement, rather than on urban growth. Migration and displacement will almost certainly escalate over the next decades because of predicted GEC, but these are not necessarily the most critical issues shaping Africa's development. Nor is an understanding of migration and displacement a sufficient preparation for responding to predicted GEC impacts. In Africa, the burden of settlement change is likely to be felt most acutely in towns and cities, which not only are increasing rapidly in size because of endogenous growth but are also potential (neglected) sites of GEC. A better understanding of the demographic dynamics of the African continent, as demonstrated in this chapter, expands the emphasis for GEC scholars from issues of migration and displacement to include the nature of permanent African urbanisation and the consequences of urban growth under conditions of GEC.

Note

1 This research was supported financially by the United Kingdom Government Office for Science through the Foresight project on environmental migration. The Foresight lead experts and project team are thanked for their suggestions and support throughout this project. This article benefited from suggestions made by two anonymous reviewers of an earlier report from this study, and from comments by participants at a Foresight workshop.

References

Agoumi, A. (2003) *Vulnerability of North African Countries to Climatic Changes: Adaptation and implementation strategies for climatic change*. Developing Perspectives on Climate Change: Issues and Analysis from Developing Countries and Countries with Economies in Transition. Winnipeg: International Institute for Sustainable Development/Climate Change Knowledge Network. Available at www.cckn.net//pdf/north_africa.pdf [accessed 14 August 2013].

Anderssen, L., J. Wilk, M. Todd, D. Hughes, A. Earle, D. Kniveton, R. Layberry and H. Savenije (2006) 'Impact of climate change and development scenarios on flow patterns in the Okavango River'. *Journal of Hydrology* 331(1–2): 43–57.

Annez, P., R. Buckley and J. Kalarickal (2010) 'African urbanization as flight? Some policy implications of geography'. *Urban Forum* 21(3): 221–34.

Awuor, C. B., V. A. Orindi and A. O. Adwera (2008) 'Climate change and coastal cities: the case of Mombasa, Kenya'. *Environment and Urbanization* 20(1): 231–42.

Barrios, S., L. Berinelli and E. Strobl (2006) 'Climatic change and rural–urban migration: the case of sub-Saharan Africa'. *Journal of Urban Economics* 60(3): 357–71.

Beall, J., O. Crankshaw and S. Parnell (2006) 'A matter of timing: migration and housing access in metropolitan Johannesburg'. In D. Bryceson and D. Potts (eds) *African Urban Economies: Viability, vitality or violation?* Basingstoke: Palgrave Macmillan, pp. 233–53.

Beauchemin, C. and P. Bocquier (2004) 'Migration and urbanisation in Francophone West Africa: a review of recent empirical evidence'. *Urban Studies* 41(11): 2245–72.

Bicknell, J., D. Dodman and D. Satterthwaite (eds) (2009) *Adapting Cities to Climate Change: Understanding and addressing the development challenges*. London: Earthscan.

Biggs, R., E. Bohensky, P. Desanker, C. Fabricius, T. Lynam, A. Misselhorn, C. Musvoto, M. Mutale et al. (2004) *Nature Supporting People: The Southern African Millennium Ecosystem Assessment integrated report*. Pretoria: Council for Scientific and Industrial Research. Available at www.unep.org/maweb/documents_sga/safma_integrated_report.pdf [accessed 3 September 2013].

Black, R., W. N. Adger, N. Arnell, S. Dercon, A. Geddes and D. Thomas (2011) 'The effect of environmental change on human migration'. *Migration and Global Environmental Change* 21(S1): S3–S11.

Boko, M., I. Niang, M. Nyong, C. Vogel, A. Githeko, M. Medany, B. Osman-Elasha, R. Tabo and P. Yanda (2007) 'Africa'. In M. L. Parry, O. F. Canziani, J. P. Palutikof, P. J. van der Linden and C. E. Hanson (eds) *Climate Change 2007: Impacts, adaptation and vulnerability. Contribution of Working Group II to the Fourth Assessment Report of the Intergovernmental Panel on Climate Change*. Cambridge: Cambridge University Press, pp. 433–67.

Bounoua, L., G. J. Collatz, S. O. Los, P. J. Sellers, D. A. Dazlich, C. J. Tucker and D. A. Randall (2000) 'Sensitivity of climate to changes in NDVI'. *Journal of Climate* 13(13): 2277–92.

Brown, O. (2008) *Migration and Climate Change*. IOM Migration Research Series No. 31. Geneva: International Organization for Migration.

Brundrit, G. (2008) *Global Climate Change and Adaptation: A sea-level rise risk assessment. Phase 1: Assessments of sea level rise for the City of Cape Town.* Cape Town: Environmental Resource Management Department.

— (2009) *Global Climate Change and Adaptation: City of Cape Town sea-level rise risk assessment. Phase 5: Full investigation of alongshore features of vulnerability on the City of Cape Town coastline, and their incorporation into the City of Cape Town Geographic Information System (GIS).* Cape Town: Environmental Resource Management Department.

Bryceson, D. and D. Potts (eds) (2006) *African Urban Economies: Viability, vitality or violation?* Basingstoke: Palgrave Macmillan.

Burke, E., S. Brown and N. Christidis (2006) 'Modelling the recent evolution of global drought and projections for the twenty-first century with the Hadley Centre climate model'. *Journal of Hydrometeorology* 7(5): 1113–25.

Chappell, A. and A. Agnew (2004) 'Modelling climate change in West African Sahel rainfall (1931–90) as an artifact of changing station locations'. *International Journal of Climatology* 24(5): 547–54.

Christensen, J. H., B. Hewitson, A. Busuioc, A. Chen, X. Gao, I. Held, R. Jones, R. K. Kolli, W.-T. Kwon, R. Laprise, V. Magaña Rueda, L. Mearns, C. G. Menéndez, J. Räisänen, A. Rinke, A. Sarr and P. Whetton (2007) 'Regional climate projections'. In S. Solomon, D. Qin, M. Manning, Z. Chen, M. Marquis, K. B. Averyt, M. Tignor and H. L. Miller (eds) *Climate Change 2007: The physical science basis. Contribution of Working Group I to the Fourth Assessment Report of the Intergovernmental Panel on Climate Change.* Cambridge: Cambridge University Press, pp. 847–940.

Clark, B. M. (2006) 'Climate change: a looming challenge for fisheries management in southern Africa'. *Marine Policy* 30(1): 84–95.

Commonwealth Secretariat (2010) *Urban Challenges: Scoping the state of the Commonwealth's cities.* London: Com-Habitat.

Crankshaw, O., T. Hart and G. Heron (1992) 'The road to Egoli: urbanization histories from a Johannesburg squatter settlement'. In D. Smith (ed.) *The Apartheid City and Beyond: Urbanization and social change in South Africa.* London: Routledge, pp. 136–46.

Cross, C., D. Gelderbloom, N. Roux and J. Mafukidze (2006) *Views on Migration in Sub-Saharan Africa: Proceedings of an African Migration Alliance workshop.* Cape Town: HSRC Press.

Crush, J., B. Frayne and M. McLachlan (2011) *Rapid Urbanisation and the Nutrition Transition in Southern Africa.* Urban Food Security Series No. 7. Cape Town: Queen's University and African Food Security Urban Network (AFSUN).

— A. Jeeves and D. Yudelman (eds) (1991) *South Africa's Labor Empire: A history of black migrancy to the gold mines.* Boulder, CO: Westview Press.

Dai, A., P. Lamb, K. Trenberth, M. Hulme, P. Jones and P. Xie (2004) 'The recent Sahel drought is real'. *International Journal of Climatology* 24(11): 1323–31.

Demeny, P. and G. McNicoll (eds) (2003) *Encyclopedia of Population.* Vol. 2. New York, NY: Macmillan Reference.

de Wit, M. and J. Stankiewicz (2006) 'Changes in water supply across Africa with predicted climate change'. *Science* 311(5769): 1917–21.

Dodson, B. (2011) 'Mobility and migration: the missing link in climate change and asset adaptation'. Paper presented to the Association of American Geographers, Seattle.

Fauchereau, N., S. Trzaska, Y. Richard, P. Roucou and P. Camberlin (2003) 'Sea-surface temperature co-variability in the southern Atlantic and Indian Oceans and its connections with the atmospheric circulation in the southern hemisphere'. *International Journal of Climatology* 23(6): 663–77.

Foresight UK (2010) 'Environment and

migration project of the United Kingdom Government Office for Science, London'. Unpublished mimeo.

Freund, B. (2007) *The African City: A history*. Cambridge: Cambridge University Press.

Hewitson, B. C. and R. G. Crane (2006) 'Consensus between GCM climate change projections with empirical downscaling: precipitation downscaling over South Africa'. *International Journal of Climatology* 26(10): 1315–37.

Hudson, D. and R. Jones (2002) 'Regional climate model simulations of present day and future climates of Southern Africa'. Technical Note 39. Bracknell: Hadley Centre for Climate Prediction and Research.

Huntingford, C., F. Lambert, J. Gash, C. Taylor and A. Challinor (2005) 'Aspects of climate change prediction relevant to crop productivity'. *Philosophical Transactions of the Royal Society B* 360(1463): 1999–2009.

Internal Displacement Monitoring Centre (2008) *Internal Displacement: Global overview of trends and developments in 2007*. Geneva: Displacement Monitoring Centre. Available at www.internal-displacement. org/8025708F004BE3B1/%28httpInfo Files%29/BD8316FAB5984142C12574 2E0033180B/$file/IDMC_Internal_ Displacement_Global_Overview_2007. pdf [accessed 20 September 2013].

IOM (2009) *Migration, Environment and Climate Change: Assessing the evidence*. Geneva: International Organization for Migration (IOM).

IPCC (2001) 'Africa'. In Intergovernmental Panel on Climate Change (IPCC) (ed.) *Climate Change 2001: Impacts, adaptation and vulnerability*. Cambridge: Cambridge University Press, pp. 489–525.

Jones, G. and S. Corbridge (2010) 'The continuing debate about urban bias: the thesis, its critics, its influence and its implications for poverty-reduction strategies'. *Progress in Development Studies* 10(1): 1–18.

Kessides, C. (2005) *The Urban Transition in Sub-Saharan Africa: Implications for economic growth and poverty reduction*. Africa Region Working Paper Series No. 97. Washington, DC: World Bank.

King'uyu, S. M., L. A. Ogallo and E. K. Anyamba (2000) 'Recent trends of minimum and maximum surface temperatures over Eastern Africa'. *Journal of Climate* 13: 2876–86.

Kraas, F. (2007) 'Megacities and global change: key priorities'. *Geographical Journal* 173(1): 70–82.

Kruger, A. C. and S. Shongwe (2004) 'Temperature trends in South Africa: 1960–2003'. *International Journal of Climatology* 24(15): 1929–45.

Lal, M. (2001) 'Tropical cyclones in a warmer world'. *Current Science* 80(9): 1103–4.

Levy, P. (2006) 'Regional climate change impacts on global vegetation'. In R. Warren, N. Arnell, R. Nicholls, P. Levy and J. Price (eds) *Understanding the Regional Impacts of Climate Change: Research report prepared for the Stern Review on the Economics of Climate Change*. Working Paper 90. Norwich: Tyndall Centre for Climate Change Research, University of East Anglia, pp. 99–108.

Lipton, M. (1977) *Why Poor People Stay Poor: A study of urban bias in world development*. London: Temple-Smith.

Lough, J. M. (2000) '1997–98: unprecedented thermal stress to coral reefs?'. *Geophysical Research Letters* 27(23): 3901–4.

Mabin, A. (1990) 'Limits of urban transition models in understanding South African urbanisation'. *Development Southern Africa* 7(3): 311–22.

Malhi, Y. and J. Wright (2004) 'Spatial patterns and recent trends in the climate of tropical rainforest regions'. *Philosophical Transactions of the Royal Society B* 359(1443): 311–29.

Marchad, R. (2006) 'Resilience of a city at war: territoriality, civil order and economic exchange in Mogadishu'. In D. Bryceson and D. Potts (eds) *African*

Urban Economies: Viability, vitality or violation? Basingstoke: Palgrave Macmillan, pp. 207–32.

McDonald, D. (ed.) (2000) *On Borders: Perspectives on international migration in Southern Africa*. New York, NY: St Martin's Press.

McDonald, R. E., D. G. Bleaken, D. R. Cresswell, V. D. Pope and C. A. Senior (2005) 'Tropical storms: representation and diagnosis in climate models and the impacts of climate change'. *Climate Dynamics* 25(1): 19–36.

McGranahan, G., D. Mitlin, D. Satterthwaite, C. Tacoli and I. Turok (2009) *Africa's Urban Transition and the Role of Regional Collaboration*. Human Settlements Working Paper Series. Theme: Urban Change No. 5. London: International Institute for Environment and Development.

McGregor, D., D. Simon and D. Thompson (eds) (2006) *The Peri-Urban Interface: Approaches to sustainable natural and human resource use*. London: Earthscan.

Monitor (2009) *Africa from the Bottom Up: Cities, economic growth and prosperity in sub-Saharan Africa*. Houghton, South Africa: Monitor Group.

Montgomery, M. (2008) 'The demography of the urban transition: what we know and don't know'. In G. Martine, G. McGranahan, M. Montgomery and R. Fernandez-Castilla (eds) *The New Global Frontier: Urbanization, poverty and environment in the 21st century*. London: Earthscan, pp. 17–36.

— R. Stren, B. Cohen and H. Reed (eds) (2003) *Cities Transformed: Demographic change and its implications in the developing world*. Washington, DC: National Academies Press.

Muhando, C. A. (2001) 'The 1998 coral bleaching and mortality event in Tanzania: implications for coral reef research and management'. In M. D. Richmond and J. Francis (eds) *Marine Science Development in Tanzania and Eastern Africa: Proceedings of the 20th Anniversary Conference on Advances in Marine Science in Tanzania*. Zanzibar: Institute of Marine Science and Western Indian Ocean Marine Science Association, pp. 329–42.

Muriuki, G. W., T. J. Njoka, R. S. Reid and D. M. Nyariki (2005) 'Tsetse control and land-use change in Lambwe valley, south-western Kenya'. *Agriculture, Ecosystems & Environment* 106(1): 99–107.

Myers, G. (2003) *Verandahs of Power: Colonialism and space in urban Africa*. Syracuse, NY: Syracuse University Press.

Myers, N. (2005) 'Environmental refugees: an emergent security issue'. Paper presented at the 13th Economic Forum, Session III – Environment and Migration, Prague, 23–27 May.

New, M., B. Hewitson, D. B. Stephenson, A. Tsiga, A. Kruger, A. Manhique, B. Gomez, C. A. S. Coelho et al. (2006) 'Evidence of trends in daily climate extremes over southern and west Africa'. *Journal of Geophysical Research: Atmospheres* 111, D14102, doi: 10.1029/2005JD006289.

Nicholls, R. (1995) 'Coastal megacities and climate change'. *GeoJournal* 37(3): 369–79.

Nicholls, R. J. and R. S. J. Tol (2006) 'Impacts and responses to sea-level rise: a global analysis of the SRES scenarios over the twenty-first century'. *Philosophical Transactions of the Royal Society A* 364(1841): 1073–95.

Nicholson, S. E., B. Some and B. Kone (2000) 'An analysis of recent rainfall conditions in West Africa, including the rainy season of the 1997 El Niño and the 1998 La Niña years'. *Journal of Climate* 13: 2628–40.

Obura, D. O. (2001) 'Differential bleaching and mortality of eastern African corals. Marine Science Development in Tanzania and Eastern Africa'. In M. D. Richmond and J. Francis (eds) *Marine Science Development in Tanzania and Eastern Africa: Proceedings of the 20th Anniversary Conference on Advances in Marine Science in Tanzania*. Zanzibar: Institute of Marine Science and Western Indian Ocean Marine Science Association, pp. 301–17.

O'Connor, A. (1983) *The African City*. London: Hutchinson.

Parnell, S. and O. Crankshaw (1996) 'Housing provision and the need for an urbanisation policy in the new South Africa'. *Urban Forum* 7(2): 232–7.

Parry, M. L., O. F. Canziani, J. P. Palutikof, P. J. van der Linden and C. E. Hanson (eds) (2007) *Climate Change 2007: Impacts, adaptation and vulnerability. Contribution of Working Group II to the Fourth Assessment Report of the Intergovernmental Panel on Climate Change*. Cambridge: Cambridge University Press. Available at www.ipcc.ch/ publications_and_data/ar4/wg2/en/contents.html [accessed 14 August 2013].

Pieterse, E. (2008) *City Futures: Confronting the crisis of urban development*. London: Zed Books.

— (2010) 'Filling the void: towards and agenda for action on African urbanisation'. In E. Pieterse (ed.) *Urbanization Imperatives for Africa: Transcending policy inertia*. Cape Town: African Centre for Cities, pp. 1–27.

Potts, D. (2005) 'Counter-urbanisation on the Zambian copperbelt? Interpretations and implications'. *Urban Studies* 42(4): 583–609.

— (2009) 'The slowing of sub-Saharan Africa's urbanization: evidence and implications for urban livelihoods'. *Environment and Urbanization* 21(1): 253–9.

— (2010) *Circular Migration in Zimbabwe and Contemporary Sub-Saharan Africa*. Woodbridge: James Currey.

— and T. Bowyer-Bower (eds) (2003) *Eastern and Southern Africa: Development challenges in a volatile region*. London: Pearson.

— and C. Mutambirwa (1990) 'Rural–urban linkages in contemporary Harare: why migrants need their land'. *Journal of Southern African Studies* 16(4): 677–98.

Rakodi, C. (ed.) (1997) *The Urban Challenge in Africa: Growth and management of its large cities*. Tokyo: United Nations University Press.

— and T. Lloyd-Jones (eds) (2002) *Urban Livelihoods: A people-centred approach to reducing poverty*. London: Earthscan.

Ruosteenoja, K., T. R. Carter, K. Jylhä and H. Tuomenvirta (2003) *Future Climate in World Regions: An intercomparison of model-based projections for the new IPCC emissions scenarios*. Finnish Environment Institute No. 644. Helsinki: Finnish Environment Institute.

Sánchez-Rodríguez, R., K. C. Seto, D. Simon, W. D. Solecki, F. Kraas and G. Laumann (2005) *Science Plan, Urbanization and Global Environmental Change*. IHPD Report 15. Bonn: International Human Dimensions Programme on Global Environmental Change.

Satterthwaite, D. (2008) 'Cities' contribution to global warming: notes on the allocation of greenhouse gas emissions'. *Environment and Urbanization* 20(2): 539–49.

— (2009) 'The implications of population growth and urbanization for climate change'. *Environment and Urbanization* 21(2): 545–67.

Schreck, C. J. and F. H. M. Semazzi (2004) 'Variability of the recent climate of eastern Africa'. *International Journal of Climatology* 24(6): 681–701.

Seto, K. (2010) 'Non-environmental drivers of change in low-lying coastal areas'. Unpublished background paper prepared for Foresight UK, London.

Shackleton, C., S. Shackleton and B. Cousins (2001) 'The role of land-based strategies in rural livelihoods: the contribution of arable production, animal husbandry and natural resource harvesting in communal areas in South Africa'. *Development Southern Africa* 18(5): 581–604.

Simon, D. (1992) *Cities, Capital and Development: African cities in the world economy*. London: Belhaven Press.

— (2007) 'Cities and global environmental change: exploring the links'. *The Geographical Journal* 173(1): 75–9.

— (2010) 'The challenges of global environmental change for urban Africa'. *Urban Forum* 21(3): 235–48.

— and H. Leck (2010) 'Urbanizing the global environmental change and human security agendas'. *Climate and Development* 2(3): 263–75.

Simone, A. (2004) *For the City Yet to Come: Changing African life in four cities.* Durham, NC: Duke University Press.

— (2010) 'Infrastructure, real economies and social transformation: assembling components for regional urban development in Africa'. In E. Pieterse (ed.) *Urbanization Imperatives for Africa: Transcending policy inertia.* Cape Town: African Centre for Cities, pp. 28–45.

Stren, R. E. and R. R. White (eds) (1989) *African Cities in Crisis: Managing rapid urban growth.* Boulder, CO: Westview Press.

Strzepek, K. and A. McCluskey (2006) *District Level Hydro-climatic Time Series and Scenario Analysis to Assess the Impacts of Climate Change on Regional Water Resources and Agriculture in Africa.* Discussion Paper No. 13. Pretoria: Centre for Environmental Economics and Policy in Africa, University of Pretoria.

Tadross, M., B. Hewitson and M. Usman (2005a) 'The interannual variability of the onset of the maize growing season over South Africa and Zimbabwe'. *Journal of Climate* 18(16): 3356–72.

Tadross, M., C. Jack and B. Hewitson (2005b) 'On RCM-based projections of change in southern African summer climate'. *Geophysical Research Letters* 32, L23713, doi: 10.1029/2005GL024460.

Todaro, M. and S. C. Smith (2009) *Economic Development.* Harlow: Addison-Wesley.

UN DESA (2010) *World Urbanization Prospects: The 2009 revision.* New York, NY: Population Division of the Department of Economic and Social Affairs of the United Nations Secretariat (UN DESA).

UNEP (2004) *GEO Year Book 2003: United Nations Environment Programme Global Environmental Outlook report.* Nairobi: United Nations Environment Programme (UNEP). Available at www.unep.org/yearbook/2003/ [accessed 14 August 2013].

— (2009) *UNEP Year Book 2009.* Nairobi: United Nations Environment Programme (UNEP). Available at www.unep.org/geo/yearbook/yb2009/ [accessed 14 August 2013].

UN-Habitat (2009) *Global Report on Human Settlements: Planning sustainable cities.* Nairobi: United Nations Human Settlements Programme (UN-Habitat).

— (2011) *Global Report on Human Settlements 2011: Cities and climate change.* London: Earthscan.

Warner, K. (2010) 'Global environmental change and migration: governance challenges'. *Global Environmental Change* 20(3): 402–13.

Wisner, B. (2003) '*Urban social vulnerability to disaster in six megacities (Tokyo, Los Angeles, Mexico City, Johannesburg, Mumbai, Manila)*'. MegaCity TaskForce of the International Geographical Union.

World Bank (2009) *World Development Report 2009: Reshaping economic geography.* Washington, DC: World Bank.

— (2010) *Cities and the Urgent Challenges of Climate Change.* Washington, DC: World Bank.

4 | Linking urbanisation and development in Africa's economic revival

Ivan Turok

Introduction

The relationship between urbanisation and development is one of the crucial questions of our time. Burgeoning urban populations in the global South often contribute to congestion, pollution, squalid housing conditions and stressed ecosystems, although in due course average living standards may rise as economies make the transition from agrarian and subsistence systems. The advantages of spatial concentration have become a major interest of mainstream economists in the global North, illustrated by the Nobel Prize recently being awarded to Paul Krugman. A range of econometric studies in Europe and North America have found that large agglomerations contribute to higher productivity and stronger growth, albeit on a modest rather than a massive scale.

Of course, the biggest economic and urban challenges lie in Africa, where there has been little comparable research. In the absence of clear evidence either way, most African governments seem sceptical of the economic gains from big cities. Faced with the visible signs of distress and decay in overcrowded informal settlements, many of them believe that rapid urbanisation makes things worse. Three-quarters of African governments actually have policies in place to reduce rural–urban migration (UN DESA 2012). They are understandably concerned that if urban economies and labour markets cannot absorb expanding populations, the pressure on poor communities without essential infrastructure is bound to heighten human misery, public health problems, social frustration and political unrest.

Over the last decade, several key international organisations have come to the conclusion that the positive developmental effects of urbanisation outweigh the human and social costs (OECD 2006; UNFPA 2007; UN-Habitat 2008; 2010; World Bank 2009). For example, UN-Habitat (2010: x) has asserted boldly that: 'The prosperity of nations is intimately linked to the prosperity of their cities. No country has ever achieved sustained economic growth or rapid social development without urbanising.' Similarly, the World Bank (2009: 24) argues that: 'No country has grown to middle income without industrializing and urbanizing. None has grown to high income without vibrant cities. The rush to cities in developing countries seems chaotic, but it is necessary.'

The arguments put forward for cities being 'engines of growth' are often rather general and imprecise. The timescales are vague and the supporting evidence from Africa is decidedly thin. The connection between urbanisation and economic growth is sometimes portrayed as automatic and inevitable, like some kind of universal law governing a single, simple process. It is striking how little attention is paid to the possibility that the character and composition of urbanisation may vary in different places, that diverse forms of economic growth can also occur, and that cities might influence growth in different ways. The impact of urbanisation on poverty and inequality, and on systems of food supply, water catchments and other natural systems, also tends to be neglected. Yet global warming, looming resource scarcity and rising social disparities mean that these issues can no longer be ignored when thinking about the processes of urbanisation and growth, let alone when formulating urban plans and policies for the future.

After a long period of stagnation, economic circumstances across many parts of Africa have improved recently. Booming exports of primary commodities and major construction projects offer tangible signs of revival. The new situation requires fresh thinking and updated evidence about the relationship between economic trends, demographic shifts and urban outcomes. There are all sorts of possibilities that require further consideration. One positive scenario is that a rising urban middle class will drive growth and spread prosperity through a consumer boom (McKinsey 2010; Ernst & Young 2011; MasterCard 2013). An alternative possibility is that growth fuelled by harvesting Africa's natural resources will produce skewed outcomes, little employment where it is needed most, and inflated urban property prices that could crowd out expansion of other productive activities.

In this chapter I seek to explore the unfolding relationship between urbanisation and economic development in Africa. The main proposition pursued is that there is no necessary or inherent connection between these phenomena. Much depends on the context in which urbanisation occurs and the form taken by economic growth. The economic environment in many parts of Africa has been insecure and unfavourable in recent decades, so it is not surprising that city economies have performed poorly, despite expanding urban populations. Indeed, urban demographic growth may have made things worse by contributing to overloaded infrastructure and general congestion.

I also touch on the policy implications. If the relationship between urbanisation and development is not close, it follows that the level or rate of urbanisation should not be an important goal of policy makers. Governments should not seek to accelerate or restrict rural–urban migration, but should rather focus on strengthening the economic base of cities and improving the 'quality' or dynamics of urbanisation. By this I mean creating and protecting all kinds of spaces for productive activities, as well as giving people meaningful choices and better access to urban opportunities.

A bleak urban future?

The United Nations (UN) predicts that Africa's current urban population of 400 million will double over the next 20 years and triple over the next 40 years (UN-Habitat 2010). This will be the result of natural growth (more births than deaths) as well as of rural–urban migration. By 2050 nearly two-thirds (60 per cent) of Africa's population are expected to be urbanised, up from 40 per cent today. Africa has been experiencing the world's fastest rate of urban population growth for decades, although the rate of growth is actually diminishing.[1] Africa also happens to be the world's poorest and most precarious continent, which raises the spectre of 'urbanisation without growth'.

Most people move to cities in the hope of finding work and a better life. It is estimated that more than two-fifths (43 per cent) of the urban population in sub-Saharan Africa live below the poverty line and three-fifths (62 per cent) live in overcrowded 'slums' lacking basic services and vulnerable to extreme hardship, illness, environmental crises and social disorder (UN-Habitat 2008). This is by far the highest proportion in the world and the trend is rising. Informal employment already accounts for some 72 per cent of non-agricultural jobs in sub-Saharan Africa (ILO 2002) and around 60 per cent of urban jobs (Kessides 2006; UN-Habitat 2008). However, informal enterprises operate with minimal capital and low skills in congested markets (UNCTAD 2011a) and therefore generate very low household incomes, little economic security and no taxes to pay for better public services. To avoid rising levels of destitution and disaffection, Africa needs to generate productive jobs and livelihoods for the 7 million to 10 million young people entering the labour force each year, a disproportionate number of whom live in cities because of the youthful profile of migration streams.

The urbanisation of poverty in Africa undoubtedly presents formidable challenges. Some external commentators have portrayed the situation as completely bleak, with no hope of improvement. For example, in his book *Planet of Slums*, Mike Davis devotes much attention to Africa's cities, which are said to be growing 'prodigiously despite ruined import-substitution industries, shrunken public sectors, and downwardly mobile middle classes' (Davis 2006: 16). He highlights extreme conditions of squalor, degradation, decay and pollution, attributable partly to globalisation and structural constraints on local actors and institutions. Davis and other observers within this mould tend to write off Africa and its cities as 'basket cases', with little sign of hope and no sense that anyone is doing anything about these problems (Freund 2007; Myers 2011).

Partly in response to such pessimism, a new group of authors has emerged who are deliberately less negative and judgemental about Africa's urban poverty

(Nuttall and Mbembe 2008; Bremner 2010; Simone 2010) and who draw particular attention to the energy and creative spirit of informality. Poor communities are not passive victims but rather active agents with resilience and imagination to negotiate and survive the tough environments of African cities. They are capable of adapting to their physical and economic constraints and making the most of the opportunities available through ingenuity and experimentation. Yet by focusing on the positive features of marginal communities and the coping strategies evident in invisible urban practices on the periphery, this literature may have failed to provide either a balanced account of the situation or a fair assessment of the consequences of large-scale urbanisation. This body of work also appears to have missed the recent wave of commodity-driven investment in many African cities, which I discuss below.

Favourable economic prospects?

In some respects Africa's economic prospects seem to be better now than they have been for many years. An unexpected upturn in many national economies during the last decade has caused a noticeable change in mood and confidence, with a renewed sense of optimism for the future. Ten years ago, Africa was usually portrayed in very pessimistic terms following two decades of structural adjustment, government debt crises and collapsing public infrastructure. As a result, labour markets and service delivery in the cities became increasingly informal, which in turn made workers and households more vulnerable by undermining the quality of jobs and social protection. This was apparent in the spheres of public transport, water, waste removal, housing and land allocation. *The Economist* magazine famously labelled Africa 'The Hopeless Continent' in 2000, yet a decade later the cover of its 3 December 2011 edition did a remarkable about-turn, describing it as 'The Hopeful Continent', with 'a real chance to follow in the footsteps of Asia':

> A profound change has taken hold. Labour productivity has been rising. It is now growing by, on average, 2.7 per cent a year. Trade between Africa and the rest of the world has increased by 200 per cent since 2000. Inflation dropped from 22 per cent in the 1990s to 8 per cent in the past decade. Foreign debts declined by a quarter, budget deficits by two-thirds. In eight of the past ten years sub-Saharan growth has been faster than East Asia's ... Over the past decade six of the world's ten fastest-growing countries were African. (Economist 2011)

Recent reports from international organisations such as the International Monetary Fund (IMF) (2011) and the World Bank (2011) and from global consultancies such as McKinsey (2010), Ernst & Young (2011) and Monitor (2009) have expressed similar up-beat sentiments. They almost seem to be competing to up the ante, with some consultancies suggesting that Africa would be one of the main sites of the next wave of global economic development. The World

Bank (2011: 2) is slightly more tentative: 'Africa could be on the brink of an economic take-off, much like China was 30 years ago and India 20 years ago.' The IMF predicts that four of the world's top ten fastest growing economies in the next five years will be in Africa. The Economic Commission for Africa (ECA) and the African Development Bank refer to the continent becoming a new growth pole in the global economy, on the back of the large savings accumulating in other emerging economies seeking returns in safe havens, and the relative stagnation of European and US markets (ECA 2012).

Africa's recent success and positive outlook appear to stem from strong global demand for primary commodities (especially oil, gas, metals and minerals such as diamonds and coal) and for agricultural products. For example, the west coast of Africa has risen rapidly to become a major supplier of oil to the USA. Africa is believed to contain around 12 per cent of the world's oil and 30 per cent of global mineral reserves. Expenditure on commercial exploration in Africa has outstripped increases elsewhere, rising from US$300 million in 2000 to more than US$2,000 million in 2008 (Harrap 2012). Large new mineral deposits are regularly being identified, such as the recent discovery of major oil and gas reserves in Tanzania, Mozambique, Kenya and Ethiopia (Economist 2012).

Some observers and organisations have also referred to the expansion of domestic consumer markets as a result of strong demographic growth and an emerging middle class (African Development Bank 2011; McKinsey 2010; Ernst & Young 2011; MasterCard 2013). This is certainly attracting the attention of multinational retailers, banks, hotel chains and other commercial operators. However, there are doubts about the genuine economic significance of this phenomenon, and whether it constitutes a sound foundation for future growth. Clarke (2012) argues that the size of the African middle class remains very small and that projections of its growth are exaggerated. Consumerism and celebrity lifestyles are confined to a tiny minority, and it would be a serious mistake for economic strategies to favour consumer-driven growth rather than investment in developing a larger productive base and encouraging higher personal savings rather than spending.

Spatial issues are also relevant to this. Historically in the global North, and now in many parts of Asia and Latin America, the cost advantages, productivity gains and dynamic effects of geographical concentration have helped spur faster growth. If resources can be found, investing in infrastructure and institutions to enable African cities to function more efficiently could secure positive urban 'externalities' and accelerate development. Critical decisions taken over the next few years on what types of infrastructure are pursued and where will define particular national growth trajectories for decades to come. They could reinforce a positive relationship between urbanisation and development, or cause urban problems to become overwhelming. Decisions on transport systems, power generation, water treatment, sanitation systems and serviced land will determine whether cities become more efficient or encounter serious social and ecological limits to growth. Africa's commodity exports could furnish some of the resources for investment in urban infrastructure, although this is not guaranteed because of many competing claims on these funds, such as agriculture, education, welfare programmes and public administration.

The need for diversification

Africa's four main exports are non-renewable and create few direct jobs, so the basis of the upturn has been narrow. To create and sustain wealth in the long term, these diminishing resources must be converted into tradable industries producing consumer and capital goods that will outlast the basic minerals; if not, the benefits may be short-lived: 'Commodity exports can lead to high but not sustained economic growth' (UNCTAD 2011a: 4). *The Economist* (2011) asked: 'Will Africa continue to rise? Or is this merely a strong upswing in a boom–bust cycle that will inevitably come tumbling back down?' Since 2008, the triple global crises of rising food prices, rising energy prices and financial turmoil have already eroded some of Africa's previous gains and exposed its vulnerability to external shocks (UNCTAD 2011a). Africa pays more for oil imports than it receives in overseas aid, according to the International Energy Agency (Mail & Guardian 2012). In addition, Africa's recent growth spurt has not helped to reduce poverty by an equivalent amount because of its composition (IMF 2011).

Africa is the least diversified region in the world in terms of its exports, and has made slow progress in the last two decades: the export diversification index improved slightly, from 0.61 in 1995 to 0.58 in 2009, while in Asian developing countries it improved from 0.32 to 0.26 and in Latin America it improved from 0.36 to 0.33 (UNCTAD 2011a). The IMF (2011) confirms that Africa's export of goods remains unsophisticated (see also African Development Bank 2007; Ajakaiye and Ncube 2010), although there has been some progress with services. The main problem is that Africa still supplies basic inputs to global value chains that are mostly located and controlled elsewhere. The pattern has not changed fundamentally since colonial times, when the continent supplied raw materials to developed economies. Diversification requires moving up the value chain by refining and processing natural resources, creating improved products, providing all sorts of services to industry, and integrating different stages of value addition to develop more rounded real economies. This is likely to be a contested process, since it will threaten foreign competitors and the tariffs that affect how African exports are treated in advanced economies.

The recent shift in patterns of foreign trade and investment from Europe and North America towards China and other parts of Asia also prompts questions about whether this is a 'new scramble for Africa' (Financial Times

2010). China could be the new imperial power exploiting African land, labour and minerals in much the same way that Europe did in the past. The latest evidence suggests that most Chinese foreign direct investment (FDI) to sub-Saharan Africa has consisted of investments in natural resources packaged with related infrastructure projects (IMF 2011). Very large investments in oil, timber, minerals and hydropower have been made in ten countries. China is also financing the building or rehabilitation of 3,000 kilometres of railway lines across the region, including reopening the Benguela railway linking Zambia and the Democratic Republic of Congo to the Angolan port of Lobito. Chinese investors and construction companies prefer to employ their own workforces, which limits the extent of technology and skills transfer to Africans. There is also a huge imbalance in the patterns of trade between China and Africa.

Yet some observers argue that there are genuine prospects for more mutually beneficial 'east–south' or 'south–south' patterns of trade and development (Ampiah and Naidu 2008; Murray 2008; UNCTAD 2011a). Asian investors, including state-owned enterprises, may well take a more patient, longer-term view of Africa's prospects than Western investors because they are less exposed to the short-term commercial pressures of American and European stock markets. And the savings being accumulated in these economies could find a worthwhile outlet in new public infrastructure in Africa, including roads, power generation, water supply and sanitation. Over time, many of the materials and other inputs for these facilities could be produced locally too. UNCTAD (ibid.) believes that in due course Africa could become a supplier of manufactured goods and of inputs to infrastructure and agro-industry to the rapidly expanding middle classes in China and India. The influential *World Investment Report* also identifies opportunities for Africa to benefit from new global trends in FDI arising from the emergence of a wider array of production and investment models (UNCTAD 2011b). These include contract manufacturing and farming, outsourcing of services (such as business process outsourcing), franchising and licensing.

Securing these parts of global value chains to strengthen domestic productive capacity will depend on appropriate policy frameworks, reliable infrastructure and sound institutions. Cheap electricity from home-grown oil and gas supplies and renewable energy will obviously help. Public procurement could also play a role, using the purchasing power of governments over infrastructure and other spending to negotiate higher levels of local production by foreign corporations, instead of relying on imported materials and components. Possible examples of technologically realistic products include fertilisers, chemicals, plastics and other petroleum products, construction materials, plant and equipment, pipes, electrical cables, pylons, buses and railway rolling stock. Governments could also seek to negotiate a progressive increase in the amount of local manufacturing content for multinationals that are seeking access to expanding African consumer markets. This could cover all kinds of consumer durables – clothing, furniture, bicycles, processed foods and even pharmaceuticals, health vaccines and medical devices, where governments are the biggest customers. Many multinationals would be open to creating joint ventures with local small- and medium-sized enterprises that would be able to offer quicker access to local consumers and established suppliers of essential inputs. At present, the stagnant markets in Europe and North America mean that foreign corporations are bound to look more favourably on African markets for growth potential.

The role of geography and urbanisation

Considerations of economic geography, space and location have barely featured in recent reports on African economies, except perhaps for the idea of infrastructure corridors and lower internal tariff barriers to promote intra-African trade (ECA 2012). UNCTAD (2011a) sets out a compelling argument for structural change from agriculture to manufacturing industry in Africa, combined with the building of stronger input–output links between sectors, general upgrading of product quality, and more efficient systems to connect producers to markets. However, it is remarkable that it does not mention how spatial proximity and urban infrastructure can contribute to these processes of economic integration. Similarly, the *World Investment Report* (UNCTAD 2011b) advocates making foreign investment 'stick' better to host economies by developing domestic suppliers, supporting technological learning, and upgrading skills and entrepreneurship. Again, no reference is made to the importance of place and space in 'embedding' external investment in dense local economic relationships, both to ensure that it does not disappear as soon as conditions change and to enlarge the multiplier effect.

The IMF economic outlook (2011) shows that, in a sample of countries, the average rate of employment growth in urban areas over the last decade was more than double the national rate (Table 4.1). Yet the accompanying analysis says little about this important tendency, and the policy recommendations ignore both urban growth opportunities and local constraints of congestion and shortages of inputs, such as electricity and clean water, that inhibit even faster growth. It is a major weakness of such reports that they neglect both the extra costs of production and trade arising from dispersed geographical patterns (the 'friction' of distance), and the multiple benefits of company co-location in strengthening industrial synergies, productivity, innovation and access to diverse skill sets. 'Place' is where complementary activities come together on the ground, where physical obstacles to growth (such as access to serviced land and clean water) are most apparent, and where business interactions are most efficient. Geography, space and cities should not be regarded as mere outcomes of industrialisation, inert containers of economic activity, or passive recipients

TABLE 4.1 Indicators of employment growth for selected African countries

Country	Period	Total employment (% annual change)	Urban employment (% annual change)	Formal employment/working age population (%)
Cameroon	2001–07	2.7	5.6	9.5
Ghana	1999–2005	3.4	6.1	13.3
Mozambique	2003–09	4.4	7.4	16.7
Tanzania	2000–09	3.3	8.8	9.5
Uganda	2002–09	7.5	9.8	13.9
Zambia	1998–2004	1.9	5.1	13.8
Overall sample		3.3	6.8	13.6

Source: IMF 2011, based on national household surveys.

of investment. When it functions effectively, the spatial economy constitutes an intrinsic part of the real economy. In short, efficient spatial patterns are crucial to promoting diversification and integrated development.

Employment is defined as all income-generating activity rather than just formal employment. Despite strong growth, the employment rate as a proportion of the working age population is still very low by standards elsewhere in the world.

African urbanisation remains a sensitive political issue because of its complicated history and the consequences for urban living conditions (Freund 2007). It is often suggested that in many countries urban growth has been driven more by political than by economic factors, such as civil wars and post-independence public spending (Bekker and Therborn 2012; Bryceson and Potts 2006; Commission for Africa 2005). Most governments are wary of appearing to encourage rural–urban migration, believing that it is not rational for households or firms, and may be harmful for the country as a whole.

However, ignoring spatial patterns can undermine the resilience of national economies and jeopardise the viability of human settlements. The cumulative effect of uncoordinated and unregulated decisions regarding the location of businesses and households may be to create bottlenecks in public infrastructure, gridlock on road networks, power and water shortages, and increased risks of environmental disasters such as flooding and pollution. A broader concern is whether the location of the population and resource-based economic growth coincide, bearing in mind the statistical probability that the distribution of minerals and other natural resources will not correspond with the location of most existing urban centres. Migration flows tend to adjust slowly and imperfectly to uneven economic growth, and impose costs of their own. This spatial misalignment means that the first priority for public investment is likely to be long-distance pipelines, transport networks and power generation to facilitate the extraction and exporting of the raw materials, rather than infrastructure to improve urban efficiency and social conditions. Governments and commercial investors will be inclined to focus on the former because these types of investment will yield the biggest financial returns in the short term.

In addition, experience suggests that growth based on extracting commodities and using the export proceeds to pay for imported consumer goods does not generate proportional employment, either within cities or anywhere else (UNCTAD 2011a). There is a large literature suggesting that mineral exploitation is a uniquely difficult and troublesome form of national development, often producing dependent or truncated outcomes rather than diversity, balance and long-term durability. For example, a 'resource curse' may undermine broad-based economic development efforts by crowding out the growth of other sectors through an inflated exchange rate, high capital intensity and barriers to entry. In addition, factional or predatory political structures often arise in the rentier economies of resource-abundant states, inhibiting other forms of economic development (Bridge 2008).

A resource curse for urban areas?

Something analogous may be occurring within many African cities. Well-endowed political and economic elites and expatriates employed by foreign oil and mining corporations tend to inflate the price of housing, vehicles, consumer goods and food. A surge in the amount of money in circulation before the real economy can respond to supply the rising demand encourages speculative land acquisition and luxury property development, in addition to a flood of imports. The effects are reinforced by land market inefficiencies and a limited supply of serviced sites for new development. Inflated property costs and higher consumer prices constrain the growth of domestic industry and raise the cost of living for ordinary citizens. Uncertain property rights and informal transfer systems can also cause distortions such as housing market bubbles. The lack of tenure security makes it easy for poor households to be evicted from well-located land, with nothing to show from the investment they have made in their homes and no share of the general rise in property prices (UN-Habitat 2010). City and national authorities often engage in property demolitions and evictions in order to make space for new buildings. They refer to the process as 'slum eradication', on the grounds that informal settle-ments are out of place and should not be tolerated in a contemporary urban setting, where general environmental standards should be higher. Of course, the social costs and the impact on people's livelihoods from dislocation and resettlement on the urban periphery are very considerable.

For example, as a result of Angola's recent oil boom, Luanda is reputed to have become the most expensive city in the world according to surveys of the cost of living produced by agencies such as Mercer. This reflects the very high cost of accommodation, groceries, fuel, restaurants, hotels, care hire and local taxes (Redvers 2012). There has been a large-scale construction boom consisting of up-market residential property and offices, with government marketing efforts describing the city as an 'African Miami' and a 'West African Dubai' under construction. Meanwhile, 75 per cent of Luanda's residents have no access to piped water on site and 90 per cent have no waterborne sewerage, despite the country's vast oil wealth (Bekker and Therborn 2012). Recognising the enormous increase in the city's land values, the government has undertaken extensive demolition of well-located informal settlements, cleared the land, and made it available for state and private developments of office blocks and flats. Some dislocated communities have been compensated and rehoused elsewhere, but many others have not. Grant (2009) and Obeng-Odoom (2011) describe similar processes in Accra, where a minority of nouveau riche Ghanaians and foreign workers live in sprawling gated communities, while the poor majority of the population is confined to severely overcrowded squatter settlements lacking rudimentary infrastructure and services.

There is a growing realisation that African economies need to add more value to their natural resources before they are exported (ECA 2012; UNCTAD 2011a; IMF 2011). Similarly, African cities need to become more than just centres of luxury consumption, public administration and informal trade. They need to make their own products and produce more of what they consume, in order to retain local spending power and increase household incomes. Diversification would involve developing upstream and downstream activities such as refining, processing, beneficiation and the supply of inputs to mining and manufacturing. Ideally, these activities would gradually move up the value chain over time, from basic production towards more technologically advanced components, producer services (such as engineering, research and marketing) and product design and development. This would create more integrated economies in terms of backward and forward links, and would ensure that any stimulus to growth generated larger multiplier effects, substantially more jobs and a broader spread of incomes throughout the economy. Diversification would also strengthen economic resilience by reducing exposure to volatile commodity prices and unpredictable levels of demand. This shift in approach would take a concerted, patient effort and extensive investment in infrastructure, institutions, skills and business development, as well as negotiations with global equipment manufacturers to invest directly in domestic production or to establish joint ventures with local firms to share knowledge, experience and risk. Governments would need to be determined and firm with foreign investors, but, given the scale of the commercial opportunities available, the potential must be considerable.

Can cities help build more integrated economies?

One of the most urgent issues to be considered is whether urbanisation can help build more coherent, durable economies based on domestic production rather than on imported goods and services. Can urban environments be created that foster local enterprise and innovation, that reduce transaction and transport costs, that facilitate more intense inter-firm trading, and that engender stronger collaboration and learning between economic agents? In short, can rapidly expanding African cities be managed in a way that strengthens local economies and progressively lifts people out of poverty-level subsistence activities?

A growing body of economic theory and evidence suggests that cities can indeed contribute to growth and prosperity in these ways (Duranton and Puga 2004; World Bank 2009; Beall et al. 2010). The concentration of people, firms, infrastructure and other institutions in one place should mean that resources of all kinds are used more productively. However, this is not inevitable, and it is important not to overstate the case. There are many powerful claims made about the far-reaching benefits of cities as 'economic generators', 'incubators of innovation' and so on. The city as a 'growth engine' has become a policy mantra that seems to ignore other conditions necessary for growth and development. The title of US economist Ed Glaeser's recent book is a good example of such hype: *Triumph of the City: How our greatest invention makes us richer, smarter, greener, healthier, and happier* (2011). Another example is provided by Monitor:

> The economic future of sub-Saharan Africa is more connected to the success of its cities than to its nation states ... Rapid urbanization turbo-charges economic growth and diversification. (Monitor 2009)

Such language is partly designed to counter the anti-urban bias that exists in many societies. This in turn reflects the social and environmental problems that for many decades afflicted old industrial cities in the North (Hunt 2004; Turok and Mykhnenko 2007) and continue to affect many cities in the South. This is understandable, but their exaggerated claims can also discredit the case for supporting urban areas, particularly in Africa.

City agglomeration economies can be summarised under three broad functions: matching, sharing and learning (Duranton and Puga 2004; Storper 2010). First, cities enable firms to match their distinctive requirements for labour, premises and suppliers better than towns, simply because markets are larger and there is a bigger choice available. Second, cities give firms access to a better range of shared services and infrastructure because of the larger scale of activity, which generates scale economies for infrastructure providers. Cities offer better external connectivity to national and global customers and suppliers through more frequent transport links to more destinations, and more efficient logistics systems to handle imports and exports. Third, firms benefit from the superior flows of information and ideas in cities, which promote more learning, creativity and innovation, and result in new and more valuable products and processes. Proximity facilitates high-level communication and enables people and firms to compare, compete and collaborate. This can create a self-reinforcing dynamic that spurs growth from within and enables adaptation to changing market conditions and technologies. These dynamic advantages are cumulative and become increasingly significant over time, compared with the one-off, static advantages gained from lower costs.

Such gains are offset by rising levels of congestion, overloaded infrastructure, air pollution, pressure on water catchments and other natural systems, and higher labour and property costs in cities. These negative externalities, or 'agglomeration diseconomies', increase as cities expand, especially if urbanisation is poorly managed and cities are deprived of essential public investment to maintain, refurbish and expand their infrastructure networks. The immediate effects of dysfunctional transport systems, unreliable power and water supplies, insecure telecommunications and degraded environments may be rising business costs, reduced productivity, and a decrease in private investment and economic growth. The balance between the agglomeration economies and diseconomies plays a big part in determining whether city economies continue to grow, stagnate or begin to decline.

Measuring the relationship between urbanisation and growth

It is difficult to disentangle and measure the impacts of agglomeration because of their complexity and because of feedback effects. The benefits are partly absorbed by higher land and labour costs, and offset by increased congestion. Consequently, they may not be evident in aggregate economic indicators such as output or employment. They may not be measurable at the level of city administrative units, for which spatial data are normally available, because of the openness of city economies, and because government transfers between areas, which are designed to compensate for economic weakness, tend to mask the underlying economic processes.

The key agglomeration outcome that should be measured is productivity. This is the single most important determinant of growth in output and income. It reflects the value of local goods and services and the efficiency with which they are produced. A variety of econometric studies in the US and Europe have been carried out in recent years to estimate the effects of agglomeration (Table 4.2). Many of them conclude that cities do offer measurable economic advantages, although they are not as substantial or widespread as often suggested. They indicate that the elasticity of city productivity with respect to city size can range widely between 0.01 and 0.2 (Rosenthal and Strange 2004; Eberts and McMillen 1999; Duranton and Puga 2004; Graham 2007; 2009). This means that doubling city size increases productivity by between 1 per cent and 20 per cent. Put differently, for a 25 per cent increase in a city's population, the output per worker (and consequently income) rises by up to 5 per cent. This is modest rather than substantial.

A novel feature of the Rice et al. (2006) study is that it also sought to measure the rate at which the economic advantages of proximity diminish with distance from the city core. They found that the benefits are greatest within 40 minutes' driving time of the central business district, tapering off quite sharply thereafter and having little or no effect beyond about 80 minutes. The effects of agglomeration are four times stronger 30 minutes' driving time away than 60 minutes away, and 17 times stronger than 90 minutes away. This means that sprawling urban areas can undermine productivity and growth by lengthening travel-to-work times. It also means that transport improvements to reduce traffic congestion and travel times in the largest cities can yield valuable productivity gains for the economy.

In summary, econometric studies have produced contrasting findings on

TABLE 4.2 Estimates of agglomeration economies in the North

Author	Units of analysis	Independent variable	Elasticity
Aaaberg (1973)	Swedish cities	City size (population)	0.02
Shefer (1973)	US MSAs	City size (population)	0.20
Sveikauskas (1975)	US MSAs	City size (population)	0.06
Kawashima (1975)	US MSAs	City size (population)	0.20
Fogarty and Garofalo (1978)	US MSAs	City size (population)	0.10
Moomaw (1981)	US MSAs	City size (population)	0.03
Moomaw (1983)	US MSAs	City size (population)	0.05
Moomaw (1985)	US MSAs	City size (population)	0.07
Nakamura (1985)	Japanese cities	City size (population)	0.03
Tabuchi (1986)	Japanese cities	City size (population)	0.04
Louri (1988)	Greek regions	City size (population)	0.05
Sveikauskas et al. (1988)	US MSAs	City size (population)	0.01
Nakamura (1985)	Japanese cities	Industry size (employment)	0.05
Henderson (1986)	Brazilian cities	Industry size (employment)	0.11
Henderson (1986)	US MSAs	Industry size (employment)	0.19
Henderson (2003)	US MSAs	Industry size (no. of plants)	0.03
Ciccone and Hall (1996)	US states	Employment density	0.06
Ciccone (2002)	EU regions	Employment density	0.05
Rice et al. (2006)	British sub-regions	Economically active population	0.05
Fingleton (2003)	British cities	Employment density	0.02
Graham (2009)	British cities	Employment density	0.07–0.19 a.

Note: MSA = metropolitan statistical area
Source: Based on Graham 2007.

the magnitude of agglomeration economies. This body of evidence is not consistent enough to justify popular claims that cities are powerful drivers of growth. According to Martin (2008: 10): 'We simply do not know enough ... to justify yet further concentration of economic activity in already congested and over-heated regions and agglomerations.'

Evidence from Africa

There have been no equivalent econometric studies of agglomeration in Africa, although there have been several other quantitative studies exploring the relationship between urbanisation and development, or comparisons with other parts of the world. Their findings have been very mixed, with at least four international comparative studies finding no connection between urbanisation and development in Africa.

A major study of 90 developing countries around the world found a positive relationship between urbanisation and poverty reduction, except in sub-Saharan Africa (Ravallion et al. 2007). Another international study concluded that: 'There is generally an unequivocal (positive) correlation between urbanisation and economic development and growth, but in Africa this appears not to apply' (Kamete 2001, quoted in Njoh 2003). A third study examined the relationship between average income and level of urbanisation for some 80 countries at two points in time – 1960 and 2004 (Bloom and Khanna 2007). It found that there was an association between urbanisation and income, particularly at higher levels of urbanisation, but the relationship was not simple or linear. This link had also strengthened between 1960 and 2004. A key conclusion was that 'the links between urbanisation and income are relatively weak at low levels of development' (ibid.: 11). The study specifically compared the impact of urbanisation on average incomes in Asia and Africa, and concluded that:

> While urbanisation in Africa over the past 45 years has been accompanied by sluggish economic growth, in Asia, where urbanisation has occurred to a nearly identical extent, economic growth has been rapid. (ibid.: 11)

Another study focused only on Africa found that nearly three-quarters (71 per cent) of the 32 countries analysed had a negative correlation between urbanisation and gross domestic product over the 1985–2000 period (Bouare 2006, quoted in White et al. 2008). This could be because people left rural areas as a result of poverty and crises, and that migration to urban areas undermined economic performance, possibly by contributing to undue congestion and diverting scarce public resources to fund social infrastructure. Similarly, the *World Development Report* for 1999–2000 argued that African cities are exceptional in failing to serve as drivers of growth: 'Instead they are part of the cause and a major symptom of the economic and social crises that have enveloped the continent' (World Bank 2000: 130). Others have suggested that Africa may have urbanised prematurely in response to push factors (rural droughts, falling agricultural prices and ethnic conflicts) rather than because of the pull of economic opportunities. This view implies that Africa is over-urbanised and that urbanisation on the continent lacks an economic logic (Beall et al. 2010; Satterthwaite 2010).

The notion that urbanisation in Africa has no economic benefits is contradicted by at least two other systematic studies that show a positive link between urbanisation and development (Njoh 2003; Kessides 2007). Njoh (2003) examined data for 40 sub-Saharan African countries and found a strong positive correlation between urbanisation and human development. In a wider-ranging study, Kessides (2007) confirmed a connection between urbanisation and growth over the period from 1990 to 2003 in 15 of the 24 African countries she examined. She also showed that national economic growth during this period was derived from urban industries, supporting the idea of cities as generators of growth. In a related World Bank report she concluded that:

> Africa cannot simply be characterised as 'urbanisation without growth', and the term does not even fit many of the countries. The economic growth that has taken place in the past decade derives mainly from urban-based sectors (industry and services), and this is especially true of the better-performing economies. But cities have clearly not lived up to their productive potential because of widespread neglect and bad management. (Kessides 2006: xxii)

Furthermore, she recognised that the advantages of agglomeration may not emerge automatically, especially if serious shortcomings in basic urban services, land, housing, transport and local government mean that the dis-economies of scale outweigh the economies:

> the simple concentration of firms and people does not guarantee that agglomeration economies will be realised. Many African firms are not experiencing the market efficiencies, ease of mobility and low transaction costs that better-managed cities could deliver, much to the detriment of the economy and competitiveness. (ibid.: ii)

After its sceptical position a decade ago, when urbanisation was seen as one of the causes of economic failure, the World Bank has become one of the strongest advocates for giving urbanisation a higher profile in African development policy. The 2009 *World Development Report* made a strong case for the role of cities in promoting economic development:

> Growing cities, mobile people, and vigorous trade have been the catalysts for progress in the developed world over the last two centuries. Now these forces are powering the developing world's most dynamic places. (World Bank 2009: 13)

Africa was singled out for special attention since it has the most dispersed and least urbanised population in the world, the highest transport costs, and the greatest institutional fragmentation and proliferation of national borders because of its colonial legacy. Consequently, the continent has to promote higher densities, shorten distances and reduce divisions between nations to stimulate economic growth. Anti-urban sentiments also need to change: 'urbanisation, done right, can help development *more* in Africa than elsewhere' (ibid.: 285). Inefficient urban land markets with informal tenure systems and poor basic services obstruct functional urban systems and development: 'Informality is a brake on land development, constraining an efficient spatial transformation' (ibid.: 241). Deficient rural facilities prompt unskilled rural–urban migration, which concentrates poverty in cities and creates squalor, social tensions and instability. And poor transport infrastructure impedes urban–rural interactions and international trade.

To sum up, there is contradictory evidence about the link between urbanisation and growth in Africa. The interpretation of this situation is controversial, with some observers attributing the finding to premature and excessive urbanisation, while others blame poor urban planning and management and lack of investment in urban infrastructure.[2] Cities in the developed North have benefited from a long history of government regulation and active investment, which cities in the global South cannot suddenly match. The main conclusion must be that the relationship between urbanisation and economic development is not automatic or straightforward, and that a range of other forces can disrupt the process.

Conclusion

The chapter develops the argument that there is no necessary or inherent relationship between urbanisation and economic development in Africa. Much depends on the context in which urbanisation occurs and the form taken by economic growth. The economic environment was very unfavourable for many years, but it has become more stable and supportive during the last decade. Yet the resource-based character of the revival is not conducive to inclusive growth and large-scale job creation. Capital investment may be focused on resource-rich regions outside cities and in export corridors linking them to coastal ports. Industrial diversification and integration seem important to add value to primary commodities prior to export and to boost the multiplier effects of resource-driven growth. Cities can perform a useful role in helping to broaden and deepen African economic trajectories, and in ensuring that the continent's diminishing stock of natural resources is used more productively and in ways that will help sustain economic growth for longer. Cities need to produce more of what they consume and to recycle income generated from commodity exports.

The fact that the relationship between urbanisation and development is not close means that the level or rate of urbanisation should not be an important goal of policy makers. Governments should not seek to accelerate or restrict rural–urban migration, but should rather focus on strengthening the economic and employment base of cities and improving the 'quality' or dynamics of urbanisation. The quality of urbanisation refers to the way in which people and firms find their place within cities. For people, this means the position they occupy in urban labour markets, housing systems, education and training systems, and social networks. For firms, this means the niche product markets, supply chains, collaborative networks and business premises they occupy.

It seems likely that urban systems that are good at accommodating and absorbing new entrants will prove to be more productive, because people and firms that find useful sites to occupy and roles to perform will tend to be more energetic, enterprising and inclined to invest. Informal settlements perform a crucial function as gateways or stepping stones to urban labour and housing markets (Turok 2012). Hence, it is vital for government policies to treat these areas sympathetically rather than to demolish them. This may mean higher levels of public investment and incremental upgrading, and an element of benign neglect where lack of affordability inhibits any immediate improvements. It is also important for governments to create and protect all kinds of spaces for productive activities within cities, to give people greater choice in deciding where to live, to assist those who want to access urban opportunities, and to avoid forced migration. In circumstances of rapid demographic and economic growth, such as in Luanda, it will always be difficult to manage conflicting requirements for land. In such situations it is all the more important that there are fair and reasonable systems of planning and regulation in place to ensure that decisions reflect a proper balance between economic, social and environmental considerations.

A final point is that further research is required into the interactions between contemporary economic and demographic changes across Africa, and into the reasons for the apparently weak historic relationship between urbanisation and economic growth. It remains unclear whether this is a statistical anomaly or is attributable to:

- premature or excessive urban population growth;
- deindustrialisation associated with structural adjustment policies;
- poor current international competitiveness in manufacturing;
- poor urban planning and management;
- lack of investment in urban infrastructure; and/or
- the predominantly informal nature of urban economies and land markets.

Notes

1 Some doubts about the reliability of these statistics and their interpretation have been raised by Potts (2012) and Satterthwaite (2010).

2 The statistics on urbanisation in Africa used to argue that there has been rapid urbanisation without economic growth have also been called into question (Potts 2012).

References

African Development Bank (2007) *African Development Report 2007: Natural resources for sustainable development in Africa*. Oxford: Oxford University Press.

— (2011) *The Middle of the Pyramid: Dynamics of the middle class in Africa*. Tunis-Belvedère: African Development Bank.

Ajakaiye, O. and M. Ncube (2010) 'Infrastructure and economic development in Africa: an overview'. *Journal of African Economies* 19, AERC Supplement 1: i3–i12.

Ampiah, K. and S. Naidu (eds) (2008) *Crouching Tiger, Hidden Dragon? Africa and China*. Scottsville: University of KwaZulu-Natal Press.

Beall, J., B. Guha-Khasnobis and R. Kanbur (eds) (2010) *Urbanization and Development: Multidisciplinary perspectives*. Oxford: Oxford University Press.

Bekker, S. and G. Therborn (2012) *Capital Cities in Africa: Power and powerlessness*. Cape Town: HSRC Press.

Bloom, D. E. and T. Khanna (2007) 'The urban revolution'. *Finance and Development* 44(3): 9–14.

Bremner, L. (2010) *Writing the City into Being: Essays on Johannesburg 1998–2008*. Johannesburg: Fourthwall Books.

Bridge, G. (2008) 'Global production networks and the extractive sector: governing resource-based development'. *Journal of Economic Geography* 8(3): 389–419.

Bryceson, D. F. and D. Potts (eds) (2006) *African Urban Economies: Viability, vitality or vitiation?* Basingstoke: Palgrave Macmillan.

Clarke, D. (2012) *Africa's Future: Darkness to destiny*. Johannesburg: Profile Books.

Commission for Africa (2005) *Our Common Interest*. London: Commission for Africa.

Davis, M. (2006) *Planet of Slums*. London: Verso Books.

Duranton, G. and D. Puga (2004) 'Microfoundations of urban agglomeration economies'. In V. Henderson and J. Thisse (eds) *Handbook of Regional and Urban Economics*. Volume 4. Amsterdam: North-Holland, pp. 2063–117.

Eberts, R. and D. McMillen (1999) 'Agglomeration economies and urban public infrastructure'. In P. Cheshire and E. Mills (eds) *Handbook of Regional and Urban Economics*. Volume 3. Amsterdam: North-Holland, pp. 1455–95.

ECA (2012) *Unleashing Africa's Potential as a Pole of Growth: Economic report on Africa*. Addis Ababa: Economic Commission for Africa (ECA).

Economist (2011) 'The hopeful continent'. *The Economist*, 3 December.

— (2012) 'Eastern El Dorado? At long last East Africa is beginning to realise its energy potential'. *The Economist*, 7 April.

Ernst & Young (2011) *It's Time for Africa: Ernst & Young's 2011 Africa attractiveness survey*. London: Ernst & Young.

Financial Times (2010) 'China's new scramble for Africa'. *The Financial Times*, 25 August.

Freund, B. (2007) *The African City: A history*. Cambridge: Cambridge University Press.

Glaeser, E. (2011) *Triumph of the City: How our greatest invention makes us richer, smarter, greener, healthier, and happier*. London and New York, NY: Penguin Press.

Graham, D. (2007) *Agglomeration Economies and Transport Investment*. Discussion Paper No. 2007-11. Paris: International Transport Forum and Organisation for Economic Cooperation and Development (OECD). Available at www.internationaltrans

portforum.org/jtrc/DiscussionPapers/ Discussion Paper11.pdf [accessed 4 September 2013].

— (2009) 'Identifying urbanisation and localisation externalities in manufacturing and service industries'. *Papers in Regional Science* 88(1): 63–84.

Grant, R. (2009) *Globalizing City: The urban and economic transformation of Accra, Ghana*. Syracuse, NY: Syracuse University Press.

Harrap, A. (2012) 'Australia supports Africa's sustainable resource extraction'. *Business Report*, 2 February.

Hunt, T. (2004) *Building Jerusalem: The rise and fall of the Victorian city*. London: Weidenfeld and Nicolson.

ILO (2002) *Women and Men in the Informal Economy: A statistical picture*. Geneva: International Labour Office (ILO).

IMF (2011) *World Economic and Financial Surveys: Regional economic outlook: Sub-Saharan Africa*. Washington, DC: International Monetary Fund (IMF).

Kessides, C. (2006) *The Urban Transition in Sub-Saharan Africa: Implications for economic growth and poverty reduction*. Africa Region Working Paper Series No. 97. Washington, DC: World Bank.

— (2007) 'The urban transition in sub-Saharan Africa: challenges and opportunities'. *Environment and Planning C* 25(4): 466–85.

Mail & Guardian (2012) 'Clean energy crucial for poor countries'. *Mail & Guardian*, 5 April. Available at http:// mg.co.za/article/2012-04-05-clean-energy-crucial-for-poor-countries [accessed 15 August 2013].

Martin, R. (2008) 'National growth versus spatial equality? A cautionary note on the new "tradeoff" thinking in regional policy discourse'. *Regional Science Policy and Practice* 1(1): 3–13.

MasterCard (2013) 'MasterCard study reveals African cities economic growth potential'. Available at http://news room.mastercard.com/press-releases/ mastercard-study-reveals-african-cities-economic-growth-potential/ [accessed 21 August 2013].

McKinsey (2010) *Lions on the Move: The progress and potential of African economies*. Washington, DC: McKinsey Global Institute. Available at www. mckinsey.com [accessed 14 August 2013].

Monitor (2009) *Africa: From the Bottom Up: Cities, economic growth, and prosperity in sub-Saharan Africa*. Houghton, South Africa: Monitor Group. Available at www.abafe.biz/fileadmin/redaktion/ pdf/WEB_Monitor_Africa_from_ bottom_up_2009.pdf [accessed 4 September 2013].

Murray, M. (2008) 'Africa's futures: from north–south to east–south?'. *Third World Quarterly* 29(2): 339–56.

Myers, G. (2011) *African Cities: Alternative visions of urban theory and practice*. London: Zed Books.

Njoh, A. (2003) 'Urbanization and development in sub-Saharan Africa'. *Cities* 20(3): 167–74.

Nuttall, S. and A. Mbembe (eds) (2008) *Johannesburg: The elusive metropolis*. Durham, NC and Johannesburg: Duke University Press and Wits University Press.

Obeng-Odoom, F. (2011) 'Developing Accra for all? The story behind Africa's largest millennium city'. *Development* 54(3): 384–92.

OECD (2006) *Competitive Cities in a Global Economy*. Paris: Organisation for Economic Co-operation and Development (OECD).

Potts, D. (2012) *Whatever Happened to Africa's Rapid Urbanisation?* London: Africa Research Institute.

Ravallion, M., S. Chen and P. Sangraula (2007) *New Evidence on the Urbanization of Global Poverty*. Policy Research Working Paper.Washington, DC: World Bank. Available at http:// documents.worldbank.org/curated/ en/2007/04/8178686/new-evidence-urbanization-global-poverty [accessed 14 August 2013].

Redvers, L. (2012) 'Living in the world's most expensive city'. BBC News website, 2 February. Available at www.bbc.

co.uk/news/business-16815605 [accessed 14 August 2013].

Rice, P., A. Venables and E. Patacchini (2006) 'Spatial determinants of productivity: analysis for the regions of Great Britain'. *Regional Science and Urban Economics* 36(6): 727–52.

Rosenthal, S. and W. Strange (2004) 'Evidence on the nature and sources of agglomeration economies'. In V. Henderson and J. Thisse (eds) *Handbook of Regional and Urban Economics*. Volume 4. Amsterdam: North-Holland, pp. 2119–71.

Satterthwaite, D. (2010) 'Urban myths and the mis-use of data that underpin them'. In J. Beall, B. Guha-Khasnobis and R. Kanbur *Urbanization and Development: Multidisciplinary perspectives*. Oxford: Oxford University Press, pp. 83–102.

Simone, A. (2010) *City Life from Jakarta to Dakar: Movements at the crossroads*. London: Routledge.

Storper, M. (2010) 'Agglomeration, trade and spatial development: bringing dynamics back in'. *Journal of Regional Science* 50(1): 313–42.

Turok, I. (2012) *Urbanisation and Development in South Africa: Economic imperatives, spatial distortions and strategic responses*. Urbanization and Emerging Population Issues Working Paper 8. London: International Institute for Environment and Development.

— and V. Mykhnenko (2007) 'The trajectories of European cities, 1960–2005'. *Cities* 24(3): 165–82.

UNCTAD (2011a) *Economic Development in Africa: Fostering industrial development in Africa in the new global environment*. Geneva: United Nations Conference on Trade and Development (UNCTAD). Available at http://unctad.org/en/Docs/aldcafrica2011_en.pdf [accessed 14 August 2013].

— (2011b) *World Investment Report 2011*. Geneva: United Nations Conference on Trade and Development (UNCTAD). Available at www.unctad-docs.org/files/UNCTAD-WIR2011-Full-en.pdf [accessed 14 August 2013].

UN DESA (2012) *World Urbanization Prospects: The 2011 revision*. New York, NY: Population Division of the Department of Economic and Social Affairs of the United Nations Secretariat (UN DESA).

UNFPA (2007) *State of World Population 2007: Unleashing the potential of urban growth*. New York, NY: United Nations Population Fund (UNFPA). Available at www.unfpa.org/webdav/site/global/shared/documents/publications/2007/695_filename_sowp2007_eng.pdf [accessed 14 August 2013].

UN-Habitat (2008) *The State of African Cities 2008: A framework for addressing urban challenges in Africa*. Nairobi: United Nations Human Settlements Programme (UN-Habitat).

— (2010) *State of the World's Cities 2010/11: Bridging the urban divide*. Nairobi: United Nations Human Settlements Programme (UN-Habitat).

White, M. J., B. U. Mberu and M. A. Collinson (2008) 'African urbanisation: recent trends and implications'. In G. Martine et al. (eds) *The New Global Frontier: Urbanization, poverty and environment in the 21st century*. London: Earthscan, pp. 302–16.

World Bank (2000) *World Development Report 1999/2000: Entering the 21st century*. Washington, DC: World Bank.

— (2009) *World Development Report 2009: Reshaping economic geography*. Washington, DC: World Bank.

— (2011) *Africa's Future and the World Bank's Support to It*. Washington, DC: World Bank.

5 | Religion and social life in African cities

Carole Rakodi

Introduction

Despite the sparse and incomplete nature of the evidence, it is clear that not only allegiance but also religious beliefs and regular practice (e.g. frequent attendance at prayers and services) are almost universal and that membership of religious groups is more common than of any other type of organisation. Religion plays important roles in the lives of most urban Africans, offering 'meaning and hope for millions of impoverished urban residents seeking solace and comfort in a heartless world' (Myers and Murray 2006: 11) and providing 'redemptive moments and spaces of spiritual and social communion' (Aina 1997b in Zeleza 1999: 55), as well as sometimes provoking rivalry and conflict. The roles of religion in social change relate to its influence on people's world views, values, behaviour and sense of identity and, in turn, to the influence of individual adherents and religious organisations on social life, through their attitudes to aspects of personal behaviour within the family and outside, perceptions of how advantage and disadvantage may be related to religious affiliation, and the charitable and service delivery activities of religious organisations. Religious groups' desire to promote their own standing and reach, influence policies on certain issues and deliver services leads them to become engaged in politics, with outcomes that vary between groups and depend on how religious and other (especially ethnic) identities are intertwined.

Attempts to describe and explain social change in African cities reflect both the continent's colonial and postcolonial history and epistemological changes in the social sciences. Both help to explain the characteristics of available data; in turn, this material influences the nature of the studies that analysts undertake. Scholarship on religion in Africa has been generated in a variety of disciplines but it has been neglected in others, including economic and development studies, and in mainstream development policy and practice, and little of the material refers (explicitly) to urban areas. While sensitivity is certainly a factor, the neglect of religion can also be attributed to the lack of appropriate conceptual and analytical tools in economics, development studies and mainstream development policy; suspicion of anthropology's methods and its links with colonialism; and the association of mainstream development policy and practice with Western countries that anticipated social secularisation and are committed to political secularism (Deneulin and Rakodi 2011). Evidence of the religious affiliation and attitudes of urban populations, the links between these and their social relationships and behaviour, and the roles played by religion in service delivery, politics and conflict is patchy, both geographically and, as with many other aspects of social change, in its emphasis on the new, spectacular or worrying rather than on the everyday and routine. The first section of the chapter will briefly explore this terrain. In the subsequent section, some of the main contours of social change will be identified, as a context for the discussion of religion that follows.

A comprehensive analysis of religion and religious groups in the towns and cities of a whole subcontinent is not possible, given the constraints of space, the limited attention paid to religion in African urban research and the variable nature of the information available. The analysis attempts to identify key trends and common characteristics, while also recognising the diversity between and within urban centres. It considers trends in religious organisation and affiliation, changing beliefs and practices, engagements between religion and politics, and the role of religious actors in providing welfare, social and economic support.

Perspectives on social change

Although there is some information from pre-colonial African cities, most of the early accounts were produced by travellers, administrators, sociologists and anthropologists, such as those employed by the Rhodes-Livingstone Institute in Lusaka, during the colonial era. They reflected the epistemological assumptions prevalent at the time. Like the Orientalist discourse that enabled European culture to represent and manage the Orient (Said [1978] 1995), colonial representations of Africa and Africans essentialised cultural and racial difference but failed to recognise the ways in which the observers' own cultural assumptions influenced their portrayal, as well as serving the interests of the colonial powers. In the later years of colonialism, and particularly after independence, it was anticipated that the objectives of prosperity and nationhood would be achieved by state-led development, underpinned, so modernisation theory asserted, by completing the socio-cultural shift from traditional to modern attitudes and social structures that was already under way. In the prevailing development discourse, thinking about goals and policies was dominated by economics, first Keynesian and later neo-liberal. Urban centres could, it was believed, contribute by maintaining the modern approaches to town planning introduced by the colonial authorities. Government agencies and academic studies sought to generate data about patterns of urban growth and change as a basis for developing appropriate policies, administering land and providing services. They did this primarily through censuses and surveys, in line with the positivistic approaches to knowledge that dominated the social sciences at the time. However, the inability of urban administrations to keep pace with the demands of urban growth led on the one hand to panic about excessive rates of urbanisation and on the other, gradually, to the gathering of information that was not captured by the official data sources, through studies of so-called informal settlements and enterprises.

The failure of post-independence economic policies to achieve sustained economic growth and poverty reduction, of political arrangements to deepen democracy and achieve stability, and of urban policies and processes to manage the rapid growth of towns and cities led not only to challenges to the assumptions and models of mainstream development policy but also to increasing recognition that positivist epistemological approaches were incapable of revealing more than a small fraction of the reality of economic and social change (Kapoor 2008; Nederveen Pieterse 2010).[1] Increasingly, analysts challenged mainstream social science methods, accusing them of failing to recognise the epistemological and methodological deficiencies of positivist knowledge and of being insufficiently self-reflexive. The value of qualitative methods was (re-)recognised, participatory appraisal approaches were increasingly adopted, and the number of ethnographic studies multiplied. However, the selection of social phenomena for study still tended to reflect the cultural and discursive assumptions of outsiders, with the result that some aspects of urban life were documented while others were neglected. It is often difficult to tell whether the features described are typical or unusual, genuinely invisible or merely puzzling to the observer (see, for example, Koolhaas 2002). This difficulty was exacerbated by the increased use of impressionistic writing in which the nature and sources of evidence are not clear (e.g. Simone 2002; 2004). In addition, the influence of postcolonial theory, which emerged out of literary studies and focuses on discourse, has increased the influence of accounts of urban change by journalists, filmmakers and writers (see, for example, Davis 2004; Fu and Murray 2007; Kehinde 2007; Mbembe and Roitman 2002; Nyairo 2006; Samuelson 2007). Often, observers' attention has been caught by the extreme, the newsworthy, the dystopian, leading to analyses that portray African cities as chaotic, unplanned, unruly and violent. Such analyses often imply that a whole city resembles the slum, social group or pattern of behaviour described, or that the city portrayed is typical of all African cities; this view is epitomised by the claim that Kinshasa or Lagos are 'quintessential' African cities (Pieterse 2010: 206). Thus, attempts to understand changing social life in African cities have often focused on the new, spectacular and worrying rather than on the everyday and routine.

This chapter acknowledges that in many cities criminality and violence are pervasive, housing and services in desperately short supply, politics dysfunctional and inequality extreme, meaning that, for many, urban life is marked by poverty, ill health and insecurity. It recognises that social change is rapid and unsettling, and that the social milieu is characterised by social disorganisation and family breakdown. Nevertheless, it also argues that most residents, most of the time, in many towns and cities, get by. They engage in multiple social and economic interactions, occupying land and building houses, markets and social facilities. They base their everyday lives on meanings, identities and social interactions that are familiar and supportive, while at the same time being constantly remade to meet the challenges of urban life. In addition, administrative processes and service delivery systems continue to function, however inadequately. Increasingly, analysts such as Myers (2011), Robinson (2006), Pieterse (2008; 2010) and Simone (2010a) have argued for accounts that seek out complementary types of knowledge, are, directly or indirectly, of practical use in identifying solutions to urban problems, and reflect the prevalence of the quotidian and mundane while acknowledging the extremes.

Religion in context

Urban lives and societies are diverse and heterogeneous. They are influenced by changing migration patterns, intra-family relationships and associational life, while aspects of social difference such as gender, generation, ethnicity and religion interact with each other and with processes of demographic, physical and economic change. Both practical arrangements and identities and meanings are constantly reproduced and remade though people's interactions with others. Religion needs to be considered within these wider processes of social change, including migration and changes in the demography of urban populations, how family life is evolving, with a particular focus on gender and generational differences, and associational life; all these elements are influenced by dimensions of difference such as ethnicity and socioeconomic status as well as by religion itself. Here, there is space to identify only a few of the most relevant trends.

Migration and demographic change Urban populations in sub-Saharan Africa continue, for the most part, to grow rapidly. This is increasingly due to high natural growth rates among urban populations, which have a relatively young age profile, despite the effects of declining fertility and increased mortality because of ill health, including HIV/AIDS. However, migration also continues to be important, although there is now evidence to show that urbanisation rates declined in some countries during economic slowdowns (Potts 2009; 2012; Zeleza 1999). For some, migration is not just a response to difficult conditions in rural areas (Annez et al. 2010) and urban economic opportunities, but also a way of escaping the stultifying sameness and boredom of village life, as well as the restrictions of a gerontocratic and patriarchal society in which older men hold power and young people and women are subordinate, and in which behaviour regarded as unconventional is disapproved of and may even lead to social sanctions (for example through witchcraft accusations).

The composition and nature of migration flows have changed over time. Trade, migration and evangelism (especially Muslim expansion) pre-dated colonialism, the latter especially in West Africa but also along the East African coast. Migration during the colonial period was both domestic and international. Migrants were initially predominantly male and migration circular, although in most countries this changed to family migration and (more or less) permanent urban settlement in the 1940s and 1950s, reinforced by the abolition of migration controls at independence. In addition, independent migration by women has become more common. Migration has never been either solely domestic or a one-way rural–urban flow (Bakewell and Jónsson 2011: 10). Even today, many migrants actively maintain links with rural kin, especially when they can make claims on rural land; many families pursue multi-local livelihoods; and some return to live in rural areas.

On arrival, migrants join an economically and socially diverse population of people born and bred in the city, including both those who claim to be indigenous and the descendants of earlier migrants. They interact not only with others from their area of origin, who may have the same religious background, to whom they may be related and who speak the same language, but also with people with very different socioeconomic characteristics and cultural practices. The nature of the interaction depends on the profile of migrants, which changes over time and varies between groups, and the evolving socioeconomic characteristics of the settled urban population, as well as on the political context. The early literature concentrated on the disruptive effects of migration on the strong social norms, kinship relations and support networks that supposedly characterised rural societies. Contemporary literature continues to express fears that traditional practices and behavioural norms are losing their influence, leading to erosion of the social fabric; that groups with different ethnic and religious identities are incompatible; and that migrants and internally displaced people compete with established urban residents, especially young people, for jobs and housing (Fielden 2008). Often, the interest of researchers has been provoked more by tensions between in-migrants and host populations than by peaceful integration (for example in Nairobi – see Campbell 2006; Johannesburg – see Afrobarometer 2010; Kihato 2007; Reitzes 2002; see also McNamee 2012). At the same time, studies continue to document the ways in which kin and fictive kin relationships still pave the way for new migrants, providing them with contacts, information and initial accommodation; associations emulate rural forms; and institutions adapted from the norms, rules and ways of operating in rural societies provide frameworks for regulating economic and property transactions in urban areas (Rakodi 2006). Recognition that 'tradition' cannot be conceptualised as primordial and unchanging has led to an improved understanding of the ways in which the norms and social relationships of rural societies are selectively adopted and adapted in urban centres with populations of mixed origin.

Changing families: gender and generational relations Towns and cities are often described by both residents and observers as places where families are breaking down, kinship obligations are no longer observed and communities no longer exist. People are portrayed as individualistic, uncaring, self-seeking and amoral and urban societies as fragmented and dysfunctional. Certainly, there is much evidence of social strain – family breakdown, high levels of crime and delinquency, widespread poverty and systematic corruption. But that is not the whole picture. Complex webs of social relationships link urban residents to many different units that are governed by continually evolving norms and rules, ranging from those that are clearly defined and tightly regulated to others that are more amorphous. There are continuous debates and contestations over the rights and obligations embedded in the relationships between parents and children, men and women, and members of extended families, leading to the emergence of different ways of accommodating individual needs for autonomy and choice while providing mutual support, attaining security and retaining a sense of belonging.

Much analysis takes the household as the primary organisational unit of urban society – essentially, this comprises the individuals who share a dwelling and pool their incomes, or at least a part of them. Even though this conceals a more complex picture in terms of the assets available to individual households, multi-spatial household arrangements, the dynamics of decision making, and the flexible nature of household composition, it has a strong logic in the urban context, and is reinforced by bureaucratic practices. However, links and mutual obligations to extended family and wider kin networks in both urban and rural areas continue to be important for most urban households. They are significant in the diversified livelihood strategies adopted by many to cope with economic shocks. The use and exchange of resources within both households and wider kinship groups are regulated by informal norms said to be characterised by trust and reciprocity, but families are, of course, sometimes in conflict and reciprocity can become a burden, especially in times of economic difficulty. In addition, access to resources is influenced by established property, power and gender relationships.

The combination of continuity and change in family patterns and relationships in urban Africa is especially evident in gender relations. There is much evidence to show that women's roles, responsibilities and influence within households have not changed, but also that traditional values and practices take on new meanings in urban settings and people become aware of the possibility for different beliefs and behaviour (van Til 2006); this can lead to the emergence of new family forms and dynamics, as well as new types of relationships based on friendship and propinquity (Werthmann 2006). Urban environments may therefore enable women to escape from the control of male lineage heads and elders and may provide new opportunities, in particular to engage in business, although this depends on a woman's access to capital and social and political networks, as well as on potential social and religious restrictions on her movements.

In addition to gender relationships (and cutting across them), both within households and in the wider society the distribution of roles between the generations and intergenerational relationships are in a state of flux, as a result of the changing age structure of urban populations, economic and policy changes, and wider cultural influences. More attention has been focused on young people than on older urban residents, partly because of their larger numbers, partly because the opportunities open to them influence their marital choices and family relationships, and partly because their social attitudes and behaviour are more likely to challenge prevailing structures of author-ity. Their general frustration may spill over into resentment of societies that remain under gerontocratic control, a search for alternative resources, and a quest for identity and belonging through membership of religious or political movements, local vigilante groups or armed militias. Today, transition from one life stage to the next seems to be increasingly problematic (Christiansen et al. 2006), giving rise to genuine concerns about the effects on young people of idleness, substance abuse and obstacles to their anticipated progress to responsible 'adulthood'.

Identity, difference and associational life The wider social relationships of individuals and households include loose associational links, membership of organisations, and/or participation in broad social and political movements. These categories overlap and are related to each other by their mutual (or conflicting) interests and common (or competitive) purposes, as well as reflect-ing broader identities that may be associated with opportunities and barriers, advantages and disadvantages (Eade and Mele 2002; Fincher et al. 2002; Simone 2010a; 2010b). While some differences may seem clear (for example, sex or age), it is increasingly recognised that even these are, in practice, socially constructed and ambiguous. In addition, people have multiple identities, and each of these is influenced by cultural and historical factors, provides a source of meaning and a basis for interaction, and may change over time (Brubaker and Cooper 2000; Puttergill and Leildé 2006). Brubaker and Cooper (2000) are critical of both solely categorical and solely constructivist approaches to identity, eventu-ally dismissing identity altogether as a useful analytical category. However, in everyday urban life, people do identify themselves with certain categories (such as men or women; members of specific kinship or wider ethnic groups; Muslims or Christians; children, youth or adults) and identity is clearly an important influence on associational patterns and, on occasion, a mobilising tool. Constructs such as 'gender' or 'ethnicity' therefore are both categorical signifiers of meaning and influences on social relationships.

In addition to gender and generation, as discussed above, the key dimensions of African social structures and identities are generally considered to be ethnicity, religion, race and socioeconomic status. Commonly, ethnicity is seen as the most foundational dimension, trumping class. It is regarded as people's primary source of identity and the main basis for the web of social relations in which they are embedded. In addition, it is the basis for much political mobilisation. The term 'commonly refers to collectivities that share a myth of origin [and] ... a "culture", the most notable aspect of which is language' (Bates 2006: 167; see also Young 2007).[2] The primordialist view takes ethnicity as a fixed characteristic of individuals and communities, but has today largely been discredited in favour of constructivist approaches that emphasise its social origins, relational nature and malleability (Agbu 2011). Often overlapping with religious affiliation to the extent that the two words are hyphenated, it has arguably become more salient since political liberalisation (Young 2007). Although national identity is still promoted and many countries forbid political parties explicitly tied to ethnicity or religion, experience of discrimination, struggles for recognition and equality, and ethnically based political rivalry may harden people's sense of ethnic identity (Dorman et al. 2007).

While race was historically significant and racial differentiation has bequeathed a spatial legacy that shapes social patterns and interactions in African cities today, its contemporary salience varies. While distinctions and tensions persist in some ex-settler colonies, race is a much less important differentiating factor in contemporary cities than it was in the colonial past, except in South Africa (see, for example, Bekker and Leildé 2006).

Religion has substantive attributes, particularly belief in a transcendental reality or spiritual being (the sacred), religiosity (signified by adherence to a set of beliefs and practices) and affiliation with a religious organisation. It also has social functions – it plays a role in the construction of people's world views and social relationships and in wider socio-political organisation. Essentially, it comprises a set of core beliefs and teachings that, among other things, specify (or suggest) how to live in accordance with the teachings of the faith and how society should be ordered. Religious teachings are promoted by religious organisations, embodied in people's lives and constantly reinterpreted and acted upon in the context in which adherents live. The dimensions of religion include belief (that texts or propositions are true), correct practice, spirituality or mysticism and ritual, with the emphasis in Christianity on beliefs, influencing European colonists' assumptions about the nature of other religions, and in Islam on rules to guide behaviour.

In parts of Africa, Islam long pre-dated the colonial era. It expanded through trade, migration and conquest and, in some parts of the subcontinent, through the establishment of Islamic states. Christianity was closely associated with European colonialism and with efforts to convert Africans not just through missionary work but also via the establishment of health and education ser-vices, the latter providing avenues for promoting cultural and linguistic changes in line with the ambitions of the colonial powers. Both of these religious (or faith) traditions share some common history, culture and body of teaching, but each comprises more than one sect or denomination, with more or less distinctive teachings, practices and organisational forms (Rakodi 2011). While Christianity and Islam have become the dominant religions (see below), some groups continue to hold traditional beliefs and practise traditional rituals, and many Christians and Muslims adhere to some of these beliefs and practices, regarding them as 'cultural' rather than 'religious', even though African tradi-tional religion(s) share many of the substantive and functional characteristics of the world religions (Alhassan Alolo 2007; Alhassan Alolo and Connell 2013; Pew Forum 2010; Rakodi 2011).

The concept of class has been problematic in the African context, where socioeconomic differentiation has typically been attributed to differential access to state resources and the associated economic opportunities (Greig et al. 2006). Political parties, even within democratic regimes, are not class-based with respect to either their ideology or their support base, while forms of mobilisation that might appear to have a class basis, such as trade unions, were in most countries more important in the years immediately after independence than they are today. Finally, it is not clear that the poor have common class interests, nor that the emerging middle socioeconomic layer of society can be considered a class (see, for example, Bekker and Leildé 2006; Dubresson 1997, on Abidjan).

Typically, conceptions of African urban societies have tended to polarise between those that depict them in a negative light, as fragmented, disorderly and dysfunctional, and those that are more positive (Harrison 2003). The former see highly mobile and differentiated urban populations, resulting in individual-isation, high turnover in social relations (Lourenço-Lindell 2001), intense com-petition and conflict (Simone 2010b) and social breakdown. In contrast, other analysts emphasise urban opportunities, the creativity that is associated with social heterogeneity and intense interaction, the resilience of reciprocal social relations and informal rules that regulate behaviour and transactions, and the many forms of associational life that are said to be repositories of social capital (Tostensen et al. 2001; Madhavan and Landau 2011). Both views capture part of the contemporary urban reality, but neither is wholly accurate.

As will be discussed in the next section, religious groups are probably the most widespread form of associational life in contemporary African cities, but they exist alongside and interact with a variety of other forms. Documentation of life in pre-colonial urban centres is limited and, although early forms of governance and organisation in some West African cities, especially those associated with Islam, continue to the present day, most of the academic literature started to be produced during the colonial period.

The early literature refers primarily to associations with socio-cultural objectives, acting as catalysts for people from the same ethnic group or area of origin in their struggle to settle in a new and hostile urban environment. They included burial societies, church associations and sports clubs. Urban associations were also generally seen as based on ideas and ideologies from the rural areas, with elders (often tribal elders) in central positions and membership being voluntary and informal ... Towards political independence ... many associations took on more political roles, developing into labour movements (as in Zambia and Kenya) or resistance movements (as in Angola and Mozambique). Leaders with traditional roots were often replaced by younger political entrepreneurs with objectives beyond the immediate social group. (Tostensen et al. 2001: 22)

Colonial administrations' attempts to control such associations continued after independence, with authoritarian regimes in particular seeking to curtail the activities of the larger associations, especially trade unions, and often banning ethnically based organisations lest they undermine the attempts of newly independent governments to forge a sense of national unity. Instead, many created branches of the ruling party to represent the interests of groups such as workers, women or young people. As a result, post-independence urban Africa saw a retreat to associations of a more private and social nature. With the exception of religious bodies, many existing civil society organisations were stifled or became dormant (Aina 1997a: 431).

New forms of organisation emerged, both to serve new interests (such as professional associations) and in response to government initiatives (such as community-based organisations in some informal settlements). The onset of urban crises in the mid-1980s, followed by economic and then political liberalisation, had a dramatic impact on the number and nature of associations (Tostensen et al. 2001). In some cities, older organisational forms gained new importance (Meagher 2010). Elsewhere, new and adapted forms emerged, sometimes autonomously and sometimes in response to changing government policies. After years of authoritarian rule in countries such as Zambia and Tanzania, the capacity of urban residents to form and operate organisations took time to develop (Andreasen 2001; Mhamba and Titus 2001; Dill 2009). The absence of comprehensive information makes it difficult to gain an overall picture, but the main forms of organisation seem to have been welfare and cultural associations, community organisations, economic networks and religious groups.

Many of the links urban residents maintain with their kin are informal, but there are more formal welfare, cultural and recreational associations in some places, generally based on a common ethnic identity and ties to a shared place of origin. Some were formed during the colonial era and some more recently. They help their members navigate the precarious and uncertain urban environment by providing practical assistance, performing ceremonial functions and organising cultural and recreational activities intended to promote shared cultural values and identities, although often only a minority belong to such associations (Adetula 2002; Landau 2010; Madhavan and Landau 2011). Rather than being primarily concerned with the interests and welfare of members living in an urban area, some ethnic associations are established to support their rural communities of origin; these are often called home town or village associations (see, for example, Englund 2001). Although such associations incorporate traditional rural characteristics and practices, these are adopted selectively, and the groups have distinctively urban features. While some ethnically based associations provide cultural activities for urban residents, many cultural and recreational needs are met by new patterns of provision or by other types of organisation, as the social relationships of urban residents widen beyond their own kin, economic crisis bites and rituals evolve in response to urban and global influences (see, for example, Aina 1997b in Zeleza 1999; Lewinson 2007).

Some ethnically based associations are formed by holders of indigenous land rights in order to subdivide land for urban development and lobby for services (Myers 2011; Grant 2009). They may contribute to the rise of urban autochthony politics, reflecting and contributing to wider political tensions between 'sons of the soil' and non-indigenes, exacerbated by constitutional arrangements that base local and national citizenship on indigeneity, as in Nigeria (Dorman et al. 2007).

Organisations and networks with mainly economic functions include rotating savings and credit associations (ROSCAs) and traders' or producers' associations. ROSCAs depend on mutual trust, so tend to be small groups formed by those who know each other, through propinquity or shared characteristics such as ethnicity or gender. Although their numbers may fluctuate, they are ubiquitous (Dill 2009; Robson 2001). While not all residents belong to them or to other savings and credit associations, in some places they have evolved into larger and more durable associations and networks, for example economic interest groups in Senegal (Abdoul 2002). Entrepreneurs often draw initially on family or ethnic group members to develop links with suppliers, intermediaries, officials and politicians. Informal cooperative arrangements may evolve into formal organisations, although the operation of market, producers' or service providers' associations may be constrained by competing economic interests and ethnic and religious polarisation, or by their vulnerability to political manoeuvring (see, for example, Meagher 2010).

Although the numbers and types of associational forms vary greatly from city to city, in most instances only a minority of residents belong to the types of organisation briefly considered above. Religious groups, as we shall see below, are a different matter.

This section shows that religion pervades urban African society, influencing residents' beliefs and world views, interacting with ethnicity and indigeneity to influence politics, and providing important sources of welfare and mutual support to adherents and urban populations more generally.

Trends in religious organisation and affiliation Evidence of the religious affiliation and attitudes of urban populations, the links between these and their social relationships and behaviour, and the roles played by religion in service delivery, politics and conflict is patchy, both geographically and, as with many other aspects of social change, in that it emphasises the new, unusual, dramatic or threatening rather than the everyday and routine. Nevertheless, it is clear that not only allegiance but also religious beliefs and regular practice (e.g. frequent attendance at prayers and services) are almost universal and that membership of religious groups is more common than of any other type of organisation. For example, about 50 per cent of the nationals and foreigners surveyed in selected Johannesburg neighbourhoods in 2006, 70 per cent or more in Maputo and 92 per cent of Kenyans in Nairobi belonged to a religious organisation (Madhavan and Landau 2011: 486).

Notable recent trends include the increased proportion of people who declare themselves to be Christian or Muslim rather than practitioners of traditional religion and the emergence of revivalist movements within both Christianity and Islam.[3] Both trends may be more pronounced in towns and cities, which are known for religious innovation (Konings et al. 2006). Many of the early mosques and established churches were located in urban areas, the former to serve pre-colonial leaders, urban residents and traders, the latter to serve colonial administrators as well as migrant populations. Many new sects, denominations, mosques and churches are also located in urban areas, where they can draw in ready audiences and cater for growing urban populations.

Individual congregations are linked in a variety of formal and informal ways to wider religious networks at the national and international levels. At one extreme, Roman Catholic parishes are organised into dioceses, and are subject to the authority of the Pope and the Vatican. Formally, most religious groups have more local, diocesan or national autonomy. However, in addition to ongoing connections to parent organisations (especially churches and mission organisations), they have important informal links through visiting preachers, access to religious media and flows of funds. Through these, ideas are channelled that may influence their religious beliefs, organisational arrangements and development activities.

Changing beliefs and practices Today, religious groups have a marked physical, visual and acoustic presence in urban areas (Aina 1997b in Zeleza 1999;

Asamoah-Gyadu 2005; de Boeck 2002; Gifford 2004; Oruwari 2001; Piot 2006). Religious buildings were among the earliest and most substantial buildings in many pre-colonial and colonial towns, and the growth and diversification of world religions have been marked by the construction of large numbers of mosques and churches, ranging from a few benches under a tree or plastic sheet to purpose-built structures capable of holding thousands. In addition, the emerging Pentecostal churches and other renewalist groups have colonised secular buildings such as cinemas, stadia, hotel halls and even night clubs. With inadequate planning, highway construction and traffic regulation, religious buildings and events add to traffic congestion at both the city and neighbourhood levels. The visual presence of religious groups is manifest in giant billboards and banners advertising preachers or religious events, as well as the ubiquitous religious slogans on vehicles, buildings and shacks. In addition, the use of loudspeakers for lengthy services, prayers and all-night vigils, as well as amplified muezzins, broadcast noisy worship well beyond the religious buildings themselves.

The established churches, which tend to be less literal in their interpretation of the Bible and more staid in their forms of worship, have lost ground to the newer churches, leading to the emergence of more charismatic clergy and congregations within the mainstream denominations. They also tend to be more bureaucratically organised than the multifarious independent and Pentecostal churches, and are sometimes more transparent and accountable to their members than churches which may appear to be more like the 'business' of an individual founder or leader. The social attitudes of some of their clergy and members may be more liberal. While most churches lobby governments to protect their own positions, roles and property, the established organisations are generally more likely than the newer churches to be involved in certain types of political activity, for example lobbying for democratic reform or advocating on behalf of the poor and against corruption. For example, Oruwari (2001) notes that the new churches in Port Harcourt were not involved in politics, although the Christian Association of Nigeria has become more politically active in response to Muslim assertiveness since political liberalisation (Best and Rakodi 2011).

In charismatic Christianity, suffering is attributed to the immorality associated with modernity and the grip of diabolic forces, and members are required to abandon their sinful lifestyles, seek salvation and regularly engage with the church. Charismatics believe that those with a strong enough faith in God and Jesus (and a willingness to make substantial donations to the church) will be granted wealth and health (the prosperity gospel), although the expected financial contributions may impoverish some instead (see, for example, van de Kamp 2010 on the Universal Church of the Kingdom of God in urban Mozambique). In face of the perceived unresponsiveness of the established churches, Pentecostal churches have attracted not just those who have been adversely affected by economic crisis and liberalisation, anonymous city life and the apparent erosion of other forms of social support, but also the upwardly mobile young and middle class, because these churches emphasise individual choices, hard work and rewards over older collective identities based on ethnicity or kinship (Dilger 2007; Ukah 2004).[4]

As noted above, despite the increased predominance of the world religions, many Africans, including urban residents, continue to hold some beliefs and engage in practices associated with traditional religions, which share the idea that the visible and invisible worlds are interconnected – invisible forces are thought to control life events and the power of traditional authorities is related in part to their connection to the spiritual forces of the invisible world (Ellis and Ter Haar 2004; de Witte 2008). Although this shared understanding has been disrupted by colonialism, evangelism, modernity and migration (Simone 2010b), it continues to exert a significant influence on many individuals, and today it remains quite common for people to explain occurrences in the visible world (for example, the acquisition of sudden wealth or misfortune) by reference to the work of invisible forces and the use of sorcery. For example, in Douala in Cameroon since the mid-1990s, 'feymen' (swindlers) who accumulate wealth quickly and mysteriously have been rumoured to use sorcery, including human sacrifice (Ndjio 2006). The ascent of powerful politicians may similarly be attributed to occult means. The predominant association of spiritual forces with misfortune can, Meyer suggests, be traced to missionaries' 'diabolisation' of traditional gods and spirits, which have been incorporated into Christian belief as demons (Meyer 2004). Indeed, the dynamic growth of Pentecostal churches is attributed by many to the ways in which they integrate a belief in malevolent witches and spirits who can cause bad behaviour and misfortune, as well as traditions of ritual and healing, into a version of Christianity that seeks to enable adherents to deal with the social, economic and spiritual problems associated with modernity and globalisation (Dilger 2007; Gifford 2004; Marshall-Fratani 1998; Maxwell 1998; Meyer 1998). This is not meant to imply that all Pentecostal churches are identical. Some condemn the appropriation of traditional religious practices (de Witte 2008) and they also appeal to different socioeconomic groups and vary in size from a single congregation to denominations with national organisations and international branches.

Within Islam, internal movements for reform and renewal have mostly been reactions against the supposed inauthenticity of the Sufi versions of Islam that are common in Africa. They have often been backed by funding from and training provided by predominantly Sunni Middle Eastern countries, particularly during the 1980s and 1990s, although these sponsors of *da'wa* (evangelism, literally 'invitation to God'), mosques and schools are distrusted by many governments and African Muslims. Many of the pietist movements emphasise individual responsibility, stressing the need for Muslims to constitute 'new personal moralities ... characterised by hard work, honesty, effort, fidelity, and education' (Simone 2010a: 16), in the absence of or as an alternative to traditional social life based on custom and reciprocity. For example, women's religious associations and learning groups have mushroomed since the mid-1980s in Mali. Although women have always had a responsibility to practise and promote their religion, these groups enable their members to access advice and teaching and to portray themselves as 'proper' Sunni Muslims, while emphasising individual responsibility both for their 'personal salvation and for societal renewal' (Schulz 2010: 82). However, this latter aim and the groups' public role have the potential to lead to conflicts between the women involved and their families and other authorities.

Other reform movements have led to intra-Muslim conflict, periodic clashes with governments and, more recently, violent attacks on Christians. In Nigeria, for example, the emergence of movements such as Izala, Maitatsine in Kano in the 1970s and 1980s and, more recently, Boko Haram is attributed by observers to the advance of petro-capitalism, the attraction of growing urban areas to migrants, periodic economic and agricultural crises, government failure and the collapse of the traditional educational system by which young male pupils of itinerant *mallams* supported themselves through informal economic activities and begging. Especially in the north of the country, there is, as a result, a large disenfranchised and disillusioned population, especially of young men (Watts 1996; 1999; Umar 2001; Best and Rakodi 2011; Aghedo and Osumah 2012). These movements pose challenges to Islamic teaching and traditional Muslim leaders and their adoption of violent tactics threatens state security. In response, they have been proscribed and subject to violent crackdowns by security forces.

Engagements between religion, politics and social change The indivisibility of religion and the state in Islamic belief has led Muslims in some parts of the subcontinent to seek the establishment of Islamic states, governed by sharia criminal as well as personal law, most notably in northern Nigeria. Even where Muslims prefer a secular constitution, their perceived disadvantage in terms of access to well-paid employment, political office and a share of government resources may lead them to be politically active at both the national and local levels. In some predominantly Muslim areas, religious leaders and organisations have long had governance functions at both city and neighbourhood levels. Cities dominated by religious bodies may have distinctive governance structures, economies, relationships with national governments, and urban and architectural features; this is the case, for example, in Touba in Senegal, the headquarters of the Mourides, a branch of the Qâddiriyya brotherhood (Gueye 2001; Cruise O'Brien 2003). More widely, some religio-civic institutions continue to operate despite the increased reach of government institutions, for example in northern Nigeria, or in self-governing Muslim strangers' quarters in Muslim minority cities such as Accra (Pellow 1991). In Niger, Olivier de Sardan identifies religious governance as one of eight modes of local governance, with its own norms, functions and legitimacy, that contribute to local political cultures formed of context-specific combinations of modes (Olivier de Sardan 2011). However, elsewhere, in both Muslim majority cities such as Mombasa and Muslim minority cities such as Johannesburg and Kumasi, Muslim organisations do not appear to be politically active at the local level (Rakodi 2004: 90).

Because of competition for converts, the emotional importance of religion and the association of religion with other sources of identity, especially ethnicity, faith is a potent mobilising tool at local and national level, making it susceptible to instrumental use by those pursuing political goals. For example, while Christian–Muslim conflicts in Jos and Kano appear to be religious, they primarily relate to rival claims to land and political power between indigenous and in-migrant groups, rather than being about different religious beliefs and practices (Best and Rakodi 2011).

Although Christianity and Islam apparently provide common overarching identities, it is clear from the discussion above that denominational and sectarian divisions within each tradition mean that they are characterised as much by rivalry and conflict as by coherence and cooperation. The relationships between gender and religion are particularly ambivalent. Although the members of some religious groups are predominantly female, the leadership of all is predominantly (and sometimes solely) male – like households, religious groups are essentially patriarchal organisations. They stress the importance of the family and emphasise women's domestic roles (Oruwari 2001). They may, therefore, block progress towards gender equality, although sometimes they can back attempts to realise women's rights if this is seen as being in the interests of the religious group and its members (see, for example, Adamu and Para-Mallam's (2012) analysis of the contrasting roles played by religious organisations in campaigns for legal change in Nigeria). Nevertheless, urban residence and migration provide women with the scope for changing some of the religious dimensions of their lives and relationships. For example, Pellow (1991) shows how migrant Muslim women in the Muslim minority city of Accra are less traditional in their social practices (seclusion, for example) than women in the Muslim majority city of Kano.

The role of religious actors in providing welfare, social and economic support Congregations and other types of religious organisation have traditionally provided day-to-day welfare and continue to do so in contemporary cities. Like Christian churches, Muslim associations were often established in urban centres with substantial migrant populations, where they provided support for those migrants; the *dairas* in Touba, Senegal are an example of this (Gueye 2001). Today, it is hard to know, in the absence of comprehensive information, the numbers of local religious groups and organisations, the overall scale and significance of the welfare they provide or how often such provision provides an incentive for people to change their religious or denominational allegiance. However, in poor neighbourhoods in Dar es Salaam, a survey in the mid-1990s found that three-quarters of registered community groups had religious affiliations (Kiondo 1994; see also Myers 2005) and that many of the larger church congregations had local groups (for example, the neighbourhood groups of 20 to 30 members associated with the Full Gospel Bible Fellowship Church studied by Dilger 2007). Such groups help members in need – including people living with HIV/AIDS (PLHA) – care for the sick and their families, assist with funerals and provide spiritual support. Oruwari (2001), for example, describes home-caring fellowships associated with the Celestial Church of Christ in Port Harcourt, which not only support their own members but also distribute charity to those in need and provide some maternal and child healthcare and nursery education.

Such religious associations are typical and widespread and can, it is often suggested, be a substitute for the family (Piot 2006; Madhavan and Landau 2011; Robson 2001). Dilger (2007: 61), for example, attributes the appeal of the two Pentecostal churches he studied in Dar es Salaam to the 'networks of healing and care' that they offer in the face of urbanisation, disintegrating kinship bonds, unequal gender relations and HIV/AIDS. He argues that they attract particularly 'younger and middle-aged women, because [they are] the most vulnerable to the erosion of kinship networks and the growing hardships of social life' in the city (ibid.: 61). The same can be said of the Malian Muslim women's associations mentioned above, which have social and financial support functions as well as pietist aims (Schulz 2010). The practical support such home or women's groups can provide to their members is influenced by their composition; they may provide bonding rather than bridging capital, and when groups (such as the Malian women's groups) do bridge socioeconomic and ethnic divisions, tensions may arise. In addition, in tandem with religious organisations' expectations that their members will make substantial financial contributions, such women's and neighbourhood groups may contribute to the disruption of social and familial life, which is, as discussed in the previous section, already perceived by some to be under threat.

Religious organisations may also take on wider roles, caring for the very poor, orphans and refugees, or promoting community development in poor localities. For example, the Central Methodist Church in Johannesburg (Bompani 2013; Kuljian 2010) has provided support for significant numbers of homeless and destitute people and refugees, sometimes leading to tensions between its leader and the members of its congregation, as well as with external agencies. Because religious bodies are perceived to have deep local roots, they are often trusted more than secular non-governmental organisations (NGOs) (Oruwari 2001; Leurs 2012). However, they may not be very distinct from other organisations if they rely on external funds (a situation that will dictate, to some extent, their choice of activities and will require compliance with standard funding criteria), and if most of the staff or volunteers of secular NGOs are religious believers (Green et al. 2012).

Religious organisations have a long history of delivering services to both their members and the wider population, especially education and health. Their roles and modes of operation vary depending on their historical evolution, organisational structures, changing volumes and sources of funds, and relations with governments. The balance varies between providing religious education as part of the socialisation of members' children and education for wider purposes. Churches took on a role in the production of colonial administrators that gave their graduates a lasting advantage in the employment market, a place within movements for political independence, and often favoured access to elite status after independence. In contrast, higher Islamic education, which had produced influential leaders and officials in predominantly Muslim states in pre-colonial times or under indirect rule, lost its value following colonisation and independence, with government-provided education, often of relatively poor quality, failing to compensate. After independence, state-led models of economic development and governments anxious to use education to forge national unity and produce workers with appropriate qualifications led to the 'nationalisation' of church schools in many countries, although the nature and extent of appropriation of responsibilities and buildings varied. Following economic crisis and liberalisation, many such governments sought to return schools to their previous owners and operators. Autonomous churches dependent on locally raised resources and declining flows of overseas funds were, however, unable or reluctant to take on rundown buildings and full responsibility for operating costs, leading to a variety of compromises, many accompanied by ongoing disagreements over matters such as curriculum content. In addition, since economic liberalisation, in many countries religious organisations have contributed to the significant increase in the number of new privately provided educational institutions at all levels.

In addition to starting schools, missionaries established health facilities, some of them in urban areas, to serve their own staff and colonial administrators and, like education, as a means of evangelisation. It was less common in the past for Muslims to be involved in healthcare, with the exception of the Ismaili community in East Africa. As with schools, the desire of post-independence governments to fulfil their independence promises by providing comprehensive services led to a takeover of many church-provided facilities, although many remained in church hands and others were returned in the 1980s. Today, increasing numbers of Muslim charities operate health facilities. Unlike private for-profit facilities, and despite a decline in flows of funds from overseas, there is some evidence that they generally continue to provide subsidised healthcare for the poor, by participating in government or externally funded programmes (Rookes and Rookes 2012a; 2012b). In particular, they have taken on roles in HIV/AIDS prevention and in the treatment and provision of care for PLHA, especially as many external funders permit them to provide only interventions that comply with religious teachings (Davis et al. 2011). However, accurate data on their current provision and reliable estimates of its overall contribution to national healthcare are not available (Olivier and Wodon 2012).

Religious organisations, especially the churches, therefore continue to play significant roles in formal educational and health provision today, with many of their higher level facilities located in urban areas. Various collaborative arrangements such as madrasa education boards and Christian health associations have been established to negotiate what are often tricky relationships with governments, and many have developed collaborative or subcontracting arrangements with government agencies, although not all coordinate their activities with each other or cooperate with government (Bano 2009; Robson 2001; Rookes and Rookes 2012a; 2012b; Taylor 2012).

Whether religious groups provide social capital that helps economic activity is more uncertain. Simone (2010b) suggests that they do (for example in Abidjan), and studies of the two main Sufi brotherhoods in West Africa (the Mouriddiya and Tiyanniya) show how in cities such as Dakar and Touba religious affiliation has been used as a basis for developing extensive national and international trading networks, through traditional institutions such as *dairas* and *zawiyyah* (lodges that offer accommodation for travelling members), new forms of organisation, and networks developed as a result of religious practices such as the *haj* (Gueye 2001; Simone 2004; 2010b). However, Deacon's study in Kibera informal settlement found that the advice offered by American Evangelicals did not translate well to the Nairobi context (Deacon 2012), and interviews with Christian traders in two Nairobi markets found that they did not use contacts made through their churches (which over 90 per cent attended every week) for business purposes, instead deliberately treating church attendance as a source of spiritual support and an enjoyable escape from trading (Lyons and Snoxell 2005).

Conclusion

African towns and cities offer many opportunities for economic advancement, social interaction and adaptation, and political debate and innovation. They are also characterised by extreme inequality and widespread poverty, frustrated ambitions, social and political tensions, and inadequate governance. Their diversity, creativity and vitality are accompanied by high levels of criminality and violence and deep social divisions. They are places where the pace of change exceeds the limited capacity of governments to cope with it, difference may lead to social exclusion, and residents face enormous problems gaining access to housing, services, adequate paid work, and safe and secure living environments. The social, economic and physical changes associated with urbanisation (heterogeneity, high densities, etc.) are said to lead to the emergence of more anonymous, transitory and superficial social relationships than those that exist in rural societies, with community ties being replaced by loose and shifting associations based on individual interests and increasingly ineffective mechanisms of social control. However, much urban analysis has now shown that the traditional portrayal of the differences between earlier or rural societies and contemporary urban societies is grossly oversimplified, and the extreme view that all African cities are unruly, conflictual and socially dysfunctional is mistaken.[5] In practice, many urban residents succeed in forging good lives for themselves and their families; families and wider social groups continue to provide social, economic and moral support; and new ways of thinking and doing things result in progressive social change. While households and families are not always harmonious and mutually supportive, they are differentiated by their characteristics, assets, lifecycle stage and aspirations, and so the outcomes of livelihood strategies and inter-gender and intergenerational negotiations vary.

In the majority of countries and urban centres, religion plays an important role in the lives of most residents and their families, providing a structure of beliefs that helps people explain the world, rules by which to live (even though these are as often breached as adhered to) and a source of personal succour and supportive social relationships. The vitality of religious groups is demonstrated by the share of wealth and organisational resources they command, which enables them to have a significant physical, social, service provision and often political presence in urban areas. Religion can be socially conservative, hindering progressive social change such as the achievement of gender equality or reduced fertility and a decrease in HIV transmission; politically disabling because of its emphasis on achieving rewards in the next world; and a source of conflict and violence because of aggressive expansionism, its association with ethnicity and indigeneity, and its potency as a mobilisational tool. However, religious groups and their leaders can also be socially progressive, encouraging moral behaviour, providing support for the vulnerable, advocating holistic models of well-being, opposing injustice, making a substantial contribution to the provision of education and healthcare, playing a role in peace building, and providing verbal and organisational backing for government initiatives ranging from health promotion to community development.

While many of these features are common to different religious groups and to many towns and cities, in various countries, such generalisations mask significant differences between and within religious traditions, countries and urban centres. Such differences result from geography, history, economic evolution, the role of religion in the wider political arena and the socio-cultural context. Inevitably, in a single chapter it is difficult to satisfactorily navigate between overgeneralisation and an awareness of specificity, between emphasising continuity and recognising the rapidity of social change, and between romanticising the positive aspects of everyday urban society and religious life and demonising their dysfunctionality.

The gaps in our knowledge are enormous, but because of the influence of recent trends in development theory, the increased acceptability of mixed methods approaches to research, and the emergence of improved conceptual and analytical frameworks for understanding religion and society (see, for example, Rakodi 2011), we are better placed today to develop an improved understanding of what religion means for its adherents; the ways in which it influences urban residents' expectations and interactions with each other; the relationships between religion and other dimensions of difference and inclusion or exclusion; the roles of religious organisations in providing welfare, social support and services, as well as in politics; and the influence of religious beliefs and actors in blocking or contributing to wider processes of urban social change.

Notes

1 Marxist and dependency approaches using historical/structural analysis emerged as an alternative, especially in Latin America, but failed to challenge the hegemony of mainstream analyses and policies and ran into a cul-de-sac by the end of the 1970s (Kapoor 2008; Nederveen Pieterse 2010).

2 Gasper (2006) defines culture as a 'way of life' sustained by a system of ideas, values, attitudes and rules and marked by a distinctive set of practices and methods through which members of a group deal with their environment. Whether religion is an aspect of culture or a distinct phenomenon is contested.

3 There are limited quantitative data on religious affiliation from some censuses and demographic and health surveys, but not all, as the sensitivity of religion means that questions on it are omitted from many censuses. Attitudinal data are available from surveys (for

example, Pew Forum 2006; 2010; World Values Surveys n.d.) and occasional opinion polls by Afrobarometer or Gallup, but the samples are not disaggregated into urban and rural respondents. In addition, the existing data have not yet been systematically mined to identify the characteristics of religious affiliation and practice in urban areas.

4 A distinction can be made between the earlier African independent churches and more recent Pentecostal churches, many of which were established or funded by Pentecostal churches overseas, especially in the US. In addition, a distinction can be made between Pentecostal churches and charismatic Christians more generally, as many of the established denominations have members and congregations who are distinguished by their charismatic beliefs and practices. Pentecostals are more likely than other Christians to report having received direct revelations from God,

experienced or witnessed divine healings, and experienced or seen exorcisms. In addition, they hold traditional Christian beliefs more intensely, including the literalism of the Bible, miracles, and Jesus Christ as the exclusive path to salvation (Pew Forum 2006).

5 See, for example, Rodgers 2010, who argues that cities are not necessarily violent merely because of their large populations, density and heterogeneity.

References

Abdoul, M. (2002) 'The production of the city and urban informalities: the Borough of Thiaroye-sur-mer in the City of Pikine, Senegal'. In O. Enwezor, C. Basualdo, U. M. Bauer, S. Ghez, S. Maharaj, M. Nash and O. Zaya (eds) *Under Siege: Four African cities – Freetown, Johannesburg, Kinshasa, Lagos.* Documenta 11_Platform 4. Ostfildern: Hatje Cantz, pp. 337–58.

Adamu, F. L. and O. U. Para-Mallam (2012) 'The role of religion in women's campaigns for legal reform in Nigeria'. *Development in Practice* 22(4/5): 803–18.

Adetula, V. A. O. (2002) 'Welfare associations and the dynamics of city politics in Nigeria: Jos Metropolis as case study'. In O. Enwezor, C. Basualdo, U. M. Bauer, S. Ghez, S. Maharaj, M. Nash and O. Zaya (eds) *Under Siege: Four African cities – Freetown, Johannesburg, Kinshasa, Lagos*. Documenta 11_Platform 4. Ostfildern: Hatje Cantz, pp. 359–80.

Afrobarometer (2010) *Tolerance in South Africa: Exploring popular attitudes toward foreigners*. Afrobarometer Briefing Paper 82. Accra: Afrobarometer.

Agbu, O. A. (2011) *Ethnicity and Democratisation in Africa: Challenges for politics and development*. Discussion Paper 62. Uppsala: Nordiska Afrikainstitutet.

Aghedo, I. and O. Osumah (2012) 'The Boko Haram uprising: how should Nigeria respond?'. *Third World Quarterly* 33(5): 853–69.

Aina, T. A. (1997a) 'The state and civil society: politics, government, and social organisation in African cities'. In C. Rakodi (ed.) *The Urban Challenge in Africa: Growth and management of its large cities*. Tokyo: United Nations University Press, pp. 411–46.

— (1997b) 'Working people's popular culture in Lagos'. Paper presented at the 24th Annual Spring Symposium, 'The Creation and Consumption of Leisure in Urban Africa', University of Illinois at Urbana-Champaign, 4–6 April.

Alhassan Alolo, N. (2007) *African Traditional Religion and Concepts of Development: Religions and development background paper*. Religions and Development Working Paper 17. Birmingham: Religions and Development Research Programme. Available at www.religionsanddevelopment. org/index.php?section=47 [accessed 14 August 2013].

— and J. A. Connell (2013) 'Indigenous religions and development: African traditional religion'. In M. Clarke (ed.) *Handbook of Research on Development and Religion*. Cheltenham: Edward Elgar, pp. 164–83.

Andreasen, J. (2001) 'The legacy of mobilisation from above: participation in a Zanzibar neighbourhood'. In A. Tostensen, I. Tvedten and M. Vaa (eds) *Associational Life in African Cities: Popular responses to the urban crisis*. Uppsala: Nordiska Afrikainstitutet, pp. 263–81.

Annez, P. P., R. Buckley and J. Kalarickal (2010) 'African urbanization as flight? Some policy implications of geography'. *Urban Forum* 21(3): 221–34.

Asamoah-Gyadu, J. K. (2005) *African Charismatics: Current developments within independent indigenous Pentecostalism in Ghana*. Leiden: Brill.

Bakewell, O. and G. Jónsson (2011) *Migration, Mobility and the African City*. Working Paper 50. Oxford: International Migration Institute. Available at www.imi.ox.ac.uk/publications/working_papers [accessed 14 August 2013].

Bano, M. (2009) *Engaged yet Disengaged: Islamic Schools and the State in Kano,*

Nigeria. Religions and Development Working Paper 29. Birmingham: Religions and Development Research Programme. Available at www.religionsanddevelopment.org [accessed 14 August 2013].

Bates, R. H. (2006) 'Ethnicity'. In D. A. Clark (ed.) *The Elgar Companion to Development Studies*. Cheltenham: Edward Elgar, pp. 167–73.

Bekker, S. and A. Leildé (2006) 'The importance of language identities in Lomé and Libreville'. In S. Bekker and A. Leildé (eds) *Reflections on Identity in Four African Cities*. Johannesburg: African Minds, pp. 189–205.

Best, S. G. and C. Rakodi (2011) *Violent Conflict and Its Aftermath in Jos and Kano, Nigeria: What is the role of religion?* Religions and Development Working Paper 69. Birmingham: Religions and Development Research Programme. Available at www.religionsanddevelopment.org [accessed 14 August 2013].

Bompani, B. (2013) 'Local religious organisations performing development: refugees in the Central Methodist Mission in Johannesburg'. *Journal of International Development*. doi: 10.1002/jid.2900.

Brubaker, R. and F. Cooper (2000) 'Beyond "identity"'. *Theory and Society* 29(1): 1–47.

Campbell, E. H. (2006) 'Economic globalization from below: transnational refugee trade networks in Nairobi'. In M. J. Murray and G. A. Myers (eds) *Cities in Contemporary Africa*. Basingstoke: Palgrave Macmillan, pp. 125–48.

Christiansen, C., M. Utas and H. Vigh (2006) 'Introduction: navigating youth, generating adulthood'. In C. Christiansen, M. Utas and H. Vigh (eds) *Navigating Youth Generating Adulthood: Social becoming in an African context*. Uppsala: Nordiska Afrikainstitutet, pp. 9–30.

Cruise O'Brien, D. (2003) *Symbolic Confrontations: Muslims imagining the state in Africa*. London: C. Hurst and Company.

Davis, C., A. Jegede, R. Leurs, A. Sunmola and U. Ukiwo (2011) *Are Faith-based Organizations Distinctive? Religious and secular NGOs in Nigeria*. Religions and Development Working Paper 56. Birmingham: Religions and Development Research Programme. Available at www.religionsanddevelopment.org [accessed 14 August 2013].

Davis, M. (2004) 'Planet of slums: urban involution and the informal proletariat'. *New Left Review* 26: 5–34.

Deacon, G. (2012) 'Pentecostalism and development in Kibera informal settlement, Nairobi'. *Development in Practice* 22(5/6): 663–74.

de Boeck, F. (2002) 'Kinshasa: tales of the "invisible city" and the second world'. In O. Enwezor, C. Basualdo, U. M. Bauer, S. Ghez, S. Maharaj, M. Nash and O. Zaya (eds) *Under Siege: Four African Cities – Freetown, Johannesburg, Kinshasa, Lagos*. Documenta 11_Platform 4. Ostfildern: Hatje Cantz, pp. 243–86.

Deneulin, S. and C. Rakodi (2011) 'Revisiting religion: development studies thirty years on'. *World Development* 39(1): 45–54.

de Witte, M. (2008) 'Accra's sounds and sacred spaces'. *International Journal of Urban and Regional Research* 32(3): 690–709.

Dilger, H.-G. (2007) 'Healing the wounds of modernity: salvation, community and care in a neo-Pentecostal church in Dar es Salaam'. *Journal of Religion in Africa* 37(1): 59–83.

Dill, B. (2009) 'The paradoxes of community-based participation in Dar es Salaam'. *Development and Change* 40(4): 717–43.

Dorman, S., D. Hammett and P. P. Nugent (2007) 'Introduction: citizenship and its casualties in Africa'. In S. Dorman, D. Hammett and P. P. Nugent (eds) *Making Nations, Creating Strangers: States and citizenship in Africa*. Leiden: Brill.

Dubresson, A. (1997) 'Abidjan: from the public making of a modern city to urban management of a metropolis'.

In C. Rakodi (ed.) *The Urban Challenge in Africa: Growth and management of its large cities*. Tokyo: United Nations University Press, pp. 252–91.

Eade, J. and C. Mele (2002) 'Understanding the city'. In J. Eade and C. Mele (eds) *Understanding the City: Contemporary and future perspectives*. Oxford: Blackwell, pp. 3–24.

Ellis, S. and G. Ter Haar (2004) *Worlds of Power: Religious thought and political practice in Africa*. London: C. Hurst and Company.

Englund, H. (2001) 'The politics of multiple identities: the making of a home villagers' association in Lilongwe, Malawi'. In A. Tostensen, I. Tvedten and M. Vaa (eds) *Associational Life in African Cities: Popular responses to the urban crisis*. Uppsala: Nordiska Afrikainstitutet, pp. 90–106.

Fielden, A. (2008) *Ignored Displaced Persons: The plight of IDPs in urban areas*. New Issues in Refugee Research. Research Paper 161. New York, NY: UNHCR, Policy Development and Evaluation Service.

Fincher, R., J. M. Jacobs and K. Anderson (2002) 'Rescripting cities with difference'. In J. Eade and C. Mele (eds) *Understanding the City: Contemporary and future perspectives*. Oxford: Blackwell, pp. 27–48.

Fu, A. and M. J. Murray (2007) 'Cinema and the edgy city: Johannesburg, carjacking, and the postmetropolis'. In F. Demissie (ed.) *Postcolonial African Cities: Imperial legacies and postcolonial predicament*. London: Routledge, pp. 121–30.

Gasper, D. (2006) 'Culture and development'. In D. A. Clark (ed.) *The Elgar Companion to Development Studies*. Cheltenham: Edward Elgar, pp. 96–101.

Gifford, P. P. (2004) 'Persistence and change in contemporary African religion'. *Social Compass* 51(2): 59–68.

Grant, R. (2009) *Globalizing City: The urban and economic transformation of Accra, Ghana*. Syracuse, NY: Syracuse University Press.

Green, M., C. Mercer and S. Mesaki (2012) 'Faith in forms: civil society evangelism and development in Tanzania'. *Development in Practice* 22(5/6): 721–34.

Greig, A., D. Hulme and M. Turner (2006) 'Class'. In D. A. Clark (ed.) *The Elgar Companion to Development Studies*. Cheltenham: Edward Elgar, pp. 67–71.

Gueye, C. (2001) 'Touba: the new *dairas* and the urban dream'. In A. Tostensen, I. Tvedten and M. Vaa (eds) *Associational Life in African Cities: Popular responses to the urban crisis*. Uppsala: Nordiska Afrikainstitutet, pp. 107–23.

Harrison, P. (2003) 'Fragmentation and globalisation as the new meta-narrative'. In P. Harrison, M. Huchzermeyer and M. Mayekiso (eds) *Confronting Fragmentation: Housing and urban development in a democratising society*. Cape Town: University of Cape Town Press, pp. 3–25.

Kapoor, I. (2008) *The Postcolonial Politics of Development*. London: Routledge.

Kehinde, A. (2007) 'Narrating the African city from the diaspora: Lagos as a trope in Ben Okri and Chika Unigwe's short stories'. In F. Demissie (ed.) *Postcolonial African Cities: Imperial legacies and postcolonial predicament*. London: Routledge, pp. 73–88.

Kihato, C. (2007) 'Governing the city? South Africa's struggle to deal with urban immigrants after apartheid'. In F. Demissie (ed.) *Postcolonial African Cities: Imperial legacies and postcolonial predicament*. London: Routledge, pp. 103–20.

Kiondo, A. S. Z. (1994) 'The new politics of local development in Tanzania'. In P. Gibbon (ed.) *The New Local Level Politics in East Africa: Studies on Uganda, Tanzania, and Kenya*. Research Report 95. Uppsala: Nordiska Afrikainstitutet, pp. 38–65.

Konings, P., R. van Dijk and D. Foeken (2006) 'The African neighbourhood: an introduction'. In P. Konings and D. Foeken (eds) *Crisis and Creativity: Exploring the wealth of the African neighbourhood*. Leiden: Brill, pp. 1–21.

Koolhaas, R. (2002) 'Fragments of a lecture on Lagos'. In O. Enwezor, C. Basualdo, U. M. Bauer, S. Ghez, S. Maharaj, M. Nash and O. Zaya (eds) *Under Siege: Four African cities – Freetown, Johannesburg, Kinshasa, Lagos*. Documenta 11_Platform 4. Ostfildern: Hatje Cantz, pp. 173–84.

Kuljian, C. (2010) 'Making the invisible visible: a story of the Central Methodist Church'. Johannesburg Workshop in Theory and Criticism. *The Salon* 3. Available at www.jwtc.org.za/volume_3/christa_kuljian.htm [accessed 14 August 2013].

Landau, L. B. (2010) 'Passage, profit, protection and the challenge of participation: building and belonging in African cities'. *Urban Forum* 21(3): 315–29.

Leurs, R. (2012) 'Are faith-based organisations distinctive? Comparing religious and secular NGOs in Nigeria'. *Development in Practice* 22(5/6): 704–20.

Lewinson, A. S. (2007) 'Viewing postcolonial Dar es Salaam, Tanzania through civic spaces: a question of class'. In F. Demissie (ed.) *Postcolonial African Cities: Imperial legacies and postcolonial predicament*. London: Routledge, pp. 43–58.

Lourenço-Lindell, I. (2001) 'Social networks and urban vulnerability to hunger'. In A. Tostensen, I. Tvedten and M. Vaa (eds) *Associational Life in African Cities: Popular responses to the urban crisis*. Uppsala: Nordiska Afrikainstitutet, pp. 30–45.

Lyons, M. and S. Snoxell (2005) 'Creating urban social capital: some evidence from informal traders in Nairobi'. *Urban Studies* 42(7): 1077–97.

Madhavan, S. and L. B. Landau (2011) 'Bridges to nowhere: hosts, migrants, and the chimera of social capital in three African cities'. *Population and Development Review* 37(3): 473–97.

Marshall-Fratani, R. (1998) 'Mediating the global and the local in Nigerian Pentecostalism'. *Journal of Religion in Africa* 28(3): 278–315.

Maxwell, D. (1998) '"Delivered from the spirit of poverty?" Pentecostalism, prosperity and modernity in Zimbabwe'. *Journal of Religion in Africa* 28(3): 350–73.

Mbembe, A. and J. Roitman (2002) 'Figures of the subject in times of crisis'. In O. Enwezor, C. Basualdo, U. M. Bauer, S. Ghez, S. Maharaj, M. Nash and O. Zaya (eds) *Under Siege: Four African cities – Freetown, Johannesburg, Kinshasa, Lagos*. Documenta 11_Platform 4. Ostfildern: Hatje Cantz, pp. 99–126.

McNamee, T. (2012) 'The real frontline of the Chinese in Africa'. *Financial Times*, 7 May. Available at www.ft.com/cms/s/0/10c9bf14-960b-11e1-9d9d-00144feab49a.html [accessed 5 September 2013].

Meagher, K. (2010) 'The tangled web of associational life: urban governance and the politics of popular livelihoods in Nigeria'. *Urban Forum* 21(3): 299–313.

Meyer, B. (1998) '"Make a complete break with the past": memory and postcolonial modernity in Ghanaian Pentecostal discourse'. *Journal of Religion in Africa* 28(3): 316–49.

— (2004) 'Christianity in Africa: from African Independent to Pentecostal-Charismatic churches'. *Annual Review of Anthropology* 33: 447–74.

Mhamba, R. M. and C. Titus (2001) 'Reactions to deteriorating provision of public services in Dar es Salaam'. In A. Tostensen, I. Tvedten and M. Vaa (eds) *Associational Life in African Cities: Popular responses to the urban crisis*. Uppsala: Nordiska Afrikainstitutet, pp. 218–31.

Myers, G. A. (2005) *Disposable Cities: Garbage, governance and sustainable development in urban Africa*. Aldershot: Ashgate Publishing.

— (2011) *African Cities: Alternative visions of urban theory and practice*. London: Zed Books.

— and M. J. Murray (2006) 'Introduction: situating contemporary cities in Africa'. In M. J. Murray and G. A. Myers (eds) *Cities in Contemporary Africa*.

Basingstoke: Palgrave Macmillan, pp. 1–29.

Ndjio, B. (2006) 'Intimate strangers: neighbourhood, autochthony and the politics of belonging'. In P. Konings and D. Foeken (eds) *Crisis and Creativity: Exploring the wealth of the African neighbourhood*. Leiden: Brill, pp. 66–87.

Nederveen Pieterse, J. (2010) *Development Theory*. 2nd edition. Los Angeles: Sage Publications.

Nyairo, J. (2006) '(Re)configuring the city: the mapping of places and people in contemporary Kenyan popular song texts'. In M. J. Murray and G. A. Myers (eds) *Cities in Contemporary Africa*. Basingstoke: Palgrave Macmillan, pp. 71–94.

Olivier, J. and Q. Wodon (2012) 'Playing broken telephone: assessing faith-inspired health care provision in Africa'. *Development in Practice* 22(5/6): 819–34.

Olivier de Sardan, J. P. (2011) 'The eight modes of local governance in West Africa'. *IDS Bulletin* 42(2): 22–31.

Oruwari, Y. (2001) 'New generation churches and the provision of welfare: a gender study from Port Harcourt, Nigeria'. In A. Tostensen, I. Tvedten and M. Vaa (eds) *Associational Life in African Cities: Popular responses to the urban crisis*. Uppsala: Nordiska Afrikainstitutet, pp. 177–89.

Pellow, D. (1991) 'From Accra to Kano: one woman's experience'. In C. M. Coles and B. B. Mack (eds) *Hausa Women in the Twentieth Century*. Madison, WI: University of Wisconsin Press, pp. 50–68.

Pew Forum (2006) *Spirit and Power: A 10-country survey of Pentecostals*. Washington, DC: Pew Forum on Religion and Public Life.

— (2010) *Tolerance and Tension: Islam and Christianity in sub-Saharan Africa*. Washington, DC: Pew Forum on Religion and Public Life.

Pieterse, E. (2008) *City Futures: Confronting the crisis of urban development*. London: Zed Books.

— (2010) 'Cityness and African urban development'. *Urban Forum* 21(3): 205–19.

Piot, C. (2006) 'Togolese cartographies: re-mapping space in a post-cold war city'. In P. Konings and D. Foeken (eds) *Crisis and Creativity: Exploring the wealth of the African neighbourhood*. Leiden: Brill, pp. 197–210.

Potts, D. (2009) 'The slowing of sub-Saharan Africa's urbanization: evidence and implications for urban livelihoods'. *Environment and Urbanization* 21(1): 253–9.

— (2012) *Whatever Happened to Africa's Rapid Urbanisation?* London: Africa Research Institute.

Puttergill, C. and A. Leildé (2006) 'Identity studies in Africa: notes on theory and method'. In S. Bekker and A. Leildé (eds) *Reflections on Identity in Four African Cities*. Johannesburg: African Minds, pp. 11–24.

Rakodi, C. (2004) 'Urban politics: exclusion or empowerment?'. In N. Devas, P. Amis, J. Beall, U. Grant, D. Mitlin, F. Nunan and C. Rakodi, *Urban Governance, Voice and Poverty in the Developing World*. London: Earthscan, pp. 68–94.

— (2006) 'Social agency and state authority in land delivery processes in African cities: compliance, conflict and cooperation'. *International Development Planning Review* 28(2): 263–85.

— (2011) *A Guide to Analyzing the Relationships between Religion and Development*. Religions and Development Working Paper 67. Birmingham: Religions and Development Research Programme. Available at www.religionsanddevelopment.org [accessed 14 August 2013].

Reitzes, M. (2002) '"There's space for Africa in the new South Africa(?)": African migrants and urban governance in Johannesburg'. In O. Enwezor, C. Basualdo, U. M. Bauer, S. Ghez, S. Maharaj, M. Nash and O. Zaya (eds) *Under Siege: Four African cities – Freetown, Johannesburg, Kinshasa, Lagos*. Documenta 11_Platform 4. Ostfildern: Hatje Cantz, pp. 215–38.

Robinson, J. (2006) *Ordinary Cities: Between modernity and development*. London: Routledge.

Robson, P. (2001) 'Communities and community institutions in Luanda, Angola'. In A. Tostensen, I. Tvedten and M. Vaa (eds) *Associational Life in African Cities: Popular responses to the urban crisis*. Uppsala: Nordiska Afrikainstitutet, pp. 250–62.

Rodgers, D. (2010) *Urban Violence is not (Necessarily) a Way of Life: Towards a political economy of conflict in cities*. Working Paper 2010/20. Helsinki: United Nations University, World Institute for Development Economics Research.

Rookes, P. and J. Rookes (2012a) 'Have financial difficulties compromised Christian health services' commitment to the poor?'. *Development in Practice* 22(5/6): 835–50.

— (2012b) *Commitment, Conscience or Compromise: The changing financial basis and evolving role of Christian health services*. Saarbrücken: Lambert Academic Publishing.

Said, E. ([1978] 1995) *Orientalism*. London: Penguin.

Samuelson, M. (2007) 'The city beyond the border: the urban worlds of Duiker, Mpe and Vera'. In F. Demissie (ed.) *Postcolonial African Cities: Imperial legacies and postcolonial predicament*. London: Routledge, pp. 89–102.

Schulz, D. (2010) 'Remaking society from within: extraversion and the social forms of female Muslim activism in urban Mali'. In B. Bompani and M. Frahm-Arp (eds) *Development and Politics from Below: Exploring religious spaces in the African state*. Basingstoke: Palgrave Macmillan, pp. 74–96.

Simone, A. (2002) 'The visible and invisible: remaking cities in Africa'. In O. Enwezor, C. Basualdo, U. M. Bauer, S. Ghez, S. Maharaj, M. Nash and O. Zaya (eds) *Under Siege: Four African cities – Freetown, Johannesburg, Kinshasa, Lagos*. Documenta 11_Platform 4. Ostfildern: Hatje Cantz, pp. 23–44.

— (2004) *For the City Yet to Come: Changing African life in four cities*. Durham, NC: Duke University Press.

— (2010a) *The Social Infrastructures of City Life in Contemporary Africa*. Discussion Paper 51. Uppsala: Nordiska Afrikainstitutet.

— (2010b) *City Life from Jakarta to Dakar: Movements at the crossroads*. London: Routledge.

Taylor, M. (2012) 'Strengthening the voice of the poor: religious organisations' engagement in policy consultation processes in Nigeria and Tanzania'. *Development in Practice* 22(5/6): 792–802.

Tostensen, A., I. Tvedten and M. Vaa (2001) 'The urban crisis, governance and associational life'. In A. Tostensen, I. Tvedten and M. Vaa (eds) *Associational Life in African Cities: Popular responses to the urban crisis*. Uppsala: Nordiska Afrikainstitutet, pp. 7–26.

Ukah, A. F. K. (2004) 'Pentecostalism, religious expansion and the city: lessons from the Nigerian bible-belt'. In P. Probst and G. Spittler (eds) *Between Resistance and Expansion: Explorations of local vitality in Africa*. Münster: Lit Verlag, pp. 415–41.

Umar, M. S. (2001) 'Education and Islamic trends in Northern Nigeria: 1970s–1990s'. *Africa Today* 48(2): 127–50.

van de Kamp, L. (2010) 'Burying life: Pentecostal religion and development in urban Mozambique'. In B. Bompani and M. Frahm-Arp (eds) *Development and Politics from Below: Exploring religious spaces in the African state*. Basingstoke: Palgrave Macmillan, pp. 152–71.

van Til, K. (2006) 'Neighbourhood (re)construction and changing identities in Mauritania from a small town perspective'. In P. Konings and D. Foeken (eds) *Crisis and Creativity: Exploring the wealth of the African neighbourhood*. Leiden: Brill, pp. 230–50.

Watts, M. (1996) 'Mapping identities: place, space, and community in an African city'. In P. Yaeger (ed.) *The*

Geography of Identity. Ann Arbor, MI: University of Michigan Press, pp. 59–97.

— (1999) 'Islamic modernities? Citizenship, civil society, and Islamism in a Nigerian city'. In J. Holston (ed.) *Cities and Citizenship*. Durham, NC: Duke University Press, pp. 67–102.

Werthmann, K. (2006) 'Urban space, gender and identity: a neighbourhood of Muslim women in Kano, Nigeria'. In P. Konings and D. Foeken (eds) *Crisis and Creativity: Exploring the wealth of the African neighbourhood*. Leiden: Brill, pp. 119–41.

World Values Surveys (n.d.) Website available at www.worldvaluessurvey.org [accessed 5 September 2013].

Young, C. (2007) 'Nation, ethnicity and citizenship: dilemmas of democracy and civil order in Africa'. In S. R. Dorman, D. Hammett and P. Nugent (eds) *Making Nations, Creating Strangers: States and citizenship in Africa*. Leiden: Brill, pp. 241–64.

Zeleza, P. T. (1999) 'The spatial economy of structural adjustment in African cities'. In E. Kalipeni and P. T. Zeleza (eds) *Sacred Spaces and Public Quarrels: African cultural and economic landscapes*. Trenton, NJ: Africa World Press, pp. 43–71.

6 | Feeding African cities: the growing challenge of urban food insecurity

Jonathan Crush and Bruce Frayne

Introduction

This chapter argues that the international food security agenda, which focuses on small farmer production as the means for alleviating poverty and hunger in Africa, is inadequate and will not achieve its objectives. This approach fails to acknowledge that within two decades Africa will be predominantly urban (see Table 6.1), following the global urban transition that is already well established. Analysis using data from the African Food Security Urban Network (AFSUN) baseline survey, which was carried out in 11 cities in nine southern African countries in 2008–09, demonstrates extremely high levels of urban food insecurity as a result of household poverty, high unemployment and limited income-generating opportunities, rather than because of food production and supply constraints. The analysis concludes that the immediate threat to food security for poor urban households is not food *availability*, but rather *access*, and that the issue of feeding the cities will become a defining development policy challenge for Africa in the coming decades.

Rural bias and urban food security The 2012 *Africa Human Development Report*, published by the United Nations Development Programme (UNDP), demonstrates clearly that Africa is the poorest and most food insecure continent. The report goes on to explain that:

> across sub-Saharan Africa, hunger prevalence is the highest in the world.
> More than one in four Africans – close to 218 million people in 2006–2008 – are undernourished, and food security is precarious. (UNDP 2012: 9)

And in concert with a broad global development community, the report argues explicitly for a solution to this persistent hunger based squarely on improved agricultural production within the continent (Crush and Frayne 2010).

Although agricultural production is emphasised as being a necessary condition for improving levels of food security in Africa, the UNDP's report also makes it clear that addressing food insecurity requires more than just a boost to production. The report recommends that food insecurity be addressed through four interrelated policy mechanisms:

TABLE 6.1 Projected urbanisation in Southern African Development Community (SADC) countries, 1990–2030 (percentage urban)

	1990	2000	2010	2020	2030
Angola	37.1	49.0	58.5	66.0	71.6
Botswana	41.9	53.2	61.1	67.6	72.7
DRC	27.8	29.8	35.2	42.0	49.2
Lesotho	14.0	20.0	26.9	34.5	42.4
Madagascar	23.6	27.1	30.2	34.9	41.4
Malawi	11.6	15.2	19.8	25.5	32.4
Mauritius	43.9	42.7	42.6	45.4	51.1
Mozambique	21.1	30.7	38.4	46.3	53.7
Namibia	27.7	32.4	38.0	44.4	51.5
Seychelles	49.3	51.0	55.3	61.1	66.6
South Africa	52.0	56.9	61.7	66.6	71.3
Swaziland	22.9	23.3	25.5	30.3	37.0
Tanzania	18.9	22.3	26.4	31.8	38.7
Zambia	39.4	34.8	35.7	38.9	44.7
Zimbabwe	29.0	33.8	38.3	43.9	50.7

Source: UN-Habitat 2008.

- increasing agricultural productivity, especially for smallholder farmers;
- strengthening nutrition, especially for women and children;
- building resilience for people and their communities; and
- promoting empowerment, especially among rural women and marginalised groups.

Even though agricultural production is seen as central to food and nutrition security, this four-pronged approach emphasises a more holistic food security strategy based on the concept of human development. While we would agree that these are important policy approaches to the problem of food insecurity in Africa, and that a human-centred development paradigm is also appropriate, what is puzzling is that the demographic reality of the urban transition taking place in sub-Saharan Africa is absent from the conceptualisation of this food security development challenge. What the report fails to recognise is the fact that sub-Saharan Africa is the fastest urbanising region in the world, at a rate about twice that of the global average, and that by 2035 more than half of the continent's population will live in cities (UN-Habitat 2010; see Figure 6.1). Within the subcontinent, southern Africa is the fastest urbanising region (UN DESA 2010). Urban growth rates in most countries are 3 to 5 per cent per annum while rural population growth rates, by comparison, are generally less than 1 per cent. Already, two southern African countries (Botswana and South Africa) are over 60 per cent urbanised. By 2030, these two countries will be over

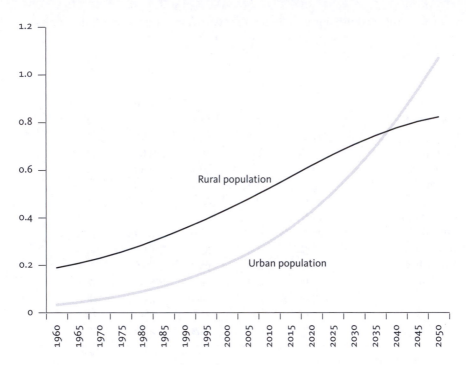

6.1 Urban and rural population in sub-Saharan Africa, 1960–2050 (billion) (*source:* Adapted from UN DESA 2010)

70 per cent urbanised, as will Angola. By then another five southern African countries (Mozambique, Zimbabwe, Namibia, Mauritius and the Seychelles) will be over 50 per cent urbanised and another four (Zambia, Lesotho, Madagascar and the Democratic Republic of Congo) will be over 40 per cent urban. Even in 'rural' countries such as Swaziland, Tanzania and Malawi, up to a third of the population will be urban. By 2050, every country in the region will be over 50 per cent urban and some (Angola, Botswana and South Africa) will be over 80 per cent urban (UN DESA 2010; see Table 6.1).

Production versus access to food While the UNDP (2012) report is in alignment with the global vision in which Africa's emancipation from poverty and hunger rests on the rapid growth of the agricultural sector (Montpellier Panel 2012), it does recognise that the ability to acquire food (access) – rather than simply the production of food – is an important dimension in understanding the dynamics and realities of food and nutrition insecurity. Indeed, purchasing power is viewed as central to acquiring food, and is the reality of a growing majority of urbanites in sub-Saharan Africa. For example, the report states that:

> households that are net food buyers are hit hardest by rising prices. In other
> regions net food buyers are mostly higher income urban residents, but in sub-

Saharan Africa they include not only the entire nonfarm population but also a majority of rural people. (UNDP 2012: 34)

As already demonstrated, this 'non-farm' population will represent the large majority of the subcontinent's population within the next two decades. Furthermore, there is no mention here of a supply constraint, even though the central food security strategy being put forward is one of increasing food production.

This lack of explicit focus on the food security of cities and towns as a fundamental development component in sub-Saharan Africa perpetuates a world view of food insecurity in Africa as being primarily a problem affecting rural populations (Crush and Frayne 2011a). Yet, in many countries, more than enough food is already being produced. South Africa, for example, produces sufficient food to guarantee an adequate diet for all. Why, then, is the incidence of under-nutrition shockingly high in that country (McLachlan and Thorne 2009; Crush et al. 2011a)? And, more generally, why do governments, international agencies and foreign donors continue to insist that increasing agricultural production by small farmers is the solution to food insecurity, even in countries such as South Africa where two-thirds of the population is already urbanised (GOSA 2002)? These questions are particularly relevant in a region and on a continent undergoing rapid urbanisation, where increasing numbers of people are leaving the countryside and relocating to urban areas, with uncertain implications for the food security of urban populations (Kessides 2005).

Many new urbanites maintain close links with rural regions but the overall trend is towards more and more people living in urban areas for progressively longer periods (Potts 2010). The majority of Africa's new urbanites live and survive in what Saunders (2010) recently called 'arrival cities' – overcrowded, low-income, informal settlements where rates of poverty and formal unemployment are extremely high. Within this context, a central development question is how Africa's rapidly growing urban populations are to be fed (Steel 2008; Satterthwaite et al. 2010). Three strategies for increasing the supply of food to African cities are commonly advocated. None pays a great deal of attention to how urban populations will actually access the food even if it is available.

Strongly influenced by the so-called 'green revolution' in the twentieth century, which improved agricultural production in much of Asia, the first strategy is the Alliance for a Green Revolution in Africa (AGRA). AGRA's principal mission is 'to achieve a food secure and prosperous Africa through the promotion of rapid, sustainable agricultural growth based on smallholder farmers' (AGRA 2010). Increased food supplies are seen as key to improving rural incomes and stabilising food prices (Diao and Headey 2008; Toenniessen et al. 2008; Sanchez et al. 2009; Ejeta 2010; Otsukaa and Kijimab 2010). International organisations, philanthropic foundations, governments, donors and researchers largely agree that the key to reducing the continent's high levels of under-nutrition is increasing technical inputs in smallholder agricultural production (World Bank 2008; FAO 2009; AGRA 2010; Wiggins and Leturque 2010; Breisinger et al. 2011). Western donors and foundations are currently promoting technical additives to small-scale agriculture in Africa in a renewed effort to achieve the kind of 'rural development' transformation that was widely reckoned to have failed only 20 years ago. Even in South Africa, where any chance of smallholder agriculture meeting the food needs of the rural (let alone the urban) poor is extremely remote, this 'solution' is being advocated by government and by some researchers (Atkinson 2006; Baiphethi and Jacobs 2009). Others are more sceptical, arguing that small-scale farming will not feed the cities and that small-scale farmers are largely excluded from the commercial supply chains that feed the cities and underwrite urbanisation (Palmer and Sender 2006; Holt-Giménez 2008; Amanor 2009; Kepe 2009; Woodhouse 2009).

Secondly, there is the alternative view that the future of urban food security in Africa does not lie in smallholder agriculture but rather in large-scale commercial agriculture and the modern agri-food supply chains that already feed the vast majority of the urbanised world, including Africa (Collier 2008; Collier and Dercon 2009; Larsen et al. 2009; Roepstorff et al. 2011; Yumkella et al. 2011). Collier (2008), citing the Brazilian case, argues that the smallholder orthodoxy is misplaced because it ignores the potential of agri-business to effect the kinds of production and productivity increases that would help feed Africa's growing cities. Supermarket expansion is rapidly changing the nature of the urban food supply in Africa, a trend that will accelerate in the future (Weatherspoon and Reardon 2003; Reardon et al. 2008; Reardon and Timmer 2008; Crush and Frayne 2011a). Modern supermarket chains increasingly control the food supply chain in the urban areas of southern Africa and beyond (Emongor and Kirsten 2009; Abrahams 2010; Crush and Frayne 2011b). Whether or not these supply chains will provide commercial opportunities for smallholder farmers is currently a matter of some debate (Humphrey 2007; Louw et al. 2007; Vorley et al. 2007). Value chains rely on supply systems that are predictable in both quantity and quality; both these factors are more difficult to ensure under the small-scale, semi-subsistence agricultural systems that are widespread in Africa.

Thirdly, there is a widespread belief that urban and peri-urban agriculture is a primary solution to urban food insecurity in the twenty-first century (Koc et al. 1999; Mougeot 2005; 2006; Van Veenhuizen 2006; Hovorka et al. 2009; Redwood 2008; Zezza and Tasciotti 2010). Contemporary policy debates are increasingly dominated by the idea that the promotion of urban agriculture is the key to ensuring food security among poor households in African cities (Drechsel and Dongus 2010; Dubbeling et al. 2010; Rogerson 2010). This argument has recently been treated with scepticism by researchers who claim that the means and motivation of the urban poor to grow their own food and derive income from its sale have been greatly exaggerated (Crush et al. 2011b; Webb 2011). City governments are also less convinced and generally adopt a laissez-faire attitude to the presence of fields and livestock in cities. In some cases, however, they actively oppose their presence as being unsuited to the urban environment (Mbiba 2000; Simatele and Binns 2008; Thornton et al. 2010).

For all their differences of emphasis and policy prescription, these three approaches to food insecurity in Africa share a productionist assumption that the answer to food security on the continent is increased agricultural output. Much of the current debate on food security in Africa therefore focuses on increasing food production, to the detriment of any serious consideration of the other dimensions of food security. However, our concern is not with how the new international agenda understands the nature and causes of rural food insecurity but rather with what it has to say about the food security of urban populations. The answer is very little, at least explicitly. In all of the policy documents and statements relating to this agenda, it is almost as if the urban does not exist in Africa.[1] Nowhere is there any systematic attempt to differentiate rural from urban food security, to understand the dimensions and determinants of urban food security, to examine the links between rural and urban food security, to assess whether the rural policy prescriptions for reducing hunger and malnutrition are relevant to urban populations, or to develop policies that are specific to the food needs of the urban poor.

The remainder of this chapter is based on findings from a household survey conducted simultaneously in 11 major southern African cities in nine countries in 2008–09 by AFSUN. The analysis of this survey data supports the view argued in this chapter that urban food security hinges on access to food rather than on the supply of food. While stable and plentiful food supplies might help to ameliorate food price changes, high levels of poverty in the region's rapidly growing cities and towns already mean that a large proportion of urbanites are chronically food insecure. A brief description of the methodology used in the AFSUN survey is followed by a presentation and discussion of the main survey findings, focusing on:

- the levels of food insecurity among poor urban households in terms of their access to food;
- the quality and diversity of urban diets;
- the relationship between poverty and food insecurity; and
- the determinants of urban household food insecurity.

Methodology

The AFSUN Urban Food Security Baseline Survey was conducted in late 2008 and early 2009 in 11 cities in nine countries in southern Africa: Blantyre, Cape

TABLE 6.2 Sample population for the AFSUN Urban Food Security Baseline Survey

City	No. of households	No. of individuals
Blantyre, Malawi	431	2,230
Cape Town, South Africa	1,026	4,177
Gaborone, Botswana	391	1,237
Harare, Zimbabwe	454	2,572
Johannesburg, South Africa	976	3,762
Lusaka, Zambia	386	1,978
Manzini, Swaziland	489	2,112
Maputo, Mozambique	389	2,737
Maseru, Lesotho	795	3,248
Msunduzi, South Africa	548	2,871
Windhoek, Namibia	442	1,848
Total	6,327	28,772

Town, Gaborone, Harare, Johannesburg, Lusaka, Manzini, Maputo, Maseru, Msunduzi (Pietermaritzburg) and Windhoek. The surveyed cities represent a mix of primary and secondary cities; large and small cities; cities in crisis, in transition and those on a strong developmental path; and a range of local governance structures and capacities as well as natural environments. These particular cities were selected on the basis of local research expertise, expressed interest and engagement from policy makers, and the fact that they collectively offer a wide platform from which to address the pressing issues of urban food security.

The survey used a standardised household questionnaire developed collaboratively by all 11 participating partners at a workshop in Gaborone, Botswana. The aim was to understand the levels and dynamics of food insecurity in poor urban neighbourhoods. In each city, one or more representative community was chosen for study by the local AFSUN partner. In the larger cities, such as Cape Town and Johannesburg, different types of formal and informal urban neighbourhoods were chosen. Within city neighbourhoods, households were sampled using a systematic random sampling technique; when it was not possible to interview people in the designated household, a substitution was made.

The resulting AFSUN Urban Food Security Regional Database contains information on 6,327 households and 28,772 individuals in 11 cities (see Table 6.2). While there have been a number of prior studies of urban food insecurity in particular cities or groups of cities within a country, this is the first study to generate a regional database and to provide a regional picture of the state of food insecurity in southern Africa.

After considering various alternatives (Webb et al. 2006; Faber et al. 2009;

Hart 2009; Labadarios et al. 2009; Barrett 2010), AFSUN selected the robust food security assessment methodology developed by the Food and Nutrition Technical Assistance (FANTA) project for its survey (Swindale and Bilinsky 2006a; Coates et al. 2007; Deitchler et al. 2010). FANTA has conducted a series of studies exploring and testing alternative measures of household food insecurity in a variety of geographical and cultural contexts and has developed various indicators and scales to measure aspects of food insecurity. These measures have previously been successfully used by other researchers in a variety of settings in Africa and elsewhere (Agarwal et al. 2008; FAO 2008; González et al. 2008; Becquey et al. 2010; Knueppel et al. 2010). Four FANTA scales and indicators for measuring food insecurity were used in the research methodology.

Levels of food insecurity in poor urban neighbourhoods

The household food insecurity access prevalence (HFIAP) indicator allocates all households to one of four food security categories according to their household food insecurity access scale (HFIAS) score. Table 6.3 shows the distribution of surveyed households between the four HFIAP categories for all 11 cities. More than half of the households (57 per cent) were 'severely food insecure' with another 19 per cent being 'moderately food insecure'. Only 17 per cent of households were food secure. In other words, over 80 per cent of poor urban households across the region experience some degree of food insecurity. In eight of the 11 cities, 60 per cent or more of the households in the sample were severely food insecure. There are important differences evident in the data between cities. For example, the proportion of households who were severely food insecure ranged from a low of 21 per cent in Blantyre to a high of 79 per cent in Manzini. In all but two of the cities (Blantyre and Johannesburg), less than 20 per cent of households were food secure. The figure was extremely low in Msunduzi (7 per cent), Manzini (6 per cent), Maseru and Maputo (5 per cent), Lusaka (4 per cent) and Harare (2 per cent).

For ease of statistical analysis, all households were recoded into two overall categories: food insecure (severe and moderate insecurity on the HFIAS, affecting 76 per cent of households) and food secure (mild insecurity and secure; 24 per cent of households). Recoding the data from four to two food security categories over-represents the levels of food security in the survey but usefully simplifies the presentation of the data without significantly changing the regional picture. Using the two computed categories of 'food secure' and 'food insecure' households, the difference between insecure and secure households is statistically significant (p<0.001, cc=0.392). Nine of the 11 cities have levels of food insecurity in excess of 76 per cent (see Table 6.4).

Another dimension of food security relates to the quality of the urban diet. The household dietary diversity scale (HDDS) attempts to provide a measure of the quality and variety of food eaten within a household (Swindale and

TABLE 6.3 Extent of urban food insecurity (percentage of households)

City	Severely food insecure	Moderately food insecure	Mildly food insecure	Food secure
Manzini	79	12	3	6
Harare	72	23	3	2
Lusaka	69	24	3	4
Cape Town	68	12	5	15
Maseru	65	25	5	5
Gaborone	63	19	6	12
Windhoek	63	14	5	18
Msunduzi	60	27	6	7
Maputo	54	32	9	5
Johannesburg	27	15	14	44
Blantyre	21	31	14	34
Total	57	19	7	17

TABLE 6.4 Levels of food insecurity by city (percentage of households)

City	Food insecure	Food secure
Harare	95	5
Manzini	92	8
Lusaka	92	8
Maseru	90	10
Msunduzi	87	13
Maputo	86	14
Gaborone	82	18
Cape Town	80	20
Windhoek	77	23
Blantyre	52	48
Johannesburg	42	58
Total	76	24

Bilinsky 2006b). In general, any increase in household dietary diversity reflects an improvement in the household's diet and reduced food insecurity. The scale is based on the number of food groups consumed within the household over a given period (in this case, the previous 24 hours) and ranges from zero to 12.

The HDDS results show that dietary diversity is inadequate in most households, with an average value of six (indicating that food from only six different food groups was consumed). When the non-nutritive food items of sugar and beverages are removed from the dietary intake of the sample, the dietary

TABLE 6.5 Dietary diversity scores

Number of food groups	Households (%)	Cumulative (%)
1	2	2
2	11	13
3	10	23
4	11	34
5	14	48
6	13	61
7	12	73
8	10	83
9	7	90
10	4	94
11	3	97
12	3	100
Total	100	

Note: n = 6,453

diversity score drops to four. Only 3 per cent of the households have an HDDS score of 12 (see Table 6.5). Over 60 per cent of the households scored six or less, and nearly a quarter scored three or less. The median HDDS for food secure households is eight and for food insecure households it is five; the difference between secure and insecure households is statistically significant ($p<0.001$, eta=0.399). This suggests that there is a strong relationship between food security (as measured by the HFIAP) and dietary diversity. In other words, as food insecurity increases, dietary diversity declines.

FANTA's months of adequate household food provisioning (MAHFP) indicator captures changes in levels of food security over the course of a year (Bilinsky and Swindale 2007). Households identified the months (in the previous 12) when they did not have access to sufficient food to meet their needs. In many rural areas, food insecurity has a clear seasonal dimension, with communities experiencing 'hungry seasons' before the new crop is harvested. Since urban food supply systems are generally able to overcome seasonality in food supply through diversification, and because urban households purchase most of their food, it was assumed that urban food provisioning would be non-seasonal. The survey found, however, that food security does vary throughout the year in these cities.

There was marked variation over the course of the calendar year in food access (see Figure 6.2). The annual period of lowest urban food shortages seems to coincide with the harvest and post-harvest period in agricultural areas, from March to May. Thereafter, through the dry and unproductive winter

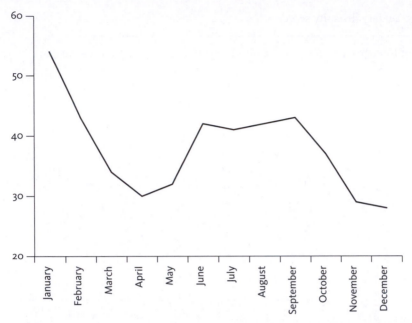

6.2 Seasonal variations in urban food insecurity (percentage of households experiencing inadequate food provisioning)

months, the levels of inadequate food provisioning rise once again, as they do in the rural areas. Part of the explanation for the apparent similarity between rural and urban cycles may lie in the fact that urban agriculture has a seasonal dimension. More important, though, is the fact that many urban households receive food direct from rural smallholdings during the harvest and post-harvest season when there are likely to be disposable surpluses. Nearly one-third of all households surveyed said they receive food direct from rural households (Frayne 2010). In cities such as Windhoek and Lusaka, the proportion was even higher, at 47 per cent and 44 per cent of households respectively. In some cities, therefore, deficits are related to the rural agricultural cycle.

Food secure households experience almost 12 months a year of adequate food access. Food insecure urban households, on the other hand, go without adequate food for an average of four months of the year (see Figure 6.3). There is a statistically significant relationship between food security status and months of adequate provisioning (p>0.001, eta=0.369). In all cities, food insecure households experience at least three months of inadequate provisioning during the year (see Figure 6.2). In some cases, such as Manzini (seven months) and Harare and Maseru (five months), the situation is even more dire for food insecure households.

The timing of the urban MAHFP cycle differs from that in rural areas. For example, a second improvement in urban food security occurs in what are normally lean months in the rural areas – from September to December. This

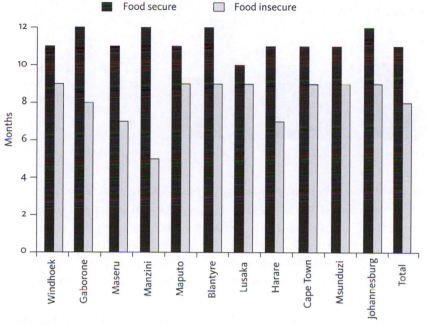

6.3 Months of adequate food provisioning by food security status

may be related to increases in spending on food towards the end-of-year holiday season and the payment of annual bonuses for those in employment. Also, the final quarter of the year is when many urbanites return home to rural areas for their annual holiday, in turn reducing the number of mouths to feed in the urban household. The worst levels of urban food insecurity occur directly after the holiday period, in January, right after the high levels of spending during the festive season. The decline in the incidence of food insecurity begins almost immediately, with the situation improving each month. This is different to the pattern in rural areas, where the pre-harvest season is often the hungriest.

Incomes and food access

As argued earlier in this chapter, households in the African urban context purchase the majority of their food. A strong association between food security and levels of household income can therefore be anticipated. The survey showed a clear relationship between the two variables, with the lowest income households experiencing the highest levels of food insecurity. The level of food security increases with income across all types of households, a relationship that is statistically significant ($p < 0.001$, cc=0.250). In addition, when income terciles are computed against food security status, households with the lowest incomes show the greatest levels of food insecurity (see Figure 6.4). More than half (57 per cent) of all food secure households are in the highest income

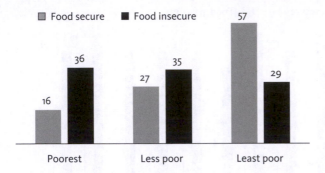

6.4 Household income terciles by food security status (percentage of households)

Food secure   Food insecure

16 36 27 35 57 29

Poorest   Less poor   Least poor

category, while the greatest proportion of food insecure households (36 per cent) is in the poorest income tercile. Blantyre has the strongest correlation between income and food security status (p<0.001, cc=0.406) and Harare the weakest (p<0.023, cc=0.132), a reflection of the collapse of the Zimbabwean economy and the generally poor levels of real income. At the same time, 29 per cent of food insecure households were in the upper income tercile and 16 per cent of food secure households were in the lowest income tercile. To explain this, further investigation would be needed to see what other pressures on income both types of households experience.

The relationship between the work status of household members and household food security was statistically significant (p<0.001), although the strength of the relationship was weak (cc=0.141). When a household has a member (or members) in full-time waged work, there is a positive correlation with improved levels of food security. However, while 46 per cent of food secure households have a wage earner, so do 35 per cent of food insecure households. This suggests that a wage earner in the household is not in itself a guarantee that the household will be lifted out of food insecurity, presumably because formal sector wages are generally so low. There was no statistically significant relationship between food security and other sources of household income, although casual work is associated more with food insecurity. Households with unemployed members who were looking for work had higher levels of insecurity.

A strong relationship between poverty levels and food insecurity was anticipated. Poverty, of course, is defined in various ways. The most common global statistical measures of poverty are those of US$1 per day (extremely poor) and US$2 per day (moderately poor). The mean monthly household income for the study sample was US$193 in the previous year. This translates into a daily per capita income of US$1.29. In only three of the 11 cities (Johannesburg, Windhoek and Gaborone), however, were mean per capita incomes above US$1 per day. At the aggregate level, 66 per cent of households live at or below the US$1 per day poverty line, and 76 per cent live at or below the US$2 per day poverty line. Given the high cost of food in African cities, it is clear that an income of US$1 per day is insufficient to meet basic needs. For example, a loaf of bread in South Africa cost approximately US$1 in 2008–09, a purchase that would leave the person with no other disposable income, yet with all other basic needs unmet. Considering that food costs approximately 30 per cent more in urban than in rural areas, income measures may therefore not be an accurate proxy for poverty (Ravallion 2007).

The study therefore used a supplementary, non-income-related measure of poverty known as the lived poverty index (LPI), a subjective experiential index (Mattes et al. 2003). The LPI has proven to be a reliable, self-reported, multidimensional measure of deprivation and is based on how often a household reports being unable to secure a basket of basic necessities of life: food, clean water, medicine or medical treatment, cooking oil and a cash income. Responses are grouped together into a single household index on a scale that ranges from zero (never going without) to four (always going without); the higher the LPI value, the greater the degree of 'lived poverty'.

The food security status of each household was cross-tabulated with its LPI score. Although the sample was split about equally between households who 'go without' on the LPI scale and those who do not, more than 91 per cent of food secure households have an LPI score of zero to one (never or seldom going without) (see Figure 6.5). In contrast, 60 per cent of those households that are food insecure are also those that 'go without' (LPI score of 1.01 to 4.0). The relationship between LPI and food security status proved to be statistically significant ($p < 0.001$), with a moderately strong correlation ($cc = 0.395$). The cities in which this poverty–food security status relationship was strongest were Blantyre ($p < 0.001$, $cc = 0.503$) and Gaborone ($p < 0.001$, $cc = 0.405$).

Strong claims are often made for social protection as a viable policy response to food insecurity. However, the survey found no statistically significant relationship between social grant income and food security status. This may be because not all countries in the survey have social protection systems. However, even in those that do, such as South Africa, social grants do not appear to impact significantly on food security. This observation holds true for the three South African cities of Cape Town, Msunduzi and Johannesburg, where about 30 per cent of households reported receiving social grants (mainly pensions and child support grants).

Food sourcing

The final section of this chapter returns to the issue posed at the outset: that is, where do poor urban households obtain their food? The survey clearly showed that modern agri-business supply chains play a critical role in provisioning the region's cities. South Africa's four major supermarket chains dominate food retailing in that country and have expanded aggressively over the last two decades both internally into poorer areas of cities and into the

TABLE 6.6 Major sources of food for poor urban households (percentage of households)

	Supermarkets	Informal economy	Small formal outlets
Windhoek	97	76	84
Gaborone	97	29	56
Msunduzi	97	42	40
Johannesburg	96	85	80
Cape Town	94	66	75
Manzini	90	48	49
Maseru	84	49	48
Blantyre	53	99	69
Harare	30	98	17
Maputo	23	98	78
Lusaka	16	100	68
Total	79	70	68

rest of Africa (Crush and Frayne 2011b). In 2007, Shoprite, Pick n Pay, Spar and Woolworths had 2,653 outlets in the countries of the SADC (Emongor and Kirsten 2009). Supermarket penetration of the urban food supply system has proceeded further in some countries than in others. The majority of the big four's outlets (85 per cent) were in South Africa itself, but all of the countries in this study had at least some outlets: Zimbabwe (129), Namibia (103), Botswana (66), Swaziland (23), Zambia (21), Lesotho (9), Malawi (5) and Mozambique (5).

Given the usual association of supermarkets with middle-class urban consumers, one of the more striking findings of the survey was the high proportion of poor urban households (over 70 per cent) that source food from supermarkets (see Table 6.6). The relative importance of supermarket sourcing varies from city to city, however, depending on the degree of supermarket penetration. In seven of the cities (in South Africa, Botswana, Lesotho, Swaziland and Namibia), over 80 per cent of households purchase food direct from supermarkets. In Lusaka, the figure is only 16 per cent, followed by Maputo (23 per cent), Harare (30 per cent) and Blantyre (53 per cent). Most households tend to patronise supermarkets on a weekly or monthly basis and food staples feature heavily in the shopping basket. Food prices are generally lower in supermarkets than in other food outlets. Emongor (2008: 122), for example, found that in both Botswana and Zambia, staples such as maize flour, bread, milk, rice and sugar, as well as fresh fruit and vegetables, were consistently cheaper in supermarkets than in small grocery stores. The primary disadvantage of supermarkets is their lack of accessibility, although there has been a recent trend to locate new stores within or close to the poorer areas of cities.

Clearly, then, commercial agriculture and modern agri-food supply chains are already playing an increasing role in feeding the region's cities.

At the same time, most cities in the region have very dynamic informal food economies (Crush and Frayne 2011b). While a smaller overall proportion of households purchases food from informal vendors (70 per cent), such outlets tend to be patronised far more frequently for vegetables and for cooked and processed food. In the cities with lower levels of supermarket penetration, patronage of the informal food economy is very high (100 per cent of households in Lusaka, 99 per cent in Blantyre, and 98 per cent in Maputo and Harare). Patronage is also significant in Johannesburg (85 per cent) and Windhoek (76 per cent) but rather less so in some of the other cities with significant supermarket penetration (Maseru, Manzini, Msunduzi and Gaborone are all at less than 50 per cent). Clearly, this pattern could change over time as competition between the formal and informal food economies intensifies. The other major source of food purchases is small formal outlets such as grocers, corner stores and fast food chains. While the overall patronage figure was 68 per cent, these sources are especially important for the urban poor in Windhoek (84 per cent), Johannesburg (80 per cent), Maputo (78 per cent), Cape Town (75 per cent) and Lusaka (68 per cent).

Without further analysis of the sourcing strategies of informal vendors and small outlets, it is impossible to say what role agri-food supply chains play in their operations. Few (except the fast food suppliers) have their own supply chains, of course, but it is clear that many source their food from supermarkets, wholesalers or fresh produce markets. In South African cities, the fresh produce markets are supplied almost entirely by large commercial farmers. In other cities with produce markets, such as Lusaka and Maputo, it is clear that some small-scale producers are able to sell their produce to urban consumers. The markets and informal vendors in the poorer areas of Maputo sell a complex mix of Mozambican rural produce, commercially produced and imported South African fresh and processed food, and foodstuffs from the global market (such as Brazilian chickens).

Urban agriculture proved to be far less important to poor households in the surveyed cities than anticipated (see Table 6.7) (Crush et al. 2011b). Around 80 per cent of households did not grow any of their own food and 97 per cent did not derive any income at all from the sale of home produce. Only cities such as Blantyre and Harare had a significant number of households engaged in urban agriculture. However, 77 per cent of those households that do engage in urban agriculture fall into the food insecure category. This figure, of course, matches the total proportion of households that are food insecure across the 11 cities, which suggests a strong association between the practice of urban agriculture and household levels of food poverty. However, the correlation between the practice of urban agriculture and food security status is statistically weak

TABLE 6.7 Urban agriculture and informal food transfers (percentage of households)

	Urban agriculture	Rural–urban transfers of food
Windhoek	3	72
Gaborone	5	70
Msunduzi	30	15
Johannesburg	8	24
Cape Town	4	14
Manzini	9	53
Maseru	47	49
Blantyre	63	38
Harare	60	37
Maputo	22	23
Lusaka	3	39

(p<0.004, cc=0.036). While only a minority of urban households produces any of their own food, a much larger number depends on informal food transfers from their rural homes. These informal food transfer channels play a very significant role in cities such as Windhoek (72 per cent) and Gaborone (70 per

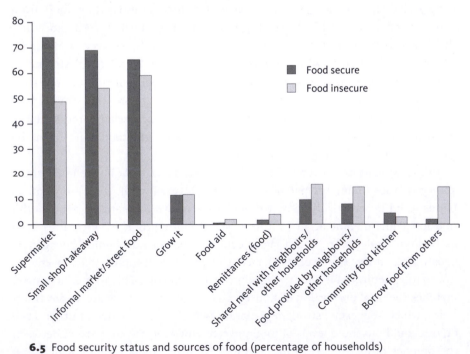

6.5 Food security status and sources of food (percentage of households)

cent), Manzini (53 per cent) and Maseru (49 per cent). Only in the three South African cities are informal rural-to-urban transfers of very little importance.

The final question is whether there is any relationship between household food security status and where the household sources its food from. In other words, do food secure households tend to source more from one type of outlet and food insecure households from another?

Notwithstanding the increasingly dominant role being played by supermarkets, it is important to note that as households become more food insecure, so they rely more on informal food sources. The correlation between supermarkets and food security status is stronger than that between all other sources of household food and security. Some 74 per cent of food secure households source some of their food from supermarkets, compared with only 48 per cent of food insecure households (see Figure 6.5). The relationship between food security status and supermarket use is statistically significant ($p<0.001$, cc=0.214). As noted above, food secure households tend to have higher incomes and members in regular waged employment. This would suggest that supermarket use increases with rising income.

Conclusion

The findings and analysis in this chapter demonstrate that food insecurity is a widespread, poverty-related phenomenon in the cities of southern Africa. These high levels of chronic hunger exist in the context of rapid urbanisation, and, in the absence of large-scale, sustained employment growth, they are likely to persist in the coming decades. While there are now substantive regional and continental initiatives to address food security (SADC 2003; AGRA 2010; UNDP 2012), these policies and frameworks have gaps that limit their potential impact, particularly with regard to *urban* food security. The urban is a critical development frontier and has particular dynamics and cross-scale links that need to be considered in order to understand – and ultimately address – the growing epidemic of urban food insecurity.

Urban food insecurity does not easily lend itself to the small farmer production orientation of the international food security agenda. Nor is urban agriculture the panacea it was once thought to be. Crush et al. (2011b) show that the extent of urban agriculture and its contribution to household food security are insubstantial in many poor areas of SADC cities. Urban food security is more about access, regularity, food safety and nutritional diversity and quality. To fully understand the complexity of urban food insecurity we need to know much more about urban food supply and distribution systems, both formal and informal (and the ways in which they interact). The informal economy is a key determinant of food access for the urban poor and needs to be better supported and less pilloried in policy. Supermarkets are rapidly emerging as a major food source for the urban poor throughout southern Africa and therefore much more attention needs to be paid to the implications of supermarket expansion for food insecurity. In policy terms, regional, national and municipal governments need to build on the evidence from a comprehensive programme of research to craft a new urban food security agenda and to formulate city-specific food security plans.

We therefore argue for a new food security agenda that takes account of rapid urbanisation and acknowledges that urban food security is the key challenge for the future. The immediate threat to food security for poor urban households in the region is not food *availability*, but rather *access*. In an urban, cash-intensive environment, income is the most important means of accessing food (as reported earlier in this chapter, improved food security status and income are positively correlated). The issue of feeding the cities will become the defining development policy challenge for Africa in the coming decades.

Acknowledgements

The authors would like to thank the following for their contributions to the AFSUN baseline survey: Caryn Abrahams, Ben Acquah, Jane Battersby-Lennard, Eugenio Bras, Mary Caesar, Asiyati Chiweza, David Coetzee, Scott Drimie, Rob Fincham, Miriam Grant, Florian Kroll, Clement Leduka, Aloysius Mosha, Chileshe Mulenga, Peter Mvula, Ndeyapo Nickanor, Wade Pendleton, Akiser Pomuti, Ines Raimundo, Celia Rocha, Michael Rudolph, Shaun Ruysenaar, Christa Schier, Nomcebo Simelane, Godfrey Tawodzera, Daniel Tevera, Percy Toriro, Maxton Tsoka and Lazarus Zanamwe. FANTA is gratefully acknowledged for providing the methodology and questions used in this survey to collect food insecurity data. The survey was funded by the Canadian International Development Agency through its University Partnerships in Cooperation and Development Tier One Program.

Note

1 For a full discussion of this agenda, refer to Crush and Frayne 2011a.

References

Abrahams, C. (2010) 'Transforming the region: supermarkets and the local food economy'. *African Affairs* 109(434): 115–34.

Agarwal, S., V. Sethi, P. Gupta, M. Jha, A. Agnihotri and M. Nord (2008) 'Experiential household food insecurity in an urban underserved slum of north India'. *Food Security* 1(3): 239–50.

AGRA (2010) 'About the alliance for a green revolution in Africa'. Kenya: Alliance for a Green Revolution in Africa (AGRA). Available at www.agra.org [accessed 5 September 2013].

Amanor, K. (2009) 'Global food chains, African smallholders and World Bank governance'. *Journal of Agrarian Change* 9(2): 247–62.

Atkinson, D. (2006) 'Is there a case for support for smallholder agriculture? A response to Palmer and Sender'. *Journal of Contemporary African Studies* 24(3): 377–84.

Baiphethi, M. and P. Jacobs (2009) 'The contribution of subsistence farming to food security in South Africa'. *Agrekon* 48(4): 459–82.

Barrett, C. (2010) 'Measuring food insecurity'. *Science* 327(5967): 825–8.

Becquey, E., Y. Martin-Prevel, P. Traissac, B. Dembélé, A. Bambara and F. Delpeuch (2010) 'The household food insecurity access scale and an index-member dietary diversity score contribute valid and complementary information on household food insecurity in an urban West-African setting'. *Journal of Nutrition* 140(12): 2233–40.

Bilinsky, P. and A. Swindale (2007) 'Months of adequate household food provisioning (MAHFP) for measurement of household food access: indicator guide'. Washington, DC: Food and Nutrition Technical Assistance (FANTA).

Breisinger, C., X. Diao, J. Thurlow and R. Al Hassan (2011) 'Potential impacts of a green revolution in Africa: the case of Ghana'. *Journal of International Development* 23(1): 82–102.

Coates, J., A. Swindale and P. Bilinsky (2007) 'Household food insecurity access scale (HFIAS) for measurement of food access: indicator guide, version 3'. Washington, DC: Food and Nutrition Technical Assistance (FANTA).

Collier, P. (2008) 'The politics of hunger: how illusion and greed fan the food crisis'. *Foreign Affairs* 87(6): 67–79.

— and S. Dercon (2009) 'African agriculture in 50 years: smallholders in a rapidly changing world?'. Paper presented at FAO Expert Meeting on How to Feed the World in 2050, Rome, 24–26 June.

Crush, J. and B. Frayne (2010) *Pathways to Insecurity: Urban food supply and access in Southern African cities*. Urban Food Security Series No. 3. Cape Town and Kingston: African Centre for Cities and Southern African Research Centre.

— (2011a) 'Urban food insecurity and the new international food security agenda', *Development Southern Africa* 28(4): 527–44.

— (2011b) 'Supermarket expansion and the informal food economy in southern African cities: implications for urban food security'. *Journal of Southern African Studies* 37(4): 781–807.

— and M. McLachlan (2011a) *Rapid Urbanisation and the Nutrition Transition in Southern Africa*. Urban Food Security Series No. 7. Cape Town: Queen's University and African Food Security Urban Network (AFSUN).

— A. Hovorka and D. Tevera (2011b) 'Food security in southern African cities: the

place of urban agriculture'. *Progress in Development Studies* 11(4): 285–305.

Deitchler, M., T. Ballard, A. Swindale and J. Coates (2010) 'Validation of a measure of household hunger for cross-cultural use'. Washington, DC: Food and Nutrition Technical Assistance (FANTA).

Diao, X. and D. Headey (2008) 'Toward a green revolution in Africa: what would it achieve, and what would it require?'. *Agricultural Economics* 39(S1): 539–50.

Drechsel, P. and S. Dongus (2010) 'Dynamics and sustainability of urban agriculture: examples from sub-Saharan Africa'. *Sustainability Science* 5(1): 69–78.

Dubbeling, M., H. de Zeeuw and R. van Veenhuizen (2010) *Cities, Poverty and Food: Multi-stakeholder policy and planning in urban agriculture*. Rugby: Practical Action Publishing.

Ejeta, G. (2010) 'African green revolution needn't be a mirage'. *Science* 327(5967): 831–2.

Emongor, R. (2008) 'The impact of South African supermarkets on agricultural and industrial development in the Southern African Development Community'. PhD thesis, University of Pretoria.

— and J. Kirsten (2009) 'The impact of South African supermarkets on agricultural development in the SADC: a case study in Zambia, Namibia and Botswana'. *Agrekon* 48(1): 60–84.

Faber, M., C. Schwabe and S. Drimie (2009) 'Dietary diversity in relation to other household food security indicators'. *International Journal of Food Safety, Nutrition and Public Health* 2(1): 1–15.

FAO (2008) *Report on Use of the Household Food Insecurity Access Scale and Household Dietary Diversity Score in Two Survey Rounds in Manica and Sofala Provinces, Mozambique, 2006–2007. FAO Food Security Project GCP/MOZ/079/BEL*. Maputo: Food and Agriculture Organization of the United Nations (FAO).

— (2009) 'World summit on food security'. Food and Agriculture Organization of the United Nations (FAO), Rome, 16–18 November. Available at www.fao.org/wsfs/world-summit/en [accessed 16 August 2013].

Frayne, B. (2010) 'Pathways of food: mobility and food transfers in southern African cities'. *International Development Planning Review* 32(3–4): 291–310.

González, W., A. Jiménez, A. Madrigal, L. Muñoz and E. Frongillo (2008) 'Development and validation of measure of household food insecurity in urban Costa Rica confirms proposed generic questionnaire'. *Journal of Nutrition* 140(3): 2233–40.

GOSA (2002) *Integrated Food Security Strategy for South Africa*. Pretoria: Government of South Africa (GOSA), Department of Agriculture.

Hart, T. (2009) *Food Security Definitions, Measurements and Recent Initiatives in South Africa and Southern Africa*. Pretoria: Human Sciences Research Council.

Holt-Giménez, E. (2008) 'Out of AGRA: the green revolution returns to Africa'. *Development* 51(4): 464–71.

Hovorka, A., H. de Zeeuw and M. Njenga (eds) (2009) *Women Feeding Cities: Gender mainstreaming in urban agriculture and food security*. Rugby: Practical Action Publishing.

Humphrey, J. (2007) 'The supermarket revolution in developing countries: tidal wave or tough competitive struggle?'. *Journal of Economic Geography* 7(4): 433–50.

Kepe, T. (2009) 'Unjustified optimism: why the World Bank's 2008 "agriculture for development" report misses the point for South Africa'. *Journal of Peasant Studies* 36(3): 637–43.

Kessides, C. (2005) *The Urban Transition in Sub-Saharan Africa: Implications for economic growth and poverty reduction*. Africa Region Working Paper Series No. 97. Washington, DC: World Bank.

Knueppel, D., M. Demment and L. Kaiser (2010) 'Validation of the household food insecurity access scale in rural Tanzania'. *Public Health and Nutrition* 13(3): 360–7.

Koc, M., R. MacRae, L. Mougeot and J. Welsh (eds) (1999) *For Hunger-Proof Cities: Sustainable urban food systems*. Ottawa: International Development Research Centre (IDRC).

Labadarios, D., Y. Davids, Z. Mchiza and G. Weir-Smith (2009) *The Assessment of Food Insecurity in South Africa*. Pretoria: Human Sciences Research Council.

Larsen, K., R. Kim and F. Theus (eds) (2009) *Agribusiness and Innovation Systems in Africa*. Washington, DC: World Bank.

Louw, A., H. Vermeulen, J. Kirsten and H. Madevu (2007) 'Securing small farmer participation in supermarket supply chains in South Africa'. *Development Southern Africa* 24(4): 539–51.

Mattes, R., M. Bratton and Y. Davids (2003) *Poverty, Survival and Democracy in Southern Africa*. Afrobarometer Paper No. 23. Cape Town: Idasa.

Mbiba, B. (2000) 'Urban agriculture in Harare: between suspicion and repression'. In M. Bakker, S. Dubbeling, U. Guendel, S. Koschella and H. de Zeeuw (eds) *Growing Cities, Growing Food: Urban Agriculture on the Policy Agenda*. Feldafing: DSE.

McLachlan, M. and J. Thorne (2009) *Seeding Change: A proposal for renewal in the South African food system*. Development Planning Division Working Paper No. 16. Midrand: Development Bank of Southern Africa.

Montpellier Panel (2012) *Growth with Resilience: Opportunities in African agriculture*. London: Agriculture for Impact.

Mougeot, L. (ed.) (2005) *Agropolis: The social, political, and environmental dimensions of urban agriculture*. Ottawa and London: International Development Research Centre (IDRC) and Earthscan.

— (ed.) (2006) *Growing Better Cities: Urban agriculture for sustainable development*. Ottawa: International Development Research Centre (IDRC).

Otsukaa, K. and Y. Kijimab (2010) 'Technology policies for a green revolution and agricultural transformation in Africa'. *Journal of African Economies* 19(2): ii60–76.

Palmer, K. and J. Sender (2006) 'Prospects for on-farm self-employment and poverty reduction: an analysis of the South African income and expenditure survey 2000'. *Journal of Contemporary African Studies* 24(3): 347–76.

Potts, D. (2010) *Circular Migration in Zimbabwe and Contemporary Sub-Saharan Africa*. Woodbridge: James Currey.

Ravallion, M. (2007) 'Urban poverty'. *Finance & Development* 44(3): 15–17.

Reardon, T. and C. Timmer (2008) 'The rise of supermarkets in the global food system'. In J. von Braun and E. Diaz-Bonilla (eds) *Globalization of Food and Agriculture, and the Poor*. New Delhi: Oxford University Press.

— and J. Berdegue (2008) 'The rapid rise of supermarkets in developing countries: induced organizational, institutional and technological change in agri-food systems'. In E. McCullough, P. Pingali and K. Stamoulis (eds) *The Transformation of Agri-Food Systems: Globalization, supply chains and small-holder farmers*. London: Earthscan.

Redwood, M. (ed.) (2008) *Agriculture in Urban Planning: Generating livelihoods and food security*. London and Ottawa: Earthscan and International Development Research Centre (IDRC).

Roepstorff, T., S. Wiggins and A. Hawkins (2011) 'The profile of agribusiness in Africa'. In K. Yumkella, P. Kormawa, T. Roepstorff and A. Hawkins (eds) *Agribusiness for Africa's Prosperity*. Vienna: United Nations Industrial Development Organization (UNIDO).

Rogerson, C. (2010) 'Resetting the policy agenda for urban agriculture in South Africa'. *Journal of Public Administration* 45(2): 373–83.

SADC (2003) 'Regional Indicative Strategic Development Plan (RISDP)'. Gaborone: Southern African Development Community (SADC) Secretariat.

Sanchez, P., G. Denning and G. Nziguheba (2009) 'The African green revolution moves forward'. *Food Security* 1(1): 37–44.

Satterthwaite, D., G. McGranahan and C. Tacoli (2010) 'Urbanization and its implications for food and farming'. *Philosophical Transactions of the Royal Society B* 365(1554): 2973–89.

Saunders, D. (2010) *Arrival City: The final migration and our next world*. Toronto: Knopf Canada.

Simatele, D. and T. Binns (2008) 'Motivation and marginalization in African urban agriculture: the case of Lusaka, Zambia'. *Urban Forum* 19(1): 1–21.

Steel, C. (2008) *Hungry City: How food shapes our lives*. London: Chatto and Windus.

Swindale, A. and P. Bilinsky (2006a) 'Development of a universally applicable household food insecurity measurement tool: process, current status, and outstanding issues'. *Journal of Nutrition* 136(5): 1449S–52S.

— (2006b) 'Household dietary diversity score (HDDS) for measurement of household food access, indicator guide, version 2'. Washington, DC: Food and Nutrition Technical Assistance (FANTA).

Thornton, A., E. Nel and G. Hampwaye (2010) 'Cultivating Kaunda's plan for self-sufficiency: is urban agriculture finally beginning to receive support in Zambia?'. *Development Southern Africa* 27(4): 613–25.

Toenniessen, G., A. Adesina and J. DeVries (2008) 'Building an alliance for a green revolution in Africa'. *Annals of the New York Academy of Sciences* 1136(1): 233–42.

UN DESA (2010) *World Population Prospects: The 2010 revision and world urbanization prospects*. New York, NY: Population Division of the Department of Economic and Social Affairs of the United Nations Secretariat (UN DESA).

UNDP (2012) *Africa Human Development Report 2012: Towards a food secure future*. New York, NY: United Nations Development Programme (UNDP) Regional Bureau for Africa (RBA).

UN-Habitat (2008) *The State of African Cities 2008: A framework for addressing urban challenges in Africa*. Nairobi: United Nations Human Settlements Programme (UN-Habitat).

— (2010) *The State of African Cities 2010: Governance, inequalities and urban land markets*. Nairobi: United Nations Human Settlements Programme (UN-Habitat).

Van Veenhuizen, R. (ed.) (2006) *Cities Farming for the Future: Urban agriculture for green and productive cities*. Ottawa: International Development Research Centre (IDRC).

Vorley, W., A. Fearne and D. Ray (eds) (2007) *Regoverning Markets: A place for small-scale producers in modern agrifood chains?* Aldershot: Gower.

Weatherspoon, D. and T. Reardon (2003) 'The rise of supermarkets in Africa: implications for agrifood systems and the rural poor'. *Development Policy Review* 21(3): 333–55.

Webb, N. (2011) 'When is enough, enough? Advocacy, evidence and criticism in the field of urban agriculture in South Africa'. *Development Southern Africa* 28(2): 195–208.

Webb, P., J. Coates, E. Frongillo, B. Rogers, A. Swindale and P. Bilinsky (2006) 'Measuring household food insecurity: why it's so important and yet so difficult to do'. *Journal of Nutrition* 136(5): 1404S–8S.

Wiggins, S. and H. Leturque (2010) *Helping Africa to Feed Itself: Promoting agriculture to reduce poverty and hunger*. Occasional Paper No. 2. London: Future Agricultures Consortium.

Woodhouse, P. (2009) 'Technology, environment and the productivity problem in African agriculture: comment on the *World Development Report 2008*'. *Journal of Agrarian Change* 9(2): 263–76.

World Bank (2008) *World Development Report 2008: Agriculture for development*. Washington, DC: World Bank.

Yumkella, K., P. Kormawa, T. Roepstrorff and A. Hawkins (eds) (2011) *Agribusiness for Africa's Prosperity*. Vienna: United Nations Industrial Development Organization (UNIDO).

Zezza, A. and L. Tasciotti (2010) 'Urban agriculture, poverty, and food security: empirical evidence from a sample of developing countries'. *Food Policy* 35(4): 265–73.

7 | Transport pressures in urban Africa: practices, policies, perspectives

Gordon Pirie

Over the years, many surveys and views about urban transport in Africa have appeared in government and consultancy reports, and in academic papers and the media. These have been filled with evidence about the condition of public transport services and the quality of travel, and discussion of the steps taken to improve mobility. The picture is seldom pleasing. The most admirable feature is often the determination and inventiveness of city residents to keep mobile in adverse circumstances. Privileged elites have struggled least.

Despite decades of surveys, research, policy making and implementation, little progress has been made on improving accessibility in African cities. Reports stretching back 20 years advocate inclusive, sustainable, pro-poor and energy-efficient urban transport. Successive governments and advisers have championed better transport (see, for example, Kwakye et al. 1996). Unattained, the same targets and hopes remain on agendas (see, for example, Sietchiping et al. 2012).

Achieving ambitious transport goals in urban Africa is worrying in view of the poor record of success. The alarm is compounded by the backlog of investment in transport and continued rapid urbanisation. This chapter sketches the current state of transport in urban Africa, focusing on the kind of transport that is provided and used, and on policies and projects intended to ease circulation in African cities. Recent headline projects are enjoying a honeymoon period with regard to their reception; however, after decades of work, neither transport bottlenecks nor mobility disadvantages in African cities have been cured and few of the smaller constituent transport obstacles have been resolved. No African cities have found a magic solution; none have devised an enviable citywide urban transport system. A second section of the chapter considers the institutional arrangements and priorities that choke transport improvements. Outdated perspectives and analyses are also unhelpful; thinking differently about African cities is a way of unblocking the logjam of ideas, information and policies relating to urban transport.

Transport and travel: practices and policies

On almost every measure of transport, African cities perform less well than their residents would wish. For example, where traffic congestion has not been alleviated temporarily (by building more roads or adding lanes to motorways), it is as bad as ever, or even worse. The world's media like to film and write about this, as if it is the single most pertinent diagnostic of urban transport. It is certainly among the most photogenic. While writing this chapter, the global CNN news channel reported on the 'daily grind of commuting in Africa's economic hubs', Johannesburg, Lagos and Nairobi. The striking headline image was a telephoto shot that, in 10 square centimetres on a laptop screen, compressed thousands of square metres of a road-cum-street market clogged with vehicles, pedestrians and street vendors under sun umbrellas.[1] Pedestrian and vehicular traffic is not segregated: whether road users are on two feet or four wheels, the only rule is to stray, bump and curse.

The chaos of public space can become iconic. African cities can be presented in a touristic and picturesque way as a tapestry of life, sound and colour, a charming and spectacular counterpoint to the regimented and sanitised mobility spaces in the cities of the global North. However, the view from behind the camera lens is not necessarily the same as on the street. In 2011, Lagos and Johannesburg were respectively placed fourth and fifth worst in a 'commuter pain survey' of 8,000 commuters in 20 cities on six continents.[2] Pricing, delays, inconvenience, discomfort and danger are sure to have been among the difficult conditions interviewees had in mind.

Conventional urban transport studies do not stoop to 'pain', but do indeed measure phenomena such as the traffic congestion that chokes efficiency and economic growth. In Dakar, it is estimated that 1 million working hours are lost per day due to congestion (Pendakur 2005). In January 2010, the South African Chamber of Commerce and Industry estimated that road traffic congestion cost the country 15 million Rand (US$2 million) per hour in lost productivity. At fault were infrastructural design and maintenance (inadequate repair of potholes, poor lighting and road marking), poor driving and slow response to accidents.[3]

Roads shoulder most of the burden of urban mobility in African cities, but, where services do exist, rail conditions may not be much better. The inefficiencies of metropolitan rail commuter services came under the public spotlight in a week-long series of social media reports in Cape Town in April 2012.[4] The special journalism supplemented regular daily radio news slots devoted to reporting and warning about traffic congestion and accidents on the motorways, out-of-order traffic lights and train delays. Delayed, dangerous and overcrowded services are among the issues that feature in the well-aired complaints from the 600,000 Capetonians who contend daily with a substandard train service. Underinvestment in railway signalling infrastructure and 50-year-old rolling stock are at the root of some of the problems, while inadequate policing and vandalism (copper cable theft and train carriage arson) contribute significant operational difficulties.

A car culture together with fragmented metropolitan transport governance also help to explain the problem. As in other 'modernising' colonial and post-colonial cities in Africa, many of Cape Town's commercial and residential activity spaces were designed to serve motorists and helped to construct the fantasy that private mobility was optimal for the city at large. A historic urban railway network, and topography that limits road building, prevented automobility becoming even more prominent. Apartheid spatial planning also presumed that poor residents confined to living on the urban periphery would mostly use public transport. Today, the economic and social burden of that inheritance is expensive long-haul transport for those urban residents least able to afford it.

Racially segregated urban settlement patterns were not unique to South Africa; there are traces elsewhere in Africa of colonial land-use organisation that dispatched poor Africans to city outskirts and that still compels them to travel long distances. Property pricing works to the same effect. Even in the newly built Nigerian capital Abuja, the central city zone (where *okada* commercial motorcycles are banned) is effectively occupied only by elites. Commuters travel in from satellite towns in 'a chaotic situation' (Sanusi et al. 2012). In reverse, the suburbanisation of residential, retail and office space has increased dependence on private transport in many African cities.

Daily commuting over long distances in cities serviced very poorly by trains helped to spawn the minibus taxi 'industry' that is so characteristic of urban Africa. From the 1960s, municipal and then privatised bus services using out-of-date technology and management were unable to handle passenger needs in rapidly expanding African cities. A key problem arose in ferrying increasing numbers of passengers between multiple origins and destinations, often from squatter camps some distance from main trunk routes. Lower capacity, more flexible minibus taxis emerged to serve the new passenger markets.

Albeit illegal in many places, unregulated and non-scheduled minibus taxis quickly became the only effective, and the preferred, form of mass public transport. One estimate is that there are 100,000 minibuses in Lagos (Kumar 2011). In Kampala, minibuses employ 60,000 people (70 per cent drivers, 20 per cent owners and 10 per cent conductors) (Kamuhanda and Schmidt 2009). Nairobi's *matatu* minibuses provide more than 90 per cent of public transport there and create between 30,000 and 40,000 jobs directly and indirectly (Gleave et al. 2005). Allied workers include vehicle repairers, washers, conductors, marshals and artists who 'pimp' the *matatus*.[5]

For all their success as a form of mass passenger transport in African cities, minibuses court criticism by being associated with reckless driving of often unroadworthy, unlicensed and overloaded vehicles. Armed violence between rival taxi drivers and groups does occur. There is tax evasion and collusion with corrupt traffic police. Pathologising minibus transport is easy; recognising the contribution it makes is harder but has underlain state efforts to re-regulate and recapitalise the minibus sector (Lomme 2008; Kumar and Diou 2010). Progress has been limited. And it is another matter entirely to transform elements of minibus taxi culture – overloading, loud music, and verbal and physical assaults by drivers and conductors can turn a relatively cheap and convenient journey into an ordeal of forbearance and calculated risk (Mungai and Samper 2006; Mungai 2010).

Partly as an attempt to organise and formalise public road passenger transport, bus rapid transport (BRT) was started in several African cities in the first decade of the twenty-first century. Following the examples of Bogotá and Medellín in particular (cities that are less well resourced than First World capitals), BRT has become the vogue in Accra, Lagos, Kampala, Dar es Salaam, Johannesburg and Cape Town (Barrett 2010; Gauthier and Weinstock 2010). Since opening in 2008, the 22-kilometre BRT-Lite scheme in Lagos has reduced fares, waiting times and journey times for some 200,000 passengers a day (Olufemi 2008; Mobereola 2009). In its second year of operation, the Lagos BRT reported 113 million passenger movements, generated 2,000 direct and indirect jobs, reduced travel time by a third, and cut carbon dioxide and greenhouse gas emissions by 13 per cent and 20 per cent respectively.[6] The politics of BRT are delicate: strong leadership is needed to deal with the vested interests of informal paratransit operators (Schalekamp and Behrens 2010). In Johannesburg this was handled by selling a half share of the BRT to minibus owners. Stressing the feeder role of minibuses is crucial, and highlighting this by using the term 'integrated rapid transit' instead of BRT can help to address sensitivities. Even so, difficult negotiations have caused expensive delays to the launch of the second phase BRT in Johannesburg.

Showpiece BRT investments provide a stark contrast to the more expensive and slower (re)investment in heavy rail networks and services. There are not many opportunities to upgrade existing metropolitan railway networks and services in African cities, but the cost of not doing so is considerable. Effective rail transport lowers the hidden costs of accommodating private cars and absorbing the effects of motor vehicle accidents and air pollution.

A conspicuous example of heavy rail investment in urban Africa is the 'Gautrain'. Partially opened in 2011, the scheduled, high-frequency train operates on 80 kilometres of dedicated double track through South Africa's economic core (Gauteng comprises the Witwatersrand conurbation, including Johannesburg, and Sandton, Midrand and Pretoria) and provides a rapid rail link with the international airport. A similar airport-anchored railway spur is planned as part of a 170-kilometre commuter rail project started in Nairobi.[7] Lagos is planning a light rail service,[8] while older suburban-type railway services persist in several South African cities. Cairo (1980s) and Algiers (2011) are the only other African cities with significant new heavy rail services.

A modernisation project second to none, the Gautrain is a signature southern hemisphere public–private partnership that enhances Gauteng's claim to 'world city' status. Inevitably, the costly investment and high ticket price of the service have attracted criticism for being exclusionary. Its narrow geographical footprint means that the train serves only a tiny proportion of the metropolitan resident and visitor population. The project aggravates mobility inequalities and entrenches the urban socioeconomic divisions cemented into South African cities by apartheid (Donaldson 2006; van der Westhuizen 2007).

When it became known that Gauteng residents who travel by road rather than by express train would face motorway tolls, the iniquity became intolerable. Mass action threatened by the country's umbrella trade union grew into a legal challenge by an unlikely alliance of labour and business. The grounds for an April 2012 court injunction delaying implementation and mandating a review of the tolling scheme included opaque costing, inflated and avoidable charges, inadequate public consultation, and unprecedented public protest. Successive concessions already made by the toll operator to meet the objections of freight and public transport passenger interests had not been enough to quash the complaints.

Motorway tolls are not primarily intended to discourage motor vehicle use. Throughout urban Africa, road building projects signal continued and deepening dependence on car transport and fossil fuels. The reticence about lessening, and then reversing, motorisation has deep roots and profound consequences. The morality of curbing actual and aspirant motorisation among the emergent middle class in urban Africa is a sensitive matter. It would not be practical, anyway, to exclude motor transport from some spheres of service: in geographically expanding cities, motor vehicles of some kind (including minibuses and motorised cycle taxis) have a role to play in serving lengthy cross-city journeys (and in facilitating geographically diffuse journeys, such as those made by women domestic workers). Nevertheless, encouraging the use of personal or shared cars only delays the transition to public and lower-carbon transport.

There is little systematic monitoring or scientific study of motor vehicle emissions in African cities, but it is clear that air pollution will be worst in urban settings where older second-hand vehicles are most affordable (van Vliet and Kinney 2007; Odhiambo et al. 2010). Indeed, in the context of relatively low rates of car ownership and use in many African cities (in Nairobi about 15 per cent of households own cars), there is an urgency to making public transport more attractive before car use spirals, worsening congestion and pollution on already overburdened roads (Salon and Aligula 2012). The relatively low proportion of private vehicles in the total transport fleets of some cities (e.g. 18 per cent in Abidjan, 13 per cent in Accra, 10 per cent in Dar es Salaam and 7 per cent in Addis Ababa) (Kumar and Barrett 2009) appears to leave room for increased motor vehicle use, but infrastructure deficiencies are an effective cap.

The use of motorcycles for commercial purposes has been booming in some African cities. Nairobi and Johannesburg are among the exceptions. The growth of motorcycling is not deliberate transport policy but a local and opportunistic market response by mostly young men. The collapse of officially organised public transport, and growing vehicular traffic congestion, created an opening for services that were quick, adaptable and offered good coverage across a range of road surfaces and widths (including rough-and-ready slum alleys). With its low capital and running costs, operating a motorcycle has created earning opportunities (invisible to the tax office) for tens of thousands of young men. In Lagos there are over 200,000 commercial motorcycles, and in 2007 there were 40,000 commercial motorcycles on Kampala's streets – a significant number were used on short trips to connect homes and work places to trunk minibus services (Kumar 2011). In 2008, it was estimated that motorbike taxis in Douala supported 30,000 direct jobs (Diaz Olvera et al. 2010).

Unregulated in respect of routes, fares and standards, commercial motorcycle services in African cities have their drawbacks. For example, they have been linked to an increase in road accidents (and injuries and death), traffic management problems, pervasive noise, and increased local air pollution and greenhouse gas emissions. In Lagos, commercial motorbikes were banned from night-time streets in 2007 because of links with criminality (Kumar 2011). The 2008 Douala study found that 17 per cent of the drivers did not hold a driving licence and that a third of the bikes had no registration documents. Only three-quarters of the drivers had at least two of the seven necessary administrative documents, and less than half had three (Diaz Olvera et al. 2010).

As with minibus taxis, there are ambivalent attitudes to the service performed by motorcycles. Users choose convenience and speed and dismiss risk, while the authorities have considered banning motorcycles as well as introducing driver registration and training. There are also calls for better enforcement of regulations on speed and the wearing of protective and reflective clothing, and for the provision of separate motorbike lanes (Ayodele 2010; Olawole et al. 2010).

As a mode of both personal and commercial transport, pedal bikes are a different proposition to motorcycles. They are used mostly for short journeys in confined city districts or in small cities. Slow, silent and inexpensive, they do not emit noxious gases. And, albeit not on a scale comparable to Asian cities, cycling provides significant direct (pedalling) and indirect (repair) jobs in some African cities, for example in Kisumu and Nakuru in Kenya (Mutiso and Behrens 2011). However, this form of non-motorised transport has been slow to catch on wherever it competes for road space with faster and more aggressively handled motorised transport. Staged provision of cycle paths is difficult in contexts where street space is rapidly appropriated by street traders (Turner et al. 1995), and few African cities have developed dedicated cycle paths or safe bike corridors in existing roadways. In relation to longer urban journeys, bicycles could play a useful role as 'last-mile' connectors from homes, schools and workplaces to train stations and bus and taxi ranks, but provision for 'carry-on' space in crowded vehicles is rare.

Recognition of the potential role of pedal cycles as a component of an affordable, clean, healthy and durable urban transport system is dawning slowly. Schemes promoting bicycle use in rural areas and small towns started in the late 1990s. In addition, hosting the fourth international Vélo Mondiale conference in Cape Town in 2006 helped spread the message. Integrating bike lanes into BRT schemes, as has happened in Latin American cities, points to new possibilities (Quarshie 2007). In Cape Town, away from the hilliest sections of the city, a bike-based affordable mobility and job-creation project was started in poor neighbourhoods in 2002. Ten years later, the Bicycling Empowerment Network was among eight finalists out of 254 entries for the 2012 Urban Age Award for the best grassroots community improvement project in Cape Town. At the time, the organisation operated 17 centres where 12,000 (foreign-donated) bikes are refurbished and repaired, and where cyclists are trained. A pedicab service is also being tested.[9]

Bicycles are the Cinderella of African urban passenger transport. Even though some potential users regard them as shameful markers of poverty (Godard 2011), bicycles have a higher status than the donkey carts, handcarts and trolleys used to carry small bundles of goods to and from street markets, to collect sellable household trash, and to make home deliveries of coal and market garden food, for example. Studies of the small, itinerant and feminised workforces in this carrying trade are rare. An eminently photogenic subject, the ancient activity of carting and head-portering is as easily romanticised as it is condemned for its abusiveness. From Cape Town to Mzuzu and Accra, this form of transportation work is a last-resort source of income for some poor citizens (Jimu 2008; Yeboah 2010). Petty traders typically carry their own sale goods to and from storage points.

The most used but most neglected form of physical mobility in cities around the world is walking. Banal it may be, but, in aggregate, more person miles are travelled on foot every day by urban residents than are travelled by any other form of transport. Walking in African cities is no exception to neglect, but it is likely that more Africans walk out of necessity than by choice, for longer distances, and in worse conditions. Poverty, coupled with the unaffordability, unreliability and poor coverage of public transport, explains the prevalence of walking, be it daily or towards the weekend when wages have been spent and there is no money left for transport fares.

Many impoverished Africans living in fringe urban settlements walk long distances on domestic errands, to work or to transport termini. All-weather surfaces are a rarity in poor and peri-urban neighbourhoods. Slow and unpleasant walking among street traders and motorised transport is made worse by fear of, and actual, attack, especially at night; women, elderly people and children are the most victimised. Provision of wider, paved and lit pavements would facilitate walking, lessen social exclusion and even ease pressure on motorised transport. Perversely, however, planners and managers in African cities continue to favour car dependency, although promoting motorised transport actively ignores and disadvantages cyclists and pedestrians (Sietchiping et al. 2012).

Aside from the supposed stigma of non-motorised transport, part of the difficulty, it appears, is 'tooling up' for multiple small-scale interventions: city transport administrations are geared towards and accustomed to more glamorous, larger-scale infrastructure bid–contract–provision processes. It is more unusual – and therefore procedurally harder – to, for example, clear ground for a short earthen cycle path using labour-intensive techniques (possibly as part of a low-skilled poverty relief programme). Similarly, retrofitting paved and shouldered pavements into urban road reservations would be a departure from conventional road contracting. Precedents do exist, however: cutting wheelchair access channels into pavements has occurred in some central areas of African cities.

Perspectives on urban transport: evidence, conscience, imagination

Several contradictory demands preoccupy urban transport administrators, consultants, planners, policy makers, practitioners and service suppliers. Since colonial times, in urban Africa there has been pressure to conform to practices and standards elsewhere; to borrow technologies and 'best practice' management; to invest and modernise. Additionally, there are now calls to minimise the exposure of transport infrastructure to climate hazard, and to switch to low-carbon transport that takes urban ecosystems into consideration and is socially just.

Balancing these expectations is tricky. In the background, often unspoken, is the imperative to use transport to create jobs, to boost productivity, and to give city residents access to work, education, healthcare and leisure facilities. A related aim is to enable wider participation in civil society, and to give poor citizens access to community social capital such as childcare, life advice and barter (Godard 2011). All this has to be achieved while bearing in mind the political feasibility of transport innovation; governments are unlikely to take unpopular steps that will put their power at risk. In addition, city governments must try to align urban transport provision and planning with new national infrastructure development plans, and with cross-border, intercity corridors intended to integrate, connect and transform Africa.[10] These schemes often pay little attention to the traffic funnels at route end points in cities. Similarly, nationally devised airport and seaport projects impose and rebound on host cities.

One of the greatest political pressures on transport policy makers in African cities is the need to help end absolute poverty. Transport is, indeed, part of the cycle of poverty; it is not only in Niamey, Dar es Salaam and Ougadougou that poor urban households cannot afford daily public transport and are stranded in peripheral settlements where there are few jobs and where they are likely to stay poor (Diaz Olvera et al. 2008; Godard 2011). Transport can produce intergenerational poverty in other ways that hurt the poor most: the injury or death of breadwinners in traffic accidents harms families' long-term life chances because of medical expenses and abandoned schooling, for example.

A related demand for policy makers is to use transport to help redress the social inequalities evidenced by mobility disparities. These are not unique to Africa; elsewhere, too, wealthy urban residents travel comfortably in private cars while masses of people struggle aboard erratic, crowded, uncomfortable public transport. Least acknowledged is the way in which inadequately designed and named streets and junctions, coupled with congestion and selfish road use, inhibit the quick response of emergency ambulance and fire services, especially in the poorest parts of cities. The dimensions of socio-spatial difference in urban Africa are particularly great, however, and carry an especially poignant emotional charge.

Persistent mobility deprivation in urban Africa has the particularly unfortunate resonance of coloniality, and illustrates the failure of successor ideologies, political formations and practices. The conundrum now is how politicians will deal with emerging middle-class car-owning aspirations that are becoming a sense of entitlement in cities with road networks that were designed for different traffic geographies and volumes. Paradoxically, however, it is possible that by virtue of 'their instantly visible manifestation of the secret and shadowy uses of power', cars may yet become 'a catalyst for real social change' (Pitcher and Graham 2007). It is unlikely that 'car wars' will be confined to Luanda, where, in a city so recently at peace, they are markedly conspicuous tokens of lavish consumerism.

The need for more dignified transport in African cities is not discussed much in planning, policy or academic circles. Unlike other indicators of transport performance (Gleave et al. 2005), the criteria are vague. Nevertheless, the notion of dignified travel is sweeping, persuasive, a handy proxy, and potentially a vote-winner. Late, draughty, dirty, overcrowded and unsafe public transport is not just a negative entry on an operator's chart of key performance indicators; it also insults and demeans people.[11] Like vandalised and inadequate roadside bus shelters, it encapsulates the de-meaning of the word 'service'. Ending harassment of passengers by taunting or inappropriate touching may not be something that is within the realm of public policy, but it is most certainly within the compass of public culture and morality.

The limits of the governability of transport in African cities are recurrent points of discussion. Institutional design, will and capacity are all called into question (Kanyama et al. 2004; 2005; Wilkinson 2010). The case of transport in Nairobi, at least, disproves the neoliberal assumption that markets can replace public institutions and can deliver public transport better. And, far from waiting for governmental institutions to produce better transport, the emphasis might be placed on improving the very transport that can help build better urban governance (Sclar and Touber 2011).

Institutional fragmentation remains a burning concern. 'Separation of expertise' in city halls plagues urbanism: for instance, building roads interrupts petty trading as well as water and sewerage services (Grieco 2012). The caution with which 'silo thinking' should be approached extends to contacts with the Africa offices of multinational civil engineering and telecommunications consultancies. Even area-wide transport governance is fragmented. The Metropolitan Area Transport Authority (2003) in Lagos is a rare attempt at multi-modal transport management in urban Africa (Mobereola 2006). Transport authorities are in their infancy in South African cities.

Vested interests and the way in which transport sensitivities, debates and policy making become part of a city government's agenda form another strand of governmentality. Clientelism and corruption are not unknown in traffic police forces and city councils. In Lagos, for example, where transport work supports more than 2 million people (15 per cent of the city population), transport owners, unions, associations and operators wield substantial political power. Elected politicians are part of this urban political economy; many have an interest in maintaining exclusive transport arrangements for their own financial gain (Kumar 2011).

A harsh spotlight illuminated the governance of urban transport in the April 2012 Gauteng motorway-toll debacle: who decides who will pay for the maintenance and upgrading of existing and future urban transport infrastructure? The genie is out of the bottle. If the Gauteng case can be generalised across urban Africa, a 'First World' model relying on overseas equipment and loan capital repayments will not be palatable in cities where significant numbers of residents and businesses feel that their mobility and livelihoods are being double- and triple-taxed. Government directives on transport for urban citizens may have become an anachronism; participatory planning and budgeting are likely to become a reality soon. Embedding and empowering citizens in informal networks and partnerships with private and public bodies in the transport sphere is an alternative to bureaucratic, opaque and token participatory planning with the state. Social media are a mobile space where information about urban transport can be exchanged rapidly and where opinions can translate quickly into action.

Transport policy makers regard information differently. In an effort to plan and deliver transport better, the temptation is to first achieve a better and comprehensive empirical grasp of the situation in African cities. Accordingly, calls are made for more systematic, sustained and comparable synoptic and time-series data about car registration, car ownership and car use (including sharing). Existing statistics about the length, number and duration of urban trips have been collected erratically and unevenly, and are biased towards men's daily work trips by vehicle. Large-scale, statistically representative household travel surveys are rare (Salon and Aligula 2012) and little information is collected systematically or published about the size of the metropolitan freight transport sector in terms of vehicles bought, sold and registered.

Massive and expensive transport surveys are conducted rarely, take a long time to analyse, and, in rapidly changing situations, soon become outdated. Routine, low-cost, automated data collection about travel patterns using mobile phones is an alternative and might generate new micro-detail that could be useful for transport planners in particular localities. Even better, perhaps, instant, inexpensive and engaged observation, listening, instinct and reason might be restored as ways of knowing about and improving urban transport.

Looking back over 50 years of transport research in African cities, the emphasis has certainly changed. Whereas roads and motor vehicles constituted and framed discussions decades ago, now urban transport is understood more holistically to touch the lives of all citizens; transport is a key element in city economies and it affects the 'liveability' of a city and the pride that citizens take in it. The proletariat is less *lumpen* than in the past, and the mobility privileges of elites are being questioned. Unequal accessibility and mobility are not new concerns, but they are penetrating the democratic agenda better than they did in the past. In an environmentally conscious age, single car occupancy and hyper-mobility are no longer taken as the default goal and yardstick of success. However, convincing the public that comfortable, safe, short-distance walking (and its health and sociability) is post-modern rather than pre-modern remains a challenge.

The language of urban transport planning and intervention has also been shifting. The talk is of privatisation, public–private partnerships, affordability, sustainability and fairness. The mobility disadvantages (including abandoned and suspended activities) and needs of marginalised women in African cities are receiving more attention (Kang 2006; Seedata et al. 2006; Venter et al. 2007; Reichenbach 2009; Salon and Gulyani 2010). The transport difficulties of elderly people are starting to be considered (Ipengbemi 2010). At the other end of the life cycle, the precarious mobility of children (Hobday and Knight 2010) has been highlighted. Like adults before them (Turner and Kwakye 1996), teenagers too have devised mobility strategies to survive in African cities (ibid.; Konings 2003; Gough 2008; Langevanga and Gougha 2009). Urban freight transport – urban food circulation in particular – still requires attention, possibly as part of policies that will make better use of urban transport facilities around the clock.

Shifts in the categories of analysis, and the increasingly interdisciplinary nature of research into mobility in African cities, are pleasing. By contrast, public conscience about the inequalities of transport in urban Africa is not what it ought to be. Discussion about mobility experiences and values remains swamped by technocratic and managerial considerations even though there is only limited ability to act conscientiously to alleviate or resolve transport and associated problems. Awareness of the depth of urban transport problems is changing, however. A puzzling question remains: are the limits of usable information about urban transport in Africa being reached? How many more case studies are needed? What comes after 'mainstreaming' gender, the environment and human rights? What if none of these actions makes a difference? When is the last throw of the dice?

Urban transport policy discourse in Africa shows signs of being stale. Although they use fresh evidence, new papers and reports mostly work within familiar frameworks of established thinking. New elements do surface, but they have not shifted the terms of debate or policy engagement. Arguably, the most dramatic crash in African urban transport is epistemic: the flaw is one of imagination, not technology and not organisation. Events on the ground in African cities might just be the spur to revitalise and deepen thinking about urban transport in Africa.

Studying, and adjusting to, so-called 'second wave' urbanisation in Africa invites new thinking about cities as economies, spaces, life worlds and policy arenas. This new urbanism is being articulated in ways that differ from 'first wave' industrial urbanism. What might be called 'monopoly urbanism' has long provided the material and conceptual template for understanding and managing cities. Instrumentalist and fundamentalist discourses and practices that have driven policy interventions in transport and mobility in African cities may be losing their effectiveness precisely because they are being directed at fading realities.

New ways of resource-constrained living and working are emerging in medium-sized cities and megacities in Africa. New civic priorities are crystalising. Residents are mobilising themselves in new ways. These novel kinds of 'cityness' present tantalising opportunities for innovative scholarship. A revolution in ideas about transport will create the perfect pressure for provoking policy that valorises, nourishes and capitalises on Africa's urban revolution.

Notes

1 http://edition.cnn.com/2012/04/05/world/africa/commuting-africa/index.html [accessed 15 August 2013].

2 www-03.ibm.com/press/us/en/pressrelease/35359.wss [accessed 15 August 2013].

3 *Business Day* (Johannesburg), 21 January 2010.

4 http://ewn.co.za/2012/04/25/The-Metrorail-Diaries [accessed 28 August 2013].

5 BBC News, audio slideshow 'Pimp

my matatu', 23 April 2012. Available at www.bbc.co.uk/news/world-africa-17600995 [accessed 15 August 2013].

6 www.lamata-ng.com/brt.php [accessed 28 August 2013].

7 *The Standard* (Nairobi), 24 May 2011.

8 www.lagosrail.com [accessed 15 August 2013].

9 www.benbikes.org.za [accessed 15 August 2013].

10 Exemplified by the multi-institutional, cross-continental 2012 Programme for Infrastructure Development in Africa. See www.afdb.org/en/topics-and-sectors/sectors/transport/ [accessed 15 August 2013].

11 Typified by May 2012 court proceedings in which South Africa's Passenger Rail Agency argued that train windows were for comfort, not safety. The legal case, which occupied the courts for six years, was brought by a passenger who lost an eye when a stone was hurled through a glassless window next to which he was seated (*Cape Times* [Cape Town], 30 May 2012).

References

Ayodele, S.-D. (2010) 'The menace of motorcycle as a paratransit mode in Lagos Metropolis'. *Journal of Estate Surveying Research* 3: 64–79.

Barrett, I. (2010) 'Development of bus rapid transit (BRT) in Africa: experience from Lagos, Accra and Kampala'. Sub-Saharan Africa Transport Programme, Annual Meeting, Kampala, Uganda, 17–19 October.

Diaz Olvera, L., D. Plat and P. Pochet (2008) 'Household transport expenditure in sub-Saharan African cities: measurement and analysis'. *Journal of Transport Geography* 16(1): 1–13.

— and M. Sahabana (2010) *Motorized Two-wheelers in Sub-Saharan African Cities: Public and private use*. 12th World Conference on Transport Research, Lisbon, 11–15 July.

Donaldson, R. (2006) 'Mass rapid rail development in South Africa's metropolitan core: towards a new urban form?'. *Land Use Policy* 23(3): 344–52.

Gauthier, A. and A. Weinstock (2010) 'Africa: transforming paratransit into BRT'. *Built Environment* 36(3): 317–27.

Gleave, G., A. Marsden, T. Powell, S. Coetze, G. Fletcher, I. Barrett and D. Storer (2005) *A Study of Institutional, Financial and Regulatory Frameworks of Urban Transport in Large Sub-Saharan African Cities*. Sub-Saharan Africa Transport Policy Program (SSATP) Working Paper No. 82. Washington, DC: World Bank.

Godard, X. (2011) 'Poverty and urban mobility: diagnosis toward a new understanding'. In H. T. Dimitriou and R. Gakenheimer (eds) *Urban Transport in the Developing World: A handbook of policy and practice*. Cheltenham: Edward Elgar, pp. 232–61.

Gough, K. V. (2008) 'Moving around: the social and spatial mobility of youth in Lusaka'. *Geografiska Annaler (Series B, Human Geography)* 90(3): 243–55.

Grieco, M. (2012) 'Transportation in African cities: an institutional perspective'. In K. Brooks, K. Donaghy and G.-J. Knaap (eds) *The Oxford Handbook of Urban Economics and Planning*. New York, NY: Oxford University Press, pp. 833–44.

Hobday, M. and S. Knight (2010 'Motor vehicle collisions involving child pedestrians in eThekwini in 2007'. *Journal of Child Health Care* 14(1): 67–81.

Ipengbemi, O. (2010) 'Travel characteristics and mobility constraints of the elderly in Ibadan, Nigeria'. *Journal of Transport Geography* 18(2): 285–91.

Jimu, I. M. (2008) *Urban Appropriation and Transformation: Bicycle taxi and handcart operators in Mzuzu, Malawi*. Bamenda, Cameroon: Langaa Research and Publishing Common Initiative Group.

Kamuhanda, R. and O. Schmidt (2009) 'Matatu: a case study of the core segment of the public transport market of Kampala, Uganda'. *Transport Reviews* 29(1): 129–42.

Kang, I. (2006) *Excluded Women's Transport Needs: The case for Johannesburg, South Africa*. Working Paper No. 129. London: Development Planning Unit, University College London.

Kanyama, A., A. Carlsson-Kanyama, A.-L. Lindén and J. Lupala (2004) *Public transport in Dar es Salaam, Tanzania: Institutional challenges and opportunities for a sustainable transport system*. Stockholm: FOI.

— (2005) 'An analysis of the situation in Dar-es-Salaam in Tanzania from an institutional coordination perspective'. In G. Jönson and E. Tengström (eds) *Urban Transport Development: A complex issue*. Berlin: Springer Verlag.

Konings, P. (2003) 'Solving transportation problems in African cities: innovative responses by the youth in Douala, Cameroon'. *Africa Today* 53(1): 35–50.

Kumar, A. (2011) *Understanding the Emerging Role of Motorcycles in African Cities: A political economy perspective*. Sub-Saharan Africa Transport Policy Program (SSATP) Discussion Paper No. 13, Urban Transport Series. Washington, DC: World Bank.

— and F. Barrett (2009) *Stuck in Traffic: Urban transport in Africa*. Africa Infrastructure Country Diagnostic, Background Paper No. 1. Washington, DC: World Bank.

— and C. Diou (2010) *The Dakar Bus Renewal Scheme: Before and after*. Sub-Saharan Africa Transport Policy Program (SSATP) Discussion Paper No. 11, Urban Transport Series. Washington, DC: World Bank.

Kwakye, E. A., P. R. Fouracre and D. Ofosu-Dorte (1996) 'Developing strategies to meet the transport needs of the urban poor in Ghana'. *World Transport Policy and Practice* 3(1): 8–14.

Langevanga, T. and K. V. Gougha (2009) 'Surviving through movement: the mobility of urban youth in Ghana'. *Social and Cultural Geography* 10(7): 741–56.

Lomme, R. (2008) 'Should South African minibus taxis be scrapped? Formal-

izing informal urban transport in a developing country'. CODATU XIII, Ho Chi Minh City, 12–14 November.

Mobereola, D. (2006) *Strengthening Urban Transport Institutions: A case study of Lagos state*. Sub-Saharan Africa Transport Policy Program (SSATP) Discussion Paper No. 5, Affordable Transport Services. Washington, DC: World Bank.

— (2009) *Lagos Bus Rapid Transit: Africa's first BRT scheme*. Sub-Saharan Africa Transport Policy Program (SSATP) Discussion Paper No. 9, Urban Transport Series. Washington, DC: World Bank.

Mungai, M. W. (2010) 'Hidden $centz: rolling the wheels of Nairobi matatu'. In H. Charton-Bigot and D. Rodriguez-Torres (eds) *Nairobi Today: The paradox of a fragmented city*. Nairobi: Mkuki na Nyota and Institut Français de Recherche en Afrique (IFRA).

— and D. A. Samper (2006) '"No mercy, no remorse": personal experience narratives about public passenger transportation in Nairobi, Kenya'. *Africa Today* 52(3): 51–81.

Mutiso, W. and R. Behrens (2011) '*Boda Boda*' Bicycle Taxis and Their Role in Urban Transport Systems: Case studies of Kisumu and Nakuru, Kenya*. 30th Southern African Transport Conference, Pretoria, 11–14 July.

Odhiambo, G. O., A. M. Kinyua, C. K. Gatebe and J. Awange (2010) 'Motor vehicles air pollution in Nairobi, Kenya'. *Research Journal of Environmental and Earth Sciences* 2(4): 178–87.

Olawole, M. O., O. A. Ajala and O. Aloba (2010) 'Risk perceptions among users of commercial motorcycles in cities of south-western Nigeria'. *Ife Psychologia* 18(2): 253–69.

Olufemi, O. (2008) 'Public transport innovation: the impact of BRT on passengers' movement in Lagos metropolitan area of Nigeria'. *Pakistan Journal of Social Sciences* 5(8): 845–52.

Pendakur, V. S. (2005) *Non-Motorized Transport in African Cities: Lessons from experience in Kenya and Tanzania*. Sub-

Saharan Africa Transport Policy Program (SSATP) Working Paper No. 80. Washington, DC: World Bank.

Pitcher, M. A. and A. Graham (2007) 'Cars are killing Luanda: cronyism, consumerism, and other assaults on Angola's postwar, capital city'. In M. J. Murray and G. A. Myers (eds) *Cities in Contemporary Africa*. Basingstoke: Palgrave Macmillan, pp. 173–200.

Quarshie, M. L. (2007) 'Integrating cycling in bus rapid transit system in Accra'. In G. M. Morrison and S. Rauch (eds) *Highway and Urban Environment: Proceedings of the 8th Highway and Urban Environment Symposium*. Berlin: Springer Verlag, pp. 103–16.

Reichenbach, R. (2009) 'Transport and the MDGs: perspectives from a Nairobi slum'. In M. Grieco, M. Ndulo, D. Bryceson, G. Porter and T. McCray (eds) *Africa, Transport and the Millennium Development Goals: Achieving an internationally set agenda*. Newcastle upon Tyne: Cambridge Scholars Publishing, pp. 67–77.

Salon, D. and E. M. Aligula (2012) 'Urban travel in Nairobi, Kenya: analysis, insights, and opportunities'. *Journal of Transport Geography* 22: 65–76.

— and S. Gulyani (2010) 'Mobility, poverty, and gender: travel "choices" of slum residents in Nairobi, Kenya'. *Transport Reviews* 30(5): 641–57.

Sanusi, O. F., I. O. Ogundari et al. (2012) *Policy Issues for Sustainable Urban Transport in Nigeria: Case study of Abuja, Federal Capital Territory*. Ile-Ife, Nigeria: National Centre for Technology Management.

Schalekamp, H. and R. Behrens (2010) 'Engaging paratransit on public transport reform initiatives in South Africa: a critique of policy and an investigation of appropriate engagement approaches'. *Research in Transportation Economics* 29(1): 371–8.

Sclar, E. and J. Touber (2011) 'Economic fall-out of failing urban transport systems: an institutional analysis'. In H. T. Dimitriou and R. Gakenheimer

(eds) *Urban Transport in the Developing World: A handbook of policy and practice*. Cheltenham: Edward Elgar, pp. 174–202.

Seedata, M., S. MacKenzie and D. Mohan (2006) 'The phenomenology of being a female pedestrian in an African and an Asian city: a qualitative investigation'. *Transportation Research Part F: Traffic Psychology and Behaviour* 9(2): 139–53.

Sietchiping, R., M. J. Permezel and C. Ngomsi (2012) 'Transport and mobility in sub-Saharan African cities: an overview of practices, lessons and options for improvements'. *Cities* 29(3): 183–9.

Turner, J. and E. Kwakye (1996) 'Transport and survival strategies in a developing economy: case evidence from Accra, Ghana'. *Journal of Transport Geography* 4(3): 161–8.

— M. Grieco and E. Kwakye (1995) 'Subverting sustainability? Infrastructural and cultural barriers to cycle use in Accra'. *World Transport Policy and Practice* 2(3): 18–23.

van der Westhuizen, J. (2007) 'Glitz, glamour and the Gautrain: mega-projects as political symbols'. *Politikon* 34(3): 333–51.

van Vliet, E. D. S. and P. Kinney (2007) 'Impacts of roadway emissions on urban particulate matter concentrations in sub-Saharan Africa: new evidence from Nairobi, Kenya'. *Environmental Research Letters* 2(4): 1–5.

Venter, C., V. Volkova and J. Michalek (2007) 'Gender, residential location, and household travel: empirical findings from low-income urban settlements in Durban, South Africa'. *Transport Reviews* 27(6): 653–77.

Wilkinson, P. (2010) 'The regulatory cycle stalled? An assessment of current institutional obstacles to regulatory reform in the provision of road-based public transport in Cape Town, South Africa'. *Research in Transportation Economics* 29(1): 387–94.

Yeboah, M. A. (2010) 'Urban poverty, livelihood, and gender: perceptions and experiences of porters in Accra, Ghana'. *Africa Today* 56(3): 42–60.

8 | Decentralisation and institutional reconfiguration in urban Africa

Warren Smit and Edgar Pieterse

Introduction

According to UN-Habitat (2010), Africa had the fastest rate of urbanisation of all regions in the world between 2005 and 2010. The virtual doubling of the urban population in sub-Saharan Africa over the next 20 years will in all likelihood involve a substantial degree of slum growth (UN-Habitat 2008). Since the majority of urban dwellers presently live in slum conditions, it is reasonable to assume that by 2030 the majority of them will still live in slums because most African cities and towns lack the institutional, financial and political resources to deal with growing levels of urbanisation. Instructively, UN-Habitat notes that:

> The growth, proliferation and persistence of urban slums in East Africa are caused and sustained by: (a) lack of urban land and planning policy; (b) unrealistic construction standards and regulations; (c) private sector housing mostly catering for high and middle-income groups; (d) lack of strategic positioning by governments and local authorities; (e) lack of public infrastructure; and (f) the politicizing of informal settlements and social housing in party lines, current in election years and forgotten as soon as the ballot count is completed. (ibid.: 14)

Slum life fundamentally represents a lack of access to a number of essential services and securities that make a productive modern life possible. It is clearly established in the literature that economic resilience and economic success depend on efficient and productive urban centres that anchor various economic sectors that extend across international boundaries (Kessides 2005; OECD 2008; Scott 2008). If such urban-based systems are non-existent or ineffective it creates a significant drag on the economy, which, in turn, undermines the national development effort. Yet, despite this relatively widespread consensus, most African governments continue to underinvest in the establishment of the institutional frameworks and systems required to enhance the productive functioning of urban platforms in their respective countries and sub-regions. International evidence suggests that at the core of such institutional frameworks is a well-resourced, capacitated, effective, relatively autonomous and democratic local government system that can ensure comprehensive service delivery to citizens and businesses, but that can also maximise distinctive competitive advantages because of intimate knowledge about local (space-economy) endowments and dynamics.

In this chapter we explore the institutional dimensions of the urban development crisis in Africa, taking account of the profound political and policy obstacles that need to be addressed. The chapter builds on other accounts in this volume on the scope, scale and dimensions of the urban development challenge in Africa. In the next section we offer a brief analysis of the institutional aspects of this crisis. From there we turn to focus on what we can learn from the uneven experimentation and implementation of decentralisation reforms over the past two to three decades across the continent in order to propose a reform agenda. This discussion is particularly germane in the light of the sustained levels of economic growth over the past decade, until the global financial crisis of 2008–09. As discussed in UN-Habitat's 2010 *State of the World's Cities* report, this economic growth did not really see any shift in the quality of life or environment in most African cities and towns:

> High slum prevalence in many African cities can also be attributed to structural and political failures in the distribution of public goods, as well as to lack of human and financial resources to address urban poverty. Against this background, economic growth in many cases has had little impact on either poverty or inequality, or both. (UN-Habitat 2010: 28)

Institutional underpinnings of the African urban crisis

It can be argued that the severe development crisis associated with urbanisation processes in Africa can largely be attributed to external forces. However, this would be disingenuous, because, despite the severe resource constraints that mark most African countries, considerably more could have been done to deal with the issue more effectively (see Chapters 4 and 13). The (in)capacity of African states to address the inevitable consequences of increased urbanisation boils down to fundamental institutional problems, such as a lack of coherent urbanisation policies and ineffective decentralisation.

National urbanisation policies Most African governments continue to execute their functions without any explicit national urbanisation strategy that can inform and guide strategic investments. This stems from a broader political sentiment that the economic future of Africa lies with improving its agricultural performance through a so-called second green revolution that will allow the continent to take its rightful place in the globally connected international economy. It is noteworthy how much of the New Partnership for Africa's Development (NEPAD) policy agenda is taken up by promoting a new agenda for agriculture. Agriculture is, of course, a vital component of a long-term development strategy, but it depends heavily on well-functioning towns and cities to get commodities to market and to absorb the produce. In other words, to plan for agricultural success without planning for effective connectivity infrastructures and for the development of cities and towns is short-sighted.

In addition, most African governments have policies that actively discourage migration into urban areas. This stems from a growing concern that their countries are urbanising too rapidly and that these dynamics need to be stemmed through active legislation. In 1996, 63 per cent of African governments responding to a United Nations (UN) questionnaire indicated a concern that their countries were becoming too urban too quickly. This figure rose to 74 per cent in 2007. Over this same period, there has been an even sharper increase in the share of African governments claiming to have policies to reduce migration to urban agglomerations – from 54 per cent in 1996 to 78 per cent in 2007 (UN DESA 2008).

Decentralisation In most African countries, the division of functions between different levels or spheres of government has been deeply problematic, leading to intergovernmental conflict, misalignment and inefficiency. Forty years ago, Richard Stren (1972: 505) noted that: 'The division of function and jurisdiction between local and central government ... leaves a great deal of room for manoeuvre, conflict, and overlap in urban policy.' This is largely still the case.

In most of Africa, urban local governments were unimportant during the colonial era (with a few exceptions), and generally became even weaker and more insignificant in the first few decades after independence. The largest cities had elected councils and elected mayors, and were responsible for a significant range of local services. However, immediately after independence, the national governments of countries such as Senegal and Côte d'Ivoire took over control of the largest cities, purportedly because of their perceived financial insolvency and administrative incompetence but implicitly in order to establish control over potential political opposition (Rakodi 1997). Similarly, in Anglophone Africa, elected local councils had been put in place by the end of the colonial period, but their performance fell far short of their responsibilities and growing demands, and their political autonomy and fiscal base were progressively eroded during the 1960s and 1970s. Central governments generally failed to give local government adequate funds or revenue-raising powers or to ensure that they had sufficient decision-making powers and trained staff to address the urban challenges they faced (ibid.). For example, local government was abolished in the early 1970s in Tanzania and replaced with direct central government administration (with some decentralisation to regions).

From the 1980s onwards, there was a shift towards decentralisation in Africa. Decentralisation is essentially any act in which a central government formally cedes powers to actors and institutions at lower levels in a political–administrative and territorial hierarchy. The key theoretical motivation behind the promotion of decentralisation was to bring decision making closer to the people, and therefore to help ensure that programmes and services better address local needs (Ribot 2001). This wave of decentralisation was widespread. Increasingly, governments and international agencies recognised that improved urban management, decentralisation and local democracy are interlinked, and there were fresh attempts at decentralisation to local government level, linked to state democratisation. Local governments were therefore established or re-established in many countries in an attempt to enhance local democracy and service delivery.

By 2000 it could be claimed that 'There is not a single country in Africa in which some form of local government is not in operation' (Oyugi 2000: 16). The implementation of decentralisation in Africa has, however, been very uneven and partial (Mabogunje 2007; Stren and Eyoh 2007). The reasons for this situation are complex and vary greatly both across the different regions of the continent and within countries. For example, UN-Habitat notes of East Africa that:

> Most of the region's central governments and local authorities claim to embrace good governance, public participation and public–private partnerships. Nevertheless, true decentralisation of powers and resources to the local authorities and participatory urban decision-making is not yet put into effect. (UN-Habitat 2008: 15)

The reasons why the actual implementation of decentralisation often lags behind decentralisation laws and policies include 'intergovernmental politics, bureaucratic politics and insufficient capacities in local governments' (Andrews and Schroeder 2003: 31). And even where decentralisation was implemented, in some cases the aim of decentralisation reforms was merely to 'reinforce vested interests in existing patterns of patronage and central–local linkage', thus having no impact on furthering a pro-poor development agenda (Crook 2003: 78). In addition, sometimes the motivations behind decentralisation were driven by self-interest, for example to shift the responsibility for unpopular structural adjustment programmes away from central government to urban local governments, which in many cases were controlled by opposition parties (Shah and Thompson 2004). Tension between national governments and urban local governments controlled by opposition parties has continued to be a common characteristic of governance in Africa (Resnick 2011).

Nigeria can be taken as a not atypical example of a stalled attempt at decentralisation, and of the impact of this on addressing urban development challenges:

TABLE 8.1 Functions of urban local government bodies in selected African countries

Function	Nigeria (local government authorities)	Cameroon (local governments)	Uganda (urban local government districts)	Tanzania (urban local governments)	Mozambique (municipalities)	South Africa (metropolitan municipalities)
Water supply	–	–	■	□	■	□
Sanitation	■	□	□	□	■	□
Refuse collection/disposal	□	□	□	□	■	□
Urban roads	–	□	–	–	■	□
Urban rail	–	□	–	–	–	–
Electricity	–	–	–	■	–	□
Housing	–	□	–	□	■	■
Urban planning	■	□	□	□	■	□
Parks and open space	□	□	□	□	■	□
Cemeteries and crematoria	□	–	□	□	■	□
Museums and libraries	–	□	□	□	–	■
Primary healthcare clinics	□	■	□	□	■	■
Hospitals	–	■	□	■	–	–
Pre-school education	□	–	□	–	■	–
Primary education	■	–	□	□	–	–
Secondary education	–	–	□	■	–	–
Fire protection	–	–	□	–	–	–
Police	–	–	–	–	–	□
Economic promotion	–	■	–	■	■	■
Tourism promotion	–	■	□	■	■	■

Key: □ Sole responsibility for providing service   ■ Responsibility for providing service is shared with other levels of government   – No information available

Source: Based on Commonwealth Local Government Forum 2008.

Local governments, although saddled with urban governance responsibilities, have never had much autonomy. Reforms have been initiated but the states maintain their holds on local authorities. Local government ability to generate revenue has collapsed, increasing their dependence and reducing their capacities to face the challenges of run-away urbanization, while lack of co-ordination increases the difficulties of urban management. (UN-Habitat 2008: 13)

Currently, the status, powers and functions of local government vary considerably across Africa. The nature of local government bodies can range from democratically elected local governments with a range of income sources and responsibility for delivering a wide range of services, to appointed local governments that depend on national government for revenue and that have only limited responsibilities.

Only in a few countries (such as South Africa and Namibia) is local government enshrined in the constitution. In most cases, local government is created by central government and therefore receives its powers and responsibilities from the enabling statutes or decrees (Wekwete 1997). While all local government bodies have at least some responsibility for functions including urban planning and refuse collection, only some have responsibility for important services such as water supply, roads and electricity (see Table 8.1). The responsibilities for core functions such as urban planning may sometimes be shared with other levels of government; for example, many countries rely heavily on centralised agencies to prepare urban and regional development plans (UN-Habitat 2008).

The widely varying powers of local government in different countries are reflected in the proportion of total government expenditure that is spent by local government. For example, local government expenditure forms only 1.3 per cent of total government expenditure in Kenya, compared with 16.9 per cent in South Africa (UN-Habitat 2009a). Government transfers are still the most significant revenue source for local governments in most countries in Africa: such transfers account for more than 90 per cent of local government revenue in Uganda, for example (ibid.). This is not ideal, as an overreliance on transfers from central government can restrict the autonomy of local government.

Simultaneously with the increased decentralisation of recent decades there has been a shift in the way in which local governments operate. As Ouedraogo (2003) notes, in the 'Anglo-Saxon' tradition, decentralisation also includes the devolution of powers and resources to local non-state bodies, such as private companies and non-governmental organisations (NGOs). In much of Africa, therefore, decentralisation has been accompanied by a strong shift towards corporatisation, privatisation and partnerships. This has been linked to a global shift to such institutional models in local government (often under the guise of implementing 'new public management' principles). The implementation of structural adjustment programmes in many countries helped introduce and legitimise these shifts. In Nigeria, for example, since the 1990s, public services that were previously administered by local governments (such as health centres, primary and secondary schools, water supply, road repairs, the management of public facilities and parks) have been privatised to a large extent (UN-Habitat 2008). In addition, in many countries in Africa, most urban development and redevelopment projects are now structured as public–private partnerships.

Institutional reform agenda for Africa

In the aftermath of the global financial crisis (of 2008–09), the rising awareness of the devastating impacts of climate variability, and a renewed commitment to systematically eradicate poverty, in the form of the Millennium Development Goals (MDGs), the importance of sustainable urban development has attracted significant attention across the world (Pieterse 2011a). The emerging development consensus on the centrality of sustainable urban development is good news for Africa because it offers an opportunity to address the institutional failures discussed above in a fundamental way. The first part of this section will therefore spell out the key tenets of a comprehensive approach to sustainable urban development, because this agenda must inform the institutional architecture at national and local levels in order to address the prevailing crisis in Africa's cities and towns. Through this discussion, it will become clear that each African country requires an explicit national urban strategy to focus and direct the efforts of a number of actors that have a role to play in the urban development agenda.

Central to such national policy frameworks is clarity on the appropriate division of powers and functions across the various levels of government, underpinned by an enabling fiscal framework. These elements assume that urban development planning is based on a rigorous and accurate understanding of systemic drivers and key trends. In other words, the data platforms in each country and city must allow for well-informed and targeted actions, which in turn can be monitored and evaluated to ensure policy implementation and effectiveness. These various national policy frameworks and local data platforms will then inform a unique infrastructure investment strategy for each city and town. However, city-level infrastructure investment strategies will go nowhere unless they are supported and enhanced by a nationally driven and funded decentralisation strategy and programme. The final aspect of the institutional reform agenda is the question of monitoring and evaluation embedded in a broader consultative process. We will now explore each of these elements of the reform agenda in turn.

Sustainable urban development framework African governments are forced to confront the challenge of sustainable urban development at a very interesting historical and global moment. It is a time in which there is widespread recognition that the resource-extractive model of economic development is no longer viable, but rather will induce a measure of climate variability and instability that will permanently disrupt societies and infrastructures (Hodson and Marvin 2009; UN-Habitat 2010). Cities are particularly important sites in responding to climate change, both in terms of mitigation and adaptation (Rosenzweig et al. 2011; UN-Habitat 2011). This heightened degree of risk is forcing a global engagement to redefine the terms of economic development by trying to identify practical measures to internalise the environmental (and possibly social) costs of production and exchange.

The environmental crisis coincides with a profound social and economic crisis. The latter came into sharp relief with the 2008–09 global debt crisis that precipitated a worldwide recession. Global economic changes over the past few decades have resulted in growing levels of income inequality in almost all regions and countries of the world, manifested most acutely in the growing urban divides (UN-Habitat 2010). In the wake of the destruction of wealth, the impoverishment of hundreds of millions of people, and the bail-out of the banks with public money, it is clear that mainstream economic activity and measurements need to be redefined (Swilling 2013). Again, cities and urban centres have emerged as key sites of economic development because the dynamics of globalisation reinforce agglomeration imperatives (of both firms and workers), and because innovation, competitiveness and productivity all depend on the advantages offered by dense settlements (World Bank 2009). Lastly, following the realisation that globalisation dynamics had been accompanied by rising levels of poverty and inequality (if China is taken out of the equation), the global community of states committed to significantly reduce physical poverty by improving access to basic services and political voice; this commitment was expressed in the MDGs for 2015 (Annan 2000). Again, in the context of rising urban poverty, cities are seen as key to making significant progress in attaining the MDGs, although the profound challenges associated with rural poverty should not be neglected (Revi and Rosenzweig 2013).

This unique global moment has forced a sharpening of our understanding of what it will take to advance and eventually achieve sustainable urban development. Figure 8.1 illustrates the four primary dimensions of sustainable urban development (Pieterse 2011a). Domain one denotes the imperative of achieving sustainable urban infrastructure transformations. A key sub-element is the raft of bio-physical network infrastructure systems such as energy, waste, water, sanitation, transport, roads, information and communication technologies, and ecological services. Another sub-element is social infrastructure sectors such as education, health and culture. Domain two denotes inclusive economies. It is now well established that formal economic metrics are wholly inadequate in capturing the diversity and dynamics of real urban

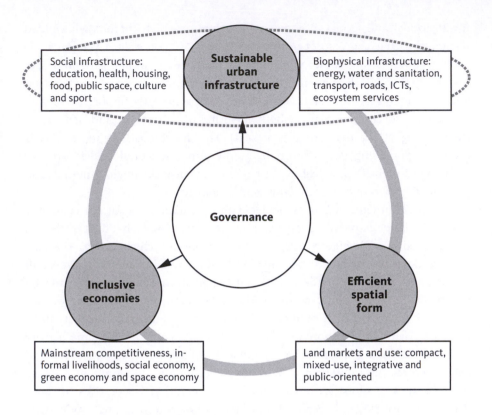

8.1 Dimensions of sustainable urban development (source: Pieterse 2011a: 313)

economies. Thus, in addition to conventional formal economic sectors, one has to identify the social economy (Amin 2010), so-called green jobs (UNEP 2011), and livelihood practices that sustain poor households without access to formal income, social security or government transfers (Moser 2008). These (new) economic dimensions need to be considered alongside the conventional economic sectors and the imperatives to recast those sectors in a low-carbon context (Kamal-Chaoui and Robert 2009). In the aftermath of the global economic crisis of recent times, the centrality of urban infrastructure to economic performance has come to the fore. In fact, economic revitalisation has been pursued through infrastructure-based investments, especially in the US and South Asia, because poor and fragmented infrastructure networks undermine economic performance (Foster and Briceño-Garmendia 2010). Domain three shows efficient spatial form as a key driver of urban development patterns and outcomes. In the wake of the sustainability critique and the worsening of urban inequalities, there is a growing consensus that the spatial form of cities and towns matters a great deal for the realisation of more sustainable urban development outcomes. Specifically, greater density through compaction is encouraged along with a much stronger emphasis on mixed-use land uses to facilitate greater efficiency and pluralism. A public-oriented approach is to be encouraged in the recalibration of land uses, as this will inform a broader agenda to foster greater cultural and social integration (UN-Habitat 2009b).

At the core of this framework is the democratic work of making decisions about key resources. Public investments are invariably rooted in public decision-making processes. With the spread of democratic local government over the past two decades in particular, there has been an ongoing refinement of policies and institutions in order to expand the domain of public influence over decisions taken, well beyond the exercise of one's franchise with every election. It is now taken for granted that urban planning and management should be designed with substantive and ongoing participation built in for very practical reasons, apart from the normative imperative of political legitimacy. Practically, in a context of limited resources and limited state capacity, it is vital that local governments work closely with civil society organisations and the private sector to co-produce development strategies and to ensure participation in various elements of the service delivery value chain. It is for this reason that institutional frameworks for decentralisation are so central to how we redefine and activate urban development processes at the local level.

Tailored national urban development strategy Very few African states have explicit policies to deal with urbanisation and intra-urban development challenges. According to Parnell and Simon (Chapter 13) this stems in part from policy neglect, rooted in a perverse sense of anti-urban bias, and confusion about the difference between urbanisation and urban policies. The former refers to explicit government policies that seek to define, understand and shape the national spatial system, including the network of cities, towns and rural settlements. Typically, this understanding informs decisions about where in the national territory investments should be concentrated and focused. National spatial frameworks also inform how migration dynamics are understood and managed. In contrast, urban policies reflect how national governments understand the role of specific cities and towns in the successful execution of national development goals. Generally, urban policies define what needs to happen with specific cities and towns with regard to various sectoral and integrative strategic objectives, whether they pertain to, for example, mobility, housing, education, health or liveability. Put differently, urban policies provide a perspective on critical city-scale issues and support the efforts of sub-national levels of government to elaborate more detailed policies and strategies for those places. Urban policies are informative and complementary to more detailed, local-level development policy processes.

Urban policies are particularly important in relation to the definition and implementation of infrastructure programmes. Depending on the economic and ecological function of a particular (urban) settlement, its relevance will vary for particular aspects of, for example, a national logistics system or water management approach. When these urban policies are not in place, most development investments are made in a space-blind fashion, which is highly inefficient and potentially unproductive from a national and regional perspective (see Chapter 4).

Keeping the importance of urban policies in mind, and mindful of the macro framework for sustainable urban development elaborated above, we now explore some of the practical steps that are required to *institutionalise* an effective policy agenda to deal with the complexities of uneven urban development in Africa.

Sound data platforms Assuming that governments accept that they need to radically adjust their approach and attitude to urban development imperatives, the essential first step is to improve the quality of data, information and analysis about the urban system and particular settlements that play a major role in the national economy. A number of considerations come into play. Most basic is the need for accurate and reliable data in the form of a periodic national census. A lot of progress has been made with regard to the execution of a national census in Africa. Onsembe and Ntozi (2006) report that 36 out of 51 countries in sub-Saharan Africa participated in the 2000 census round (which started in 1995). Of the 15 countries that did not participate, they observe that 'two-thirds of the countries were engaged in conflicts and hence were not stable enough to plan and execute a census programme' (ibid.: 13). Apart from undertaking regular censuses that are credible, it is particularly important to ensure that these instruments are based on enumerator areas that will allow decision makers and citizens to extrapolate meaningfully at the urban scale. Often, surveys that complement the census, such as labour force surveys or firm competitiveness surveys, are not calibrated to allow meaningful extrapolation for urban areas or, more significantly, intra-urban areas. It will be important for national statistical agencies to work closely with local government associations and urban development bodies to develop a shared approach to the collection and collation of data.

A second dimension of the data agenda is local institutional data (Robinson 2009). Most government departments, local authorities, regional agencies, parastatals, development agencies and large NGOs collect their own data on a range of urban development issues. It is vital to develop an overview of what data exist, their robustness and how they can be related to other data sources. Acknowledging these other repositories of information can also be an effective means of building an intergovernmental and interagency awareness of national urban policy goals and strategies. Some recent technological advances in democratising access to spatial data platforms, such as Google Earth, create substantive opportunities for data pooling and comparisons.

In recent years, various grassroots organisations such as Slum Dwellers International and StreetNet have adopted various enumeration processes to underpin their claims and strategies. This source of grassroots intelligence and information, typically from neighbourhoods and contexts that are difficult to access for the state, is a vital component of an overall urban data system. It also offers promising opportunities for government officers to better understand, from a different angle, the contexts they are seeking to impact. Discrepancies between community data sets and official statistics provide an excellent entry point for reaching an agreement on what the actual local context may be.

Recent advances in the geospatial representation of various data sets have the potential to provide the glue to cohere and relate multiple categories of data. Moreover, geographic information system (GIS) representations can support administrative decision-making processes to improve prioritising and targeting, as well as potentially helping to facilitate the public's engagement with the data.

Finally, it is important to recognise and engage with the significant movement to standardise the relevant indicators that deal with sustainable urban development. In this regard, it is important to mention the Global Urban Observatory capacity within UN-Habitat and the Global City Indicators Facility, which aims to provide a framework for a consistent and globally comparable collection of city indicators.[1] In tandem with this trend, many municipalities, with the support of local government associations, are embarking on processes to establish local urban observatories. It is vital that these initiatives are integrated into national urban policy frameworks.

Infrastructure investment strategy and plan As a result of the post-Washington consensus that now dominates development thinking in most agencies, the central role of the state in the development process is again being recognised. This revalorisation coincides with a so-called 'infrastructural turn' in policy debates and the broader academic literature (Swilling and Annecke 2012). Informed by the experiences of the successful South-East Asian economies, the central role of infrastructure for economic, social and environmental development has become a focus of attention during the past few years (Lee 2007; World Bank 2004; 2009). It is also noteworthy that the stimulus packages introduced in many parts of the world (for example, the United States) after the economic crisis of 2008–09 included large infrastructure investments. These investments aimed to kick-start economies, generate a new generation of 'green' jobs and form the foundation stones for a much more wide-ranging transition to low-carbon economies (Swilling 2013). It is also important to note that China, India, Brazil and South Africa are all heavily reliant on national infrastructure programmes to enhance inclusive growth and to prepare for ongoing demographic and economic pressures.

It is against the backdrop of these trends that African governments need to work out how best they can address the profound infrastructural deficit in both urban and rural areas, as well as prepare for future growth and demand. This exercise needs to be undertaken with a sober understanding of how economic development, basic services and ecological protection development goals can be integrated, balanced and negotiated. Tough trade-offs will be inevitable. The World Bank's authoritative *Africa Infrastructure Report* suggests that investment in infrastructure can both 'guarantee sustainable urbanization and social equity' and 'improve productivity in the modern sector and connectivity with and across locations' (Foster and Briceño-Garmendia 2010: 128).

If the balancing act between basic services and economic infrastructure is not complex and challenging enough, it is now irrefutable that African governments and cities will also have to factor in how best to adapt to and mitigate climate change impacts. These considerations hinge on the successful management of infrastructural transitions. For example, smart and strategic infrastructure planning and investment should facilitate:

- greater transport energy efficiency due to reduced distances and greater shares of green transport modes;
- greater energy efficiency in buildings (both heating and cooling) due to the lower surface-to-volume ratios of more compact building typologies and urban vegetation;
- more efficient use of grid-based energy systems such as combined heat and power;
- lower embedded energy demand for urban infrastructure; and
- greater energy efficiency in operating a range of utilities (UNEP 2011).

On a more practical note, this discussion illustrates that it is simply not possible for African governments to leave infrastructure planning and management in the hands of sectoral interests that benefit from the status quo. A strategic national policy framework on infrastructure is required. Such a framework must spell out how national, urban and rural infrastructure deficits will be assessed, defined, analysed and addressed through short, medium and long-term programmes. The framework will have to specify how best to aggregate particular infrastructure sectors into bundles that can enhance the economic potential of certain territories, while forming part of a national and regional whole. Furthermore, it will have to address the institutional modalities of infrastructure provision, technology, maintenance and financing. Traditional privatisation models tend to reinforce a sectoral approach and produce extremely negative social and environmental consequences. In contexts where state capacity is under strain, investment capital limited and the capacity of citizens to pay for the services restricted, hybrid institutional forms will have to be developed.

Decentralisation policy and operational strategy In this chapter we have intimated that one of the key institutional difficulties associated with decentralisation efforts in Africa is the problematic division of powers and functions between different levels of government. In most African countries the problem is that not enough powers have been assigned to sub-national and, especially, local levels of government. In cases where administrative decentralisation has been instituted, it has often occurred without concomitant powers to raise local revenues to execute the requisite functions, or with inadequate intergovernmental transfers to enable local authorities to fulfil their mandates. This problem is widespread and systemic.

The dimensions of sustainable urban development, along with the imperatives of a strategic approach to infrastructure investment and extension, should inform national approaches to the division of powers and functions across levels of government. There is no single recipe or formula that can be applied to all African contexts. What is required is a strategic understanding of how limited resources can best be deployed to advance the national development project in the context of specific urban and rural settlements, correlated with (local) state capacity and the institutional modalities of service provision. For example, the national urban policy framework should present a clear description and analysis of the national space economy. This should include details of where formal and informal economic sectors (and clusters and value chains) are located in relation to demographic patterns and resource flow patterns, and the implications of this for various categories of settlement as well as for specific urban centres where the bulk of the national economy is anchored. Such an understanding will provide an indication of how the infrastructure deficits can best be tackled in a differentiated manner, building on local capacity and responding to key nodes with the potential to advance the overall development prospects of the country and its broader region. It would be foolish to undertake this kind of analytical or planning exercise in the absence of sound data or without the active participation of local actors (mayors, local authorities, business interests and civil society organisations). A sensible approach to the division of powers and functions across different levels of government and across diverse institutional forms (e.g. national or local utilities) cannot be achieved without an awareness of the unique developmental roles of various local settlements.

The second step in developing a decentralisation policy framework is to define an overall governance system that could give expression to the objectives of a national urban policy and any associated infrastructure investment strategy. Given the historical context of institutional reform and the persistence of national political and economic control, it is important to be realistic about phasing in decentralisation reforms and to create incentives for all vested interests to maintain the momentum over time. One of the errors that must be avoided is the imposition of a uniform system to assign powers and functions to lower levels of government. It is important to differentiate between different categories of local government in relation to their capacity, revenue-raising potential, and population size and density.

A national decentralisation policy framework needs to clarify the government's thinking and intent with regard to addressing basic needs, economic development, citizen empowerment and environmental protection through a sensible division of powers and functions across different levels of government. This implies that there is a clear policy argument that tackles the balances and trade-offs between these different categories of development based on available resources, potential development paths and opportunities for synergy between the government, private sector, civil society organisations and citizens.

The third step in developing a decentralisation policy is having an explicit focus on democratic enhancement tools that foster state responsiveness, legitimacy, accountability and enrolment of civil society and citizens in development programmes. There is now a relatively mature body of global experience and relevant literature on the range of policy instruments that are available to substantiate democratic decentralisation (Amis 2008; Gaventa 2006; Manor 2004; Fung and Wright 2001) and it is not necessary to rehearse all those policy options here. However, it is relevant to simply list the dimensions of democratic decentralisation:

- Local elections: It is important to decide on the form of elections and how they will relate to the system of executive power; for example, will mayors be directly elected or appointed, and so on. In many African countries there remains important foundational work to be done to make local elections transparent, fair and free of violence.
- Traditional authorities: A decision needs to be made about how best to incorporate various categories of traditional authorities that continue to exercise profound influence at the local level. Since these authorities are typically not elected, their interface with the democratic system needs clarity as well as recourse for citizens who choose to live outside the jurisdictional claims of these bodies. Most importantly, the role that traditional authorities play in regulating land use and occupancy needs deliberate attention so that it does not impede inclusive economic and social development (Berrisford 2011).
- Citizen voice: It is vital that citizens and civil society organisations have a variety of means to engage with the policy development process, programme and project implementation, and review or auditing aspects of sound urban management. There is a variety of tools available to facilitate and enhance the quality of citizens' engagement with the research and framing dimensions of policy development (Fung and Wright 2001; Goetz

and Gaventa 2001). In a context of limited resources, vast need and a variety of local compensatory strategies to deal with service deficiencies, it is essential that service delivery – especially in the domain of basic services and social development functions – is undertaken within a partnership framework. Lastly, citizen voice can also be enhanced through various monitoring and review techniques that allow citizens to give their opinion about the quality and effectiveness of service delivery. The most potent forms of citizen voice and engagement with local development processes are through avenues that allow citizen engagement with the planning and budgeting processes, because these go to the heart of resource prioritisation (Pieterse 2011b). The Municipal Development Partnership in Harare, for example, has been building up a significant body of knowledge and experience in working with local authorities and communities across east and southern Africa to explore the potential of participatory budgeting in particular.[2]

The fourth dimension of an effective decentralisation policy and programme is performance. State effectiveness depends on institutional clarity of purpose, effective leadership, capacity, resources, democratic pressure, and continuous feedback to indicate whether goals are being met.

Conclusion

In this chapter we have provided a contextualised discussion of the institutional dimensions of decentralisation in Africa. The discussion started off with a reminder of the negative development trends associated with poorly managed urbanisation: slum growth associated with massive basic service deficiencies, underperforming economies, informalised livelihoods, rising urban inequality and serious environmental degradation that makes these settlements extremely vulnerable to heightened climate variability. Against that introductory backdrop, the first section explored the institutional underpinning of the urban development crisis in Africa. This provided a good platform from which to review the experience of decentralisation efforts across the continent over the past three decades or so. This is also a disheartening narrative. In most postcolonial contexts there was a move towards significant decentralisation, not least because of the ideological tenets of some of the liberation parties at the time, but this was soon reversed and replaced with increasing centralisation of power and resources. This is a dynamic that remains by and large the dominant institutional tendency in most African countries, even though there has been a widespread re-experimentation with decentralisation models since the 1980s. The attempts at decentralisation during the height of the structural adjustment programmes have not been particularly effective because they often promoted institutional approaches that excluded the majority of urban citizens in Africa. The uneven and problematic history of decentralisation and urban management has produced a very complicated knot of policy problems, which now require radical and far-reaching reform. In the last section we put forward a conceptual framework for thinking about the primary dimensions of policy priorities for advancing sustainable urban development. In practice, it implies that national governments need to commit to developing a trio of policy reforms:

- a national urban policy framework;
- a national infrastructure policy agenda; and
- a revitalised decentralisation policy framework and operational strategy.

Throughout the chapter we have been at pains to highlight the fact that, for institutional reform to achieve sustainable urban development, it cannot proceed as a top-down endeavour. It must be rooted in genuine bottom-up interventions. There are two dimensions to this. Firstly, local authorities and governments must be supported to put their agendas and interests into the public arena for discussion and debate. Moreover, civil society organisations – especially those that champion the interests of slum dwellers – must also be given meaningful opportunities to be part of these processes. Real progress will be achieved only when national governments and elites recognise that everyone's long-term interests lie in creating a dynamic institutional framework that allows for an appropriate division of powers and capacities across all levels of the governance system.

Notes

1 For more information, see www.city indicators.org [accessed 19 August 2013].

2 For more information, see www. mdpafrica.org.zw [accessed 19 August 2013].

References

Amin, A. (2010) 'Locating the social economy'. In A. Amin (ed.) *The Social Economy: International perspectives on economic solidarity*. London: Zed Books.

Amis, P. (2008) 'New aid modalities and local government: are they supporting or hindering processes of decentralization'. *Commonwealth Journal of Local Governance* 1: 115–25.

Andrews, M. and L. Schroeder (2003) 'Sectoral decentralisation and inter-governmental arrangements in Africa'. *Public Administration and Development* 23(1): 29–40.

Annan, K. (2000) *We the Peoples: The role of the United Nations in the 21st century*. New York, NY: United Nations.

Berrisford, S. (2011) 'Why it is difficult to change urban planning laws in African countries'. *Urban Forum* 22(3): 209–28.

Commonwealth Local Government Forum (2008) *The Commonwealth Local Government Handbook 2009*. London: Commonwealth Local Government Forum.

Crook, R. C. (2003) 'Decentralisation and poverty reduction in Africa: the politics of local–central relations'. *Public Administration and Development* 23(1): 77–88.

Foster, V. and C. Briceño-Garmendia (eds) (2010) *Africa's Infrastructure: A time for transformation*. Washington, DC: World Bank.

Fung, A. and E. O. Wright (2001) 'Deepening democracy: innovations in empowered participatory governance'. *Politics and Society* 29(1): 5–41.

Gaventa, J. (2006) *Triumph, Deficit or*

Contestation? Deepening the 'deepening democracy' debate. IDS Working Paper No. 264. Brighton: Institute for Development Studies.

Goetz, A. and J. Gaventa (2001) *Bring Citizen Voice and Client Focus into Service Delivery*. IDS Working Paper No. 138. Brighton: Institute for Development Studies.

Hodson, M. and S. Marvin (2009) '"Urban ecological security": a new urban paradigm?'. *International Journal of Urban and Regional Research* 33(1): 193–215.

Kamal-Chaoui, L. and A. Robert (eds) (2009) *Competitive Cities and Climate Change*. Paris: Organisation for Economic Co-operation and Development (OECD).

Kessides, C. (2005) *The Urban Transition in Sub-Saharan Africa: Implications for economic growth and poverty reduction*. Africa Region Working Paper Series No. 97. Washington, DC: World Bank.

Lee, K. N. (2007) 'An urbanizing world'. In L. Starke (ed.) *State of the World 2007: Our urban future*. New York, NY: W. W. Norton & Company.

Mabogunje, A. (2007) *Global Urban Poverty Research Agenda: The African case*. Urban Update No. 10. Washington, DC: Woodrow Wilson International Center for Scholars.

Manor, J. (2004) 'Democratisation with inclusion: political reforms and people's empowerment at the grassroots'. *Journal of Human Development* 5(1): 5–29.

Moser, C. (2008) 'Assets and livelihoods: a framework for asset-based social policy'. In C. Moser and A. Dani (eds) *Assets, Livelihoods and Social Policy*. Washington, DC: World Bank.

OECD (2008) *Cape Town, South Africa*. OECD Territorial Reviews. Paris: Organisation for Economic Co-operation and Development (OECD).

Onsembe, J. O. and J. P. M. Ntozi (2006) 'The 2000 round of censuses in Africa: achievements and challenges'. *African Statistical Journal* 3: 11–28.

Ouedraogo, H. M. G. (2003) 'Decentralisation and local governance: experiences from Francophone West Africa'. *Public Administration and Development* 23(1): 97–103.

Oyugi, W. O. (2000) 'Decentralization for good governance and development'. *Regional Development Dialogue* 21(1): 3–22.

Pieterse, E. (2011a) 'Recasting urban sustainability in the South'. *Development* 54(3): 309–16.

— (2011b) 'Building brave new worlds: design and the second urban transition'. In C. Smith (ed.) *Design with the Other 90%: Cities*. New York, NY: Cooper-Hewitt National Design Museum.

Rakodi, C. (1997) 'Conclusion'. In C. Rakodi (ed.) *The Urban Challenge in Africa: Growth and management of its large cities*. Tokyo: United Nations University Press.

Resnick, D. (2011) 'In the shadow of the city: Africa's urban poor in opposition strongholds'. *Journal of Modern African Studies* 49(1): 141–66.

Revi, A. and C. Rosenzweig (2013) 'The urban opportunity to enable transformative and sustainable development'. Background paper for the High-Level Panel of Eminent Persons on the Post-2015 Development Agenda. New York, NY: Sustainable Development Solutions Network.

Ribot, J. C. (2001) *Local Actors, Powers and Accountability in African Decentralizations: A review of issues*. Washington, DC: World Resources Institute.

Robinson, J. (2009) 'State of cities reports: briefing document'. Unpublished report for African Centre for Cities.

Rosenzweig, C., W. D. Solecki, S. A. Hammer and S. Mehrotra (2011) *Climate Change and Cities: First assessment report of the Urban Climate Change Research Network*. Cambridge: Cambridge University Press.

Scott, A. J. (2008) *Social Economy of the Metropolis: Cognitive-cultural capitalism and the global resurgence of cities*. Oxford: Oxford University Press.

Shah, A. and T. Thompson (2004) *Implementing Decentralized Local Governance: A treacherous road with potholes, detours and road closures*. World Bank Policy Research Working Paper 3353. Washington, DC: World Bank.

Stren, R. (1972) 'Urban policy in Africa: A political analysis'. *African Studies Review* 15(3): 489–516.

— and D. Eyoh (2007) 'Decentralization and urban development in West Africa'. In D. Eyoh and R. Stren (eds) *Decentralization and the Politics of Urban Development in West Africa*. Washington, DC: Woodrow Wilson International Center for Scholars.

Swilling M. (2013) 'Economic crisis, long waves and the sustainability transition: an African perspective'. *Environmental Innovation and Societal Transitions* 6: 96–115.

— and E. Annecke (2012) *Just Transitions: Explorations of sustainability in an unfair world*. Cape Town and Tokyo: UCT Press and United Nations University Press.

UN DESA (2008) *World Population Policies 2007*. New York, NY: Population Division of the Department of Economic and Social Affairs of the United Nations Secretariat (UN DESA).

UNEP (2011) *Towards a Green Economy: Pathways to sustainable development and poverty eradication*. Nairobi: United Nations Environment Programme (UNEP). Available at www.unep.org/greeneconomy/greeneconomyreport/

tabid/29846/default.aspx [accessed 5 September 2013].

UN-Habitat (2008) *The State of African Cities 2008: A framework for addressing urban challenges in Africa*. Nairobi: United Nations Human Settlements Programme (UN-Habitat).

— (2009a) *Guide to Municipal Finance*. Nairobi: United Nations Human Settlements Programme (UN-Habitat).

— (2009b) *Global Report on Human Settlements: Planning sustainable cities*. Nairobi: United Nations Human Settlements Programme (UN-Habitat).

— (2010) *State of the World's Cities 2010/2011: Bridging the urban divide*. Nairobi: United Nations Human Settlements Programme (UN-Habitat).

— (2011) *Global Report on Human Settlements 2011: Cities and climate change*. London: Earthscan.

Wekwete, K. H. (1997) 'Urban management: the recent experience'. In C. Rakodi (ed.) *The Urban Challenge in Africa: Growth and management of its large cities*. Tokyo: United Nations University Press.

World Bank (2004) *World Development Report 2004: Making services work for poor people*. Washington, DC and Oxford: World Bank and Oxford University Press.

— (2009) *World Development Report 2009: Reshaping economic geography*. Washington, DC: World Bank.

9 | The challenge of urban planning law reform in African cities

Stephen Berrisford

Introduction

The call for legal reform to realise a new vision for African cities is heard with increasing frequency. Since most African[1] countries became independent there has been a concern among officials, professionals and international development agencies that better planning laws are needed.[2] This concern has, however, seldom translated into new law that has been implemented successfully, or, where there has been implementation, it has not been for the purposes originally envisaged for that law. In many cases inherited colonial planning laws remain on the statute books, largely unchanged. In both the cases where new law has been enacted and where the old law remains in force there have been increasingly publicised cases of governments using those laws to justify large-scale eviction and demolition campaigns.[3] The legislation has also been unable to check excessive developments driven by the private sector. Therefore, planning law has tended to have the effect of being no more than an irritant to developers but an oppressive force for the poor, without yielding any significant societal benefits.

Currently, efforts to continue to revise the planning legislation in African countries are generally funded by international agencies and donors. This chapter asks why it is so difficult to effect these revisions. It then concludes with ideas for improving these efforts. At the heart of the question is the principle that planning law is meant to reflect and assert the public interest. It mitigates and directs the impacts of private interests, especially in relation to land development. It balances private rights in property with the public interest in having a safer, more efficient and more equitable urban environment. Under the various colonial regimes in place in different African countries, planning law was used to assert the interests of a small minority, often not of the city's residents but of representatives of the colonial power, against those of the majority. Planning laws effectively drew the lines around those parts of the city in which the development and use of land was permitted. These laws set standards for use and construction as well as plot size and land tenure that were never going to be affordable for the majority. The law thus excluded the citizenry from participating in the benefits of urban planning.

Since independence, all indications are that this situation has endured, albeit with a different minority elite reaping the benefits.

It is trite to say that African countries are diverse and varied. From the perspectives of both law making and the practice of planning there are widely different traditions, histories and experiences, not to forget very different economic, social and political contexts. Nevertheless, experiences with planning law reform are remarkably similar. The success rate is poor across the board.

The hypothesis that this chapter examines is that the drafting processes in most cases fail on two counts:

- Firstly, they fail to identify the key stakeholders in the drafting and imple-mentation of a new planning law and to identify each set of stakeholders' economic and political interests accurately and openly.
- Secondly, they assume that planning law reform in Africa is somehow easier, more susceptible to a relatively simple technocratic approach to law making than is the case in other, more developed, countries, and so any need to follow the basic principles of law making that most developed countries at least try to follow[4] is seen as superfluous.

These failures are not the results of bad intentions on the part of any person or organisation. And similar mistakes are made in many developed countries and other parts of the world. However, the failure to address these shortcomings means that future attempts to reform, update or even completely transform planning laws in African countries are unlikely to succeed. The argu-ment proposed here is that the effort currently invested in planning law reform is almost always misdirected. Firstly, many of the legal instruments proposed are not suited to the context in which they will have to be implemented. The legal instruments inevitably overestimate the professional and techni-cal capacity of the officials required to put them into practice and they also rely on technological systems that are not available. There is also a striking tendency for the new legislation to propose compliance standards concerning, for example, building materials, coverage and urban design that are unafford-able for the vast majority of citizens. Secondly, the primary concern of many of the drivers of planning law reform is the challenge of bringing the poor, generally in informally constructed structures, in line with regulatory norms and standards. In other words, this entails imposing a regulatory burden on those least able to bear it, often with negligible public interest benefits. The puzzlement of planning law reform protagonists when it transpires that these approaches are unpopular is disingenuous. Why should poor people want to invest more in their homes or businesses than they are currently doing purely to satisfy a planning vision? Thirdly, while the focus remains on the challenge of imposing planning standards on the poor, scant attention is paid to the regulation of the powerful players in the land development field: developers, commercial farmers, traditional leaders and wealthy citizens. The elephant in the room is the ability of the powerful – often including planning officials and related professionals – to escape the application of planning laws that would in any way diminish or restrict their capacity to obtain capital growth as well as rental income from their property.

Systems of planning law are necessary to provide a framework of rules to mediate and regulate competing pressures and interests. A proper understanding of these pressures and interests is thus a prerequisite for making progress in planning law reform. A proper understanding entails looking beneath the surface. While a particular stakeholder or type of stakeholder may well profess, or even believe, that they pursue regulatory change for a particular reason, there may well be other less obvious, or less palatable, motivations as well. Understanding these at the outset is important in order to avoid issues emerging at a late stage in the process, ambushing the final passage of a bill into legislation. In a context of high social inequality, the threat of elite capture of a law-making process has to be confronted squarely. Where organs of civil society are weak and stretched – and the resource being regulated is as valuable as urban land – it is inadequate simply to ensure that opportunities for participation in a law-making process are provided. Similarly, where elite groups, which may include traditional leaders as well as wealthy citizens and developers, ignore such a process there has to be a concern that this is because they believe that their social and political power will invariably allow them to proceed with their activities unhindered by the new legislation.

Planning law reform is difficult in any context, in any country, anywhere in the world. By its nature it is a complex area of law, having to mediate the competing interests of stakeholders seeking to maximise their own opportunities. It has the potential either to be redistributive or to consolidate existing privilege. Planners cannot anticipate the future any better than a layperson, yet planning law provides the profession with legal instruments to restrict household and business activities in order to achieve future objectives. Crucially, planning law determines which buildings are legal and which are not. When this final characteristic of planning law is seen alongside insecure and unpredictable land rights, it represents an important fault line running through society. As countries become more urban and as urban land assumes an increasingly important economic role – for both households and firms – and as competition for land on which to build and invest intensifies, so planning laws assume a fundamental importance. These laws establish the regulatory hurdles that have to be cleared for a parcel of land to enter the formal land supply chain and so they contribute to constraining that supply, and thereby push up the price of urban land, reduce affordability and restrict access for the poor. The application of planning laws thus becomes, albeit sometimes indirectly or covertly, the determinant of who benefits from participation in the urban land market and who loses, whose asset values increase and whose prospects of acquiring a formal right to hold or develop land in the city are diminished.

Does it matter that efforts to reform planning laws in Africa have failed? Inadequate, ineffective planning law is hardly the greatest of the problems facing the continent. One could also argue that there is so little capacity – technical or political – to implement planning law in most countries that the quality of the law is neither here nor there. This would effectively be advocating a 'do nothing' approach: leave things as they are and wait until there is capacity to implement the laws. The great risk involved in the drafting of a planning law (as opposed to, for example, a planning policy or even a plan that is not likely to be implemented soon) is that one's outputs assume the force of law. Moreover, creating a law that is incapable of being implemented (in the hope that one day circumstances will change to allow for it to blossom according to its original design) is unhelpful. Following this approach diverts scarce human and financial resources into a futile endeavour, rather than towards areas in which real, albeit perhaps modest, achievements are possible.

Questions that need answers

The thinking behind this chapter was seeded by three discussions I had with knowledgeable and enthusiastic proponents of planning law reform; these are described elsewhere (Berrisford 2011).[5] The essence of each of these discussions was a sincerely held belief that new urban planning legislation for African countries could be designed and drafted both quickly and easily, primarily on the basis of legislation used successfully elsewhere or by using a model law that could be crafted for widespread application across the continent. While nobody disputed the complexity of the urban situation, they harboured a confidence that at least the urban planning side could be fixed with a cleverly written law. This has prompted me to explore answers to the question of why the design of new planning laws for African countries is more complicated than it apparently seems. Why do we need a new approach to urban planning law reform? By asking why it is difficult to change planning laws in Africa I am not suggesting that it is easy anywhere else; rather, I am countering the view that in Africa it might be easy, or at least easier than it is in other countries, that in Africa it is simply a case of finding a law that works elsewhere and then pursuing its implementation and enforcement.

In doing so I tread in the footsteps of Professor Patrick McAuslan, who has consistently argued against the practice of simply lifting a law from one context and expecting it to work in another, particularly in the context of planning and land law in Africa (McAuslan 2003). His work demonstrates the shortcomings of the 'one size fits all' approach to planning legislation as well as the need to keep a firm rein on the gap between what the law prescribes and what is in fact possible. He also reminds us that such an approach is not new. In the late 1940s the British Colonial Office developed a 'model town and country planning law' for use across Africa and the Caribbean (ibid.: 92). McAuslan concludes that:

> the diaspora of town and country planning law has been used in country after country to keep the urban masses at bay; to deny them lawful homes and livelihoods; to reinforce the powers of officials; and to weaken the institutions of civil society. (ibid.: 103)

He argues for a new model, one that has to 'address the democratic deficit' (ibid.: 104). It also needs to be in line with a number of other trends that are emerging and that bring the question of appropriate planning law in Africa into sharp focus. Among these are:

- the renewed interest in making markets – in this case (mainly urban) land development markets – work better for the poor;[6]
- the interest in governance, which is necessarily determined by the laws in terms of which governing takes place, and which need to 'support each state's democratic philosophy' (ibid.: 105);
- the pressure of Millennium Development Goal 7, Target 11, which requires improvements in slum dwellers' lives;
- the sharper gaze, both internationally and domestically, on the demolition of structures that do not comply with applicable planning or building laws (Du Plessis 2005);
- the rising value of urban land in many cities in Africa as a result of economic growth, which increases the pressure on government and the private sector to invoke the non-compliance mentioned above to clear land for commercial development (Lall et al. 2009); and
- the importance placed on decentralisation in Africa by international organisations and major donors, with the consequent need to review and change planning laws to accommodate the decentralisation of planning powers and functions (UN-Habitat 2012a).

The need therefore arises to revive the debate on what constitutes an effective planning law, why new planning laws in most African countries are ineffective, and how the process of planning law reform might be undertaken in a different and better way. As Ann and Robert Seidman wrote in 1996, 'the complaint "we have good laws, but bad implementation" constitutes an oxymoron' (Seidman and Seidman 1996: 27). It is no good to draft a law that appears to address a wide range of concerns yet is incapable of being implemented, not just because 'capacity is limited' or 'there is no political will' but rather – or also – because it fails to address the reasons why people, whether they are politicians, officials, planners or individual households or firms, behave in particular ways. Many of the efforts to write new planning law for African countries are dead in the water, as is often quietly, if sheepishly, acknowledged by participants. In order not only to achieve more efficient law-making processes but also, importantly, to create better and more effective laws, the way in which new planning laws are conceptualised, drafted and implemented has to change.

Who thinks that planning laws should change?

There is little disagreement among the main proponents in the international urban development discourse that planning laws (among many others) should change. As to how to effect that change, there is not a great deal of dispute either. The generally supported method is one where the government of a country requests assistance with the revision of its planning laws. The donor or other organisation responds positively, there not being much dispute that the laws need to change. A consulting firm is then appointed, a work plan drawn up and the process commences. These processes can take anything from six months to a couple of years. The work plan will meticulously record that, at the culmination of the consultancy, a bill will be presented to the country's parliament – and duly enacted after deliberation and debate.

UN-Habitat reports have consistently called for the reform of planning laws, particularly the regulation of land use and development. *State of the World's Cities 2012/2013: Prosperity of cities* (UN-Habitat 2012a: 114) argues strongly for the rationalisation of planning and building codes to unleash economic potential, while the 2009 *Global Report on Human Settlements: Planning sustainable cities*, equally strongly affirms that: '[a]n important precondition for more effective urban planning is that national legislation is up to date and is responsive to current urban issues' (UN-Habitat 2009: 215).

The World Bank's 2009 urban strategy document asks:

> How then should cities proceed? Experience suggests that only a few regulations are critical: minimum plot sizes and minimum apartment sizes, limitations on floor area ratios, zoning plans that limit the type of use and the intensity of use of urban land, and land subdivision ratios of developable and saleable land in new greenfield developments. Cities can use urban planning audits to determine which regulations should be changed to enable density and urban form to move in tandem with urbanization. (World Bank 2009: 16)

The African Development Bank's 2011 *Urban Development Strategy* commits the bank to:

> [i]mprove the investment climate by providing technical assistance to municipalities and other sub-national governments for reform of their legal and regulatory frameworks. (African Development Bank 2011: 14)

All the major donors, as well as bodies such as the Cities Alliance, when they mention the issue are united in their concern that law reform in urban (and rural) planning is important. Many donors have funded programmes to effect law reform in the sector.

The governments of African countries are also generally consistent in their statements on the subject: better planning law is needed to bring order and control to an illegal, informal, untidy and out-of-control situation; it is needed to modernise the society and to enable governments to exert a stronger influence over spatial patterns. Within the international organs of civil society there is increasingly a call for laws and regulations to respect and give value to 'the right to the city' (Sugrayes and Mathivet 2010).

Generally, there is thus a solid chorus at the outset of any initiative to change the law. As the process unfolds and gaps start to emerge between what the government and the donors or international organisations anticipate, so unease on the part of donors and international organisations begins to appear and the positions of the government representatives start to diverge and to harden. From the government's side, this arises from a growing realisation of the potential impacts of the sorts of changes envisaged by the donors on key constituencies, especially on elite sectors such as wealthy citizens, developers and traditional leaders. The consultants – generally a foreign technical expert or a multinational team including 'local' experts – are left to mediate the increasingly difficult and charged situation while constantly keeping a weather eye on their contractual obligations to speedily deliver new draft law. This is not a good recipe for international development cooperation, nor for good law making.

The importance of planning law in Africa

Planning law has a poor record in Africa. It has provided oppressive regimes, whether colonial or independent, with a legal mechanism for restricting social and economic opportunities for most people and controlling urban land supply as a way of limiting urbanisation. Not infrequently it has been used even more directly to justify campaigns of demolition or eviction, as was notoriously the case with Zimbabwe's Operation Murambatsvina (UN-Habitat 2005; Ocheje 2007; Berrisford and Kihato 2006).

The call for new, revitalised, modernised planning laws grows ever louder. This call is motivated by a growing sense that the laws, many of which are based on (if not direct copies of) laws drawn up for use in the colonial powers' own countries, are out of date and inappropriate. It is also fuelled by the persistent and often desperate belief that, if only new, more easily implemented laws could be written, then a beleaguered state would be able to police its way to a more orderly and efficient urban future.

As one approaches the question of what planning law would be good for

Africa, it is important to identify the ambit of planning law. Traditionally, and globally, planning law has fulfilled two main functions. Firstly, it provides the legal framework in terms of which plans are made, who makes the plans, what processes have to be followed in the plan making, what is the content of the plan, and what is its legal effect. Secondly, it regulates the process of approving the development or change of the use of land: what land use changes or land developments require permission and in which areas; the process to be followed by a person wishing to obtain approval for a proposed land use change or land development; the factors to be taken into account by decision makers when considering an application for permission, including the effect of any approved plan; and the legal consequences of a decision to approve an application for permission, such as the payment of infrastructure and service charges and compliance with specified conditions relating to environmental protection, the need for any additional approvals, or time limits within which to exercise the newly granted rights. This function is generally described as 'development control' or 'development management'. In general, the planning laws currently in place set out to tackle all of these functions. In practice, they fail to achieve any of the apparently desired outcomes, hence the shared appreciation that the laws need to change.

There are a number of assumptions that underpin the generally accepted ambit of planning laws described above and that could be applied to any planning system in the world. These assumptions include that:

- planning laws (or indeed any laws) enjoy legitimacy in the eyes of the public;
- there are legitimate and effective structures of government able to carry out the functions described above in an impartial and reasonable manner;
- planning law is needed to control development, and that unrestricted development is acknowledged to be a 'public bad' that must be fought rigorously;
- people value the benefits of a planning system and so are willing to invest time and money in participating in the legal process in order to improve the value of their land or buildings; and
- government authorities are able to appreciate the benefits of a planning system for, inter alia, budgeting for infrastructure investment or establishing the land values needed to support a property tax.

In African cities, however, few of these assumptions hold true. In the paragraphs below I will describe the ways in which each of the five assumptions described above falters.

Legitimacy of the legislation Not all planning laws are inherited from colonialism. Over the past 50 years, most countries have amended or even replaced those laws. In some cases the changes have seemed dramatic, at least on paper. In practice, however, the grip of the colonial legislation over professional practice and profession mindsets, particularly within government bureaucracies, remains strong. Officials see themselves as a bastion against informality, illegality and anarchy. Their views are often complemented by those of their political principals, who see the laws as serving very much the same purposes as their colonial forebears did: to protect elite neighbourhoods and to punish transgressors for failing to comply with the often arcane prescriptions of the law. This leads inexorably to a situation in which there is a widespread perception that there are 'two laws': one for the well-to-do and another for the rest. Consequently, there is very little respect for the law from either the wealthy or the poor and it enjoys very little legitimacy.

Legitimate and effective structures of government Democracy has spread over the past 20 years. This has improved, but not done away with, the problem of widely held views that African governments' legitimacy is compromised by both questionable electoral practices and corruption. The problem is particularly acute in relation to local government, which is frequently appointed rather than elected. Donor-driven efforts to strengthen local government and decentralise functions are widespread. A growing trend is that political parties in opposition to a government at a national level are strengthening their representation in local government, in many cases assuming power over important cities.[7] The inevitable political tension that then arises between national and local government has the effect of weakening the legitimacy of both, and of weakening national governments' support for decentralisation. In a multiparty context, and especially where different parties control national and local government, the argument for decentralisation is less compelling for those holding power at the centre.

Development control is a public good In a context where land markets are often dysfunctional, at least when seen through a conventional market lens, where poor people battle tremendously hard to save enough money to invest in larger, more comfortable – but often unlawful – homes, and where business investment by local and international investors is both scarce and scared off by government regulation, it is very difficult to make the case for more control over land development. While there is no doubt that control is necessary to protect public rights of way (roads, railway lines and access for emergency vehicles) as well as to minimise the risk of natural disasters such as flooding or landslides, the tendency in current planning law is to try to control every aspect of land development. The impossibility of achieving this objective defeats the purpose of development control on a day-to-day basis, although the residual power to control development is retained. The pre-existing risk of natural disaster is then compounded by the risk of politically driven eviction or demolition campaigns, all contributing to a highly insecure situation for most urban citizens. Developers operate in a system where opportunistic planning officials easily succumb to the temptations of bribery and corruption.

There is value in participating in the planning system Either as an applicant or an objector in a planning permission process, or as a participant in a plan-making process, there is generally very little value in participating. The process of obtaining planning permission is widely held to be corrupt, with the outcome determined more by the payment of bribes or the exertion of political influence than by any consideration of 'planning' issues. The making of a local plan is equally widely considered to be an exercise in futility, as the final output of the exercise is seldom, if ever, applied to future decision making over land development in the area. Although some current planning laws require public participation in plan making, the cases where individuals or communities are willing or able to influence the outcome of the plan are exceptional. The model process for plan making remains one in which the technical work is carried out by expatriate consultants, flown in for the purposes of that particular project, working with a handful of officials.

The planning system forms part of a virtuous cycle of urban management The weak capacity of local government in particular, and government in general, coupled with the high levels of absolute and relative poverty make it almost impossible for a functional planning system to play the supportive role required by a well-managed town or city. Infrastructure provision is programmed according to budget availability, which in turn is frequently determined by the availability of finance from an external source, by way of either a loan or grant from a donor or international organisation. A scenario in which a local council is able to align infrastructure programming with planned expansion or in which the probable future consumption of municipal services can be anticipated by monitoring the operation of the development control system is simply not realistic, even in the most well-managed African towns and cities. Similarly, local property-based taxation systems are weak, revenue collection rates are low and there is seldom any formal or informal connection between the granting of development rights through the planning system and the revaluation of property via the property taxation system.

Going forward: can planning law reform be improved?

The premise behind this work is that planning law reform processes can be improved. Not only *can* they be improved but also they *must* be improved. Laws aiming to promote forward planning and to regulate the development of land are not going away. In the absence of improvements and changes to these laws, their many negative consequences will continue to be felt and are likely to worsen.

In the sections below, three broad themes are explored. The first looks at the importance of better understanding the interests of the stakeholders in the resulting planning system while designing that system through the drafting of a new law. The second looks at five 'principles of good regulation' and assesses them in the light of the constraints generally experienced when trying to change planning laws in African countries. The third, using those five principles, starts to look at ways in which the law reform process can be designed differently. The suggested way forward outlined below echoes the work of Farvacque and McAuslan, who crisply asked the following questions of policy makers reviewing land use regulations in 1992:

- What purpose(s) do the existing regulations serve?
- How much do they cost?
- How many households cannot afford to pay the cost of meeting these regulations?
- What will happen to these households?
- What would be the impact of not having these regulations (Farvacque and McAuslan 1992: 69)?

Identifying the interests of stakeholders effectively The Seidmans make the important point that 'behaviour in the face of the rule of law, like all behaviour, invariably has complex, multiple causes' (Seidman and Seidman 1996: 26). The behaviour to be shaped and regulated by planning law is extremely complex and never static, as it adapts constantly and often rapidly to changing conditions. As the 2010 State of World's Cities report *Bridging the Urban Divide* concludes: 'Two cross-cutting factors implicit in ... much of this Report are political will and human agency' (UN-Habitat 2010: 165). These factors are both ultimately the expression of the interests and concerns of stakeholders. They represent the non-negotiable determinants of what is and what is not possible in the implementation of legislation. If they are not understood in the making of a law, then that law has little prospect of achieving its objectives. In the context of rapidly growing, weakly managed towns and cities operating in often volatile political circumstances, understanding these interests and concerns – and the conflicts between those of the different stakeholders – is inherently difficult. Notwithstanding the difficulty, a failure to reach this understanding will result in an inappropriate legal and regulatory outcome.

At least the following groups' interests and concerns have to be well understood:

- Politicians: The excuse for failed policies that political will is lacking is not convincing. Political will is neither mysterious nor unfathomable.

Understanding the particular forces that impel politicians in a particular context is the first step towards legislation that is likely to win political support.

- Officials: In practical terms, the people with the most personal investment in the planning system are the officials. In most countries there is a strong correlation between the officials responsible for the planning system and the planning profession. It is essential to appreciate and understand their interests in, on the one hand, securing and protecting a set of rules with which they are not only familiar but also in which they have unsurpassed expertise and, on the other, in driving through selective changes that will enhance their decision-making powers vis-à-vis politicians.
- Investors and developers: The interests of these participants in the urban development sector are often the easiest to anticipate from the outset but are paradoxically the most difficult to elicit in practice. While in theory they have the most to gain from an effective urban planning system, in reality they are in general the most reluctant to commit resources to a process of change. They are, it seems, most comfortable with the status quo – a system that is known – despite always being ready with a trenchant critique of that system when the opportunity demands it.
- Citizens: It is a fundamental principle of good law making that citizens should participate in the process. In a typical African city the two key citizen groupings are civil society bodies representing the urban poor and associations of the urban elites. In practice, notable by their relative absence are the civil society bodies and groups that in another context might be expected to play a central role. Individual poor citizens or households never have the time or the willingness to participate. These organisations are either too weak or too few to participate meaningfully or, where they exist, are too stretched by existing programmes to commit resources to participate in law reform processes. With the emergence of new, globally and regionally linked movements such as Shack/Slum Dwellers International, it is hoped that this situation will improve, allowing for an essential voice to be heard.[8] On the other hand, the interests of elite groups are no less opportunistic than those of any other grouping. They tend to support the maintenance of planning standards that contribute to keeping intact the barriers to entry, especially to elite neighbourhoods, while resisting fiercely measures that might allow for land uses that threaten the market values of their properties. Their preferred tactic is to remain aloof from any planning law reform, confident that a weak process will best maintain the status quo.

Principles of good regulation Although writers such as the Seidmans, McAuslan and others mention many principles of good regulation, the United Kingdom's Better Regulation Task Force[9] codified a set of widely applicable principles that provide a useful starting point. These principles are used not because they are intrinsically better or more appropriate than any others, but to illustrate the ways in which methods used in developed countries are capable of being reinterpreted in the context of a developing country.[10] These principles are set out below:

- Proportionality: Regulators should only intervene when necessary. Remedies should be appropriate to the risk posed and the costs identified and minimised.
- Accountability: Regulators must be able to justify decisions and be subject to public scrutiny.
- Consistency: Government rules and standards must be joined up and implemented fairly.
- Transparency: Regulators should be open and keep regulations simple and user-friendly.
- Targeting: Regulations should be focused on the problem and minimise side effects.

Each of these principles is examined in detail elsewhere (Berrisford 2011). However, any consideration of a set of principles such as these has to bear in mind the limitations in transferring a model method, which can be just as hazardous as transferring a model law. Minogue and Cariño deal with this issue extensively:

The conditions in which the 'best practice' model of regulation is located include:

- a stable macroeconomic environment, to reduce uncertainty in economic decision-making;
- a redistributive tax base, to fund strong social protection arrangements through a well-developed social security system;
- a rules-based system supported by an effective legal infrastructure and the rule of law;
- a transparent and accountable public policy process;
- a clear separation of administrative and political roles within a democratic constitutional framework;
- appropriate financial and human resources to ensure that regulatory agencies can work effectively. (Minogue and Cariño 2006: 74)

Development agencies are still inclined to proffer models based on conditions and practices such as these in high-income economics and then become frustrated when such models do not seem to work elsewhere, or receive little more than diplomatic lip service. There is a reality gap here between donor ideas of best practice, and the actual legal, administrative, political and economic processes that exist in low- and middle-income countries.

Designing the law reform process From the above, it is clear that planning law reform is important in Africa. It is also very hard to do. Crafting a planning law is effectively the act of designing a planning system through the back door. This is not a straightforward task. It is particularly difficult where government officials see planning law as a source of direct power and influence, wealthy individuals and investors see it merely as red tape to be evaded by fair means or foul, and the poor see no benefit in any compliance with it and fear its enforcement.

Deep attitudinal shifts are required if a new model is to arise. These shifts cannot be prescribed. They have to emerge, they have to be grounded in the different logics and interests of the various stakeholders and they will not all happen simultaneously. It is salutary to look at the example of the Brazilian City Statute; this emerged after more than 30 years of efforts by different stakeholders with widely divergent interests, the process was interrupted by dramatic political events such as the military regime, the result was made possible by a particular political moment, and the final product is still re-garded as being inadequate in certain respects (Cities Alliance 2010). From the experience of Brazil we can see that the outcome generally preferred in Africa – a wholesale rewriting of complex legislation and its recodification into something new and better – is not realistic. Perhaps it is not desirable either. The enormity of the challenge does not necessarily call for bigger budgets for legal consultants or more in-house government lawyers. However, it does call for a more measured approach, where the different interests of stakeholders are weighed up appropriately and where the implementation opportunities and costs are assessed carefully. It requires a sober assessment of the realities of the regulatory context, both present and future, remembering that:

> poverty, corruption and bureaucratic pathologies are the products rather than
> the causes of underdevelopment ... and ... that local political cultures will
> shape and mediate externally derived economic and managerial reforms, rather
> than being transformed by them. (Minogue and Cariño 2006: 78)

Much of the writing on the need for legislative change is premised on an assumption – primarily on the part of donors and their consultants – that new planning laws will reflect an entirely new understanding of cities, of poverty and of planning. In reality, such a law would be out of step with profes-sional practice (in both the planning and the legal professions) and with the personal and economic interests of most of the personnel responsible for its implementation, as well as with the financial and human resources available for that implementation. The International Finance Corporation's work on regulatory reform confirms this when it argues that it is unhelpful to believe that 'complex systems are self-correcting and that only by changing the rules inside the system can the behaviour be changed' (IFC 2010a: 38).

Obviously there is a risk of overgeneralisation given the wide range of different contexts in African countries, but nevertheless there is an inescapable and significant chance that most work on reforming planning laws is ultimately going to be irrelevant. That does not mean that the need for that change is negligible – it has never been stronger – but it does mean that new methods are needed to determine which and how much of existing laws should be changed, as well as the ways in which law reform processes are designed. Some examples of what could be done differently are described elsewhere (Berrisford 2011), but all of them point to the need to build, carefully and practically, a new set of methods and techniques for urban planning law reform.

Conclusion

It is too easy for researchers, officials and citizens to conclude that better legislation, or even better implementation of legislation, will solve the African urban crisis. Law, in many ways, is part of the problem, dividing the lives and livelihoods of rich and poor and strengthening the power and interests of unaccountable groupings. Many of the legislative prescripts advocated for African cities are likely to perpetuate these dimensions of the problem, especially in relation to urban planning law and access to urban land for use and development.

Urban legal reform has to emerge from an understanding of the role of law in perpetuating unequal access to urban resources and in weakening the prospects of the poor and marginalised. It is precisely because of planning law's position at the bedrock of urban division and injustice that efforts to change that law are invariably thwarted by vested interests, with the blame conveniently allocated to the state, characterised as incapable of leading what should be a straightforward law-making process.

This is no reason to step back in despair from urban legal reform. But it is a reason to be more circumspect and, in most cases, to stand back from attempts to reform comprehensively the entire urban legal order in one blow. Legal reform has to focus on those areas of change that will strengthen the bargaining positions of the poor in the urban land markets and will curb the excesses of large-scale land developments in relation to their impact on the livelihoods and environmental conditions of ordinary citizens. Similarly, reforms that lower the barriers to entry to the market and that enhance rather than constrain the supply of opportunities to use and develop land should be supported. Legal reform can play a constructive role in addressing the African urban crisis only where it is grounded in an understanding of the interests, competing and complementary, of the different groups and sectors in the urban management system as well as of the different groupings within a rapidly changing and growing urban citizenry.

Acknowledgements

I am grateful to Susan Parnell for helpful and thoughtful comments on an earlier draft.

Notes

1 This chapter uses the term 'African' broadly. However, it refers primarily to the regions of the continent where I work: southern and eastern Africa, and mainly the Anglophone countries in that region.

2 The term 'planning law' here refers to the body of laws (national statutes, ministerial proclamations, state/provincial laws and local by-laws or regulations) that govern both the making of spatial plans – at a city, town, village or district level – and the regulation of land use and land development.

3 See, for example, Ocheje 2007.

4 These rules vary from country to country but there are many similarities. One example is the UK's five 'Principles of Good Regulation'.

5 This chapter emerged while on a sabbatical from my usual occupation as an independent consultant working in South, southern and eastern Africa on the revision of planning laws and policies. This chapter draws heavily on an article published after that sabbatical (Berrisford 2011).

6 Key Issue 5 raised at the 2012 World Urban Forum was that '[l]egal and regulatory frameworks aimed at giving access to land for the urban poor should be based on clear understanding of how urban land markets work' (UN-Habitat 2012b).

7 Examples include Addis Ababa, Harare, Lusaka and Cape Town. See also UN-Habitat (2008: 156).

8 McGranahan et al. (2009) provide an indication of how these organisations are increasingly able to play a constructive role in policy development.

9 This was an advisory body originally linked to the UK Cabinet Office. The function has since been shifted within the UK government structure.

10 For another perspective, see IFC (2010b: 30), which cites the 'principles of good regulation' set out in the Organisation for Economic Co-operation and Development's (OECD's) 1997 *Report to Ministers on Regulatory Reform* as follows: 'Good regulations should: (i) be needed to serve clearly identified policy goals and effective in achieving those goals; (ii) have a sound legal basis; (iii) produce benefits that justify costs considering the distribution of effects across society; (iv) minimize costs and market distortions; (v) promote innovation through market incentives and goal-based approaches; (vi) be clear, simple and practical for users; (vii) be consistent with other regulations and policies; and (viii) be compatible as far as possible with competition, trade and investment-facilitating principles at domestic and international levels.'

References

African Development Bank (2011) *Urban Development Strategy*. Tunis: African Development Bank.

Berrisford, S. (2011) 'Why it is difficult to change urban planning laws in African countries'. *Urban Forum* 22(3): 209–28.

— and M. Kihato (2006) 'The role of planning law in evictions in sub-Saharan Africa'. *South African Review of Sociology* 37(1): 20–34.

Cities Alliance (2010) *The City Statute of Brazil: A commentary*. São Paulo: Cities Alliance.

Du Plessis, J. (2005) 'The growing problem of forced evictions and the crucial importance of community-based, locally appropriate alternatives'. *Environment and Urbanization* 17(1): 123–34.

Farvacque, C. and P. McAuslan (1992) *Reforming Urban Land Policies and Institutions in Developing Countries*. Washington, DC: Urban Management Program.

IFC (2010a) *Regulatory Governance in Developing Countries*. Washington, DC: International Finance Corporation (IFC), World Bank.

— (2010b) *Regulatory Capacity Review of Zambia*. Washington, DC: International

Finance Corporation (IFC), World Bank.

Lall, S. V., M. Freire, B. Yuen, R. Rajack and J.-J. Helluin (2009) *Urban Land Markets: Improving land management for successful urbanization*. New York, NY: Springer.

McAuslan, P. (2003) *Bringing the Law Back In: Essays in law and development*. Aldershot: Ashgate Publishing.

McGranahan, G., D. Mitlin, D. Satter-thwaite, C. Tacoli and I. Turok (2009) *Africa's Urban Transition and the Role of Regional Collaboration*. Human Settle-ments Working Paper Series. Theme: Urban Change No. 5. London: Inter-national Institute for Environment and Development.

Minogue, M. and L. Cariño (eds) (2006) *Regulatory Governance in Developing Countries*. Cheltenham: Edward Elgar.

Ocheje, P. D. (2007) 'In the public inter-est: forced evictions, land rights and human development in Africa'. *Journal of African Law* 51(2): 173–214.

Seidman, A. and R. B. Seidman (1996) 'Drafting legislation for development: lessons from a Chinese project'. *American Journal of Comparative Law* 44(1): 1–44.

Sugrayes, A. and C. Mathivet (2010) *Cit-ies for All: Proposals and experiences towards the right to the city*. Santiago: Habitat International Coalition.

UN-Habitat (2005) *Report of the Fact-finding Mission to Zimbabwe to Assess the Scope and Impact of Operation Murambatsvina by the UN Special Envoy on Human Settlements Issues in Zimbabwe Mrs Anna Kajumulo Tibaijuka*. Nairobi: United Nations Human Settlements Programme (UN-Habitat).

— (2008) *The State of African Cities 2008: A framework for addressing urban chal-lenges in Africa*. Nairobi: United Nations Human Settlements Programme (UN-Habitat).

— (2009) *Global Report on Human Settlements: Planning sustainable cities*. Nairobi: United Nations Human Settle-ments Programme (UN-Habitat).

— (2010) *State of the World's Cities 2010/11: Bridging the urban divide*. Nairobi: United Nations Human Settlements Programme (UN-Habitat).

— (2012a) *State of the World's Cities 2012/2013: Prosperity of cities*. Nairobi: United Nations Human Settlements Programme (UN-Habitat).

— (2012b) 'Summary of key messages from the sixth session of the World Urban Forum held in Naples, Italy, from 1–7 September 2012'. Statement issued by the Advisory Group for the Sixth World Urban Forum, 6 Septem-ber 2012.

World Bank (2009) *Systems of Cities: Harnessing urbanization for growth and poverty alleviation*. Washington, DC: World Bank.

10 | The education and research imperatives of urban planning professionals in Africa

James Duminy, Nancy Odendaal and Vanessa Watson

Introduction

The pace with which the African urban revolution is unfolding and its consequences are difficult to pinpoint and predict. Many megacities, secondary cities and towns will grow rapidly for the foreseeable future, although in other places urbanisation levels will be more stable, perhaps even subsiding as patterns of circular migration between urban and rural areas change and intensify (see Potts 2012). This spatially and temporally uneven process of urban transformation presents an immense set of acute challenges to urban practitioners of all sorts. A glimpse at the policy landscape reveals that planning is increasingly recognised as a way of contributing to sustainable urban development (see UN-Habitat 2009). As such, the current juncture is a key moment or leverage point to reform planning education in order to make it more relevant and effective in producing professionals to manage Africa's many diverse and fluid urban transformations, within a proactive equity agenda. This is the understanding and optimism that drives the vision and project work of the Association of African Planning Schools (AAPS), a 50-member peer-to-peer network of mostly Anglophone sub-Saharan African universities that teach urban and regional planning.

The purpose of this chapter is to discuss a set of imperatives that face urban planning professionals on the continent, particularly from a research and educational perspective. For the purposes of setting up our argument, we start with a basic hypothesis: that is, urban planning in Anglophone sub-Saharan Africa has been relatively ineffective in delivering sustainable and equitable urban development (Watson 2009a). We propose that several imperatives need to be addressed before planning practice can be made more relevant and effective. These relate to the need for different types of data, skills and ethical subjectivities to guide and assist practice. Specifically, we argue that contemporary African planners require:

- more and better data and knowledge to assist planning practice and policy development;
- planners who are innovative problem-solvers, capable of collaborating with

many different actors involved in the development process (including local affected communities);

- planners with an explicit and progressive value base (an advocacy or activist agenda); and
- teaching methods that promote the development of these skills and ethical positions through experiential learning.

The first section of the chapter therefore seeks to explain why these imperatives exist and why they need to be addressed, mentioning various issues relating to urban planning governance systems, as well as more subjective factors – including the ethics, ideologies and power relations that characterise many (but not all) of the actions and sensibilities of planning professionals in Africa. We argue that the promotion of case study research, and teaching methods drawing on case study approaches, is one way of addressing these imperatives. The second section of the chapter considers the contribution that the case study research methodology can make to planning education and practice, and its potential to foster a professional planning sensibility that is attuned to local needs and issues while retaining a critical reflexivity informed by progressive values. We hold that the case study research methodology, as a broad set of ideas, theories and methods, offers benefits on at least two levels. The first concerns the *type of knowledge* produced by case study research and its relationship to questions of learning and praxis. Case study research generates the concrete, contextual data that are necessary for enhanced social practice, by fostering a nuanced understanding of why certain phenomena exist and 'how it came to be that way'. This sort of knowledge is well suited to feed back into education and teaching courses, where it can be used to develop skills in problem analysis and creative solution making. The second set of benefits concerns the *process* of doing case study research, specifically that which encourages the researcher to engage with many different actors, especially local communities and members of the urban poor. We further highlight the effects that this process of discovery may have on the values and attitudes of the learner. The discussion reflects on these issues in relation to the actions and experiences of AAPS, which included operating a case study research and documentation project from 2009 to 2011.

The state of planning systems in Africa

The reasons for the fact that planning has been relatively ineffective in confronting the challenges of urban transformation are complex, and the blame cannot be laid squarely with planning itself (ibid.). Nevertheless, it is worthwhile providing some indication of how the actions of urban planning professionals working in Anglophone sub-Saharan Africa are often circumscribed by outdated institutional systems, policy and data gaps, and severe capacity deficiencies. Planning in many African urban contexts operates within legislative systems that have been inherited from earlier colonial governments (see Chapter 9). Colonial-era planning law has proved to be particularly resilient and difficult to change in many African countries, a topic that was the subject of a recent special issue of the journal *Urban Forum* (see Watson 2011). Where legislative reforms have been undertaken, changing the attitudes and practices of government officials has proven difficult, as was recently the case in Zambia (Berrisford 2011). Despite profound changes in the rate, scale and nature of urbanisation on the continent, inherited planning systems and approaches have largely remained unchanged, often adhering to a highly technocratic and bureaucratic mode of operation.

The persistence of master planning and other highly inflexible, top-down planning approaches is merely one aspect of this institutional inertia, which has proven largely incapable of dealing with the pace, mobility and fluidity of the urbanisation that affects many parts of Africa. That being said, there have been recent attempts to engage with more strategic and inclusive models of planning decision making, where planning is often seen as a useful tool in the integration of public sector functions. The experiment with integrated development planning in South Africa and the adoption of similar approaches in Tanzania and Zambia are examples of this (ibid.). The United Nations (UN) Urban Management Programme is another such initiative. A collaborative effort between UN-Habitat, the United Nations Development Programme (UNDP) and the World Bank, it largely followed a strategic planning approach, encouraging participatory decision-making approaches while insisting that local governments link their policies to implementation through budgets and action plans. Although the programme has been largely successful in renewing forward planning processes in the participating cities, it has attracted critique from various quarters for failing to impact positively on urbanisation processes, and for failing to change the ways in which many local governments 'do business' (Watson 2009b). In the Tanzanian cities involved in the project, reforms largely ignored the regulatory land use management tools that are key to implementation. In effect, two parallel systems came into being, with the real power remaining in the hands of those administering the zoning system (ibid.).

The lack of success attending planning reform programmes such as the Urban Management Programme is related to a host of structural political and economic factors and other obstacles, which have undermined local state capacity to conduct accountable participatory planning and to finance and regulate the implementation of urban development plans (ibid.). A particularly insurmountable set of obstacles relates to the lack of political will among African leaders to deal with urbanisation in a concerted manner. Edgar Pieterse suggests that 'the dominant policy response to the deepening crisis associated with [African] urban growth and expansion is inertia' (Pieterse 2010a: 8). This is fostered by a 'widespread denial' of the realities of urbanisation among African political leaders, if not an outright anti-urban stance, creating a 'policy vacuum' that leads to unmanaged urban processes. The economic and environmental crises affecting African cities have thus been matched by a 'political and policy crisis' (ibid.: 8). One aspect of this policy inertia has been the general absence of coordinated urban policy positions at the national level, and central government strategic guidance and support for local planning initiatives have often been lacking (Parnell and Simon 2010). Civil society has largely been unable to provide coherent challenges to this inertia, as, in many cases, it remains fractured along ethnic and religious lines (see Gandy 2006 for a discussion of the case of Lagos).

One of the major structural impediments to the development of effective planning systems relates to a general lack of data on the rate, scale and trajectories of African urbanisation. In most cases, such data simply do not exist, or national survey instruments are not calibrated to provide useful in-depth information on complex urban changes (Pieterse 2010a). This has effectively meant that many assumptions about African urbanisation (i.e. that it is a ubiquitously rapid process, driven by permanent population migrations from rural areas to large urban centres) have gone unchallenged for decades (Potts 2012). Where censuses have been carried out by African nations, political interference and difficulties pertaining to the precise definition of 'the urban' have meant that, to a large extent, these data are not reliable. In any case, they offer us very little in providing 'a rounded conceptualisation of cityness' that is essential to developing a 'fully fledged conception of African urbanisms' (Pieterse 2010b: 209).

So, despite the fact that recent policy documents such as UN-Habitat's 2009 *Global Report on Human Settlements* highlight the crucial role that planning should play in managing a sustainable form of urbanisation, clearly practice and implementation have often been constrained by structural and institutional factors. Even if steps have been made towards developing appropriate policies and plans for urbanisation, local state capacity is often so lacking, crippled by human and financial resource deficiencies, that implementation has proven extremely difficult and vulnerable to takeover by power interest groups. Aside from these structural constraints, from an educational perspective it is imperative that we ask questions about the concurrent state of professional planning practice, in terms of the ideologies, skills and ethics that planners carry and express in their work. Therefore, the following section turns to the available literature from Africa that focuses on planning practice, highlighting aspects of poor or unethical methods that can potentially be addressed through education processes and a renewed agenda for planning research.

The state of professional planning in Africa

When making statements about the state of the urban planning profession in Africa, the concession has to be made that it is difficult to generalise across a highly diverse continent affected by a range of colonial histories and post-independence trajectories. In Africa, 'planning' refers to a wide range of activities, and people who call themselves 'planners' possess very different educational backgrounds, professional ideologies, cultural affinities, types and refinements of skills, and so on. Our concern here is not to unnecessarily misrepresent and critique the (often extremely good) work of our colleagues. Instead, we hold that educational procedures could take greater steps to promote a critical and reflective capacity on the part of graduates; a willingness to engage with localised initiatives and livelihood strategies, and to incorporate and accommodate these in official planning in a way that can promote principles of spatial and social justice. In this section we wish to address the lingering view and function of planning as a technical, bureaucratic and ultimately value-neutral practice, obsessed with control and the biased enforcement of petty regulations. Some evidence of the problems associated with this perception can be found in published examples of research conducted into planning practice in Africa.

Fred Lerise's (2005) in-depth case study of land use planning in a Tanzanian village is a good place to start. By following the actors and actions involved in the process of land and water management in post-independence Chekereni, on the slopes of Mount Kilimanjaro, Lerise reveals that the mismatch between plan objectives and outcomes was largely due to the persistence of 'centralized top-down land-use planning' as the main mode of decision making, driven by persistent beliefs that the state 'is the only agent that can bring modernization and development' and that 'is able to define public interests and pursue them for the benefit of all'. Lerise argues that 'these notions crumble in the face of the Chekereni evidence' (ibid.: 165). Only some groups benefited from the planning process, particularly 'the leaders or experts' and a 'few powerful individuals whose interests were primarily served by the state'. Indeed, 'often experts and decision-makers used plans to legitimize their decisions and interests in land and the determination of access to water-use rights' (ibid.: 167). Lerise uses these experiences to argue for a more participatory planning practice, one no longer perceived as a 'technical activity ... confined to the state and its experts' but rather as an inherently complex political activity involving bargaining, conflicting interests and power games (ibid.: 167).

Another Tanzanian example is the work of Tumsifu Jonas Nnkya (2008). It is worth quoting the general conclusions of his study of urban planning in Moshi at some length:

[T]he unmanaged urban spatial change which characterizes urban places in [Tanzania] is a result of undemocratic planning practice; disregard of residents' rights; inability of the planners to recognize and make use of opportunities for shaping the built environment; lack of motivation and/or capacity, and subsequently lack of skills for inclusive planning. The unmanaged urban change is also a consequence of technocratic, unlawful, and corrupt practices characterized by lack of transparency and accountability in the planning system, so that sometimes the system is misused and abused to justify [the] self-interest of a few more powerful, influential, and well-to-do individuals, at the expense of the society at large. The poor are particularly affected because they are either unaware of their rights or they are aware but unorganized and lack economic capacity to pursue such rights in the appropriate political–administrative and legal organs of the state. Even when the poor can do so, power is sometimes used to suppress their voices, delivery of justice is delayed, the consequence being despair and hopelessness, increased poverty, loss of confidence and trust in the government. (ibid.: 9)

On a positive note, he also points out that 'the courage to organize and confidence to speak the truth to power' have led some Tanzanian planners to engage in more 'inclusive and collaborative' modes of practice, which respect the rights and interests of the urban poor (ibid.: 9). Nevertheless, the quote above paints a bleak picture of the state of the planning profession, which is certainly not unique to the Tanzanian context.

Another, possibly more damning, reference point for the state of planning practice in Africa is presented by the work of Amin Kamete, who takes a Foucauldian perspective in examining issues of power and governmentality in African planning. His research on the role of planners in the devastating 2005 Zimbabwean urban 'clean-up', Operation Murambatsvina (or Operation Restore Order), reveals that the planning system was intimately enrolled in the 'techno-legal articulation', de-politicisation and legitimation of the operation (Kamete 2007), concluding that planners have a lot to answer for as the 'handmaiden of state repression' (Kamete 2009). Writing of the state of public planning in parts of southern Africa, he notes:

> Legitimized and empowered by the state, qualified planners believe they have the capacity to decide for others. This capacity is legitimized by reference to the possession of essential specialist skills based on acquired technical and scientific knowledge. (Kamete 2007: 156)

The dominance of instrumental rationality within planning, and a professional self-image legitimated by the possession of technical expertise, can lead to pernicious results for the urban poor. Kamete and Lindell (2010) speak of 'nonplanning' interventions that masquerade as sanitising practices in Zimbabwe and Mozambique. In the process, informal housing and economic activities are deemed nuisances to be relocated away from prime urban areas. Marginalised residents living in areas with a high proportion of illegal land use activities suffer the brunt of sovereign and disciplinary forms of power, often involving the use of outright state-sanctioned violence, while 'gentler, less explicitly directive, pastoral controls' are reserved for the wealthy and powerful (Kamete 2012).

So we have a prevailing image of planning as a disengaged, technical and apolitical process, serving elite interests under the neutral guise of technical arguments and scientific truth claims, with planners assigned varying degrees of guilt and complicity. However, the academic work of planners and their association with technocratic officialdom, if not outright repression of the poor, only begin to represent the clichéd image of the paper-pushing planner, obsessed with procedures, and relatively immune to the creativity and moral character of the urban poor. On a recent field trip to a fishing community in the Makoko area of Lagos, in which two of the chapter's authors were involved, a state planning official alerted the attendants (all African planning academics) to what might be seen in the field later that day, and in doing so hinted at a personal justification for 'doing what he does'. Speaking of Makoko's local residents, he explained:

> They don't value possessions; they don't value motorcycles ... they don't value their lives. Are you with me? And you see people parking on the streets, hooking on the streets, doing every ... playing draughts, recreating ... playing draughts on the streets. Doing everything they like on the streets. And when you just press your horn, they just look at you and say, 'what is happening?' ... So they don't value their lives ... Ah, but there is a need to have to take care of them, because, uh ... they are frustrated somehow.[1]

Bearing in mind these realities, which are counterbalanced in many contexts by the highly talented, creative and progressive advocacy planners and planning educators who give the profession some semblance of a positive identity, numerous challenges face the planning profession as its members attempt to become more effective facilitators and servants of the public interest within urban development processes. It may well be too late to ever convince practitioners such as the Lagosian state planner quoted here of the benefits of close engagement with local communities and means of livelihood as a way of delivering more sustainable urban outcomes. However, planning education is a key leverage point for shifting the professional attitudes and skill sets of future urban planners towards a more engaged, value-based mode of practice. The following section therefore discusses several key imperatives of planning professionalism that can be addressed through educational reform and teaching.

The imperatives of planning practice in Africa

The previous two sections outlined several factors that have constrained the efficacy of urban planning interventions in Africa, related both to structural and institutional limitations, and to the current state of professional ideologies. This section channels these constraints and issues into three basic imperatives that need to be addressed in order to make planning practice more effective. These imperatives relate primarily to the need for data, skills and ethical subjectivities among planning graduates.

Imperative 1: Produce more and better data to assist planning practice Previously this chapter highlighted the extreme difficulty urban planning researchers face in accessing reliable data with which to develop theory or guide decision making. Where censuses have been conducted and results are accessible to researchers without political interference, these data are largely insufficient in terms of providing a complete picture of the ephemeral dynamics of urban life on the continent. As a result, authors have issued repeated calls for African urban scholarship to engage with the rationalities that frame the decisions and actions of urban residents (Mbembe and Nuttall 2004; Simone 2004; Pieterse 2008). The quest to 'understand and appreciate the terms on which they seek to make viable lives for themselves' is increasingly seen as a prerequisite for developing more effective ways of conceptualising and responding to African urban dynamics (Beall et al. 2010: 198). Therefore, in the African context, planners and decision makers urgently need accurate and regular data, ranging from quantitative data on the systemic trends pertaining to urbanisation to detailed substantive knowledge about how people live and survive in the city, and how formal and extra-formal systems of settlement, land management, economic production and service provision relate to and produce one another. It follows that a robust methodological frame is required to allow for various types of data to be analysed and discussed in a complementary manner.

Imperative 2: Develop better professional skills and competencies Recent debates within planning theory have emphasised the changing roles fulfilled by professional planners in the workplace, and hence the need to redesign curricula to promote the development of certain graduate skills (see, for example, Sandercock 1999; Ozawa and Seltzer 1999). We emphasise the fact that, in addition to imparting extremely competent skills in technical design and an acute critical knowledge of how legislative and institutional systems function and change, educational approaches need to produce planners who are innovative problem solvers, capable of collaborating with many different actors involved in the development process, including local affected communities. Planners therefore require skills in fostering public participation, conflict resolution, information management and communication, in addition to a critical awareness of how power is expressed through planning procedures and the production of knowledge. A crucial aspect of this enhanced problem-solving potential is the analytical capacity to articulate everyday urban practices with longer-term system dynamics that affect the development of cities. Furthermore, and importantly in the context of Africa and other parts of the global South, these general competencies must be complemented by an enhanced capacity to plan within environments characterised by severe poverty, social conflict and violence.

Imperative 3: Produce planners with reflexive and progressive values Although it is widely recognised that 'fundamental ethical dilemmas underpin both planning practice and theory' (Campbell and Marshall 1999), there have been relatively few discussions surrounding the ethics of planning as represented and encouraged by education. Sandercock (1999) has previously argued that educational programmes should be devised to reflect planning as an exercise in ethical inquiry and judgement. Watson (2006: 46) implies that the realities of 'deepening difference' and 'the aggressive promotion of neoliberal values' within many southern urban contexts require the encouragement of values that are primarily concerned with the equitable outcomes of planning rather than with the process. The basic point of much of this work is that effective planning needs an explicit value base – but one that is not necessarily rooted in 'a universal set of deontological values, shaped by the liberal tradition' (ibid.: 46).

In his study of planning in Tanzania, Fred Lerise (2005) draws on the work of Patsy Healey to argue in favour of a 'reflexive and critical capacity' or 'moral consciousness' that may counteract the dominance of 'individual experts' private interests in decision-making debates'. However, we argue that planning ethics have to go beyond this sort of reflexive attitude, especially in the African context. Here, planning ethics need to engage with an overtly activist and advocacy agenda, explicitly located within a rights-based understanding of urban sustainability (Parnell et al. 2009) that sees planning as worthwhile only if it seeks out and serves the voice of the poor in the face of power, securing their 'right to the city' and delivering improved outcomes for their lives and general prosperity. We argue the need for planners with both a critical openness to 'the way things are' and a creative anticipation in speculating on 'how things could be'.

The three points outlined above are by no means an exhaustive list of the challenges and imperatives facing African planners; rather, they serve as the basis for developing an argument in favour of alternative approaches to research and education. Indeed, one way of delivering on these imperatives more or less simultaneously is through the promotion of case study research and case study-based teaching methods.

The case study methodology in research and education

Developing knowledge that can make planning practice and education more relevant to African contexts is a major challenge facing researchers and educators on the continent. The issue of producing knowledge attuned to the particularities of African urbanisation is also embroiled within the wider dilemma of how to conduct research that links the descriptive, analytical or explanatory question of 'what is' to the prescriptive or normative question of 'what ought to be' (Campbell 2012). Recently, the case study research methodology has attracted favourable attention as a means of producing 'nuanced' analyses of urban processes, and of generating knowledge that has greater relevance to planning practice. This section discusses some of these beneficial aspects, which in 2009 led AAPS to devise and operate a two-year project to revitalise planning research and education in Africa through case study research and teaching. The project took as its starting point the idea that case study methodology potentially enables urban practitioners to understand and intervene in the complexities of African urbanisms in a more effective manner.

Of all the proponents of case study research in the social sciences, Bent Flyvbjerg (2001; 2006; 2011) has developed the most sophisticated argument as to why the case study is suited to the broad intellectual domain of planning. He sees case study research as a way of driving a reorientation of planning research towards a pragmatic, rather than normative or utopian, position and as a way of challenging the 'rationalist' approaches underpinning most dominant schools of planning thought. His argument for a 'phronetic planning research' agenda is, therefore, an argument for a disciplinary refocus on issues of practical judgement, on the values that drive practice, and especially on issues of power (Flyvbjerg 2004).

A classic case study pays close attention to reality and focuses on the details of events as they actually happened. The real value of the case study is its capacity to show what has happened in a given setting, and how. Given this close attention to empirical detail and process, case study research is eminently suited to the analysis of the complex causality, material and power relations, ethics and judgements that give rise to real-world planning outcomes. From the perspective of learning, the good case study enables 'the development of a nuanced view of reality', and produces the concrete, context-dependent knowledge and experience that lie 'at the very heart of expert activity' (Flyvbjerg 2011: 303).

Flyvbjerg and other advocates resist the common tendency to associate the case study approach with qualitative data analysis exclusively, and instead hold that the case study research methodology (understood as a broad set of methods and principles) is robust and flexible enough to accommodate a variety of analytical approaches and data types within a single research frame or inquiry. These approaches may include more localised and qualitative approaches (for example, ethnographic and local historical analysis) alongside quantitative data analysis, as well as institutional systems and network analysis. Case study research can therefore be an important means of interdisciplinary engagement and analytical innovation, offering a methodological space in which medium and long-term structural dynamics may be understood and contextualised within the specifics of a local site or event. This close attention to context allows insights to be gained into the broad variety of the continent's urban spaces and livelihoods, while keeping in check the tendency to recite uncritical generalisations about the continent, often stemming from long-held disciplinary mantras.

These convictions led AAPS to embark on a project aimed at advancing the use of the case study methodology in teaching and research. Funded by the Rockefeller Foundation and starting in 2009, the project had a number of objectives, fitting within the Association's wider agenda around promoting relevant and contextualised curricular reform within African planning schools. The first main objective was to enhance the research skills and methodological knowledge of planning academics through the organisation of three case study research workshops, facilitated by experienced case study researchers (see Odendaal 2012). The second objective was to promote the production and distribution of published research on urban planning in Africa.

As a network of educational institutions, AAPS built on the argument that the analysis of a well-documented, strategically selected case study, and the experiential learning obtained from this immersion, can be used as a powerful teaching aid (Barnes et al. 1987). There was thus a pedagogical motivation. In terms of a research agenda, telling the 'story behind the statistics' through case studies, and in the process gaining insights into the rapid manifestation of global trends on a local scale, were seen as worthy inputs into the ongoing research inquiry surrounding African and southern urbanisms. There was also a transformative agenda in the selection of the case study method: a well-constructed narrative from case study documentation has the potential to challenge assumptions and preconceived notions of events and trends in the public sphere (see Flyvbjerg 2001). Considering the continued anti-urban and anti-poor bias shown by many African national and local governments, the case study was therefore seen as a way of generating specific knowledge to inspire legislative change (see Watson 2011).

At the three case study workshops, each organised in a different region of sub-Saharan Africa, participants produced an impressive array of case study work. Many of these studies focused on informal modes of economic activity, revealing processes of exclusion and resistance, and the subtle ways in which informal operators engage flexibly and strategically with government and civil society actors.

In general, workshop participants were accustomed to producing empirical (usually quantitative survey-based) urban research in the synchronic style of a report, where discussion is divided into sections presenting context, findings, conclusions and recommendations. Their involvement in the AAPS case study project required a shift in this approach to gathering and presenting data. This proved difficult to execute for various reasons: personal histories of education and training, questions of familiarity, writing style and language, as well as institutional and economic pressures to do outside work (necessitating a high proportion of consultancy work compared with published academic research). In reality, their experiences tended to lie somewhere between in-depth case study research and case-based empirical work.

Several participants gave presentations on their adoption of a case study approach in teaching. In particular, the 'live case' or 'studio' approach was identified as being a rewarding teaching method; this approach involves students working closely with a real client (often a community) in the field to produce solutions to a particular pre-existing problem. This recognition was due to the studio's potential to change student perspectives on issues such as informality, to foster dynamic and creative responses to real-world urban problems, and to promote collaborative interpersonal skills between planners and local community members. These findings highlight advantages associated less with the type of knowledge produced than with the skills and subjective transformative benefits gained from the actual process of conducting in-depth case study research or learning through a case study approach.

The importance of experiential learning to planning education is well recognised (see Tyson and Low 1987; Kotval 2003). It is seen as a means of enabling self-examination of mindsets and values in relation to real planning problems. By engaging with case study actors and affected local communities in the course of a studio approach, the researcher or student is forced to confront, manage and respond to the intractable ethical dilemmas and 'wicked problems' (Balassiano 2011) that often characterise professional practice. Students learn how to work in and lead groups, to organise and facilitate community meetings, to negotiate tricky politics and conflicting interests, and ultimately to manage extreme uncertainty and complexity in the challenges presented by urban change. Another point relating to experiential learning, which we wish to highlight here, is its capacity to challenge and perhaps destabilise the student's and/or educator's attitudes and thereby have an impact on value constructs. A participant in the AAPS's southern African workshop discussed how her students had retrospectively assessed a project conducted as part of the course on housing, focusing on informal recyclers in the city of Johannesburg. Students were encouraged to engage with recyclers and to find creative ways of recording and presenting their findings using various media. One commented on the course:

> This project constantly raises the question of what determines one's rights to the city. Does someone have to participate in the formal housing and employment market to be able to operate in the city? What determines how one

can use public space? And furthermore what determines 'the public'? ... This project has highlighted that there are a group of people, who are by no means an homogenous group, that are directly contributing to the economic output and the improvement of the city, but they are constantly in a struggle for use of space in the city, both in how they work and where they reside. Surely their operations should not be neglected and ignored?

These are the critical and reflexive questions that future planners should be asking themselves: difficult moral questions concerning notions such as rights, equity and public interest. These sorts of inquiries are associated with affective moments of moral liminality that arise when a severe mismatch of knowledge and reality becomes apparent through one's immersion in the reality of highly complex urban situations and problems. We wish to argue for more fieldwork and engagement in African planning education – for teachers, researchers and students to 'get their shoes dirty' from long, dusty twilight trudges through our many townships and settlements; for them to discover more about the materialities, spaces and narratives of everyday life in urban Africa as a route towards greater efficacy and credibility in practice. As put by Nnkya:

> For planners to justify what taxpayers are spending on them, the materials being used for making plans, they must make an about-turn, stop prescriptions, leave their offices, and go where development is taking place. There they will meet the real world, with real stakeholders and thus real and not imagined interests. Negotiations and agreements should proceed there ... Short of that, planners and planning will increasingly lose credibility, as is the case at the moment, and [be] marginalized at their own expense and that of the environment. (Nnkya 2008: 311)

We ask for planners to 'leave their offices' as part of a concerted effort to shift the image and function of planning – from being a technocratic, value-neutral process of legitimising elite interests to encapsulating a set of principles and practices seeking to promote urban equity and the empowerment of the urban poor within a rights agenda. On the other hand, case study research and teaching are not only about 'navel gazing' questions of moral value, but also concern the production of solutions to seemingly impossible problems – and therefore of creativity and innovation in both analysis and prescription. The capability of the case study research and teaching approach to build a link between questions of 'what is' and 'what ought to be' (Campbell 2012) is not a topic that can be covered in full detail here. It is, however, an issue that relates in part to the virtue of phronesis, the 'art of judgement', and of how we balance instrumental rationality with value rationality (Flyvbjerg 2004: 285). Again, the case study approach is eminently suited to promoting this style of learning, and is thus highly relevant to the African context, where the efficacy and moral character of public planners has, on occasion, been subject to severe public disaffection.

In line with all of these arguments and agendas, since 2011 AAPS has specifically sought to encourage a 'live case' teaching approach among its members. Through a memorandum of understanding signed with Shack/Slum Dwellers International (SDI) in 2010, planning students at various AAPS member schools work with local SDI affiliates and federations to engage with real planning problems in the field, thereby encouraging the co-production of planning analyses and solutions. Further partnerships and engagements are hoped for, through agreements signed with international advocacy organisations such as Women in Informal Employment: Globalizing and Organizing (WIEGO).

A final point concerns the need for educational reform alongside other efforts to promote wider systemic change for planning practice, especially legislative reform (see Chapter 9). It is unlikely that changing modes of planning education will be sufficient to drive a reorientation of planning values and skills by itself. Even graduates from the most progressive of planning schools may still find themselves, as practising professionals, boxed in by entrenched interests and bureaucratic modes of operation that tend to resist changes to the way in which plans are made and implemented. Efforts aimed at reforming planning legislation, practice and education must therefore proceed hand in hand. This recognition has led AAPS to pursue an agenda of changing planning legislation in Africa through the promotion of published research into legislative change, and through an engagement with a variety of influential thinkers and policy actors on the continent. Such international engagements within and beyond educational networks, drawing in and collaborating with professional, advocacy, policy and donor networks, form part of a workable strategy for recasting the urban planner within contemporary processes of urban change.

Conclusion

This chapter has argued that urban planning practitioners and educators in sub-Saharan Africa need to engage with different styles of research and teaching in order to enhance the effectiveness with which planning responds to Africa's urban revolutions. Specifically, it has suggested that planners face imperatives relating to the production of new knowledge that is relevant to their practice, skills and competencies, as well as the values they exemplify in the course of their professional work.

Case study research and teaching was proposed as a key means of directly addressing these three concerns – albeit one that should be supplemented by other forms of research to guide analysis and decision-making practice. As a way of producing data and knowledge on African urbanisation, case study research allows the interweaving of qualitative and quantitative data in order to present nuanced explanations of how planning interventions intersect with everyday urban practices. This sort of detailed, context-dependent knowledge is essential to enable planners to develop phronetic sensibilities of how to interpret and respond to complex urban challenges. Furthermore, the process of conducting case study research, or learning in case study-based teaching fieldwork, can simultaneously promote skills in communication, conflict management and community facilitation, as well as critical reflexive value-based and attitudinal shifts on the part of the researcher.

Finally, these initiatives raise important issues regarding the power of educational networks, such as AAPS, to inspire change. Many of the underlying imperatives facing urban practitioners on the continent remain in place and are difficult to address due to the many political and institutional factors. Closer engagement between the organised profession, civil society groups and the policy environment is therefore necessary in order to realise the values that inform the vision of planning practice outlined in this chapter. Ultimately, the success of AAPS initiatives in tackling the challenges that confront contemporary urban planning will be measured by the capacity of future planners to deliver relevant and sustainable design and policy solutions with equitable development outcomes, within the immense urban transformation that frames our values, limitations and opportunities.

Note

1 Recorded with permission at Makoko, Lagos, 6 December 2011. Authors' notes.

References

Balassiano, K. (2011) 'Tackling "wicked problems" in planning studio courses'. *Journal of Planning Education and Research* 31(4): 449–60.

Barnes, L. B., C. R. Christensen and A. J. Hansen (1987) *Teaching and the Case Method: Text, cases and readings*. 3rd edition. Boston, MA: Harvard Business School Press.

Beall, J., B. Guha-Khasnobis and R. Kanbur (2010) 'Introduction: African development in an urban world: beyond the tipping point'. *Urban Forum* 21(3): 187–204.

Berrisford, S. (2011) 'Revising spatial planning legislation in Zambia: a case study'. *Urban Forum* 22(3): 229–45.

Campbell, H. (2012) 'Planning to change the world: between knowledge and action lies synthesis'. *Journal of Planning Education and Research*. Published online, 7 March. doi: 10.1177/0739456X11436347.

— and R. Marshall (1999) 'Ethical frameworks and planning theory'. *International Journal of Urban and Regional Research* 23(3): 464–78.

Flyvbjerg, B. (2001) *Making Social Science Matter: Why social inquiry fails and how it can succeed again*. Cambridge: Cambridge University Press.

— (2004) 'Phronetic planning research: theoretical and methodological reflections'. *Planning Theory and Research* 5(3): 283–306.

— (2006) 'Five misunderstandings about case-study research'. *Qualitative Inquiry* 12(2): 219–45.

— (2011) 'Case study'. In N. K. Denzin and Y. S. Lincoln (eds) *The Sage Handbook of Qualitative Research*. 4th edition. Thousand Oaks, CA: Sage Publications.

Gandy, M. (2006) 'Planning, anti-planning and the infrastructure crisis facing metropolitan Lagos'. *Urban Studies* 43(2): 371–96.

Kamete, A. Y. (2007) 'Cold-hearted, negligent and spineless? Planning, planners and the (r)ejection of "filth" in urban Zimbabwe'. *International Planning Studies* 12(2): 153–71.

— (2009) 'In the service of tyranny: debating the role of planning in Zimbabwe's urban "clean-up" operation'. *Urban Studies* 46(4): 897–922.

— (2012) 'Interrogating planning's power in an African city: time for reorientation?'. *Planning Theory* 11(1): 66–88.

— and I. Lindell (2010) 'The politics of "non-planning" interventions in African cities: unravelling the international and local dimensions in Harare and Maputo'. *Journal of Southern African Studies* 36(4): 889–912.

Kotval, Z. (2003) 'Teaching experiential learning in the urban planning curriculum'. *Journal of Geography in Higher Education* 27(3): 297–308.

Lerise, F. S. (2005) *Politics in Land and Water Management: Study in Kilimanjaro, Tanzania*. Dar es Salaam: Mkuki na Nyota Publishers.

Mbembe, A. and S. Nuttall (2004) 'Writing the world from an African metropolis'. *Public Culture* 16(3): 347–72.

Nnkya, T. J. (2008) *Why Planning Does Not Work: Land-use planning and residents' rights in Tanzania*. Dar es Salaam: Mkuki na Nyota Publishers.

Odendaal, N. (2012) 'Reality check: planning education in the African urban century'. *Cities* 29(3): 174–82.

Ozawa, C. P. and E. P. Seltzer (1999) 'Taking our bearings: mapping a relationship among planning practice, theory, and education'. *Journal of Planning Education and Research* 18(3): 257–66.

Parnell, S. and D. Simon (2010) 'National urbanisation and urban policies: necessary but absent policy instruments in Africa'. In E. Pieterse and S. Parnell (eds) *Africa's Urban Revolution: Policy pressures*. London: Zed Books.

— E. Pieterse and V. Watson (2009) 'Planning for cities in the global south: an African research agenda for sustainable human settlements'. *Progress in Planning* 72(2): 233–41.

Pieterse, E. (2008) *City Futures: Confronting the crisis of urban development*. London: Zed Books.

— (2010a) 'Filling the void: towards an agenda for action on African urbanization'. In E. Pieterse and S. Parnell (eds) *Africa's Urban Revolution: Policy pressures*. London: Zed Books.

— (2010b) 'Cityness and African urban development'. *Urban Forum* 21(3): 205–19.

Potts, D. (2012) 'Challenging the myths of urban dynamics in sub-Saharan Africa: the evidence from Nigeria'. *World Development* 40(7): 1382–93.

Sandercock, L. (1999) 'Expanding the "language" of planning: a meditation on planning education for the twenty-first century'. *European Planning Studies* 7(5): 533–44.

Simone, A. (2004) *For the City Yet to Come: Changing African life in four cities*. Durham, NC: Duke University Press.

Tyson, B. T. and N. P. Low (1987) 'Experiential learning in planning education'. *Journal of Planning Education and Research* 7(1): 15–27.

UN-Habitat (2009) *Global Report on Human Settlements: Planning sustainable cities*. Nairobi: United Nations Human Settlements Programme (UN-Habitat).

Watson, V. (2006) 'Deep difference: diversity, planning and ethics'. *Planning Theory* 5(1): 31–50.

— (2009a) 'Seeing from the South: refocusing urban planning on the globe's central urban issues'. *Urban Studies* 46(11): 2259–75.

— (2009b) '"The planned city sweeps the poor away …": urban planning and 21st century urbanisation'. *Progress in Planning* 72(3): 151–93.

— (2011) 'Changing planning law in Africa: an introduction to the issue'. *Urban Forum* 22(3): 203–8.

11 | Filling the void: an agenda for tackling African urbanisation

Edgar Pieterse

Maybe Kinshasa shouldn't even try to follow the West. We could not catch up with it even if we tried. We would do better to follow the last one in the race, the hungry one, and follow the rhythm of his footsteps, the time of that hungry one. Of course, hunger signifies a lack of freedom. Somehow we have lost the equilibrium between the physical question and the beyond that creates the freedom. Ready to accept and eat about anything, hunger reduces one to mere survival. But beyond that hunger lies something else. Kinshasa is not only stomach. We have the capacity to open up to that something else, but we haven't yet managed to surpass the problem of hunger, of death, of illness, of suffering. We haven't yet overcome the rupture.

And then, hunger and death do not only signify closure, they also enable the creation of an opening, if not physically then at least mentally. There are such streams of energy running through this city and we have not yet sufficiently explored them. Hunger might help us to learn how to do that, it offers a possibility. Hunger is a good starting point for the incessant search for a beyond, for it reveals the paradox in which we are living: a country so rich, with water, rivers, sun, forests, and yet with inhabitants so miserable. There is a hiatus somewhere, a void, and this void needs to be filled. It has to be filled by us, the inhabitants of this city, the initiated, the *shege*, the expatriates, the multitudes of people that make up this city. The city belongs to all of them. And they all have to constantly reinvent their own myths, their own stories of the street, to keep going and to offer themselves a semblance of direction for this world that keeps slipping through their fingers. The city is indeed a never ending construction.

Vincent Lombume Kalimase (cited in De Boeck and Plissart 2004: 261)

In most African cities and towns, slum life is the norm. As the opening vignette about Kinshasa intimates, this translates into a harsh, complex (because it is also interlaced with the energies and ingenuity of people living their lives) but ultimately unacceptable condition for humans making their way in the world. However, UN-Habitat (2008) informs us that almost all of the projected urban growth in Africa over the next two decades will take the form of slum growth, because this is what the evidence from previous years demonstrates.

This is a startling assertion given that routinised exploitation – in the form of insecure tenure, evictions or threats of eviction, and generalised extortion for access to any basic services or economic opportunity – dominates the lives of slum dwellers.[1] The urban poor who eke out a livelihood in Africa's slums arguably pay the highest transaction costs to be in the city: a clear manifestation of the systematic failure of states and the market. It goes almost without saying that this scale of abuse cannot simply reproduce itself indefinitely. It is already clear, as second- and third-generation urbanites reach adulthood in African cities, that social unrest and generalised volatility will become features of everyday life, threatening not only the well-being of slum dwellers but the political stability of the city and the private market interests that agglomerate there. This tendency will be accelerated by the exponential growth of social media among the youth.

Even though no one can predict how long this state of affairs can continue without erupting into outright violence and social disruption, there seems to be no discernible sense of urgency or concern among the political and business elites about this condition. In fact, evidence suggests that the dominant policy response to the deepening crisis associated with urban growth and expansion is inertia.

This stems primarily from the fact that most political leaders in Africa continue to refuse to accept that their societies are urbanising at a rapid and irreversible pace. This widespread denial, which is both tragic and dangerous, creates a public policy vacuum that leads to unregulated and unmanaged processes of surreptitious urbanisation. These dynamic processes lead to the majority of African urbanites carving out extremely precarious and degrading existences – a sure recipe for continuous uneven development, economic exclusion of the majority, and violence. A further problem stemming from political neglect is the absence of credible data and analysis about the rate, dynamics and consequences of differential urbanisation processes across the continent. While this state of affairs continues, African societies will remain without the basic platform in place from which to define and drive effective public policy responses to the complex and intractable problems associated with rapid urbanisation. In response, this chapter seeks to offer a series of reflections and proposals about how we can shake off this deep-rooted inertia and lay the foundations for effective local, national, supranational, continental and global actions that are mutually reinforcing.

The chapter builds on the trend data about urbanisation pressures and dynamics set out in the Introduction and in the preceding chapters. The next section explores five underlying drivers of urban policy failure in Africa, in order to focus our more propositional arguments set out in the section 'Building blocks of a new urban practice'. The final part deals with the institutional implications of taking this agenda forward in a variety of political and policy arenas.

Drivers of urban failure

The easy approach in seeking drivers of current urban policy failure in Africa would be to blame predominantly external factors for African countries' failure to deal effectively with their urban development crises, especially in a context of systematic economic marginalisation that stems from the current status quo in terms of global investment and trade. However, this would be convenient and easy reading, and inappropriate given the scope that exists for Africans to take stock of their situation and respond decisively. This section prioritises five primary drivers of urban policy failure in Africa, without suggesting that the list is exhaustive or that they are necessarily the most important factors. However, they seem to be at the core of the generalised problem of policy inertia with regard to urban development.

First and foremost is the prevailing governmental attitude that urbanisation is something bad or undesirable that needs to be prevented and, failing that, reversed through effective rural development policies, leading to a refusal to provide for the 'illegal' urban dwellers. We recognise that this attitude arises from the particular blend of national liberation ideologies that accompanied the postcolonial era in Africa – ideologies that were built on the valorisation of a 'return' to the land, to rural lifestyles and to traditional harmony. As a result, many national governments and former liberation movement political parties hold a deep disdain for urban life and the 'modern corruption' and defilement of pure African identities found there, which are seen as essentially a product of the exploitative colonial experience. From this perspective, African urbanism is a material expression of Western dominance and vice, and therefore something that is only grudgingly acknowledged and engaged with.

However, as with so many other aspects of contemporary African life, there is a deep ambivalence towards Western modernity, because the political elites embrace the very same culture to symbolise their power and dominance over society (Deutsch et al. 2002). Paradoxically, what is often found in many African countries is a split condition whereby the elites embrace modern consumerism and its built expression in the form of mansions, condominiums and skyscrapers to reflect their power, but at the same time trade on a rural identity of purity and tradition as a way of culturally re-embedding themselves in a unique nationalist project that is ultimately about control and continuity of that power (Mbembe 2007). In this context, poor urban dwellers, who are largely excluded from modern consumerism, dislocated from the land and a threat to the order of the city, are regarded with deep suspicion and loathing. It is from this perspective that the utter neglect of the urban poor, who, by and large, live in unacceptable makeshift conditions, can be partially understood.

202

Second, political elites in many African countries have grown up and consolidated their positions through the effective nurturing of political cultures of authoritarianism and sectarianism. Commentaries on African politics tend to focus narrowly on the functioning and performance of formal state institutions. However, it is much more important and insightful to appreciate the internal nature of dominant political parties in Africa, whose dynamics and cultures overdetermine the functioning of the state at national, regional and local levels (Stevenson 2011). Practically, what this means is that the interest of the party always trumps the interest of the state or of society at large (see Chabal 2009). As a consequence, policy agendas, priorities and resource allocation are driven by narrow party interests (and especially those of party leaders and their networks), as opposed to a democratically negotiated consensus around public interest and value. In urban areas this often means that the need for control of local neighbourhoods and resources comes before the empowerment of local actors, whether they be local state institutions or autonomous civil society organisations. The shortage of resources, and a small tax base to address vast urban needs through government programmes, exacerbate this dynamic (Bayat and Biekaarts 2009). In light of this, it is no surprise that political decentralisation, linked to robust multiparty democracy and local fiscal responsibility, has been slow in achieving traction, despite the bullish rhetoric of various African governments. Yet it is clear that, because of the complexity and local specificity of Africa's urban problems, empowered decentralisation is essential to ensuring an effective institutional response (see Chapter 8).

Third, it is important to highlight the centrality of limited public funding for urban development programmes in constraining urban development. In a recently published report, *Africa's Infrastructure: A time for transformation* (Foster and Briceño-Garmendia 2010), a detailed account is provided of the overall infrastructure trends in Africa, including both urban and rural areas. According to this report, Africa's infrastructure needs are US$93 billion per annum (see Table 11.1), twice as much as the current spending levels of US$45 billion.

Fourth, another crucial systemic failure in the African response to the challenges of urbanisation is the weakness of civil society institutions that are compelled to function in fragile democratic political spheres, a situation that drains cities of accountability. The scale of urban neglect over the past four decades means that we will be confronted with a situation of need far outstripping the capacity of available resources to address it. Such a context is a recipe for conflict, abuse and routine exploitation of the destitute, unless it is managed sensitively and strategically.

Whether one is in favour of state-driven development or not, it is self-evident that a large part of the resolution of the African urban crisis will come from the efforts of the urban poor themselves. Some ideas about how best to advance such efforts will be elaborated later in this chapter. At this point

TABLE 11.1 Overall infrastructure spending needs for sub-Saharan Africa (US$ billion annually)

Infrastructure sector	Capital expenditure	Operation and maintenance	Total spending
ICT	7.0	2.0	9.0
Irrigation	2.9	0.6	3.4
Power	26.7	14.1	40.8
Transport	8.8	9.4	18.2
Water and sanitation	14.9	7.0	21.9
Total	60.3	33.1	93.3

Source: Foster and Briceño-Garmendia 2010: 7.

I want to highlight the fact that civil society action falls into two categories: self-empowered activities driven by the poor through their democratic organisations; and effective engagement with the (local) state to access entitlements and resources, in order to give expression to democratic citizenship (Pieterse 2008). Such an institutional culture in civil society can only really emerge and consolidate itself if there is a national commitment to democratisation and to the maintenance of functioning political spheres that allows for contestation, negotiation, agreements and oversight of decisions taken. There is very little evidence from across the continent of any appetite for this vital aspect of the democratisation process. If local participation is allowed, it is generally restricted to micro-project design or management decisions, and far removed from resource allocation processes that determine the size and shape of the overall envelope for urban development.

These factors – wanton governmental neglect of the urban question linked to short-sighted imperatives to maintain political control of ideas and spaces, together with very limited financial resources and ineffectual civil society voices – add up to a context with no, or very limited, political accountability. Without accountability there is simply no incentive system in place to devise, sustain or deepen a meaningful urban policy reform agenda. This analysis brings us to the point where we can explore a proposal about what the most strategic agenda for action could be in seeking to arrest and reverse the crisis of urbanisation in Africa.

Taking action

The first step in addressing the crisis of urbanisation in Africa is to accept the need for a paradigm change in how we think about and respond to this complex and challenging phenomenon.

At the heart of this new paradigm is the subversive idea that our greatest resource and opportunity to solve the African urban crisis lies with the people who effectively build the cities through their tenacious efforts to retain a foothold there – the agents of slum urbanism. In other words, instead of regarding the urban poor and excluded urbanites as the problem, we should recognise the energies and ingenuity that they marshal to retain their place in the city, despite the odds against them. Bringing about this paradigm shift in the minds of African governments and politicians will be a gargantuan challenge, but one we need to meet through careful argument, backed by evidence, and effective coalitions of interests to advance the agenda simultaneously on multiple fronts. The lines of action and research elaborated here capture some of the interventions that can be pursued.

A major implication of this paradigm adjustment is that the urban poor who live in informal settlements and on occupied land must be *recognised* and afforded security in our cities. Once this happens, it opens up the possibility of urban consolidation, which, in turn, is a precondition for investment and asset growth. If the urban poor are protected from forced evictions and extortion by unregulated (informal) landlords and rent-lords, they are more likely to prioritise the education of their children, which is the only long-term path to economic inclusion and the empowerment of whole populations. Furthermore, if the urban poor are protected against arbitrary violence and abuse, they are more likely to invest in social formations and organisations that can play a pivotal role in improving health and social well-being. The more the health status of the urban poor improves, the greater the likelihood of small-scale enterprises and savings associations flourishing. And the more the urban poor are enrolled in economically viable and growing concerns, the greater their aggregate contribution to the urban economy will be. This will generate demand for more services and finance in the economy, which in turn has the potential to grow the tax base and resource pool for city-wide infrastructure development, benefiting the entire economy at a city region and national level. But this virtuous circle begins by fundamentally changing mindsets among political and administrative leaders – a task more difficult than it seems.

Joel Bolnick refers to a wry observation by one of the Asian leaders of Slum/Shack Dwellers International (SDI), Jockin Arputham, in which he presciently captures the difficulty political elites have in recognising the poor:

> If you go to the government and ask for a cigarette and a match they will swear at you and call you a bloody beggar. If you go to them with a cigarette in your mouth, they will light it for you without even thinking.[2]

The point of this comment is that dominant powers in our cities speak a language of arrogance and dismissal. This is, in part, related to issues around the contemporary role of political parties in many African contexts, but it also

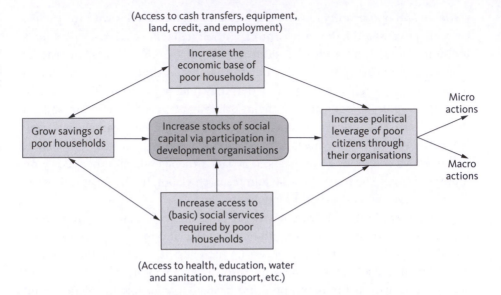

(Access to cash transfers, equipment,
land, credit, and employment)

Increase the
economic base of
poor households

Grow savings of
poor households

Increase stocks of social
capital via participation in
development organisations

Increase political
leverage of poor
citizens through
their organisations

Micro
actions

Macro
actions

Increase access to
(basic) social services
required by poor
households

(Access to health, education, water
and sanitation, transport, etc.)

11.1 Developmental links at the micro scale (*source*: Pieterse 2008: 171)

underscores the deep-seated belief that nothing good or valid can come from the messy, unsightly, stinking, foul neighbourhoods that make up large parts (sometimes most) of the built fabric of our cities and towns. It is therefore important to understand that one cannot rely on rational persuasion or a moral sense of compassion to change the mindset and behaviours of political elites. Instead, what one needs to focus on is how to promote legitimate and mainstream institutional systems that will compel such a paradigm shift. This pertains to accountability mechanisms, and to more precise and effective policy agendas that place the urban poor at the centre of the analysis.

It is imperative that local-level interventions address the concrete needs or wants of the urban poor, while making sure that the processes of addressing these needs also unlock a wider set of developmental dynamics that visibly contribute to the strengthening of local institutions, empowerment of communities and individuals. In urban contexts dominated by a lack of work or access to productive opportunities, this locally legitimate leadership is often the lead mechanism to unlock developmental processes in poor communities. Experience of and research on organisations such as SDI and StreetNet suggest that fostering savings that are held collectively is often the most effective way of stimulating access to productive assets and employment opportunities (Appadurai 2002; Chen 2012).[3] Figure 11.1 captures the dynamism of the proposed interactions.

This empowerment paradigm argues that the biggest asset a poor community has is its stock of social capital, which allows it to carry out collective actions on the basis of solidarity. Social capital is best enhanced through collective actions that address the physical well-being of the participating individuals (and households) in one form or another. The experience of achievement that comes from positive collective action provides a useful foundation to promote political agency aimed at powerful local actors and the government, depending on the issues at hand. Local interventions also require a keen understanding of how the specific action will link up with contiguous processes at the micro and macro scales. In other words, how do the experiences of local development processes, with all their frustrations and achievements, directly inform advocacy and lobbying processes at national and international levels? This is the intersection point where the micro *informs* the macro and the macro can, potentially, *enable* local action, which in turn can empower poor households, citizens and their organisational formations. This approach rests on a more fully elaborated political theory of relational politics (see Pieterse 2006; 2008).

What this approach suggests is that it is imperative to recast all of the conventional aspects of urban development – decentralisation, infrastructure investment and local economic development – from the perspective of empowering the urban poor as an integral part of the urban development agenda. In exploring the implications of this agenda, we now turn to seven action areas that flow from the argument presented up to this point.

Building blocks of a new urban practice

There are seven dimensions to reimagining and rebuilding the African urban agenda so that it addresses the systemic drivers of dysfunctionality explored above:

1 open-source social infrastructures;
2 jobs linked to the crisis of social mal-development and the growing environmental crisis;
3 infrastructure-led actions and urban reforms to simultaneously address economic, social and environmental challenges that coalesce in cities;
4 appropriate land use and land value policies and regulation;
5 effective accountability to ensure a correlation between democratic deliberation and negotiation and resource allocation decisions;
6 robust institutions, networks and learning as the preferred means to address knotty urban problems that manifest uniquely in different urban settings; and
7 effective data collection and analysis to inform processes, decisions and action on an ongoing and recurrent basis.

We now explore each of these issues in turn.

Action front 1: Open-source social infrastructures Some of the most effective and impressive social formations that have come to the fore in the past decade are SDI and StreetNet. These organisations seek to use the autonomous actions of the poor to improve their livelihood contexts as a means of addressing multiple developmental objectives at the same time. For example, the immediate living conditions of the participants are improved by giving them access to pooled resources and vital intelligence about how best to survive in adverse conditions. Furthermore, the neighbourhoods or quarters where the members reside tend to improve because of the collective impact of the improvement in living conditions and the constant, simultaneous effort to access opportunities for betterment. Moreover, these households and communities have a higher chance of leveraging state resources because evidence of their success or improvement gives them a better chance of attracting more resources, since they now represent a lower risk profile for investors. As these links take effect, they also enhance the political confidence of the members of the organisations of the poor, who now see that political responsiveness is possible and so, invariably, set their sights on more ambitious claims with greater resources; this in turn allows the organisations to attract more members, as the benefits of participation visibly outweigh the risks of collective action.

Another positive spin-off of this approach to social capital expansion is the greater prospect of government policies and programmes being adapted to the particular conditions of poor neighbourhoods. This is very important because too often, when (local) governments have slum upgrading or public housing programmes, the terms of engagement undermine the livelihood practices of the poor or criminalise their survival mechanisms.

It is possible to think of these dynamics as an alternative operating system for our cities. Similar to the ubiquitous Windows computer platform that is premised on proprietary rights and therefore restricted to those who can afford to pay, we regard the dominant model of urban development and management as exclusionary and structured by the ability to pay. It is possible to envisage a more democratic, horizontal, network-based 'Wiki' model of urban development that takes the collective efforts of the urban poor to address their needs as an inspirational starting point for how to design appropriate urban interventions. This model, which centres on autonomy, democratic exchange, learning and joint priority setting between the local state and the urban poor (without excluding other actors who have a role to play in the city), provides the key to the creation of the institutional framework required to address our urban crisis (Appadurai 2002; Swilling 2011).

Action front 2: Addressing the crisis of youth unemployment The evidence is now fairly clear that Africa is currently experiencing its demographic bulge. The population cohort between the ages of 12 and 24 (from puberty to economic independence) represents a demographic plateau, as fertility rates decline and make the current group the largest it will ever be – hence the notion of a youth or demographic bulge.[4] Usually this represents an economic windfall because a number of economically productive actors enter the economy, raising investment levels, productivity and competitiveness, which in turn leads to higher growth rates. As this cohort moves through its productive life cycle, it becomes a long-term source of prosperity – at least in theory. However, in the African context the youth bulge seems to represent a 'demographic curse' as most young people are without the requisite skills and resources to enter the formal labour market, which has become increasingly demanding in a globally integrated economy. Instead, most African youth fail to complete their school education, end up in low-wage and precarious employment, and, typically, remain on the lookout for opportunities to migrate (within a country, to neighbouring countries or beyond the continent).[5] Culturally, the youth are continuously bombarded by ubiquitous advertising messages promoting expensive consumer desirables that accompany contemporary Western life-styles. Unsurprisingly, these markers of style and identity become an important motivation to do whatever it takes to acquire cash or the opportunity to participate in such consumption-driven lifestyles (Diouf 2003).

Increasingly, this cohort represents second- and third-generation urban dwellers, which suggests a qualitatively different social outlook and disposition – one that is more open and susceptible to involvement in violent and criminal socioeconomic practices that can secure (non-familial) ties and access to desirable and elusive urban opportunities. On the one hand, sections of this cohort are enrolled in the political processes of victimisation and election stealing, reinforcing the authoritarian political cultures mentioned above. On the other hand, they also represent a measure of volatility and anger that will become increasingly impossible to contain or channel. There is, therefore, a direct self-interest for urban elites and political classes in finding ways to offer innovative large-scale programmes to enrol young people into forms of employment and sociality that can serve the broader interests of inclusive urbanism.

There are three kinds of urban services that are desperately needed to mend and extend the tattered fabric of our cities: a) labour-intensive jobs to install, maintain and revitalise urban infrastructure, especially in informal settlements but also along the strategic transport corridors required to capitalise on the global demand for African commodities; b) social development services to address the home-based care needs of AIDS sufferers, orphaned children, preschool children and the elderly who have been left redundant; and c) environmental services related to recycling economies and regeneration of the degraded ecosystem services on which our cities and towns rely. All three of these areas of public service activity can be designed and rolled out at scale, creating a mechanism to channel large numbers of youth into the formal labour market via the social economy (Amin 2012).

Action front 3: Infrastructure-led growth Many African countries that are endowed with non-renewable resources needed by the rapidly expanding economies of the world, especially China, India, Indonesia and Turkey, have experienced an unprecedented boom over the past decade. In fact, average growth rates for Africa have been 4.5 per cent since the mid-1990s (Cheru 2008). This trend represents an extraordinary opportunity that may already be fading as the recent global financial crisis continues to reverberate, depressing global demand. Nevertheless, as the world economy re-centres itself over the next 30 years, moving away from the US–EU–Japan nexus to the BRICS countries (Brazil, Russia, India, China and South Africa), the extensive raw materials of Africa will remain in demand (Wilson and Purushothaman 2003). The question is whether this unique windfall will be used strategically to broaden the base of African economies, improve Africa's terms of trade and allow millions more into the formal labour market. It is by no means a foregone conclusion that African lives will get better through this commodities boom. On the contrary, current evidence suggests that many African countries endowed with natural resources are becoming even more unequal and poor (African Development Bank 2007).

The strategic challenge is to recognise the need for *targeted* infrastructure investments to improve the logistical efficiency of African economies. This will ensure more widespread and equitable access to urban services for local labour forces, helping to grow labour absorption and enhance productivity. There is an undeniable opportunity for synergy between addressing the fundamental needs for safe water, decent sanitation and affordable energy of urban populations (often the majorities in African cities) who live without these essentials, and the imperative to improve the logistics of getting products and services to regional and global markets. In other words, we need to focus our strategic sights on how to simultaneously address growth imperatives and ensure access to urban opportunities for the urban poor and under-serviced.

The problem has been that urban and political elites tend to take a much narrower view than this. Their preference is to focus on providing services only to middle-class and elite areas, and to support pockets of commercial activity, in order to link them to information and communication technologies and key transportation hubs. A hard economic calculus underpins this tendency: if people cannot afford to pay for the services provided by the state, they should not be given access to such services. Also, economic imperatives tend to take preference over other, less financially sustainable infrastructure investments, because, it is argued, a growing economy is the surest way of producing the tax revenue needed to undertake more redistributive or loss-making investments in the infrastructure. Of course, the point of sufficient tax surpluses never arrives, and a game of continual deferral follows its course. In the absence of meaningful political forums where these investment decisions can be contested and debated, it is unlikely that this practice will shift at all. It is for this reason that one has to treat these various action fronts as interdependent.

In seeking the appropriate balance between growth and access imperatives, urban infrastructures need to be planned and instituted in the following order of priority:

- water and sanitation, as part of a broader public health agenda;
- public transport within a larger connectivity agenda, to satisfy the mobility requirements of key economic sectors that sustain regional growth;
- access to land and tenure security within a wider framework of land use management imperatives that is suitably flexible for the diverse needs of African urban dwellers; and
- expanded investment in public infrastructure, before provision of individual services for the middle classes is undertaken.

This prioritisation can only be considered feasible if there is a broader agenda for institutional reform (explored more fully below). A tailor-made urban infrastructure strategy is most likely to succeed if governmental institutions are appropriately devolved, i.e. with the requisite resources and/or taxation powers to carry out locally negotiated plans. But this is not enough. A number of intermediary institutions and appropriate coordination and alignment mechanisms are required to ensure that national, provincial/regional and local infrastructure plans and investments come together to optimise the development strategies of cities and towns.

At the urban scale, it is important to create critical institutional planks that

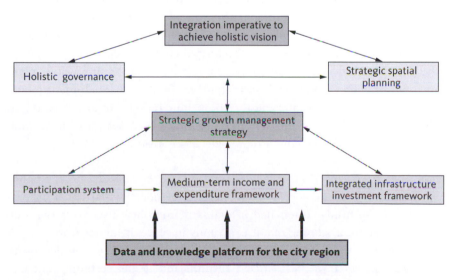

11.2 Policy and institutional dimensions of the sustainable city (*source*: Author)

link infrastructure planning with long-term growth management imperatives. In other words, going forward, the sustainability and inclusivity imperatives for urban areas are forcing a tighter and more realistic integration of governance, planning, management, infrastructure investment and democratic oversight (see Figure 11.2).

As this figure illustrates, the assumption is that effective local government institutions are in place and have the capacity to establish these systems and policies. It further assumes that there is the political maturity and confidence to operate these institutions in a participatory fashion. It is clearly beyond the scope of this chapter to discuss the feasibility of this.

Action front 4: Appropriate land use One of the most devastating and pernicious systems of urban exclusion in many African countries is the approach to land use management and land rights (see Chapter 9). State and market failure with respect to investment in housing that is suitable for the needs of the urban poor throughout their lives is at the heart of the slums crisis, according to Nicholas You, former Special Adviser in the Office of the Executive Director, UN-Habitat. Working from the proposition that 'the demand for housing solutions among the urban poor is much more differentiated than with middle or higher income groups', You critiques the simplistic policy agenda that seeks to promote home ownership for all slum dwellers (You 2007). Instead, he argues for a response that takes seriously the preference among most slum dwellers for access to rental housing, so that they can apportion the bulk of their irregular and low incomes to other priorities such as education and mobility. However, an alternative approach to housing and shelter also requires an innovative attitude to broader land use regulation and urban planning. Here, the argument turns to a method of regulation that can simultaneously address the unique needs of the urban poor who live in ill-defined legal contexts, and those of the formal city that depends on clear-cut rules. One practical instrument to overcome this divide is 'innovative planning zones or action plans for slum upgrading' (ibid.: 219). Such instruments allow municipalities to advance better urban integration, but also investment frameworks that allow for the systematic upgrading of services in informal settlements without producing a new cycle of exclusion.

Action front 5: Effective democratic deliberation and accountability The policy ideal of vibrant local democracy characterised by effective participatory processes is now so firmly entrenched in mainstream policy discourses that one can be forgiven for assuming that it is actually in place. Evidence from various sources makes it clear that the growing movement for democratic decentralisation has delivered, at best, mixed results, and it has certainly failed to deliver more responsive institutions from the perspective of the urban poor (see Chapter 8). In fact, what is more common is political capture by powerful political parties who use control of local government as an instrument in a larger game of patronage, extortion and selective development. At the core of this political rot is the absence of effective countervailing institutions and organisations, in particular autonomous organisations of the urban poor, who have a vested interest in making these fledgling institutions work.

Consequently, we need to think about deepening the democratic agenda in Africa's cities and towns along three tracks that reinforce one another. The first and most urgent priority is to create an explicit incentive system for the urban poor to organise themselves effectively in order to advance their own social and economic reproductive interests. The model we have in mind is the work of SDI, which uses the ritual of daily savings by its members as the primary rationale for enrolling people into the movement. In other words, they address a very practical material need for access to capital and mutual support for people who are persistently economically vulnerable (Bolnick 2009). At the economic reproductive end, StreetNet follows a very similar model of organisa-tion, but its mobilisation is focused on improving the regulatory environment within which its members struggle to keep their micro-enterprises alive. In both cases the urban poor find their voice and confidence in numbers and around very pragmatic and focused campaigns. Each small victory provides the fuel to grow the movement, and, through small incremental gains, the organisations are also able to insinuate themselves into the governance pro-cesses of the cities where they operate. Over time, the remit of their influence and engagement spreads, and soon links are drawn between the immediate needs of their members in a particular quarter of the city and the long-term strategy and investment programme for the territory.

However, urban reforms driven forward by the campaigns of community-based organisations (CBOs) focused on pragmatic 'life space' questions are not enough. What is ultimately needed is a range of formalised institutional mechanisms that draw citizens into deliberations about the long-term strategic direction and programme of the city, in order to realise the full potential of all citizens and businesses who operate there (whether they be formal or informal). International evidence suggests that this imperative is best advanced when democratic deliberation focuses on competing needs and the necessity of making choices about trade-offs for clearly defined reasons, and then ties this to specific decisions about the mobilisation and allocation of resources for those priorities and trade-offs (Fernandes 2010). The best illustration of this is the participatory budgeting experiments undertaken across Latin America, and increasingly in Europe and Asia (UN-Habitat 2004). In the African context, the Municipal Development Partnership, based in Harare, has been driving engagement with this methodology in southern and eastern Africa.[6]

However, it is important to anticipate the possibility that participatory

budgeting or other tools for democratic deliberation around resource allocation priorities can fail, if they are not linked to an explicit engagement with
the spatial form and dynamics of the city. All public and private investment
has spatial consequences – certain parts of the city become valorised and
others are rendered obsolete or left to decline. The uneven and always shifting
distribution of value to different parts of the city has great consequences for
the realisation of the urban poor's right to that city. Thus, another important
agenda for democratic reform is the democratisation of planning in general,
and specifically of more recent innovations such as city development strategies
(CDSs) that aim to forge a shared agenda for long-term urban investment and
development (Pieterse 2008). What would it take to have the leaders of slum
dwellers and informal sector workers become central actors in CDS processes?
How can such leadership be secured?

The promotion of organisations of the urban poor and the institutionalisation
of city-wide decision-making mechanisms for agreeing on strategic resource
allocation priorities both depend on confident local states that take democratic
processes and accountability seriously. The key question is, given the nature of
the political culture in many African countries, how does one nurture capable,
dedicated and corruption-free local government? The answer to this question
continues to be elusive, but what is clear is that one must stop thinking in
terms of capacity building alone and rather focus collective energies on building
robust democratic counterpoints – that is, effective and free media, monitoring
instruments in the public domain and leadership from across society, including
within the political parties that occupy office at local and national levels. This
notion of a dispersed coalition of interests takes us to the next domain for action.

Action front 6: Robust institutions, networks and learning Despite the scale
of the challenges confronting us, and the great variety of national and local
circumstances, it does seem possible to delineate elements of a soft institutional architecture that should be fostered in order to create the basis for
taking the urban debate forward at a country and city level, which in turn
can fuel a continental conversation. This institutional architecture includes
the following requirements:

- In each country, build the institutional capability and readiness to advance
  the local (and regional) case for the urban agenda among core institutions such as: national ministries dealing with urban issues (finance,
  infrastructure, economic development, planning, environment, etc.), local
  government associations, universities, non-governmental organisations
  (NGOs), social movements of the urban poor, and enlightened businesses.
  The programme driven by Cities Alliance to generate country-level State of
  Cities reports is an important step promoting this culture.[7]

214

- Invest in long-term capacity to build durable institutions that can respond to the knowledge, policy development, training and implementation challenges associated with the urbanisation question: scholars, researchers in think tanks, effective knowledge networks and forums linking policy analysts and decision makers, and cross-country networks that focus on the general problems and that may be thematically connected.
- Incubate innovation by providing appropriate and multidimensional support (finance, technical advice, organisational development support, etc.) for initiatives that show vision, promise and endurance. Examples of this are the new public transport initiatives that the Institute for Transportation and Development Policy is involved with in Tanzania, Ghana, Senegal and South Africa; partnership-based models of delivering affordable and safe water and sanitation services as pioneered by the Water & Sanitation for the Urban Poor programme;[8] mutual protection and savings models for enhancing community empowerment as reflected in the methods and practices of movements such as StreetNet and SDI; and ecologically sound infrastructural and design solutions for the urban poor as pioneered by the Development Bank of Southern Africa (with the Sustainability Institute) in Grabouw and Cape Town (South Africa). What is noteworthy about these examples of innovation is that they share some, if not all, of the following characteristics:
  - They are driven forward by a strong endogenous or bottom-up energy.
  - They are capable of fostering and sustaining sound partnerships.
  - They solve the financing dimension of their initiative or activities.
  - They hold the potential for replicability and/or for being rolled out on a larger scale.

The key question that remains is: how does one create a system of institutions, vibrant networks and sound knowledge that not only incubates innovation and disseminates findings but also becomes mainstream? Since this system must involve an institutional mesh of state leadership, sound data/knowledge platforms, a series of intermediary institutions (universities, think tanks, NGOs), a shared long-term strategy for cities and towns at the local level, epistemic communities and policy networks with leaders, skilled managers and CBOs held together by shared objectives, and an intelligent process of capacity development, the question can be rephrased as: how can these elements be brought to life and sustained? I will return to this in the conclusion.

Action front 7: Effective data collection and analysis The dominant tendencies discussed earlier, such as political denial of the scale and seriousness of rapid urbanisation, the phenomenon of policy inertia, and the systematic marginalisation of slums in terms of public investment priorities and political inclusion, contribute to a lack of commitment to obtaining accurate data about the state of Africa's cities, regions and (trans)national urban systems. As urban policy makers and activists, we are operating with blindfolds on because most national survey instruments are not calibrated to give us a depth of understanding of rapidly changing urban dynamics in terms of economies, ecological systems, social structures, infrastructural coverage and so on.[9] Unless we are able to systematically remedy this situation, urban policies will continue to run aground on the rocks of unexpected outcomes and unacceptable levels of risk.

Over and above the problem of basic data availability, we are also confronted by an intellectual legacy in the urban field that is atheoretical, aspatial and often even ahistorical (Pieterse 2011). Instead, urban research suffers from a 'relevance' reflex. A number of urban scholars and activists pride themselves on the fact that they are interested only in practical policy questions that can solve real problems. The difficulty with this approach is that it fails to appreciate that all data must be interpreted, and interpretation depends on theoretical assumptions; the more one renders those assumptions invisible, the greater the likelihood that analysis will be incorrect or partial (Flyvbjerg 2001). As is suggested by our opening vignette, African cities are characterised by profound levels of hybridity and complexity and will remain impervious to understanding and effective policy action unless we can promote the creation of a richer, more nuanced and context-specific lexicon on African urbanism (Pieterse and Simone 2013).

Taking this agenda forward

Systemic change in the direction argued for in this chapter will most likely come about if we pursue reform at multiple levels – continental, country level and city or town level – in manners that are mutually reinforcing. It is therefore vital that we reflect on what is required at each of these scales of policy development and institution building, with a sense of how these requirements should be prioritised. This concluding section sets out some broad options for actions that key institutional actors could undertake at various levels.

At an Africa-wide level, it seems essential that continental institutions such as the African Development Bank, African Union, African Ministerial Conference on Housing and Urban Development, Cities Alliance and United Cities and Local Governments – Africa, in conjunction with UN-Habitat, provide the leadership in this regard. We need to reflect on whether the efforts under way in these forums are robust and focused enough to have impacts on national governments (and especially on the political parties that dominate national political systems) that will lead them to take the urban question seriously. For example, how can we strategically engage with the African Development Bank's urbanisation strategy development process to ensure that it addresses tough policy challenges and does not slip into a mode of making vague policy suggestions? Similar questions can be asked about the policy processes of other pan-African organisations and initiatives such as the African Union and the New Partnership for Africa's Development cities programme.

At the national level, it is essential to consciously work towards having a sustained national debate on the nature of the urban system and on the priority issues that arise in various categories of cities and towns, based on evidence gathered. In this light it seems opportune to build on the State of African Cities process that UN-Habitat undertook in 2008, 2010 and 2013. Similarly, it would seem strategically useful to explore how the Cities Alliance methodology of country-level State of Cities reports can be deployed to set out the urban agenda. One of the most valuable spin-offs of these processes is the collation, sifting and verification of available data on urban issues. This prepares the ground for the conceptualisation and promotion of interventions in the various action areas explored above. The African Centre for Cities (ACC) and its partners are therefore engaging with these processes to explore how the proposals mooted here can be taken up and consolidated in ongoing country-level efforts.[10] Over time, it will also be possible to exchange practical information about how to establish and sustain such national processes and institutions.

At city and town level, the priority must be to build vibrant and effective grassroots organisations that can combine autonomous mutual support initiatives to strengthen livelihood imperatives with more politically engaged work to challenge the (local) state to provide access to a minimum level of universal services. Furthermore, the key priority must be to use the general move towards city-scale development strategies as an opportunity to include the interests and agendas of the urban poor alongside those of the political and economic elites and the middle classes in these cities. It would also be of great value to look at when and where there may be scope to connect development strategy and prioritisation exercises with resource allocation processes, through experiments such as participatory budgeting in its various incarnations. It is also at this scale that university-based and independent knowledge institutions including NGOs can position themselves more effectively to produce evidence-based analyses of urban priorities and appropriate responses. Finally, at the city scale, it is imperative for regulatory systems relating to land use, taxation and financial investment to be strengthened and brought into line with the overarching development trajectory of the city, which will invariably be unique and place-specific.

There are two important cross-cutting considerations that apply to all three levels of urban review and transformation: the role of political parties, and the need for informed and diverse public discourse facilitated by effective and autonomous media. One of the most difficult issues confronting the continent is the lack of mature leadership from the leading political parties, which have often had to make the transition from liberation movements into modern, professionally organised party structures. In a context of economic scarcity and patronage-based distributive mechanisms, political parties are often part of the problem rather than the solution. There is an urgent need for greater internal democracy, transparency to minimise systemic corruption, which often spills over into the state, and a willingness to be subjected to peer review by, for example, autonomous civil society actors or even other political parties in other countries grappling with many of the same challenges. We are unlikely to see the emergence of effective local government, coherent urban development policies or meaningful city strategies if we do not address the decay in our political cultures. It goes without saying that autonomous, vigorous and diverse media are essential stimuli for such political reform.

Conclusion

This chapter puts forward an African civil society perspective on the urbanisation crisis facing our societies. The chapter started with a warning that newfound economic growth is highly skewed and at risk because of its dependence on global demand and the narrow economic base in most countries. In particular, I demonstrated how these contextual drivers produce an urban setting dominated by the effects of unregulated and surreptitious urbanisation, manifested most dramatically in the predominance of slums with alarming levels of deprivation in almost all of our cities and towns. In the interest of promoting a realistic and clinical discussion about how to address these structural conditions at their root, the chapter has suggested five reasons for urban policy failure in Africa. The purpose of this was to identify a strategic agenda that flows from a paradigm shift – putting the urban poor at the centre of our strategy – in how we define the African urbanisation challenge. The final sections of the chapter considered concrete interventions and the kinds of institutional scaffolding that would be required to translate this agenda into a dynamic, evolving reality. In this way, I hope to have provided food for thought on how the 'void' at the heart of our societies and cities can be filled with audacity and an appreciation of the centrality of the urban. For, indeed, as Vincent Lombume Kalimase (cited in De Boeck and Plissart 2004) reminds us, we are caught up in this terrible

> paradox in which we are living: a country [or continent] so rich, with water, rivers, sun, forests, and yet with inhabitants so miserable. There is a hiatus somewhere, a void, and this void needs to be filled. It has to be filled by us, the inhabitants of this city ... The city is indeed a never ending construction.

Notes

1 For a visceral account of this, see the documentary film, *Living with Corruption* by Sorious Samura (2007), which offers an insider account of daily life in Kibera, Nairobi, Kenya.

2 This was relayed in the presentation by Joel Bolnick at the African Urban Innovations Workshop convened by the African Centre for Cities (ACC) in October 2008.

3 SDI is a transnational network of local slum dweller organisations that have come together at the city and national level to form federations of the urban poor; see www.sdinet.org. The StreetNet International alliance of street vendors was launched in Durban, South Africa, in November 2002. Membership-based organisations (unions, cooperatives or associations) directly organising street vendors, market vendors and/or hawkers are entitled to affiliate to StreetNet International; see www.streetnet.org.za.

4 More technical background can be obtained from World Bank (2007).

5 These trends are carefully mapped in World Bank (2009).

6 The Municipal Development Partnership for Eastern and Southern Africa is an active and hands-on capacity-building facility whose aim is to enable effective self-governance at the local level in sub-Saharan Africa. It promotes alternative development approaches to problems and issues that affect local authorities, by placing emphasis on the ownership and direct participation of key stakeholders. See www.mdpafrica.org.zw.

7 ACC works with Cities Alliance to implement this programme. Typically, local universities are used as intermediaries to bring together these actors and undertake the research to inform the State of Cities report.

8 Water & Sanitation for the Urban Poor is a non-profit partnership based in the United Kingdom but working across various African countries and Bangladesh. See www.wsup.com [accessed on 29 August 2013].

9 ACC has embarked on a collaborative process with various agencies and governmental units to establish an integrated data platform for the Cape Town metropolitan region through a facility called the Cape Urban Observatory. This mirrors a similar experiment in the north of South Africa, called the Gauteng City-Region Observatory. Similar initiatives are being undertaken across Africa and a lot of potential exists to dovetail this with the work of UN-Habitat's Global Urban Observatory and the emerging Sustainable Urban Development Network (SUD-Net) platform.

10 In March 2013, ACC, the Association of African Planning Schools and Cities Alliance convened a workshop in Addis Ababa, Ethiopia to moot and establish the African Urban Research Network. More information on this initiative is available from the author.

References

African Development Bank (2007) *African Development Report 2007: Natural resources for sustainable development in Africa*. Oxford: Oxford University Press.

— (2009) *African Statistical Year Book, 2009*. Tunis: African Development Bank.

Amin, A. (2012) *Land of Strangers*. Cambridge: Polity.

Appadurai, A. (2002) 'Deep democracy: urban governmentality and the horizon of politics'. *Public Culture* 14(1): 21–47.

Bayat, A. and K. Biekaarts (2009) 'Cities of extremes'. *Development and Change* 40(5): 815–25.

Bolnick, J. (2009) 'A tale of all cities: a short history of the evolution of Shack Dwellers International'. Unpublished paper. Cape Town: African Centre for Cities.

Chabal, P. (2009) *Africa: The politics of suffering and smiling*. London: Zed Books.

Chen, M. (2012) *The Informal Economy: Definition, theory and policies*. WIEGO

Working Paper No. 1. Cambridge, MA: Women in Informal Employment: Globalizing and Organizing (WIEGO).

Cheru, F. (2008) *Africa's Development in the 21st Century: Reshaping the research agenda*. Current African Issues 41. Uppsala: Nordiska Afrikainstitutet.

De Boeck, P. and M. Plissart (2004) *Kinshasa: Tales of the invisible city*. Brussels: Ludion.

Deutsch, J.-G., P. Probst and H. Schmidt (eds) (2002) *African Modernities: Entangled meanings in current debate*. Portsmouth, NH: Heinemann.

Diouf, M. (2003) 'Engaging postcolonial cultures: African youth and public space'. *African Studies Review* 46(1): 1–12.

Fernandes, E. (2010) 'Participatory budgeting processes in Brazil – fifteen years later'. In C. Kihato, M. Massoumi, B. Ruble, P. Subrirós and A. Garland (eds) *Urban Diversity: Space, Culture, and Inclusive Pluralism in Cities Worldwide*. Washington, DC and Baltimore, MD: Woodrow Wilson Center and Johns Hopkins University Press.

Flyvbjerg, B. (2001) *Making Social Science Matter: Why social inquiry fails and how it can succeed again*. Cambridge: Cambridge University Press.

Foster, V. and C. Briceño-Garmendia (eds) (2010) *Africa's Infrastructure: A time for transformation*. Washington, DC: World Bank.

Mbembe, A. (2007) 'Why am I here?'. In L. McGregor and S. Nuttall (eds) *At Risk: Writing on and over the edge of South Africa*. Johannesburg: Jonathan Ball Publishers.

Pieterse, E. (2006) 'Building with ruins and dreams: exploratory thoughts on realising integrated urban development through crises'. *Urban Studies* 42(2): 1–20.

— (2008) *City futures: Confronting the crises of urban development*. London: Zed Books.

— (2011) 'Grasping the unknowable: coming to grips with African urbanisms'. *Social Dynamics* 37(1): 5–23.

— and A. Simone (eds) (2013) *Rogue Urbanism: Emergent African cities*. Johannesburg: Jacana.

Stevenson, T. (2011) 'African politics: is there any hope?'. In B. Breytenbach (ed.) *Imagine Africa*. Brooklyn, NY and Dakar: Island Position and Gorée Institute.

Swilling, M. (2011) 'Reconceptualising urbanism, ecology and networked infrastructures'. *Social Dynamics* 37(1): 78–95.

UN-Habitat (2004) *72 Frequently Asked Questions About Participatory Democracy*. Nairobi: United Nations Human Settlements Programme (UN-Habitat)

— (2008) *State of the World's Cities 2008/9: Harmonious cities*. London: Earthscan and United Nations Human Settlement Programme (UN-Habitat).

Wilson, D. and R. Purushothaman (2003) *Dreaming with BRICs: The path to 2050*. Global Economic Paper No. 99. New York, NY: Goldman Sachs.

World Bank (2007) *World Development Report 2007: Development and the next generation*. Oxford: Oxford University Press.

— (2009) *Africa Development Indicators 2008/9: Youth and employment in Africa*. Washington, DC: World Bank.

You, N. (2007) 'Sustainable for whom? The urban millennium and challenges for redefining the global development planning agenda'. *City* 11(2): 214–20.

12 | Infrastructure, real economies and social transformation: assembling the components for regional urban development in Africa

AbdouMaliq Simone

Introduction: development through infrastructure

Critical questions concerning sustainable urbanisation in Africa centre on how individual cities in the region – continental Africa – can connect to each other and strengthen ways of working together. As a result, future African regional economic development will require a more elaborate latticework of connectivity. The current limited circumference and trajectories of inflows and outflows, of articulations among territories, of integration among diverse functions, populations and sectors will be rectified only by a series of coordinated infrastructure interventions on many fronts. This is more than simply building new roads, railways, power lines and telecommunications. It is more than just a matter of constructing synergies between the physical, the institutional, the economic and the informational.

These interventions and synergies are no doubt necessary. But in order for them to do their job, they must take into consideration the impetus, practices and movements adopted by Africans across the region as they construct new spaces of operation, habitation and transaction. The extensiveness of need, the impact of global economic change and the urban social transformations under way combine in ways that require new thinking and expectations about what is possible and how to make it happen. Only by identifying more comprehensive ways to map, understand and engage urban real economies can the momentum for infrastructure-led and environmentally sustainable economic growth be maintained.

In addition, more comprehensive knowledge is needed about how resources and materials actually flow through cities. Infrastructure largely exists to bring water, power, people, materials and waste from one place to another. While infrastructure inadequacies are conventionally calculated in terms of access, there is often limited understanding of the exact volumes, directionalities, flows, uses and links involved. A range of new mapping devices, planning techniques and financial modelling can support strategic decisions about how to maximise the productive impact of new infrastructure investments (OECD 2012). These attempt to capitalise on various specificities of African cities –

particularly the ways in which apparent and long-term dysfunction has given rise to an urban resourcefulness that is usually underplayed in other cities of the world – but also on the ways in which much of what takes place is not radically dissimilar to urban situations elsewhere.

There has been widespread optimism during the past few years that sizeable increases in infrastructure investment can not only build on favourable economic growth rates but can also provide substantial increases in the sustainable livelihoods available to urban residents, address serious environmental deficits and realign the region's position in global economic hierarchies. Some of this optimism is warranted: total multilateral and bilateral infrastructure investment commitments amounted to US$12.4 billion in 2007; commitments for power generation went from US$1 billion per year in 2005 to US$2.3 billion in 2007 (Foster and Briceño-Garmendia 2010). Fifteen per cent of the region's gross domestic product (GDP) already goes to covering infrastructure deficits and US$30 billion of the US$45 billion spent annually on infrastructure is generated domestically (ibid.).

Additionally, as land production and delivery are the critical underpinnings of urban development, advances in how land is identified – now increasingly through spatial data-processing systems – registered, valued and used should translate into more robust economic opportunities. Of course, this is premised on land being well governed, secured through transparent tenure frameworks, and capable of being developed through multiple forms of investment, remuneration and securitisation that ensure its access by different actors and for various uses.

Much of the improvement in infrastructure coincided with accelerating growth rates throughout much of the past decade. Despite the global economic crisis of recent years, overall investment interest in infrastructure development seems to be sustained. As the crisis has had substantial deleterious effects in the region, part of the sustained interest may be attributed to the potential profitability of high-profile, large-scale projects in a high-risk environment when they do finally come on line (PPIAF 2009). But clearly the fluid, even precarious, nature of future economic trajectories will result in investors being extremely cautious. The African Development Bank indicates that real aggregate GDP growth fell to 2 per cent in 2009 from 6 per cent in 2008, with an optimistic projection of 3.9 per cent for 2010, and with the fastest growing countries having taken the greatest hit. There has been a 10 per cent increase in unemployment just in 2009 alone, and aggregate fiscal balances for the entire region went from a 3.3 per cent surplus in 2008 to a 4.2 per cent deficit in 2009 (Kasekende et al. 2010).

The demographic composition of Africa's population, while becoming more urban, is also becoming more differentiated and unstable – in terms of mobility, occupation and sustainable livelihood. The United Nations Human

Settlements Programme (UN-Habitat) estimates that the urban population in the region will double from current levels to 759 million by 2030 (UN-Habitat 2009). But, perhaps more importantly, there appears to be a greater diffusion of household livelihoods geographically as a means of accessing and protecting against oscillating employment opportunities and sources of income. Individuals go back and forth between different cities, between cities and rural areas, between regional and international destinations, and between different parts of the same city (Beauchemin and Bocquier 2004). This mobility not only exerts intense pressure on existing infrastructure but also intensifies the marginality of those unable to move. In addition, the mobility of residents means that they do not use their resources in an attempt to cultivate opportunities locally, but rather devote their efforts to an opportunistic and constant hunt for possibilities elsewhere.

Clearly, the probable levels of leveraged finance available for infrastructure investment will come nowhere near what is required to address existing needs. To compensate for the shortfall, multilateral agencies try to propose a different scenario by arguing that the potential of combined reform measures such as an improved regulatory environment, greater cost savings, efficiency gains, new financial instruments and enhanced competitiveness could generate significant improvements. At the same time, the increasing volatility of urban life itself, which is both productive and harmful, generates wide-ranging political, social and cultural impacts that are difficult to predict and assess. As such, despite these scenarios envisioned by the multilaterals, municipalities and states are obliged to govern much more mobile, differentiated and contested societies, where the practicalities of consensus and consolidation are more difficult, despite clear changes in the capacities and technologies of government management at all levels (de Sardan 2009).

Despite the skills they have demonstrated over time and in the face of numerous disadvantages, African urban residents are clearly not able to make maximum use of their capabilities Here, the story is well known: densely populated environments lacking a wide range of facilities; infrastructure and services that depend on labour-intensive maintenance activities; and too many residents vulnerable to health problems and a concomitant loss of livelihood. Insufficient investment in energy, transportation, telecommunications and financial regulation and support inflate transaction costs and thus depreciate the value of local production. Inefficient systems of revenue management short-circuit necessary provisioning and investment.

Given this situation, attention must be paid to the ways in which everyday urban practices question how wealth is presently redistributed and security ensured. African infrastructure needs are enormous. The lack of sufficient generation of electrical power means that existing economic capacity is underutilised. Intermittent access to essentials makes planning, scheduling, forecasting and marketing unreliable. Proven skills that otherwise would be dedicated to long-term development and growth are tied up in adapting to unpredictable conditions and mitigating unforeseen circumstances.

The challenges of urban 'real' economies

Given the disparities between need and available finance, and given the complexity of the political, demographic and social terrain, how can progress be conceptualised and translated into policy and project form? Critical decisions have to be made as to which needs, locations and sectors to prioritise. As an initial step, it is important to get to grips with urbanising processes across the region. Of course, these processes have different shapes and histories in different cities, but for the most part, whatever the national context, geographical location or economic position, Africans are trying to forge productive connections with places and processes beyond their immediate locations. They are migrating between and sojourning in different cities; they are trading goods across a variety of boundaries and in a range of markets; and they are using skills and experiences beyond those contexts to which they are accustomed. They often do so with great difficulty and risk, with frequent interruption and constraints – and yet they persist.

Across the region, agricultural products, minerals and other commodities originating in specific points can pass through vastly divergent trade networks, towns, national territories and ports on their way both to the same and to different destinations. While this diversity may reflect various political instabilities and the lack of regulatory structures and accountability, it is also often used instrumentally to tie together actors and places that otherwise would have no reason to be in relationships with each other. By trying to forge such provisional relationships, a platform is established from which collaboration can be expanded to other areas or sectors. Specific economic activities can become the object of intense dispute, even prolonged violent conflict. Such contestation, while no doubt full of destructive implications, nevertheless can ensure that a broader range of actors and places are brought into the orbit of economies centred on a particular commodity or activity (Raeymaekers 2002; Boone 2003; Bayart and Warnier 2004).

The composition of infrastructure investment will inevitably reflect the exigencies and motivations of powerful economic interests, and, in doing so, reiterate some of the insularity of the past. If this insularity is not attenuated by a heightened commitment to maximising the density of interconnections between territories, people and activities, a critical opportunity for development will be lost. In many respects, Africans are leading the way 'with their feet' – by their own efforts to intensify the connections between any given location and a wider world of economic activity. The implantation of infrastructure – roads, optic cables, satellite transmission, solar power and hydroelectric systems

– creates important opportunities to define and institutionalise significant articulations among places and economic activities. Given the high capital costs involved, maximising the long-term productivity of this infrastructure, in addition to realising the potential for eventual cost recovery, necessitates a high degree of consonance between the articulations infrastructure puts in place and the diverse patterns of connectivity being generated by African entrepreneurs, traders, farmers and retailers themselves.

Of course, not every circuit or trajectory can be addressed; infrastructure will alter routes and ways of life and establish new ones. Many existing circuits of transaction are arduous, diffuse and time consuming. They often reflect the trajectories of resource exploitation from the colonial era, with its frontiers and often senseless administrative boundaries. Enhanced and established connectivity may also lessen the vulnerability of certain areas to protracted struggles over resources and territorial control by extrajudicial forces.

Still, the transnational character of commodity flows, population movements and entrepreneurial activities requires regional approaches to and interconnections between infrastructure. National frameworks will be developed, but the efficacy of infrastructure developments depends on broad-based recognition of the increasing links between national territories and the promotion of new economic regions.

National urban development frameworks will be centred on the more efficient and just functioning of cities – ensuring more proficient services for and governance of heterogeneous city populations. Region-wide considerations can elaborate an important set of principles for setting viable agendas in this regard, sharing experiences and capacity, and harmonising policy frameworks. But the most important consideration of a region-wide urban development agenda will emphasise how the differentiated resource bases, histories and geo-economic positions of cities and towns could be most productively connected in order to create regional domains – crossing distinct national territories or rural–urban divides – with a density of synergistic relationships between diverse economic activities.

The most obvious and frequently cited example is how transactions of all kinds could be maximised between Abidjan, Accra, Lomé, Cotonou, Lagos and Ibadan – long imagined to be the elements of a mega-urban region – in ways that enhance the income and capacity of each individual city. But a similar logic exists more widely across Africa and along various corridors – such as Douala to Aba, Nigeria, which crosses some of the most densely populated rural areas in Africa; Lilongwe through Nampula to the port of Beira; or from Eldoret or Mombassa through Nairobi, Tanga and Dar es Salaam to Kigoma and then onward through the Great Lakes region; or the circuit that runs from Niamey, Zinder, Kano and Katsina to Jos, where it crosses routes from Aba to Enugu to Jos, and where the intersection of such circuits plays out in apparently religious conflict. In West Africa, there are Sahelian trajectories that run west to east – Dakar to Khartoum to Port Sudan or Djibouti – along historical routes of religious migration, with multiple points of intersection to transit southward.

While sub-regional bodies such as the Economic Community of West African States, the Southern African Development Community, the Economic Community of Central African States, the East African Community and the Arab Maghreb Union work to harmonise and coordinate economic policy between contiguous nation states, resident populations are reworking historical transit and trade routes that invoke pre-colonial circuits and cultural domains. They do this in order to maximise their exposure and access to a larger world and to generate value in economic transactions that commerce within the formal boundaries of national economies and economic sectors either does not recognise or cannot take advantage of. It may be that existing regional organisations are not the most effective vehicles through which to concretise urban regional links, and that, instead, new collaborating city-to-city networks are required.

Responsibility for managing infrastructure inputs will, of course, largely fall to national governments. In the end, they retain the right to sovereignty and thus to the management of the ways in which their territories are dedicated to specific functions. Nevertheless, a region-wide urban development perspective must not only chart and attain buy-ins for potential networks within a region. It must also realise the potential links between national infrastructure projects, both planned and implemented, filling in any gaps with various feeder systems and connectors. A large portion of available investments would be directed towards the fluid export of natural resources targeted as being essential for economies elsewhere. This is an inevitable implication of bilateral accords, which would be pursued regardless of overarching regional interests. Truncated systems and a lack of connectivity will persist as a result. But even if regional coordinating investment mechanisms must coexist with such bilateral mechanisms, there are still opportunities to 'fill in the gaps' – to develop connections that promote new networks between previously disconnected regions. Here, cities become a means of anchoring such intersections – giving new importance to a wide range of secondary cities and border towns that straddle the divide between the usually coastal metropolitan regions and the inland, often hard-to-reach, resource-rich areas.

Maximising the affinities between infrastructure and existing economic practices is vital within metropolitan regions. How are productivity gains substantiated in Africa's largest cities? How are city spaces better integrated as economic machines and thus made into better places of habitation? In part, this is a matter of effectively assessing the positive impacts that the most resourceful aspects of urban economies have on other towns and cities and then using this as a basis to make new links and transactions between them a reality.

The dilemmas of 'real' governance

Still, the development of strategy, policies and projects must take into consideration how African cities are actually governed today. No matter how much donor and private finance for urban development is available, much is asked from municipal and national government. Even when they do not assume direct responsibility for project implementation or management, government is expected to ensure proper accountability and an adequate regulatory environment. While technical competencies, political will and financial transparency are often cited as major challenges for African governance, there is rarely sufficient appreciation of the complexities of just what it takes to administer African cities; Africa's urban political cultures, replete with diverse historical antecedents and contemporary conditions, encompass very different modalities for mobilising and administering populations.

On the one hand, it was rare for any given segment of society to attain the control of cities needed to impose either a unifying vision or overarching rules. Even when specific regimes exercised national power for long periods of time and kept national capitals, in particular, on a tight rein, they often had limited traction in the day-to-day operations of a heterogeneous urban population. Policing the streets and the airwaves was not the same thing as securing the functional cohesion of an urban population that largely had to make its own way, its own livelihood and its own methods of dealing with each other. The fundamental challenge was always who could do what, with whom and under what circumstances, and what could ensue from the resulting actions (Coquery-Vidrovitch 1991; Marie 1997).

In such a situation, security was produced through a process of 'joining the dots', of extending the ways in which different actors, their interests and ways of doing things became implicated with each other in expanding circles of relationships. Different social statuses, associations, ascriptions, ways of earning a living and economic sectors had to find ways to become actively interconnected without overarching political or cultural guidelines. While conventional ideas about the control of populations seem to prioritise a system whereby individuals are assigned specific positions and roles in various hierarchies of responsibility and authority, most African cities relied on the promotion of cross-cutting interdependencies and the bringing together of people and things that on the surface would seem to have nothing to do with each other.

This does not mean that the everyday organisation of urban societies did not have its hierarchies. Urban politics and economies are full of patronage. Individuals will 'hitch' themselves to a 'big figure', with loyalty traded for opportunity. These patronage relationships anchor individuals in a clear framework of reciprocal obligations. However, these systems, while important in organising urban neighbourhoods and districts, were seldom sufficient for governing relationships across the entirety of the city.

Of course, such a complex network of relationships required incessant negotiations and flexible measures for taking account of events and attributing responsibility, and negotiations could often break down into prolonged periods of conflict. Across urban Africa, then, there are many forms of contestation. There is contestation in terms of the fundamental rights and obligations embedded in relationships between children and parents, between extended family members, between men and women, patrons and clients, citizens and government officials. Basic questions as to the place of self-initiative, individual decision making and the conditions of belonging to family and to other social groups are debated intensely. People are finding many different ways of working out an accommodation between the needs of autonomous individual action and the security of life that largely remains rooted in long-term forms of social belonging (Cline-Coles and Robson 2005).

Given the critical state of urban infrastructure and economy in Africa, efficiency gains, cost savings and resource mobilisation will take place only by intensifying and extending the participation of residents in concrete activities where they feel that they are not simply being consulted or manipulated. Rather, residents must be convinced that participation advances the larger project of inclusive nation building and region building. The greater visibility of demands for justice, democracy, efficiency and morality that are taking place across African cities presents a fruitful place to support political contestation that can be waged on behalf of those who have previously been kept out of the process. But what the poor actually win largely depends on the existence of political parties and institutionalised policies that back up their claims for rights. Here, the problem is that the more powerful political forces can define the categories and identities through which these claims can be made. These forces are usually constituted in the alliances cemented between particular national ruling elites, using the apparatus of the state to consolidate and prolong their power, and large established and emerging non-African national powers, as well as with multinational companies. They are also constituted in networks of African elites that cross national boundaries and that have deals to support each other regardless of internal legitimacy. Whereas economic elites often played the game of national politics in order to create favourable conditions for enhancing accumulation, a new generation of businesspeople is plying the more globalised networks of interchange as a means of carving out spaces of operation that try to pay as little attention as possible to political competition (Hyden 2006; Igué 2010; Onamo 2011).

In part, this power is reproduced through governments actively complicating the lives of residents, undermining 'real' economic activities, and intensifying

228

the labour required to get things done. Residents are actively 'disadvantaged' by having to wait unnecessarily for the delivery of services and assistance to which they are entitled, in an arduous, time-wasting process of repeated visits to bureaucratic offices. It is displayed in the ways in which evictions are decided and practised, demonstrations are broken up, and people are arrested arbitrarily and harassed over minor infringements. It is displayed in the dispossession of the spaces and practices through which intricate webs of support had been cultivated by turning participants into the objects of entrepreneurial development through microenterprise. This wear and tear on the patience and energies of a significant part of a city's population dissuades people from taking authority seriously when it does appear to act in their interests.

It also takes away the desire and confidence of citizens to take concrete steps to organise in ways that would improve everyday living conditions. Reducing vulnerability is often tied to making daily events less visible to the authorities, therefore taking away the mutual recognition that is an important element of building collaboration. Historically, the management of the streets has long relied on a punitive attitude. Long-term efforts to remove trade, hawking and public assembly from the streets and to assign such activities a designated place end up diminishing the value of street networks (Mitullah 2003). These are the domains in which the heterogeneity of the city has the most potential to be mobilised as a facilitator of both social safety and movement across the city. It is understandable that municipal administrations want to introduce order into large trading areas, especially those hijacked by various mafias and delinquents. Still, while the spatial systems of cities emphasise both fluid circulation and coherent integration of activities and populations, the streets are where these two dimensions intersect. The more that neighbouring streets evidence different but complementary degrees of activity and traffic flow, the more dynamic local centres will emerge (Hillier 2009).

Given these realities, it is important to enrol advocates and champions for new urban development ideas and practices from a wide range of quarters. Public services are often handicapped by problems of moral hazard, delivering the minimum because those for whom they provide services do not have the tools or expectations to evaluate what constitutes adequate performance. Too often, providers and decision makers have inadequate incentives to align their interests with those of their clients; therefore, important improvements in social welfare may be brought about in situations where there are strong moral connections between people and where providers and decision makers have a large degree of autonomy in how they act upon those connections.

That these situations now often relate to contexts outside the local public sphere – in the domains of religious, activist and even traditional associational groupings – should not be a deterrent to their engagement by development actors. In this regard, the numerous transnational trading networks that ensure the supply of car parts, electronics and other household items, as well as managing the export of large volumes of agricultural products and minerals outside official state channels (often with the state's complicity), constitute a largely untapped wealth of expertise and financial capital. How they are incorporated into above-board development collaborations remains to be worked out, but the important first step is at least to include them conceptually as possible actors.

Conceptualising a way forward

Given the preparedness of a larger number of urban residents to take on the challenges of development and growth, what can be done in the near future? Programmes and policies must reflect an intelligent willingness to grapple with the infrastructure deficit, better understand the operations of a 'real' economy, and foster institutions or networks that will enhance innovation in a context of dire need, too little money and perverse political incentives.

Network-centric development intervention Given the fragmentary character of African urban development politics, interventions aimed at leveraging economic and social links for growth are critical. In order to build on existing capacity and entrepreneurial initiatives, it is important to ensure a flow of information that gets to the right people at the right time. As indicated above, increasing numbers of urban residents are demanding to be 'part of the loop', to have more direct, unmediated access to information about how resources are acquired and used at the municipal level. While maintaining relationships with local networks remains critical, residents are also increasingly dissatisfied with seeing the city through the eyes of local chiefs and power brokers. This dissatisfaction partly accounts for the growing popularity of radio and television programming – both that of local media markets and web-based programming – that demonstrates a critical perspective on municipal affairs and often presents itself as the 'voice of the people'.

At the same time, urban 'popular economies' centred on small-scale services – repair, internet or retail – are often limited because they are situated within a network of family and extra-familial relationships that make claims on the services provided as well as on the limited profits generated by them. Being sited within a broad network of relationships enables individuals to diversify greatly, manoeuvring for opportunities and services, and to establish reciprocities of support. However, small enterprises are constantly forced to cover the various immediate needs of the network as well as to provide employment to individuals who add little to the running of the business itself.

That said, despite clear inefficiencies in infrastructure, services and labour markets, what often does work in the densely populated small and medium-sized urban production districts are the different forms of labour practices at work. Textiles, shoes, furniture, car parts and repair, household goods, hardware, catering, transport, electronics and second-hand IT products are significant sectors of the urban economy, often concentrated in specialised districts that absorb tens of thousands of workers in a mix of small and medium-sized enterprises. Many different kinds of work exist – fabrication, repair, marketing, invention – in the same setting, so there can be a built-in flexibility applied to the specifications of different orders and consumer needs. As the bulk of consumers at this level are based locally, there can be a continuous flow of information between end markets and producers. The key is how to build up from these local-level proficiencies to address potential markets on a much larger scale.

In such situations, a full range of activities and services are required to take a service or product from concept to final sale – i.e. financial, regulatory, supply, support services, etc. The key strengths of African urban production are the strong ties that exist at the local level and the ways in which these ties support links between different kinds of work and skills. But accessing larger markets requires the development of a wide range of connections that are often more fluid and short term. Customer needs vary, preferences come and go, orders are not necessarily continuous and production centres must be prepared to adapt their lines to a broader range of tastes and situations. Given the excess capacity that already exists in many parts of the thoroughly industrialised world, African cities are not going to compete anytime soon in terms of mass-produced items such as electronics, textiles and household goods. But they do have a potential comparative advantage in producing for a wide range of niche markets, both domestic and international, in which craftsmanship, cross-component assembly of machinery and electronics, back-office operations, small-scale innovative technologies, agricultural and bio-product processing or piecework have substantial value. As customer requirements become increasingly differentiated, they need to be addressed in specific ways, and this requires a systematic assessment of available local capacity, skill and experience among a *network* of qualified suppliers.

Entrepreneurs of various types have long cultivated relationships with suppliers, customers and collaborators that cut across local contexts to include both other parts of their own cities and different cities. Long-term circuits of exchange, which are used to move goods and people, involve dense networks of contacts. At the same time, the shape of these networks can often be quite circumscribed, relying on longstanding social, religious, ethnic or family ties that keep entrepreneurs from exploring new relationships and opportunities. In many cases, businesspeople complain about being 'locked into' often very parochial circuits of exchange and collaboration. While these circuits sometimes provide extensive reach across cities and countries, they may, simultaneously, restrict the kind of synergies that are possible within the home city.

Therefore, substantial added value to existing economic capacity could be attained through investments in network hubs that mediate between and join different links on the value chain. The question is how the different strands of the 'concept to end use' trajectory can be efficiently interwoven in order to reach new markets. At present, the number of bottlenecks is legendary. Costly time lags continue to persist between offloading at ports and onward shipment by rail or truck; the absence of storage facilities results in spoilage; sporadic power and other service supplies interrupt production schedules; and lack of adequate sanitation and healthcare result in unpredictable labour availability. A more seamless movement of goods and services is crucial to market expansion, and this will necessitate substantial investment in infrastructure. But more extensive exposure to information – in terms of both potential markets and existing productive and support capacity – could contribute to an increase in African market share domestically and internationally.

More proficient matching of networks of workshops producing similar items (or whose existing operations could easily be converted to either short- or long-term production of different commodity lines) with local business and advertising services, custom clearance brokers, container lines and air freight could expand volume and secure delivery efficiencies. Local expertise on trade fairs, niche markets, online marketing, consumer inventories and retail diversification could be connected to networks of different local producers. Here, hubs operate to identify the distribution of particular activities and resources across specific locations; they act as an intersection between different data and knowledge bases. While the earnings of expatriate Africans are remitted in large amounts back home, there are few ways in which to consolidate and utilise their accumulated experiences and their knowledge of the areas in which they operate, apart from sector-specific entrepreneurial networks. Hubs could be one way of achieving a better synthesis of these disparate 'exposures' to international settings, in order both to enhance knowledge about international markets and to increase the number of 'weak' network ties, which are usually seen as being important to market expansion.

As hubs are intended to maximise the circulation of information and knowledge available to various components of the value chain, so too would information about the operation of hubs be widely available to a broad range of actors. While it is impossible for any operating hub not to privilege particular networks and connections, not to rely on specific configurations of relationships between various producers and service providers, it is critical that such hubs do not become yet another sphere of clientelism. The assumption here is that, while various forms of patrimonial governance have to some extent secured stability in often precarious and volatile urban environments, they also do not make efficient use of the existing resources and abilities. It is a system that over-includes – it draws too many financial and human resources into a limited range of activities – and over-excludes – unnecessarily and without economic justification. As such, it keeps too many actors from using their full potential.

Hubs, then, are one modest way of recalibrating resource and opportunity flows and of involving a larger proportion of the urban population in value-added economic activity attained through market expansion. Of course, this is an approach to urban management that poses significant challenges to 'business as usual', where local authorities often use their position to steer resources and opportunities into specific networks of support. Therefore, the operation of hubs would require public accountability and reporting, as well as commitment at a national level in the form of a dedicated state agency to mobilise the technical assistance, policy support and international connections that only the state can provide.

Intraregional and inter-sectoral approaches to infrastructure financing Given the highly constricted financial space in which African cities presently operate, there are few viable avenues through which to pursue the mobilisation of funding for infrastructure, particularly in the prolonged aftermath of the global economic crisis. Given the increasing parallelism of finance and productive/commodity capital, Africa has little choice but to rapidly develop its financial sector – an enormous challenge given the small size, illiquidity and inadequate market infrastructure that characterises national capital markets. Given these constraints, strategies that enable the interlinking of bond and equity instruments issued by national and municipal governments are required in order for the financial sector to attain sufficient scale. It is important to continue with innovations in hybrid delivery value chains that meld together different scales of housing finance and production to enhance affordability, as well as to use the full range of 'mix and match' opportunities to secure land and provide differentiated access to housing, from sites and services to fully extended social housing schemes and segmented rental markets.

Connections among different ways of mobilising finance need to be explored. At local district levels, residents are sometimes proficient at raising money for various projects to improve their livelihoods and built environment but then receive little support from financial institutions. Sometimes, major informal trading groups have access to significant amounts of money but find that municipal and national governments either put too many impediments in the way of systematic investment in infrastructure improvement or extort too high a price for their cooperation. These funds then end up going elsewhere, particularly in property development outside Africa. The proficiency and speed shown by large informal groups in moving money around are rarely matched by formal institutional mechanisms. While accountability and legitimacy are important considerations, these values are often deployed as a way of 'getting a piece of the action' rather than as devices for adequately socialising financial flows.

Conclusion

Any urban development strategy must be built around the aspirations, capacities, practices and histories of a city's majority. In significant ways, that majority is yet to be discovered, as it has seldom expressed or recognised itself as a coherent political entity. Municipal elections have taken place, of course, and most mayors and regional governors are now democratically elected, and so in some sense a 'majority' has spoken. But the sort of majority we are discussing here goes beyond the statistical count or composition of electoral victories. Rather, it highlights how much is still unknown about the ways in which civil servants, bureaucrats, artisans, workers, labourers, salespeople, traders and entrepreneurs – all with their specialisations and sectoral interests – have continued to think of and make use of each other as complementary resources in order to carve out a viable life in the city. All the ups and downs in the development of public institutions, commerce, manufacturing, service industries and enterprise have often meant that staying strictly within the confines of a particular sector of work is not sufficient in order to make a life for themselves. As a result, these differentiated actors have to find various ways to work together, to intersect their opportunities and resources.

This coming together has rarely assumed a stable, continuous form; it has been something to be negotiated and reworked time and time again. Still, these efforts give rise to a 'majority' – neither strictly poor nor middle class, yet sufficiently stabilised to create urban lives. An urban politics and an approach to development that make use of these histories of mobilising an urban majority are therefore crucial elements of any urban transformation in Africa today. The intelligence honed from these efforts, as well as respect for the sacrifices made, must be critical elements of any strategic approach. Decentralised local councils may be the most salient venues in which to foster participation and manage local services, but city-wide politics remains the arena for tapping into and harnessing the majority, not as vote banks, but through the capacity of different segments, backgrounds and ways of life to come together and push through changes of orientation and administration. This city-wide politics requires its space, and thus a freeing of public activity and expression in a range of dedicated public spaces is a crucial component of such politics.

Finally, Africa is a striking example that urbanisation does not equate precisely with city life. If urbanisation entails thickening intersections and restructurings of spaces, actors and materials in ways that intensify their interdependencies, then the urbanisation of Africa goes beyond simply the enormous growth of cities. The intensive ways in which rural and underdeveloped areas of the region have been directly incorporated into highly experimental circuits of commodity trade and production networking, the reworking of low-density savannah lands and deserts into highly contested routes for trade and population movement, and the well-worn migratory paths between city and rural areas all point to processes of urbanisation that exceed the scale of the city. The growth of so-called secondary cities and the prolific trade flows between them give rise to urbanised regions largely based on complementary circulations of agricultural commodities. In addition, sizeable numbers of Africans are always in motion, as migration and sojourning become a way of life, and these personal trajectories constitute new links between places.

This diffusion of urbanisation processes raises important questions about the scale at which things are done, combined and changed. While a tendency towards subsidiarity and decentralisation has been critically important, life for increasing numbers of African households means dividing their time and resources between divergent places, sectors and domains. If many Africans are propelled out into the wider world because there are few opportunities to construct a sustainable livelihood locally, then it will be increasingly difficult to consolidate localities within cohesive 'local' frameworks, since their residents follow such diverse and individual trajectories.

What this means when considered in the context of all the circulations and movements taking place in the region today is that, with few exceptions, African cities may still have highly circumscribed and limited economic, political and cultural relations with a globalised world, but that households and localities within those cities often participate in a large number of relationships with spaces, actors and processes that exceed the territorial and jurisdictional boundaries of a given district, municipality or even region. Everyday life may be widely urbanised, even if the terms of that life as viewed through the lens of one specific locality may appear to be quite limited, even impoverished. With such a distribution of attention and effort across often highly differentiated contexts, directing households 'back' into a more concentrated focus on the development of something called 'their neighbourhood' or 'their city' will undoubtedly need to be persuasive. This does not mean that most city residents are not largely stuck in redundant routines and locations, not in need of massive economic and political transformations. Rather, it highlights the many ways in which African spatial organisation has exceeded its colonial legacies and exceeds the various postcolonial efforts to configure new regional economic and trading blocs. In any formulation of urban development strategy, then, considerations of scale become important. Policy makers, investors and researchers cannot simply assume a universal city to which similar strategies will apply. Of course, some common approaches can be generalised. But if critical concerns and struggles for many Africans today are precisely at what scale it is possible to conceive and realise a viable life and how the definition and location of that scale are always changing – from the level of the family to that of national identity – what takes place between cities, between cities and rural areas, and between Africa and the rest of the world, is as important as what takes place within the city.

References

Bayart, J.-F. and J.-P. Warnier (2004) *Matiére á politique: le pouvoir, les corps, et les choses*. Paris: Karthala.

Beauchemin, C. and P. Bocquier (2004) 'Migration and urbanisation in francophone West Africa: a review of the recent empirical evidence'. *Urban Studies* 41(11): 2245–72.

Boone, C. (2003) *Political Topographies of the African State*. New York, NY: Cambridge University Press.

Cline-Cole, R. and E. Robson (2005) *West African Worlds: Paths through socio-economic change, livlihoods and development*. Upper Saddle River, NJ: Pearson Education

Coquery-Vidrovitch, C. (1991) 'The process of urbanization in Africa (from the origins to the beginning of independence)'. *African Studies Review* 34: 1–98.

de Sardan, J.-P. O. (2009) *Les huit modes de gouvernance locale en Afrique de l'Ouest*. Power and Politics in Africa, Working Paper No. 4. London: Department for International Development and the Overseas Development Institute.

Foster, V. and C. Briceño-Garmendia (eds) (2010) *Africa's Infrastructure: A time for transformation*. Washington, DC: World Bank.

Hillier, B. (2009) 'Spatial sustainability in cities: organic patterns and sustainable forms'. In D. Koch, L. Marcus and J. Steen (eds) *Proceedings of the Seventh International Spatial Syntax Symposium*. Stockholm: KTH.

Hyden, G. (2006) *African Politics in Comparative Perspective*. Cambridge: Cambridge University Press.

Igué, J. (2010) 'A new generation of African leaders: what issues do they face'. *International Development Policy* 1: 115–33.

Kasekende, L., Z. Brixova and L. Ndikumana (2010) 'Africa's counter-cyclical policy responses to the crisis'. *Journal of Globalization and Development* 1(1): 1–20.

Marie, A. (ed.) (1997) *L'Afrique des Individus: Itineraires citadins dans l'Afrique contemporaine (Abidjan, Bamako, Dakar, Niamey)*. Paris: Karthala.

Mitullah, W. (2003) 'Street vending in African cities: a synthesis of empirical findings from Kenya, Cote d'Ivoire, Ghana, Zimbabwe, Uganda and South Africa'. Background case study for *World Development Report 2005: A Better Investment Climate for Everyone*.

OECD (2012) *Mapping Support for Africa's Infrastructure Investment*. Paris: Organisation for Economic Co-operation and Development (OECD).

Onamo, A. (2011) *The Politics of Property Rights Institutions in Africa*. Cambridge: Cambridge University Press.

PPIAF (2009) *Annual Report 2009*. Washington, DC: Public-Private Infrastructure Advisory Facility (PPIAF).

Raeymaekers, T. (2002) *Network War: An introduction to Congo's privatised conflict economy*. Amsterdam: NOVIB.

UN-Habitat (2009) *Planning Sustainable Cities: Policy directions*. London: Earthscan.

13 | National urbanisation and urban strategies: necessary but absent policy instruments in Africa

Susan Parnell and David Simon

Introduction

Consciously or unconsciously, governments and their bankers make decisions on a daily basis that impact on the vitality of cities and towns. This is nowhere more obvious than in Africa, the most rapidly urbanising continent in the world (World Bank 2009). The associated demographic transitions in Africa now mean that the embedded urban policy positions of governments, whether or not they are defined as such, are among the most important in determining the well-being of the population and also the continent's economic and ecological resilience. Despite their obvious importance, national urbanisation and national urban strategies in Africa receive remarkably little policy attention today – a situation that, we argue in this chapter, must change, not least by means of a shift in the focus of development bank lending priorities to become more consciously 'urban sensitive' in terms of urban–rural interactions and integration at national and supranational levels.

Embracing African cities does not imply abandoning the rural agenda. On the contrary, what we are suggesting is that effective national planning and investment hinge on complementary and differentiated urban and rural strategies. Conscious and transparent policy formation is necessary because there are some trade-offs that will have to be made, and policy positions must be politically defensible. It is important to have explicitly linked but differentiated policy agendas, because the urban and rural circumstances are hugely variable and governments' success in delivery will depend on their being responsive to local circumstances. As Africa enters a period of heightened opportunity and risk, the blunt policy instruments that have persisted over the last half century of independence are neither practically nor politically robust. Outdated national development policy positions – some now existing more in name than in substance – must give way to sharper strategic interventions that address the dilemmas of the day and speak to the challenges of the future. In this context, how to address the challenges posed by African cities represents a key policy question.

One of the problems one encounters in trying to construct a coherent discussion about African urban futures is that there are ambiguities in the policy discourses; these stem, at least in part, from the confusion between *urbanisation policy* (i.e. how to guide the national urban spatial system or the network of cities and towns, or the process of rural–urban demographic shift) and national *urban policy* (i.e. what sovereign states aspire to through and in their major settlements). Both are important, and they are certainly related, but they present very different policy choices. Urbanisation or spatial frameworks hinge on where investment and people are concentrated (and will be concentrated), while urban policy debates are about what happens within, especially the largest, cities. In order to avoid the common mistake of conflating the issues, perpetuated most obviously in the Lipton-inspired debate about urban bias (Corbridge 1982; Lipton 1977; Varshney 1993; see also Jones and Corbridge 2010 for a recent appraisal), we highlight the role of national government with respect to the movement of people from rural areas to towns and the emerging urban system on the one hand, and the role of national government departments in cities and towns on the other hand. If anything, we would suggest that the issue of how central governments act (or do not act) in the cities and towns of Africa should be given increasing priority over the often unproductive debate on the urban versus the rural or on urbanisation that has tended to dominate both the academic literature and political discussion. In this chapter we do not address the burgeoning literature on city development strategies (CDSs) in Africa (Boraine et al. 2006; Robinson 2011) as, while national government is sometimes involved in these city-level regional strategic planning processes, where they happen at all they tend to reflect locally driven agendas in places where city governments have significant strategic capacity. The CDS-type process, despite its donor-driven origins in the neoliberal devolution of planning and marketing roles, often has significant local legitimacy and thus represents an ideal opportunity for national governments to engage in bottom-up urban change and avoid being sidelined by the major cities.

Following recent calls for more, not less, government involvement in African development and planning (Gandy 2005; Parnell and Pieterse 2010; Parnell et al. 2009; UN-Habitat 2009; 2010a; Van Donk et al. 2008) and the more specific arguments of Turok and Parnell (2009) that cities are far too important to be left entirely to the devices of local government, the purpose of this chapter is to suggest a greater and expanded role for the central state in city development. Targeted infrastructure investment is one obvious opportunity for national governments to intervene in the urban system and to make cities work better and more sustainably. Especially in Africa, where outdated institutional systems of governance and an ill-equipped civil service militate against effective and resilient urban management, it is often only the centre that can stimulate the kinds of reforms (for example in tax and law) that are needed to complement

enhanced local governance performance. The proposition that national governments should do more both *for* cities and *in* cities should not be confused with
a centralising agenda. Indeed, many of the reforms that national governments
might wish to consider would involve greater autonomy or differentiated and
more appropriate systems for urban governance.

The remainder of this chapter comprises three parts. The next section
provides a historical context to the current policy environment, and draws
out the principal politico-economic forces underpinning the evolving postcolonial urbanism in Africa and its relationships to other world regions in
a period of deepening economic and social globalisation (see, for example,
Simon 1992). The major point made in this section is that the African urban
present is locked into the dysfunctionalities of the past. For this to change
on a city scale requires transformational policy change, principally, though
not exclusively, at the central government level. The developmental barriers
include the fact that there has generally been negligible reform of the internal
management of cities, because of nationally imposed institutional constraints
and the negative economic impact of previous spatial development and industrial policies that have eroded confidence in national spatial planning. In
the second part we explore more contemporary dynamics, arguing that global
environmental changes, including climate change, the internal transformation
of African economies, and especially the dramatically altered demographic
profiles of countries and cities heighten the need for a more overt focus on
cities, both in national settlement systems and in the work of national line
departments. The third and concluding section reflects on recent work that
has called for a move 'beyond urban bias', and proposes tangible areas for
greater involvement by African governments (and their financial supporters)
that are willing to reform their engagement in the national spatial system
and the internal functioning of cities in the interests of enhanced and more
sustainable development.

A discredited legacy: national urbanisation and urban strategy failure and omission

UN-Habitat's *Global Report on Human Settlements* (2009) provides an exceptionally clear exposition of the dysfunctional internal management of cities,
especially in Africa, a view that is widely reflected in the academic literature
(see Pieterse 2008). While it is far from clear how this dire position is to be
rectified, there are ideas that we can draw on about the genesis of the contemporary urban crisis in Africa. Significant structural problems in African cities
can be linked to widespread experiences of war and drought (see Jenkins and
Wilkinson 2002; Simon 2008), but the personal and infrastructural strains that
are evident in the continent's urban areas, large and small, are also tied to the
uncoupling of urbanisation and industrialisation, which can be attributed in

large part to Africa's global economic marginalisation (Simon 1992; UN-Habitat 2010a). External factors aside, major institutional failures also underpin the urban malaise, a situation not helped by neoliberalism's impact on African cities; this further eroded already weak state structures through structural adjustment programmes in the 1980s, followed by some privatisation and corporatisation (Rakodi 1997; Simon 1995; Stren and White 1989). Even without neoliberal efforts to decentre the state and create commercial rationalities in government, in general African urban planning and management systems are outmoded, ineffective, corrupt, dysfunctional or absent. It is our proposition that some of the crisis in cities stems not from globalisation or privatisation, but simply from national government neglect, benign or otherwise, of the institutional framing of urban development.

Other than stipulating the terms of local government elections, few African governments have done much to overturn the colonial dual-city planning structure that characterises cities across the continent, a legacy that still accounts for much of the profile of inequality in these cities today (Freund 2007; King 1976; Myers 2003; O'Connor 1983; Simon 1992). Until recently, and then only when pushed by neoliberal decentralisation initiatives, post-independence governments rarely altered their national planning and fiscal systems to allow for improved city revenue collection or for city-scale redistribution (see Chapters 9 and 10; Stren and White 1989). As a result, systems of city government have not been developed properly and informality is now the dominant experience of African urban residents, with the possible exception of South Africa (Chabal and Daloz 1999; Iyenda 2007; Simone 2004; Simone and Abouhani 2005). Even the self-conscious efforts of the relatively well resourced South Africans to transform their cities have had limited success, in large part because of the reluctance of national government to address the needs of cities or to reform the contradictions in the underlying planning and fiscal regimes in sub-national government (Turok and Parnell 2009).

By leaving in place the colonial/traditional planning regimes that are ill-suited to the complex demands of urban management, national governments in countries such as South Africa, Botswana and Tanzania have not only compounded sprawl and informality but have failed to create conditions that are conducive to poverty reduction, growth or environmental sustainability (see Myers 2005). Peri-urban areas across the continent are largely unplanned and ungoverned, either because of the failure to incorporate them into working urban local authorities that are capable of service provision, or because of the pressures from below to stay out of formally governed territory where municipal service costs erode already stretched household incomes (McGregor et al. 2006; Simon 2008). Thus, for diverse reasons, much of Africa's urban development of the last 50 years has been poorly integrated into either local or national systems of urban regulation. As these settlements grow, as demand for formal service provision mounts, and, critically, as developers begin to demand a more predictable planning environment for large-scale commercial and industrial developments, the lacuna in the conceptual thinking about urban management in Africa becomes more apparent. It is partly for this reason that there has recently been a shift beyond the narrow development focus on the African slum to a systematic reconsideration of the role of urban planning in Africa (Parnell et al. 2009; Pieterse 2008; UN-Habitat 2009; 2010a; 2011).

Whereas policy about the internal management of cities in the post-independence period was generally characterised by neglect and oversight, the same is not true of African governments' attention to urbanisation. The questions of where development assistance should be provided and what it should focus on have been a dominant motif of the independence era for governments, donors and bankers. During the 1960s and 1970s, national urban (development) strategies informed by modernisation approaches to development comprised an integral feature of state policy and planning in most parts of the global South, including Africa. In fact, with the notable exceptions of South Africa (1910) and Egypt (1922), this period coincided with the wave of decolonisation across Africa that commenced in Ghana in 1957. The immediate post-independence period was imbued with optimism that poverty, illiteracy and underdevelopment could rapidly be overcome by the twin motors of the rapid worldwide economic growth then occurring and the grand modernist nation-building visions led by the indigenous elites newly come to power.

Axiomatic to modernisation theory and its practical application in a development context was the view that large-scale industrial projects deploying new technologies could serve as focal points for economic development and capital accumulation. Located principally in urban areas, these would attract new investment funds and migrants, giving rise to urban growth and generating economies of scale. In time, congestion and other diseconomies of scale would become significant, triggering a trickle down through the urban hierarchy and rural space economy, providing employment, raising incomes and ultimately increasing welfare. Through this process, regional and urban–rural inequalities, initially sharpened by the strongly centripetal forces of early-stage urban development, would decline and the periphery would progressively be incorporated into the modern economy.

Neoclassical economists argued that increasing spatial and socioeconomic inequalities during the agglomeration phase were necessary for rapid capital accumulation and urban development, and that the tipping point towards outward diffusion would occur spontaneously when the disadvantages of further agglomeration outweighed the benefits. Conversely, Keynesian economists held that the processes could be optimised and inequalities kept within

TABLE 13.1 Summary of the different imperatives defining national urbanisation and urban strategies in late twentieth- and early twenty-first-century Africa

	Urbanisation policy	Urban policy
The colonial and postcolonial legacy of retarded and defunct policy	Discredited urban and industrial incentives fail to stimulate urban growth, and are blamed for rural deprivation. See Table 13.2 for variations in urbanisation policy (Rogerson 2009).	African economies are weak and based on agriculture, not on manufacturing or urban sectors. Interests of the urban elite are protected by colonial systems that are left intact while the needs of the new urban poor are ignored, resulting in pervasive informality. Cities are small and not politically important nationally. Neoliberal devolution puts the focus on local government.
New imperatives for African urbanism	Demographic changes – migration and urban growth are changing settlement systems. Agriculture cannot sustain large rural populations.	The majority of the national population is urban. Bigger urban populations present new markets. Larger cities are at greater ecological risk. Major city regions compete in the global economy.
Substantive opportunities for urbanisation and urban policy formation	Ecological vulnerabilities. Large infrastructure. Land use management reform.	Legal and institutional reform to ensure the appropriate size and shape of government. Tax reform to ensure that resources follow responsibilities.

acceptable limits by means of careful state intervention to prevent extreme urban economic overheating and agglomeration, and to promote regional and urban development across the space economy by redistributing investment and economic activity. Different combinations of public and private investment were advocated on ideological or pragmatic grounds, and decentralisation incentives were often combined with restrictions on new investment or industrial expansion in core urban areas. Generally, more authoritarian regimes of all ideological orientations were able to implement harsher penalties, including often draconian restrictions on urban residence for incoming migrants.

Based largely on such 'Western' economic precepts and on previous experience in the Organisation for Economic Co-operation and Development (OECD) countries which served to define the norms, considerable research effort was therefore devoted in different regions to identifying 'optimal' city sizes; missing links in urban hierarchies that could be targeted for filling; and the most efficient strategies for state-directed and urban-led regional development, which differed principally in the degree of concentration or dispersal of urban investment in such growth poles or centres. Different strategies (or sometimes successive phases of a single country's strategy – as in South Africa or Kenya) prioritised secondary cities that already had infrastructure, resources and 'critical mass'; intermediate cities that were perceived as needing stimulation as a precondition for self-sustaining growth; and/or smaller rural service centres (see, for example, Berry 1973; Friedmann 1973; Perroux 1950; Richardson 1972; 1973; 1976; 1981; 1987; Rodwin 1987; Simon 1990). Table 13.1 provides a typology of such past and current urban development strategies, highlighting the way in which attitudes and practices shift over time.

Since very few newly independent countries could afford such investment programmes from endogenous sources, donor funds and foreign direct investment were prerequisites. Accordingly, urban (development) strategies became de rigueur either as stand-alone documents or as components of national five-year or other development plans. Success was variable and often limited, and frequently came at disproportionate cost to the exchequer or aid donors. Some critics calculated that the opportunity cost of lost investment, employment and national income in core cities through the disincentives outweighed the decentralisation gains. Arguably the best-documented example is South Africa, where the policies were manipulated by the white minority government to serve its racially motivated agenda of territorial apartheid. State-led programmes in countries professing Marxist or African socialist ideologies, such as the Republic of Congo and Tanzania, bore considerable similarities to those in overtly capitalist states, although the emphasis was more on rural service centres and villagisation to facilitate infrastructure and social service delivery, but also on political control.

During this period, several African countries sought to reduce the dominance

TABLE 13.2 Typology of national urbanisation strategies

Strategy	Description
1. Laissez-faire	The 'do nothing' strategy is one with no set spatial policy, which allows urban patterns to reflect the play of market forces. Urban infrastructure investments are allocated on the basis of existing population and no linking occurs between patterns of urban development and broader societal goals.
2. Polycentric development of the primate city region	This efficiency-oriented strategy is premised on the assumption that the agglomeration economies of primate cities offer unrivalled advantages and that the major issue of national urban policy is to avert the diseconomies of urban growth. Building on the agglomeration advantages of primate cities, this strategy involves the planning of sub-centres or satellites linked to the metropolitan core via a city region-wide transport system.
3. Leapfrog decentralisation within the core region	This strategy is an extension of the core region strategy 2. The development of satellites would take place, however, outside the contiguously developed metropolitan region. The strategy therefore involves an extension of the existing city region with the development of the immediate hinterland.
4. Counter-magnets	In sharp contrast to the concentrated patterns of urbanisation that would flow from strategies 1–3, the strengthening of counter-magnets would result in a greater dispersion of urban development. The key point is using a form of polarised development to combat polarisation towards the primate centre. Inherent difficulties of this strategy are the requirement that counter-magnets be relatively large and the danger of merely replicating elsewhere the negative traits of polarisation, which this strategy is designed to overcome in the primate centre.
5. Small service centres and rural development	This strategy is often viewed more as a complement to a national urban policy than a variant of it. The policy thrust is towards retaining rural migrants in country areas by providing support for agrarian improvement and opportunities for non-farm employment.
6. Regional metropolis and sub-system development	This strategy involves a melding of strategies 4 and 5 across the urban hierarchy of a single region. Emphasis is on the largest city in a region, promoting its role as regional metropolis but simultaneously treating it as the pinnacle of the urban hierarchy in its region and planning development in order to maximise spillover effects into smaller centres.

7. Growth centres	Strategy 7 involves the selection of urban centres on the basis of their potential for accelerated development. Growth centres are meant to function as loci for decentralised industrial development and as regional centres for rural–urban migrants. Implementation of this strategy is hindered by the political temptation to select too many centres.
8. Development axes or corridors	The promotion of development axes aims to achieve mutually reinforcing cities by stimulating axes of urban development along intercity transportation corridors. Often these axes evolve de facto; however, their planning may be a means of building up the economies of adjacent but economically unequal regions.
9. Provincial capitals	A policy for activating growth in provincial capitals is a kind of dispersed urban strategy. Often it is attractive politically because it may eschew development potential.
10. Secondary cities	An increasingly popular strategy is one of promoting growth at a limited number of secondary cities, which might be a subset of provincial capitals (strategy 9), but where developmental potential is an important criterion for selection. Secondary city strategies are distinguished from growth centres (strategy 7) in that they focus on the promotion of indigenous development rather than on attracting large-scale industrial development.
11. Hybrid	The final kind of national urban development strategy involves a combination of two or more of strategies 2–10.

Source: Rogerson 2009: 15.

of colonial-era capital cities – which were often marginal to the national territory – and to promote regional development and national integration through the establishment of new, more centrally located and politically neutral capitals. The best examples are Abuja (Nigeria), Dodoma (Tanzania), Lilongwe (Malawi) and Yamoussoukro (Côte d'Ivoire). These swallowed vast capital investments, often mirrored by underinvestment and deterioration in the former capitals and other cities, and have been only partially successful at best. Several decades later, Lagos and Dar es Salaam continue to host some traditional capital city functions.

By the early 1980s, such policies and programmes had lapsed or been abandoned virtually everywhere. There was a combination of reasons for this, including excess cost, limited achievement, corruption in allocation of incentives or ability to evade restrictions, government indebtedness, and the severe central, regional and local government budget cutbacks that occurred under structural adjustment programmes that imposed neoliberal economic policies. The failure of these plans was also a result of concerns that many longstanding policies had contributed strongly to 'urban bias', a term popularised by Michael Lipton's (1977) study of India. Accordingly, the emphasis of donors shifted strongly to rural-based regional development (see, for example, Riddell 1985), which spawned intense debates over the merits and effectiveness of state-led, top-down versus community-driven or bottom-up approaches (Friedmann and Weaver 1979; Stöhr and Taylor 1981). In many African countries, this shift in emphasis was reinforced by the regional or rural orientation of traditional elites or particular ethnic groups who were against economic concentration in metropolitan areas beyond their territory, or regarded urbanisation and modernisation as a threat to 'tradition' and hence to their control. The focus then turned to debt relief (the Jubilee 2000 campaign) and poverty reduction through the mainly nationally and sectorally oriented Millennium Development Goals (MDGs) adopted by the United Nations (UN) in 2000. These targets now drive most development and poverty reduction policy in poor countries. Few of the MDGs are explicitly urban but most do have significant urban dimensions (UN-Habitat 2010a; Chapter 1).

In place of national urban policies and strategies, from the late 1980s and early 1990s the emphasis shifted to decentralisation and local economic development. Central governments in Africa all but abandoned the policy arena to provincial or regional governments and local authorities, which – where resources and incentives permitted – became increasingly competitive domestically and internationally, using place marketing, local 'boosterism' and their own packages of infrastructural or fiscal incentives (see Rogerson 2009 for a comprehensive review). Less proactive cities often stagnated, especially if lack of urban investment led to deteriorating and outdated infrastructure, the inadequate provision of shelter and the loss of competitive positions.

TABLE 13.3 Levels of African urbanisation, 2010

Country	Urban population (%)
Burundi	11.0
Uganda	13.3
Niger	16.7
Ethiopia	17.6
Rwanda	18.9
Malawi	19.8
Burkina Faso	20.4
Eritrea	21.6
Kenya	22.2
Swaziland	25.5
Tanzania (United Republic of)	26.4
Lesotho	26.9
Chad	27.6
Guinea-Bissau	30.0
Madagascar	30.2
Mali	33.3
Congo (Democratic Republic of)	35.2
Guinea	35.4
Zambia	35.7
Namibia	38.0
Mozambique	38.4
Sierra Leone	38.4
Central African Republic	38.9
Mauritania	41.4
Benin	42.0
Mauritius	42.6
Egypt	42.8
Senegal	42.9
Togo	43.4
Sudan	45.2
Nigeria	49.8
Côte d'Ivoire	50.1
Ghana	51.5
Seychelles	55.3
Morocco	56.7
Gambia	58.1
Cameroon	58.4
Angola	58.5
Cape Verde	61.1
Botswana	61.1
Liberia	61.5
South Africa	61.7
Congo	62.1
São Tomé and Príncipe	62.2
Algeria	66.5
Tunisia	67.3
Libyan Arab Jamahiriya	77.9
Gabon	86.0
Djibouti	88.1

Source: UN-Habitat 2010b, based on data for 2007.

Imperatives for a new generation of national urbanisation and urban policies

Conditions in the new millennium have again changed, and as a result there is renewed interest from governments in the increasingly complex settlement systems that are emerging in Africa. The acknowledgement that Africa, and many of its coastal and inland cities, are among the most vulnerable to climate risk has increased the focus on the capacity of the state in African cities to put in place policies such as coastal management, food security and disaster risk reduction plans, further revitalising the notion of nationally led planning (Simon 2010; UN-Habitat 2009; 2010a). The single most important driver of a policy shift in favour of cities, however, is the demographic change that is taking place on the continent, making it more populous and more urban.

The rate of growth of the African urban population is the highest in the world (at over 3 per cent), and while many of the countries on the continent remain predominantly rural, there are already many nations, including some of the largest in population terms, that are more urban than rural (Table 13.3). Unsurprisingly then, the next generation of Africans are projected to have an urban future (Table 13.4). These figures, which are regularly produced as a motivation for more careful and more explicit attention to be given to African cities, should speak for themselves and there should be no need to make the case for nation states to give greater attention to their cities. That the urbanisation trend is so widely ignored is a result of negligence on behalf of governments and major players such as the African Development Bank, donors and the UN; the legacy of deep-seated rural bias in policy; or vested interests (such as those of traditional authorities) that need to be exposed in the wider interests of development.

In practice, what African demographic transitions mean is not just many more millions of people, but a totally different social, economic and spatial or settlement structure. Africa is emerging as a continent with a few very large 'megacities' and a significant number of large metropolitan centres (many of them primate centres). Often these cities are associated with a highly dynamic and expanding semi-formal peri-urban hinterland. Finally, a significant proportion of the population lives in small towns and rural areas, either on traditional commonage or on commercial farms. In this regard, the current South African settlement typology (Table 13.5) is not atypical of an emerging pattern, although the country has one of the continent's few megacities and it also has a higher than average level of urbanisation for Africa (Figure 13.1).

Many authors caution against too static a depiction of the settlement system in Africa, pointing to widespread oscillating migration and the strong links between rural and urban livelihoods. Net outmigration was experienced from some capitals and other core urban areas during the recession of the 1980s and early 1990s, often in favour of secondary cities or rural areas (see Briggs and

TABLE 13.4 Trends in African urbanisation in a global context, 1950–2050

Region	Urban population (millions)						Urban population (%)					
	1950	1975	2007	2025	2050		1950	1975	2007	2025	2050	
World	737	1,518	3,294	4,584	6,398		29.1	37.3	49.4	57.2	69.6	
More developed regions	427	702	916	995	1,071		52.5	67.0	74.4	79.0	86.0	
Less developed regions	310	817	2,382	3,590	5,327		18.0	27.0	43.8	53.2	67.0	
Africa	32	107	373	658	1,233		14.5	25.7	38.7	47.2	61.8	

Source: UN DESA 2008: 3–5.

TABLE 13.5 Typology of South African settlements, 2008

	Population (% of national)	Economic activity (% of national GVA)	People living below a minimum level of living (% of national)
Gauteng city region	22	39	13
Coastal city regions	16	26	10
Cities	6	5	5
Regional service centres	14	16	14
Service towns	3	3	3
Local and niche settlements	9	2	13
Subtotal: urban (% of national)	72	94	60
Clusters and dispersed rural settlements	21	2	31
Farms/rest of South Africa	7	4	9
Subtotal: rural (% of national)	28	6	40

Note: GVA = gross value added.
Source: SACN 2008.

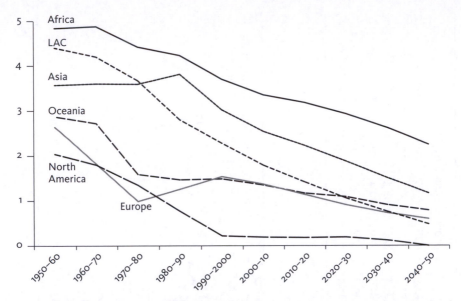

13.1 Distribution of urban population by city size in sub-Saharan Africa (percentage of urban population) (source: UN DESA 2008: 222)

Mwamfupe 2000; Potts 1995; 1997; Simon 1995), but this has generally now been reversed and urbanisation levels are rising again, with some exceptions such as Zimbabwe, where the governance crisis has profoundly distorted migration patterns. But it is a spurious logic that suggests that either the fact of ongoing deep rural poverty or the reality of the integrated or interdependent urban/rural livelihoods of many African people should justify urban neglect. What high levels of transnational and oscillating migration in Africa do point to is the imperative of national governments' urban policies accommodating migrants' needs, whether they are voluntarily migrant or not, when they are based in the cities where they spend a large proportion of their lives (see Chapter 12).

For now, Africa is still usually depicted as a rural continent, as a continent of refugees and displaced people, or of migrants to chaotic and unruly cities, but already it has a number of differentiated urban systems, with cities far larger than most European capitals occurring across the continent. This characteristic of Africa's urbanity has gone virtually unnoticed. Notwithstanding the obvious importance of these metropolitan cores to a country's national identity and economic profile, national governments are sometimes reluctant to acknowledge and facilitate big-city growth, South Africa being a prime example of this anti-urbanism or anti-metropolitanism (Turok and Parnell 2009). In looking forward to an urban African future, it would be naïve to anticipate that there will be no opposition, especially from national governments that stand to be eclipsed by increasingly powerful cities that are better able to position themselves in the global economy (Segbers 2007).

Significant African city regions have begun to emerge that not only dominate their national space economies but also serve as continental and even global hubs, presenting a modern consumer entry point for global capital. The corporate consultancy Monitor, for example, argues that:

> the economic future of [sub-Saharan Africa] is more connected to the success of its cities, and the competitive clusters based there, than to its nation states. Cities today generate most of the subcontinent's wealth, with many thriving despite obvious challenges. Rapid urbanization turbocharges economic growth and diversification, enhances productivity, increases employment opportunities, and improves standards of living. (Monitor 2009: 8)

Ironically, the three main interventions that the corporate consultancy identifies as key to making African cities competitive are actions that, in general, are the responsibility of national governments: the upgrading of large-scale infrastructure (power, transport, bulk services); skills development for a knowledge economy; and foreign direct investment.

Progressive urban metropolitanisation and city-centric globalisation have renewed concern about regional inequalities and urban (over-)concentration, but now in the context of increasing transboundary movements of people, goods, services, funds and even economic development along urban corridors. These corridors represent a contemporary form of what were termed development axes in the 1970s: in other words, linear development spines along which urbanisation flourishes and investment agglomerates. Prominent African examples include the Maputo Development Corridor linking Mozambique's capital with Gauteng, South Africa's industrial heartland, and the Greater Ibadan–Lagos–Cotonou–Lomé–Accra corridor linking four adjacent West African countries (UN-Habitat 2010a).

For national governments, especially smaller states that lack a large city or port, a national urbanisation strategy needs to define how it will integrate into the neighbouring countries' urban space economies. Information and communications technology (ICT) and the reduced real cost of surface and air transport have played important roles in linking city regions across political boundaries. Some of these trends, over which banks have significant influence, have also been encouraged by initiatives to reduce trade barriers and facilitate mobility undertaken by regional economic communities such as the Economic Community of West African States (ECOWAS), the Common Market for Eastern and Southern Africa (COMESA), the East African Community (EAC) and the Southern African Development Community (SADC) (see Chapter 12).

New spatial and socioeconomic inequalities are therefore becoming entrenched on different geographical scales, and policies are once more being sought to guide and moderate the vicissitudes of rampant market-led economic development. However, the technological revolutions and processes of trans-nationalisation just described make for a very different policy environment from that prevailing in the 1960s and 1970s. National sovereignty has been reduced by the progressive evolution of international and intergovernmental organisations and obligations in terms of international conventions and treaties from above, and the rise of civil society and non-governmental organisations from below.

While national urban policies are therefore important, they are inadequate on their own. Realistically, therefore, they will need to be complemented by compatible regional policies to address transboundary urban zones and corridors linking neighbouring states or groups of states, and also continental policies to address interregional interactions in a context where a small number of metropolitan areas serve as regional hubs and foci for interregional and global flows through highly connected airports, ports and ICT. At least five such primary hubs have emerged in Africa – Cairo (North Africa), Nairobi (East Africa), Johannesburg (southern Africa), and Lagos and Dakar (West Africa) – but Cape Town and Durban (southern Africa), Dar es Salaam and Addis Ababa (East Africa) and Accra (West Africa) also have strong interregional and intercontinental connectivity. In other words, the nation state and national policies need to be situated within regional and continental urban systems, which in turn articulate with the world economy. These are already, and will increasingly become, the gateways through which to maximise the benefits and to mediate the disadvantages of Africa's engagement with globalisation.

Conclusion: opportunities and scope for national urbanisation and urban policies

Notwithstanding the fact that cities (and local governments) in Africa play a possibly larger than usual regional economic development role, there are important aspects of national policy formation that will shape the developmental path of settlement systems and individual cities. This section focuses specifically on the opportunities and scope for national governments to influence urbanisation strategies and mould urban policy on critical issues such as industrial policy, poverty relief and climate change.

Debate on the form of a national urban spatial development framework has moved beyond the spatial concentrations talked about in the 1970s and 1980s (see Table 13.2). Today, national urban policy must not only define service nodes and economic corridors but also facilitate the creation of polycentric city regions that are located within regional and global economies and that may transcend national boundaries. With ecological and economic footprints that inevitably exceed their physical boundaries, and as the sites of critical infrastructure and intellectual investment, these city regions have to assume far greater national and regional policy prominence. Implied in this agenda is a clear understanding of the formal and informal urban space economies that drive African economies.

National urban policies should do more than address the national urban or settlement system, giving due weight to natural resource constraints and ecological vulnerabilities of cities and towns, especially along the coast. The increasing importance of the urban relative to the rural, and the economic dominance of cities, means that it is imperative that all national policies should work in the urban context, and this entails much more than national spatial planning. However, as stated above, there should not be a return to earlier dichotomous urban–rural policies. The importance of integrated national policy spanning urban, peri-urban and rural areas is underlined by the growing challenge of national food security in the face of continuing migration to towns and cities.

Speaking as part of the South African debate about the role of national government in urban development, Turok and Parnell (2009) have made a series of recommendations that could have general applicability in other African contexts (Box 13.1).

Box 13.1. Seven arguments for a national urban strategy to complement and reinforce essential action at the local scale

1. Signal a consistent message of conviction to key departments, state agencies and the private sector about development priorities.
2. Streamline the powers of public bodies over the built environment in order to organise these functions more efficiently and to strengthen city leadership.
3. Extend financial freedoms and flexibilities to competent municipalities in order to accelerate progress in addressing infrastructure bottlenecks, backlogs and neglected repairs.
4. Instigate changes in the national land management system to promote densification and to gradually reconfigure the urban form.
5. Coordinate the policies of different parts of government with a spatial dimension and align their investment programmes in order to get more consistency around major priorities such as poverty reduction, worklessness and climate change.
6. Initiate capacity building to overcome the deficient skills and experience among many municipalities, which are a barrier to basic service delivery and business support.
7. Improve knowledge and understanding of the challenges facing the country's cities and towns, including their economic and demographic links with other parts of the region.

Source: Adapted from Turok and Parnell 2009.

Finally, there are two crucial differences between the first generation of such plans tabled in the 1970s and 1980s and what we are advocating here. The first is that the dichotomised thinking about the urban and rural as somehow being in structural and functional opposition to each other is no longer tenable. The recent blossoming of research and policy on peri-urban interfaces or zones has demonstrated clearly that there are continua, not dichotomies, between them. Moreover, these continua are highly dynamic, especially under conditions of rapid urbanisation, with particular places changing their character and functional links with remarkable speed. In order to have a reasonable chance of shaping these changing spatial, socioeconomic and environmental relationships, the new generation of such plans must avoid the blueprint tradition in which spatial fixes are just that – rigid. Instead, more flexible and readily updated approaches are needed, starting not from an idealised planner's drawing board but from an understanding of the profound fluidity and dynamism of urbanisation processes. Instead of seeking to restrict and restrain through rigid zoning, they need to provide permissive guidelines and criteria that are appropriate to local conditions, and that factor in environmental change and the associated challenges of mitigation and adaptation.

The second key difference is that such national planning can no longer ignore transboundary processes and interactions. As we have indicated above, globalisation creates its own set of dynamics, often volatile and unpredictable. Again, these require flexibility rather than rigidity. However, appropriate national plans and guidelines will need coordination with those of neighbouring states if the dynamic potential of transboundary metropolitan areas and development corridors is to be guided rather than stifled. Indeed, to have contradictory policies and plans on either side of an economically integrated border would be very much worse than having none at all.

References

Berry, B. J. L. (1973) *The Human Consequences of Urbanization: Divergent paths in the urban experience of the twentieth century*. London: Methuen.

Boraine, A., O. Crankshaw, C. Engelbrecht, G. Gotz, S. Mbanga, M. Narsoo and S. Parnell (2006) 'The state of South African cities a decade after democracy'. *Urban Studies* 43: 259–84.

Briggs, J. and D. Mwamfupe (2000) 'Peri-urban development in an era of structural adjustment in Africa: the city of Dar es Salaam, Tanzania'. *Urban Studies* 37(4): 797–809.

Chabal, P. and J.-P. Daloz (1999) *Africa Works: Disorder as political instrument*. London: James Currey.

Corbridge, S. (1982) 'Urban bias, rural bias and industrialisation: an appraisal of the work of Michael Lipton and Terry Byres'. In J. Harriss (ed.) *Rural Development: Theories of peasant economy and agrarian change*. London: Hutchinson.

Freund, B. (2007) *The African City: A history*. Cambridge: Cambridge University Press.

Friedmann, J. (1973) *Urbanization, Planning and National Development*. London: Sage.

— and C. Weaver (1979) *Territory and*

Function: The evolution of regional planning. London: Edward Arnold.

Gandy, M. (2005) 'Learning from Lagos'. *New Left Review* 32: 37–53.

Iyenda, G. (2007) *Households' Livelihoods and Survival Strategies among Congolese Urban Poor: Alternatives to Western approaches to development*. Lewiston, NY and Lampeter: Edwin Mellen Press.

Jenkins, P. and P. Wilkinson (2002) 'Assessing the growing impact of the global economy on urban development in southern African cities: case studies in Maputo and Cape Town'. *Cities* 19: 33–47.

Jones, G. and S. Corbridge (2010) 'The continuing debate about urban bias: the thesis, its critics, its influence and its implications for poverty-reduction strategies'. *Progress in Development Studies* 10(1): 1–18.

King, A. (1976) *Colonial Urban Development: Culture, social power, and environment*. London: Routledge and Kegan Paul.

Lipton, M. (1977) *Why Poor People Stay Poor: A study of urban bias in world development*. London: Temple-Smith.

McGregor, D., D. Simon and D. Thompson (eds) (2006) *The Peri-Urban Interface: Approaches to sustainable natural and human resource use*. London: Earthscan.

Monitor (2009) *Africa from the Bottom Up: Cities, economic growth and prosperity in sub-Saharan Africa*. Houghton, South Africa: Monitor Group.

Myers, G. (2003) *Verandahs of Power: Colonialism and space in urban Africa*. Syracuse, NY: Syracuse University Press.

— (2005) *Disposable Cities: Garbage, governance and sustainable development*. Aldershot: Ashgate Publishing.

O'Connor, A. (1983) *The African City*. London: Hutchinson.

Parnell, S. and E. Pieterse (2010) 'The "right to the city": institutional imperatives of a developmental state'. *International Journal of Urban and Regional Research* 34: 146–62.

— and V. Watson (2009) 'Planning for cities in the global south: a research agenda for sustainable human settlements'. *Progress in Planning* 72(2): 233–41.

Perroux, F. (1950) 'The domination effect and modern economic theory'. In K. W. Rothschild (ed.) *Power in Economics*. London: Penguin.

Pieterse, E. (2008) *City Futures: Confronting the crisis of urban development*. London: Zed Books.

Potts, D. (1995) '"Shall we go home?" Increasing urban poverty in African cities and migration processes'. *Geographical Journal* 161(3): 245–64.

— (1997) 'Urban lives: adopting new strategies and adapting rural links'. In C. Rakodi (ed.) *The Urban Challenge in Africa: Growth and management of its large cities*. Tokyo and New York, NY: United Nations University Press.

Rakodi, C. (ed.) (1997) *The Urban Challenge in Africa: Growth and management of its large cities*. Tokyo: United Nations University Press.

Richardson, H. W. (1972) 'Optimality in city size, systems of cities, and urban policy: a sceptic's view'. *Urban Studies* 9(1): 29–48.

— (1973) *The Economics of Urban Size*. Farnborough: Saxon House.

— (1976) 'Growth pole spillovers: the dynamics of backwash and spread'. *Regional Studies* 10: 1–9.

— (1981) 'National urban development strategies in developing countries'. *Urban Studies* 18: 267–83.

— (1987) 'Whither national urban development strategies in developing countries?'. *Urban Studies* 24: 227–44.

Riddell, R. (1985) *Regional Development Policy: The struggle for rural progress in low-income countries*. Aldershot: Gower.

Robinson, J. (2011) 'The spaces of circulating knowledge: city strategies and global urban governmentality'. In E. McCann and K. Ward (eds) *Mobile Urbanism: Cities and policy-making in the global age*. Minneapolis, MN: Minnesota University Press.

Rodwin, L. (ed.) (1987) *Shelter, Settlement*

and Development. London: Allen and Unwin.

Rogerson, C. (2009) *International Policy Review: National spatial development planning*. Johannesburg: South African Cities Network.

SACN (2008) *Towards a National Urban Development Framework*. Johannesburg: South African Cities Network (SACN).

Segbers, K. (2007) *The Making of Global City Regions: An exploration of Johannesburg, Mumbai/Bombay, Sao Paulo, and Shanghai*. Baltimore, MD: Johns Hopkins University Press.

Simon, D. (ed.) (1990) *Third World Regional Development: A reappraisal*. London: Paul Chapman.

— (1992) *Cities, Capital and Development: African cities in the world economy*. London: Belhaven Press.

— (1995) 'Debt, democracy and development: sub-Saharan Africa in the 1990s'. In D. Simon, W. van Spengen, C. Dixon and A. Närman (eds) *Structurally Adjusted Africa: Poverty, debt and basic needs*. London: Pluto Press.

— (2008) 'Urban environments: issues on the peri-urban fringe'. *Annual Review of Environment and Resources* 33: 167–85.

— (2010) 'The challenges of global environmental change for urban Africa'. *Urban Forum* 21(3): 235–48.

Simone, A. (2004) *For the City Yet to Come: Changing African life in four cities*. Durham, NC: Duke University Press.

— and A. Abouhani (eds) (2005) *Urban Africa: Changing contours of survival in the city*. Dakar, London and Pretoria: CODESRIA, Zed Books and UNISA Press.

Stöhr, W. B. and D. R. F. Taylor (eds) (1981) *Development from Above or Below? The dialectics of regional planning in developing countries*. Chichester: John Wiley & Sons.

Stren, R. E. and R. R. White (eds) (1989) *African Cities in Crisis: Managing rapid urban growth*. Boulder, CO: Westview Press.

Turok, I. and S. Parnell (2009) 'Reshaping cities, rebuilding nations: the role of national urban policies'. *Urban Forum* 20: 157–74.

UN DESA (2008) *World Urbanization Prospects: The 2007 Revision*. New York, NY: Population Division of the Department of Economic and Social Affairs of the United Nations Secretariat (UN DESA).

UN-Habitat (2009) *Global Report on Human Settlements: Planning sustainable cities*. Nairobi: United Nations Human Settlements Programme (UN-Habitat).

— (2010a) *The State of African Cities 2010: Governance, inequalities and urban land markets*. Nairobi: United Nations Human Settlements Programme (UN-Habitat).

— (2010b) Global Urban Observatory (GUO): current database. Nairobi: United Nations Human Settlements Programme (UN-Habitat).

— (2011) *Global Report on Human Settlements 2011: Cities and climate change*. London: Earthscan.

Van Donk, M., M. Swilling, E. Pieterse and S. Parnell (eds) (2008) *Consolidating Developmental Local Government: The South African experience*. Cape Town: UCT Press.

Varshney, A. (ed.) (1993) 'Beyond urban bias'. *Journal of Development Studies* 29(4, special issue): 3–258.

World Bank (2009) *World Development Report 2009: Reshaping economic geography*. Washington, DC: World Bank.

14 | Urbanisation as a global historical process: theory and evidence from sub-Saharan Africa

Sean Fox

The process of urbanisation has traditionally been understood as a natural by-product of economic development. While there is no doubt that economic expansion in the urban sector can stimulate rural-to-urban migration, hence urbanisation, a strictly economic theory of the process fails to account adequately for the phenomenon of 'urbanisation without growth' observed in sub-Saharan Africa in the 1980s and 1990s (Fay and Opal 2000). Inspired by this apparent anomaly, I propose an alternative, historically grounded theory of urbanisation and deploy it to explain the stylised facts of Africa's urban transition, namely the late onset of urbanisation vis-à-vis other major, less developed world regions and the persistence of both urbanisation and rapid urban population growth in the late twentieth century despite economic stagnation (see Table 14.1).

TABLE 14.1 Demographic and economic trends in less developed regions, 1960–2005

	1960	1975–2005		
	Urban population (%of total)	Urban growth rate	Urban-isation rate	GDP growth rate
Sub-Saharan Africa	14.8	4.4	1.7	−0.1
East Asia and Pacific	20.5	3.5	2.1	3.1
South Asia	16.7	3.4	1.2	3.7
Middle East and North Africa	35.1	3.6	0.9	1.2
Latin America and Caribbean	48.9	2.8	0.8	1.2

Notes: Gross domestic product (GDP) growth rate estimates are based on real GDP per capita (constant 2000 US$). Throughout this chapter, 'urban growth rate' refers to the compound average annual rate of population growth in urban areas; 'urbanisation rate' refers to the compound average annual rate of change in the percentage of a country's population residing in urban as opposed to rural areas.

Source: Calculation based on data from the World Bank's World Development Indicators Database, accessed January 2012.

I argue that urbanisation should be understood as a global historical process driven by population dynamics associated with technological and institutional change. While urban settlements emerged in many regions before the nineteenth century, the proportion of the global population residing in urban areas remained low. Historical evidence indicates that urban population growth in the pre-industrial era was ultimately restricted by two factors: 1) the scarcity of surplus energy supplies (primarily food) to support non-agricultural populations; and 2) an inability to control infectious and parasitic diseases, which thrive in densely populated settlements. In other words, limitations on the availability of food supplies coupled with high disease burdens in urban settlements imposed a natural ceiling on urban population growth and hence urbanisation in the pre-industrial era.

A combination of technological and institutional innovations in the eighteenth and nineteenth centuries began to alleviate these constraints. While these emerged primarily in Europe, they were later diffused worldwide through colonialism, trade and, in the postcolonial period, international development assistance, thereby setting in motion an inexorable process of world urbanisation. Crucially, many of these innovations have contributed directly to both mortality decline (hence population growth) and economic development, leading to the spurious conclusion that economic development is the motive force behind urbanisation. Although there is no question that structural shifts in labour markets contribute to rural-to-urban migration, the historical record indicates that ultimately improvements in disease control and food security underpin urbanisation.

Applying this thesis to the African case, the late onset of the region's urban transition can be attributed to natural geographic endowments that rendered the local production and acquisition (through trade) of surplus food supplies, as well as disease control, especially difficult. The rapid pace of urban growth in Africa since 1960 is explained by mortality decline and improved access to surplus food supplies made possible by the application of technologies and the consolidation of institutions introduced through colonialism, trade and international development assistance. Countries that have experienced more rapid economic and demographic growth have urbanised more quickly in the era following World War Two, but the absence of economic growth has not been sufficient to arrest urban population growth wherever mortality has continued to fall and sufficient food supplies have remained available. In short, the seemingly unique characteristics of Africa's urban transition are explicable within the framework of the historical theory of urbanisation proposed here.

This chapter proceeds as follows. I first provide a critical review of economic and demographic theories of urbanisation. Drawing on the work of economic historians and historical demographers, I sketch the stylised facts of world urbanisation in the pre-industrial era and articulate an integrated, historically grounded explanation of urbanisation based on these observations. I then apply this theory to urbanisation trends in Africa. First, I offer statistical evidence that cross-country variation in colonial experience – an important historical determinant of institutional and technological change – accounts for a significant proportion of the variation in patterns of early urbanisation in the region. Second, I examine the dynamics of African urbanisation in the postcolonial era and demonstrate empirically that 'urbanisation without growth' and exceptionally rapid urban population growth are largely accounted for by sub-Saharan Africa's unique historical circumstances and population dynamics. I conclude with a brief comment on the policy implications of the theory and evidence presented here.

Economic and demographic theories of urbanisation

The traditional economic theory of urbanisation, which has dominated in both academic and policy circles since the 1950s, revolves around the relationship between structural economic change and the spatial dynamics of the labour market. The premise is straightforward: as the modern urban sector (i.e. manufacturing and services) expands, surplus labour from the 'backward' rural economy (i.e. agriculture) is drawn to towns and cities, attracted by higher wages (Lewis 1954; Fei and Ranis 1964). In other words, this economic model suggests that urbanisation is fundamentally driven by rural-to-urban migration stimulated by a wage gap between rural and urban areas that arises in the early stages of industrialisation.[1]

As early as the 1950s, however, scholars recognised that rates of urbanisation in many developing countries were not commensurate with the growth of wage-based employment opportunities in urban areas, resulting in under- and unemployment – a phenomenon dubbed 'over-urbanisation' (Davis and Golden 1954). To explain this deviation from the classic dual-economy model of urbanisation, and the implied failure of the market to allocate labour efficiently between rural and urban areas, Harris and Todaro (1970) proposed a revised model in which migration decisions are influenced by expected, as opposed to actual, earnings in the urban sector. Over-urbanisation is explained in the Harris–Todaro model as a consequence of wage-distorting government interventions in the labour market that inflate the wages of a few and raise the expectations of the masses. In such contexts, the model suggests, policies of wage equalisation or mobility restriction will lead to net welfare improvements.

While decades of research have consistently demonstrated a strong cross-sectional association between indicators of economic development (e.g. income per capita and structure of output) and levels of urbanisation at the national level, empirical tests of the wage-differential mechanism assumed in both the classic and the Harris–Todaro models have produced ambiguous results, explaining only a small fraction of the variation in rates of urbanisation across countries (see Mazumdar 1987; Weeks 1995; Becker and Morrison 1995; Fay and Opal 2000; Lall et al. 2006). This outcome may reflect the failure of these models to take account of the role of the urban informal sector (the 'third sector'), which is where most migrants (especially in Africa) are found (Bhattacharya 1993).[2] It may also be a consequence of a narrow focus on economic incentives for migration.

Qualitative and quantitative studies conducted in the 1960s and 1970s identified many non-economic motives for migration, such as the desire of youth to escape the control of older generations; of women to escape gender discrimination, join husbands in town, or take advantage of the market for spouses in urban areas; and of others to acquire the social prestige associated with urban life or to pursue their aspirations in the 'bright lights' of the big city (see Byerlee 1974; Mazumdar 1987; Becker and Morrison 1995). More recent studies have explored the impacts of ethnic conflict, war and climatic changes in spurring migration to urban areas (Fay and Opal 2000; Barrios et al. 2006).

Given the many reasons people have for leaving the countryside for the city, it is not surprising that studies have failed to confirm the primacy of the wage-differential mechanism. But few alternative explanations have been proposed. For example, in their effort to solve the paradox of urbanisation without growth in sub-Saharan Africa throughout the 1980s and 1990s, Fay and Opal (2000: 25) note that in Africa, and in many other regions, 'urbanisation continues even during periods of negative (economic) growth, carried by its own momentum'. The only explanation the authors provide for this momentum is a vague speculation that external forces (such as globalisation) may be at work.

A missing consideration in most studies is the potential role of population dynamics. In fact, the process of urbanisation has received marginal attention in demography and, notably, there has been little cross-country research on the topic (Dyson 2011). The few studies that have sought to explain the variation in rates of urbanisation and urban population growth emphasise the dynamics associated with the demographic transition. There are essentially two sources of urban population growth: natural increase in urban areas and rural-to-urban migration (Cohen 2003).[3] The onset of mortality decline ahead of fertility decline in urban areas raises the rate of natural increase, and urban populations expand regardless of whether they are net recipients of rural migrants. Urbanisation, of course, could occur in a population without rural-to-urban migration if urban natural increase were to occur faster than rural natural increase over a sustained period, but in reality this has rarely happened.[4] With regard to rural-to-urban migration – the proximate cause of urbanisation – it has long been assumed among demographers influenced by Malthusian arguments that rapid population growth in rural areas (stimulated by mortality decline) places a strain on natural resources (e.g. land and water), resulting in declining living standards and thereby contributing to the 'push' factors that drive people into cities (Preston 1979; Kelley and Williamson 1984).

There is robust empirical evidence that mortality decline and the acceleration in population growth that follows are important determinants of urban population growth. Preston (1979), for example, demonstrated a strong one-to-one correlation between total population growth and urban growth, and many studies have observed that urban natural increase generally contributes more to overall urban population growth than does rural-to-urban migration, although the relative contribution of each tends to shift as a country urbanises, with natural increase playing an increasingly important role (see, for example, Davis 1965; Preston 1979; Cohen 2003; Lall et al. 2006). By contrast, evidence on the relationship between rates of population growth and rates of urbanisation is virtually non-existent.

Whether the onset of the demographic transition is a necessary and/or sufficient condition for the urban transition to occur is difficult to deduce from cross-country research. Hypothetically, both urbanisation and urban growth could occur solely through rural-to-urban migration in a context of zero overall population growth and rapid economic growth. Conversely, if the Malthusian arguments are right, rapid urbanisation in Africa against a backdrop of economic stagnation might be explained by the region's exceptionally rapid population growth – a possibility that has never been empirically tested. However, the work of historical demographers supports the view that the onset of the demographic transition is a necessary and possibly sufficient condition for urbanisation.

Towards a historical theory of world urbanisation

Abstracting from historical accounts of the emergence, growth and decline of cities across the world over the past 6,000 years, one can glean two key theoretical insights concerning the underlying factors that drive urbanisation. Both insights relate to the question of why the world's urban population remained small and static (hovering around 5 per cent of the world population) for thousands of years, before experiencing a rapid and sustained expansion beginning in the late nineteenth century (see Figure 14.1).

The answer provided by historical demographers is that cities were deadly places in which to live until recently. Before the nineteenth century, urban settlements with rudimentary water and sanitation infrastructures were especially conducive to the spread of infectious and parasitic diseases. As a consequence, death rates tended to exceed birth rates, turning cities into 'demographic sinks' (Graunt 1662/1964; de Vries 1984; Bairoch 1988; Lowry 1990; Dyson 2011). With negative rates of natural increase, cities depended on a constant inflow of rural migrants to sustain their populations. This suggests that the propensity to migrate from rural to urban settlements has been a

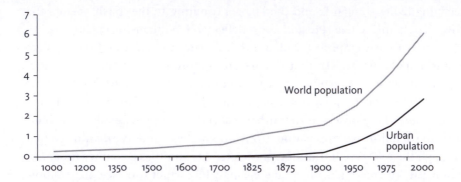

14.1 World population and urbanisation, AD 1000–2000 (billions) (*sources*: Population estimates from Maddison 2009; urbanisation estimates from Grauman 1977 and UN DESA 2010)

consistent feature of human behaviour for as long as cities have existed – even when migrants stood to suffer from higher rates of morbidity and mortality than they would have done in the countryside. The important implication is that any realistic model of the urbanisation process should assume some constant rate of rural-to-urban migration, all other things being equal.

This disease constraint on urban growth also helps explain the mechanism linking the demographic transition to urbanisation by identifying mortality decline stimulated by disease control as the demographic dynamic of greatest causal significance. Where the burden of disease is eased, mortality decline contributes to urban population growth in three ways:

- by raising the rate of urban natural increase above zero;
- by increasing demographic pressure in rural areas, potentially spurring migration; and
- by transforming rural migrants into a source of urban population growth instead of mere population maintenance.

Although evidence to support the disease constraint argument comes primarily from a handful of historical case studies, it is compelling enough for Dyson (2010: 126) to claim that 'no population that has experienced a reduction in its death rate from a high level to a low level has failed to urbanize'. In other words, mortality decline is a necessary precondition for urbanisation and urban growth to occur. Moreover, if some constant net positive rate of rural-to-urban migration is assumed, mortality decline (and the rapid population growth that follows immediately in its wake) can also be interpreted as a sufficient condition.

Economic historians provide a complementary explanation for the limited scale of urbanisation prior to the nineteenth century based on a persuasive logical premise: cities can exist only where a surplus of energy (i.e. food and fuel) is available to support a large non-agricultural population (Lowry 1990). It follows that the size of the urban population in any given region is a function of the quantity of surplus energy it is able to acquire, which in turn is jointly determined by agricultural productivity and transportation costs (Bairoch 1988).

The limitations imposed on urban population growth by agricultural productivity and transport costs largely explain the geography of early cities, which emerged almost exclusively in areas naturally conducive to surplus food production (such as fertile river valleys) or in locations with naturally low trade costs (i.e. on coasts and along rivers) (Childe 1950; Davis 1955; Bairoch 1988). Indeed, it is still possible to detect the profound and long-lasting influence of natural geography on patterns of urbanisation using a simple ordinary least-squares (OLS) regression analysis in which a country's level of urbanisation and urban population size in 1960 (the earliest date for which comprehensive data are available) are modelled as a function of relatively time-invariant geographic characteristics that influence agricultural productivity and transportation costs. Table 14.2 presents the results of such an analysis based on a sample of 126 countries.[5] Independent variables include soil quality (measured as the percentage of a country's land area with soils that are very or moderately suitable for six key rain-fed crops), length of coastline in kilometres and total length of navigable waterways in kilometres. A control for GDP per capita in 1960 is included to capture the inevitable mediating effects of technological and institutional changes prior to 1960 on natural geographical constraints. In the second specification, in which the dependent variable is the total size of the urban population (as opposed to the percentage of the national population residing in urban areas), an added control for national population size

TABLE 14.2 Effect of geographic characteristics on the percentage of the population that is urban and the urban population size, based on a sample of 126 countries, 1960

	Urban population (%)	Urban population size
Ln coastline (km)	.058[b] (.030)	.055[a] (.016)
Ln waterways (km)	.049[b] (.024)	.034[b] (.014)
Soil potential	.026[a] (.110)	.013[a] (.004)
Ln GDP per capita, 1960	1.794[a] (.095)	.678[a] (.050)
Ln national population		.975[a] (.035)
R-squared	.801	.941
Observations	126	126

Notes: Standard errors are in parentheses. Significance at the 1% and 5% levels are indicated by [a] and [b].

Sources: See Table A.2.

is included because of the natural correlation between total population and urban population size (Davis and Henderson 2003).

The results confirm that countries with better soil quality and more extensive 'natural' transportation infrastructure were both more urbanised (column 1) and had larger overall urban populations (column 2) in 1960 than countries that were less favourably endowed, as predicted. There is some collinearity in this model: countries with longer coastlines tend to have more kilometres of navigable waterways. While this obscures accurate interpretation of effect magnitudes for these variables, it does not affect the overall fit of the model.

The case for causality in this model is strong: the time-invariant characteristics of coastline, waterways and soil potential are clearly exogenous to urbanisation and urban population size in 1960. Moreover, the inclusion of GDP per capita in 1960 as a control variable is likely to capture the influence of any omitted variables, given the strong correlation between GDP and urbanisation.

The history of ancient Rome provides a useful illustration of how physical geography affected access to surplus energy supplies and hence shaped the fortunes of urban settlements in the pre-industrial era. At its peak in AD 200, Rome is estimated to have contained over 1 million residents (including both citizens and slaves), a population size that far exceeded the total surplus production capacity of the Italian peninsula. To satisfy its energy requirements, Rome was forced to import anywhere from 75 to 95 per cent of its wheat supplies from distant territorial possessions. Given the state of transportation technology at the time, this was an extremely costly means of surplus acquisition that contributed to the eventual financial ruin of the empire. With the shift of the imperial centre to Constantinople in AD 330 and the subsequent collapse of the publicly financed system of interregional grain distribution, Rome's population plummeted to just 50,000 inhabitants by AD 700 – a size more in line with the productive capacity of its hinterland (see Bairoch 1988; Reader 2004).

Low agricultural productivity and high transportation costs in the pre-industrial era also explain why the proportion of the world's urban population remained unchanged for so long. Increasing agricultural output in the pre-modern era was driven primarily by bringing more land under cultivation rather than by intensifying yields. Thus, although the global urban population may have risen in absolute terms, it could not expand in relative terms because of very limited improvement in surplus output.[6] Moreover, the potential for regional specialisation and exchange in agricultural goods was very limited, since transportation costs remained well above the threshold that would have made such trade economically viable (Braudel 1984; Bairoch 1988).[7]

A binding 'surplus constraint' would indicate that the expansion of a food surplus is a necessary condition for urban populations to grow.[8] The rise and fall of cities in the pre-industrial era could therefore be understood as a reflection of both shifting disease burdens and fluctuations in the capacity of individual settlements to acquire surplus food supplies.

Both the disease constraint and the surplus constraint arguments trace the origins of world urbanisation to a confluence of social and technological changes in northern Europe in the eighteenth and nineteenth centuries. Innovations such as nitrogen fertiliser, crop rotation and mechanisation drove a surge in agricultural productivity (Bairoch 1988; Cameron 1997; Maddison 2007). The harnessing of inanimate sources of energy to fuel railways, steamships and eventually automobiles led to a dramatic reduction in transportation costs (Bairoch 1988; Crafts and Venables 2003). Improvements in hygiene, medical knowledge, maternal education and urban planning practices and the expanded availability of healthcare led to a gradual decline in mortality rates (Szreter 1997; Bloom and Sachs 1999; Reher 2004; Livi-Bacci 2007). Political-institutional changes such as the consolidation of private property rights, improved third party contract enforcement, and an expansion of the role of governments in the provision of public goods (notably healthcare, education and infrastructure) reinforced and sustained these trends (Szreter 1997; Cameron 1997; Maddison 2007). Collectively, these changes catalysed a permanent shift in Europe from a Malthusian economy characterised by stagnant per capita income growth and high mortality to a modern growth regime typified by secular rises in factor productivity and life expectancy (Galor and Weil 1999).

Against a backdrop of growing surpluses, intensified regional trade and falling mortality, the stage was set for European urbanisation.[9] Between 1800 and 1900, the proportion of Europe's population living in cities nearly tripled (growing from around 10 per cent to 30 per cent), and by the turn of the millennium approximately 70 per cent of Europe's population lived in urban areas (Bairoch and Goertz 1986; UN DESA 2010). Through trade, colonialism and, in the latter half of the twentieth century, international development assistance, the key technological and institutional developments that propelled Europe's urban transition were disseminated to other regions, stimulating urbanisation there as well. The onset of the urban transition in any given country or region should therefore be understood as part of a global historical process linked to technological and institutional change and diffusion, not simply as a product of endogenous economic and demographic forces.

Figure 14.2 provides a stylised diagram of this historically grounded theory of urbanisation. In brief, the underlying causes of the urban transition are the advent of technologies and institutions that facilitate disease control and surplus energy availability (i.e. productivity growth and reductions in transport costs). These factors stimulate mortality decline in both rural and urban areas.[10] Mortality decline facilitates urban population growth directly by raising the rate of urban natural increase and indirectly by raising the rate of rural-to-urban migration.

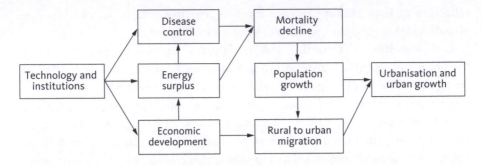

14.2 Historical theory of urbanisation

Technological and institutional changes also promote economic development, which exerts a positive effect on urbanisation and urban growth by further stimulating rural-to-urban migration as demand for labour in non-agricultural sectors expands. However, economic growth is not a necessary condition for urbanisation to occur. Given that non-economic motivations for migration are ever present, countries may experience net positive rates of urbanisation as long as disease control and food security are maintained in urban areas.[11]

The fact that many of the technological and institutional changes that drive mortality decline and facilitate surplus expansion also drive economic development is the source of the spurious conclusion that urbanisation is fundamentally a by-product of economic development. These two processes can become decoupled – as is illustrated by the case of sub-Saharan Africa, to which I now turn.

Geography, colonialism and early urbanisation in sub-Saharan Africa

Archaeological evidence and oral histories confirm the presence of urban settlements in sub-Saharan Africa for over 2,000 years (Anderson and Rathbone 2000). However, these settlements remained relatively small, few and dispersed in comparison to those in other regions of the world, and most proved ephemeral. As Figure 14.3 illustrates, the region's urban transition did not begin until the middle of the twentieth century.

Drawing on the earlier discussion of constraints to urban growth, the late onset of Africa's urban transition can largely be explained by natural geographic conditions. Africa's climate, soils, topography and disease ecology represent considerable obstacles to surplus agricultural production (Diamond 1997; Bloom and Sachs 1999). A high ratio of land area to coastline, few navigable rivers and low population densities are significant natural barriers to trade, contributing to exceptionally high transportation costs in the region even today and limited scope for specialisation and innovation (Bloom and Sachs 1999). Climatic and ecological characteristics render the region especially susceptible

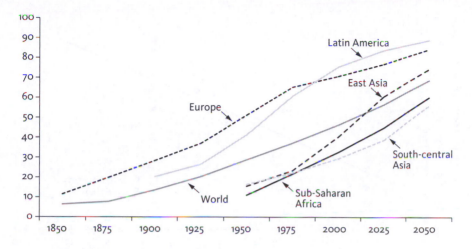

14.3 Urban population (%) by major world regions: estimates and projections, 1850–2050 (*sources*: Grauman 1977; UN DESA 2010)

to infectious and parasitic diseases. As a result, countries in sub-Saharan Africa have consistently exhibited some of the highest mortality rates in the world since comparable records became available in the 1950s (ibid.; Acemoglu et al. 2001; Iliffe 2007).

The alleviation of geographical constraints on urbanisation began in the colonial era. In the early colonial period, the slave trade, violent conflicts, the introduction of foreign pathogens and the disruption of traditional systems of production and networks of trade contributed to a shrinking of the region's population (Iliffe 2007). After World War One, however, colonial governments began to invest more heavily in primary commodity production, launched health campaigns to combat epidemic diseases, expanded transport infrastructure, and introduced new agricultural technologies and cultigens such as cassava, which is drought resistant and has become an important anti-famine crop across Africa (ibid.; Clapham 2006). While these changes collectively improved surplus availability and stimulated a secular decline in mortality rates, urbanisation remained limited because of colonial restrictions on African mobility and residence in urban areas, poor urban living conditions and limited waged employment opportunities.

After World War Two, the colonial powers, especially Britain and France, changed tack and launched a 'modernisation' drive designed to prepare colonies for eventual independence. This involved a significant expansion of public education and health services, further infrastructure development and limited industrial investments (Cooper 2002; Iliffe 2007). Vaccination schemes led to sharp reductions in mortality associated with epidemic diseases; child mortality rates began to fall because of better treatment for polio, measles, diarrhoea and malnutrition; and improved road and rail transport contributed

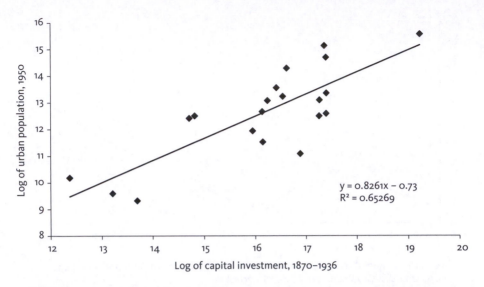

Note: The 1950 population data have been aggregated to conform to colonial territory boundaries.

14.4 Capital investment (£ thousand) in the colonial period and total urban population in 20 sub-Saharan African territories, 1950 (*sources*: Colonial investment data from Frankel 1969; population estimates from UN DESA 2010)

to reductions in famine-related mortality by making affected areas more accessible to emergency aid (Iliffe 2007). As mortality rates fell, Africa's population began to grow rapidly. The gradual relaxation of government restrictions on African mobility, coupled with higher demand for labour in urban areas during and immediately after World War Two, accelerated rural-to-urban migration. Rapid urban expansion exacerbated poor housing conditions and led to consumer price inflation and unemployment – factors that proved instrumental in catalysing the growth of labour unions, which played a pivotal role in securing independence in the region (Cooper 2002; Iliffe 2007).

In sum, Africa's urban transition was set in motion by technologies and institutions introduced in the late colonial period that facilitated mortality decline (and a subsequent population boom in the region) and increased the availability of surplus food supplies. However, the nature and impact of colonialism varied widely across countries, and this variation provides a means of assessing the relative impact of colonialism on urbanisation. A plausible hypothesis is that those countries in which colonial powers were more economically and politically assertive experienced higher degrees of technological and institutional transfer and diffusion, thereby creating more favourable conditions for urbanisation and urban growth. To test this hypothesis, I use capital investment during the colonial period as an indicator of colonial influence.

Figure 14.4 presents evidence that variation in levels of colonial capital investment in sub-Saharan African territories is correlated with the variation in early urbanisation in the region. The x-axis represents log-transformed values of the total amount of publicly listed capital invested in individual European colonial territories between 1870 and 1936, as catalogued by Frankel (1969). The y-axis represents log-transformed values of the total urban population of each corresponding territory in 1950. Although only 20 observations are available, the figure shows a clear correlation between early colonial investment and early urbanisation.[12]

Additional evidence of colonial influence on patterns of early urbanisation in the region can be drawn from two other indicators: the relative degree of 'indirect rule', based on legal records, and a measure of administrative depth, for which the proportion of civil servants in the population is used as a proxy. An analysis of their effects is set out in the appendix.

While no single piece of this statistical mosaic provides definitive confirmation that urbanisation in Africa was historically inhibited by unfavourable geographic conditions and was ultimately set in motion by technologies and institutions introduced by European colonisers, collectively the evidence provides significant support for these arguments.

Urbanisation and urban growth in the postcolonial era

The growth in urban populations that began in the late colonial period accelerated in the independence era owing to a confluence of demographic, political and economic factors. The mortality decline that began in the late colonial era continued, while fertility rates remained exceptionally high, resulting in a population increase on a historically unprecedented scale.[13] Many countries experienced a surge in rural-to-urban migration in the early independence period due to the elimination of residence restrictions on Africans in urban areas and a sharp increase in urban employment opportunities, which can be attributed to the expansion and 'Africanisation' of civil service administration and investment in urban public works (Miner 1967; Stren and Halfani 2001; Iliffe 2007). I refer to this phenomenon in the statistical analysis below as a 'postcolonial adjustment effect'. Economic growth rates in the region reached historic highs, fuelled by a boom in public and private investment (much of it provided by international actors) and strong growth in commodity exports (Miner 1967; Stren and Halfani 2001; Iliffe 2007). As a result, rates of urbanisation and urban population growth reached extraordinarily high levels between 1960 and 1975 (see Table 14.3).

Subsequently, unsustainable fiscal expansion, poor macroeconomic management, deteriorating terms of trade, and a global recession following the 1973 oil price shock resulted in a region-wide economic crisis. By the early 1980s, sub-Saharan Africa was experiencing negative per capita income growth and fiscal retrenchment in the form of donor-imposed structural adjustment programmes. The consequences in urban areas were severe. Public and private

TABLE 14.3 Demographic and economic trends in Africa, 1960–2005 (percentage per annum)

	1960–75	1975–90	1990–2005
Urban population growth	5.1	4.6	4.0
Rate of urbanisation	2.5	1.8	1.5
GDP per capita growth	2.1	-0.6	0.5
Population growth	2.5	2.8	2.6

Notes: GDP growth rate estimates are based on real GDP per capita (constant 2000 US$).

Source: Calculation based on data from the World Bank's World Development Indicators Database, accessed January 2012.

sector employment contracted sharply, real wages declined, investments in housing and urban infrastructure came to a virtual standstill, and the rural/urban wage gap that arose in the early independence era essentially vanished (Potts 1995; Weeks 1995; Becker and Morrison 1995). Yet urbanisation and urban population growth rates remained generally high in Africa, with a few notable exceptions. This can be explained by continued mortality decline and by steady surplus expansion sustained by imports and aid. Figure 14.5 shows that surplus food supplies (measured in tonnes of cereals and starchy roots) generally kept

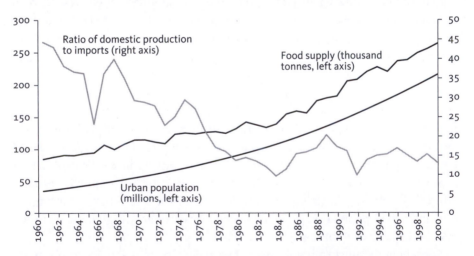

Note: Food supply data include both domestic production and imports of cereals and starchy roots.

14.5 Urban population growth (millions) and surplus food supply (thousand tonnes) in sub-Saharan Africa, 1961–2000 (*sources*: Food supply data from FAOSTAT [the Statistics Division of the Food and Agriculture Organization of the United Nations] online database, accessed June 2010; population figures from the United Nations)

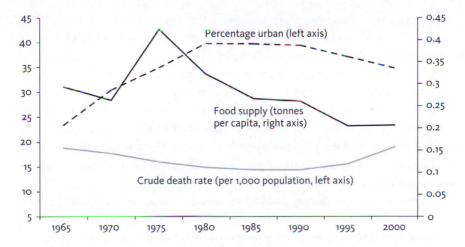

Note: Food supply data include both domestic production and imports of cereals and starchy roots.

14.6 A case of de-urbanisation: food supply, mortality and the urban percentage of the population in Zambia, 1965–2000 (*sources*: Food supply data from FAOSTAT online database, accessed June 2010; population figures from the United Nations)

pace with urban population growth, even in the crisis years of the 1980s and early 1990s. It also shows that this growth was made possible by imports more than by productivity growth.

Perhaps the most well-known exception to this narrative is Zambia, which experienced de-urbanisation in the 1980s and 1990s. This anomaly is generally attributed to a severe economic downturn and the effects of structural adjustment on urban livelihoods (Potts 1995), yet many other countries experienced similar crises without de-urbanisation. However, Zambia also experienced a sharp decline in food supplies and a reversal in the trend of declining mortality beginning in the late 1970s as a result of a crisis in the public health sector, deteriorating nutrition and increases in mortality related to malaria and HIV/AIDS in particular (Dyson 2003; Garenne and Gakusi 2006). Moreover, under-five mortality rates rose much faster in urban than in rural areas between the mid-1970s and early 1990s and fell faster (from the mid-1990s) in rural areas than in cities (Garenne and Gakusi 2006). As Figure 14.6 illustrates, de-urbanisation in Zambia was preceded by an abrupt and sustained contraction in per capita food supplies and was accompanied by rising mortality rates. While some of the factors that contributed to rising mortality rates were a direct consequence of Zambia's economic failures, others (such as rises in malaria and HIV/AIDS mortality) were independent of it (ibid.). In other words, Zambia experienced a unique combination of misfortunes that led to the resurgence of the surplus and disease constraints that inhibit urbanisation – and in this case resulted in a rare episode of de-urbanisation.

To summarise, Africa's urban transition in the postcolonial period was driven by a combination of rapid population growth set in motion in the late colonial period, a postcolonial adjustment involving the 'Africanisation' and expansion of employment opportunities in urban areas, and early international aid and investment. Through the recessionary years of 1975 to 1990 and the slow-growth recovery of the 1990s, the transition was sustained by persistent demographic expansion. In other words, both urbanisation without economic growth and exceptionally high urban growth rates in the late twentieth century are explicable once Africa's unique post-war political and population dynamics are taken into account.

As a test of this argument, and of the broader theory of urbanisation outlined above, Table 14.4 presents the results of an OLS regression analysis in which average annual rates of urbanisation and urban growth are modelled as a function of: 1) average annual rates of population growth; 2) average annual rates of per capita income growth; and 3) the sectoral composition of output, measured as the average percentage contribution of agriculture to GDP over the relevant period. According to the theory outlined above, population growth and economic growth rates should both be positively correlated with rates of urbanisation and urban growth, while agriculture as a percentage of GDP should be negatively correlated (as a result of labour being retained in the rural sector). The model also incorporates a dummy variable for sub-Saharan African countries to determine whether they share some unobserved characteristics that account for persistent urbanisation in the absence of economic growth and for exceptionally high urban population growth rates.

The data consist of an unbalanced panel dataset with 353 observations from over 150 countries and spanning three 15-year intervals that roughly correspond to global economic trends (1960–75, 1975–90 and 1990–2005), in order to limit the influence of short-term fluctuations in economic and demographic conditions. This arrangement also permits the inclusion of two more control variables: interactive regional dummies to determine whether there was a significant postcolonial adjustment effect (see Fay and Opal 2000). These are AFRICA*P1 and AFRICA*P2, where P1 and P2 represent dummy variables for the 1960–75 and 1975–90 periods respectively. Finally, the initial level of urbanisation in each period is controlled for.

As expected, population and per capita GDP growth rates are both positively and significantly correlated with urbanisation and urban growth rates, while the contribution of agriculture to GDP is negatively and significantly correlated. The 'Africa' dummy is insignificant; however, the period interactive dummies are both positive and significant. The fact that the coefficient on the first interactive dummy (AFRICA*P1) is larger than that of the second (AFRICA*P2) is indicative of the postcolonial adjustment effect noted in the historical narrative presented above. The models have near-identical coefficients because of

TABLE 14.4 Determinants of urbanisation and urban growth rates, 1960–75, 1975–90 and 1990–2005

	Urbanisation rate	Urban growth rate
Population growth	.139[a] (.043)	1.139[a] (.043)
Per capita GDP growth	.126[a] (.024)	.126[a] (.024)
Agriculture (% of GDP)	-.015[a] (.006)	-.015[a] (.006)
AFRICA	.058 (.195)	.056 (.195)
AFRICA*P1	1.509[a] (.256)	1.510[a] (.256)
AFRICA*P2	.689[a] (.236)	.690[a] (.236)
Urbanisation$_{t1}$	-.469[a] (.050)	-.469[a] (.050)
R-squared	.586	.821
Observations	353	353

Notes: Standard errors are in parentheses. Significance at the 1% level is indicated by [a].

Sources: See Table A.2.

the naturally strong correlation between rates of urban population growth and rates of urbanisation.

The design of this model precludes definitive statements about causation: it merely confirms contemporaneous correlation between the variables of interest. It is possible that omitted variables or reverse causality is driving the results. However, there is nothing in the quantitative literature to suggest that significant determinants of urbanisation or urban growth are omitted from these models, and there is little reason to suspect reverse causality. Higher levels of urbanisation are generally associated with lower fertility rates, hence lower population growth rates. Consequently, if rates of urbanisation or urban growth were having an effect on population growth rates, it would most likely be a negative effect. Similarly, all of the existing empirical evidence suggests that GDP growth drives urbanisation, and there is no evidence that levels of urbanisation affect GDP growth rates (Bloom et al. 2008).

Nevertheless, a second test examining the determinants of changes in levels of urbanisation and urban population size serves as a check for robustness. In this case, the model is designed to test whether lagged values of the independent variables of interest add predictive power to a model that includes lagged values of the dependent variables as independent variables.[14] I examine whether population and GDP growth rates between time t_1 and time t_2 help to predict levels of urbanisation and urban population size at time t_2 when levels of urbanisation and urban population size at time t_1 are controlled for. As in the previous model, the data are divided into three 15-year periods. Given that past levels of urbanisation and urban population size explain over

TABLE 14.5 Determinants of changes in relative and absolute size of urban populations, 1960–2005

	Level of urbanisation$_{t2}$	Urban population$_{t2}$
Population growth$_{t1 \to t2}$	.082^a (.017)	.142^a (.007)
Per capita GDP growth$_{t1 \to t2}$	.049^a (.010)	.019^a (.004)
Agriculture (% of GDP)$_{t1 \to t2}$	−.008^a (.002)	−.002^a (.001)
AFRICA	.057 (.077)	.016 (.029)
AFRICA*P1	.254^b (.101)	.163^a (.039)
AFRICA*P2	.197^b (.093)	.086^b (.035)
Urbanisation$_{t1}$	.881^a (.020)	
Ln urban population$_{t1}$		.804^a (.019)
Ln national population$_{t2}$		.188^a (.020)
R-squared	.953	.992
Observations	353	353

Notes: Standard errors are in parentheses. Significance at the 1% and 5% levels are indicated by ^{a} and ^{b} respectively. 'Urbanisation$_{t1}$' refers to the level of urbanisation in a given country at the beginning of the 15-year period examined (i.e. 1960, 1975 or 1990). The same principle applies to the variables 'Log of urban population' and 'Log of national population'.

Sources: See Table A.2.

90 per cent of variation in contemporary levels, the independent variables of interest must be correlated robustly with the dependent variables to exhibit statistical significance. The results of this test are presented in Table 14.5.

Again, the results are consistent with the hypotheses: population growth and economic growth continue to exhibit positive and significant effects on levels of urbanisation and urban population size, while the share of agriculture in GDP remains negative. There is also no evidence of an 'Africa' effect, but there is significant evidence of a postcolonial adjustment effect as captured by the two interactive dummies. The fact that these results echo those of the previous model lends further support to the theory outlined above. Moreover, given that, logically, levels of urbanisation and urban population size at time *t2* cannot have influenced rates of urbanisation or GDP growth in the previous 15-year period, this model offers further evidence of a causal relationship between population growth and GDP growth (on the one hand) and urbanisation and urban population growth (on the other).

Conclusion

Urbanisation should be viewed as a global historical process propelled by technological and institutional changes that alleviated the surplus and disease constraints that limited urban population growth in the pre-industrial era.

These changes initially emerged in Europe and subsequently spread, albeit unevenly, through conquest and trade. This historically grounded view of urbanisation stands in contrast to the traditional view that urbanisation is a by-product of industrialisation. While it is true that mortality decline and expanded access to surplus food supplies – prerequisites for urbanisation – often go hand in hand with economic development, they do not always do so.

In the case of sub-Saharan Africa, colonisers introduced key technological and institutional innovations that alleviated geographically determined surplus and disease constraints, which had previously inhibited urban population growth in the region. Colonial influence varied significantly between countries within the region, and this variation accounts for a significant proportion of the variation in patterns of early urbanisation across countries.

In the years after World War Two, gains in life expectancy and increased access to surplus food supplies occurred more rapidly than economic development in sub-Saharan Africa. As a result, many countries in the region experienced urbanisation without economic growth. Moreover, rapid mortality decline coupled with minimal fertility decline led to population increases on a historically unprecedented scale – increases that largely account for the extraordinary urban growth rates in the region.

There is, in short, nothing particularly unusual about Africa's urban transition when viewed through the historical lens outlined here. The implication of this theory, from a practical policy perspective, is that the process of urbanisation cannot be restrained. For governments interested in alleviating demographic pressure in urban areas, the only humane policy option is one targeted at encouraging fertility decline in order to reduce population growth rates. While fertility decline is a natural consequence of urbanisation, targeted interventions such as family planning initiatives may serve to accelerate the process and ease the social strains associated with rapid urban population growth.

Appendix

This appendix offers further evidence of colonial influence on urbanisation. Table A.1 presents bivariate correlations between two indicators of colonial influence (the independent variables) on the one hand and variables related to disease control, food security and early urbanisation (the dependent variables) on the other. In the upper half of the table, the independent variable is a measure of 'indirect rule' in 33 former British colonies worldwide developed by Lange (2004). The indirect rule index reflects the percentage of legal cases settled by traditional authorities as opposed to formal courts in 1955. The higher the percentage, the greater the extent to which British authorities relied on local powerbrokers to maintain order in their territories. Using this index, Lange (ibid.) demonstrated that higher degrees of colonial indirect rule resulted

TABLE A.1 The colonial origins of variations in mortality, food security and early urbanisation trends

	IMR (1960)	Calories per capita (1960)	Doctors per 1,000 (1960)	Δ IMR (1960–75)	Urbanisation (1960)	Urban population (1960)
Former British colonies worldwide						
	(1a)	(2a)	(3a)	(4a)	(5a)	(6a)
Indirect rule	.012[a] (.002)	−.002[a] (.001)	−.023[a] (.004)	.026[a] (.007)	−.044[a] (.008)	−.022[a] (.005)
Ln population						1.091[a] (.073)
R-squared	.654	.259	.576	.299	.462	.889
Observations	33	31	33	33	33	33
Former British and French territories in sub-Saharan Africa						
	(1b)	(2b)	(3b)	(4b)	(5b)	(6b)
Colonial civil servants	−.088[c] (.044)	.090[a] (.029)	.690[a] (.177)	−.458[a] (.140)	.600[b] (.271)	.429[b] (.187)
Ln population						1.137[a] (.129)
R-squared	.120	.252	.352	.269	.144	.735
Observations	31	31	30	31	31	31

Notes: Standard errors are in parentheses. Significance at the 1%, 5% and 10% levels are indicated by [a], [b] and [c] respectively.

IMR = infant mortality rate.

Sources: See Table A.2.

in less effective public institutions in the postcolonial period. In the lower half of the table, the independent variable is the number of colonial civil servants per capita in British and French territories in sub-Saharan Africa circa 1936, as calculated by Richens (2009). This serves as a proxy for administrative depth. As with capital investment, it is reasonable to suppose that higher degrees of direct political rule and administrative depth resulted in greater technological and institutional transfer and diffusion, hence more favourable conditions for early urbanisation.

The dependent variables in Table A.1 include the infant mortality rate in 1960, food supply in 1960 (measured in calories per capita per day), the number of registered doctors per thousand population around 1960, the average annual rate of change in the infant mortality rate in the 15 years after 1960, the level of urbanisation in 1960, and total urban population in 1960. Controls (apart from the inclusion of national population in column 6) are omitted because of the small sample sizes of the colonial data.

The results indicate that higher degrees of indirect rule are associated with higher infant mortality, smaller food surpluses and fewer doctors per capita in 1960 (columns 1a–3a), while greater administrative depth is associated with lower infant mortality rates, greater food surpluses and more doctors per capita in 1960 (columns 1b–3b). The direction of causality in these correlations is not necessarily clear. As Acemoglu et al. (2001) have argued, patterns of colonial settlement may have been influenced by the region's disease environment and agricultural potential, so these correlations could be interpreted as indicative of reverse causality. In other words, colonial rulers may have invested economically and politically in territories with lower disease burdens and greater agricultural potential.

On the other hand, there is no theoretical reason to believe that mortality decline following independence was driven by anything other than the further diffusion of technologies and the consolidation of institutions introduced during the colonial period that affected public health. As column 4 shows, African countries that had more robust colonial legal institutions and greater colonial administrative capacity experienced more rapid declines in infant mortality in the early postcolonial period. In this case the direction of causality is clear: postcolonial changes in mortality cannot logically have driven colonial settlement patterns. Finally, columns 5 and 6 confirm the association demonstrated above between colonial capital investment and early urbanisation: the indicators of indirect rule and administrative depth are both significantly correlated with the size and percentage of a country's urban population in 1960.

TABLE A.2 Data sources

Variable	Description	Source
Level of urbanisation	Percentage of national population residing in urban areas	UN DESA (2010)
Log of urban population	Log of the absolute size of a country's urban population in thousands	UN DESA (2010)
Log of national population	Log of the absolute size of a country's population in thousands	UN DESA (2010)
World population (Figure 14.1)	Population in millions	Maddison (2009)
Historical urbanisation estimates (Figures 14.1 and 14.3)	Percentage of the world population residing in urban areas	Grauman (1977)
Log of coastline (km)	Log of kilometres of coastline	CIA World Factbook (various years)
Log of waterways (km)	Log of navigable waterways	CIA World Factbook (various years)
Soil quality	Percentage of land area with soil very or moderately suitable for six key rain-fed crops	Gallup et al. (1999)
GDP per capita	Real GDP per capita in 1990 international Geary–Khamis dollars	Maddison (2009)
Colonial investment, 1870–1936	Sum of publicly listed capital invested in African colonial territories between 1870 and 1936, calculated in pounds sterling	Frankel (1969)
Indirect rule	Percentage of legal cases adjudicated by 'traditional' authorities in British colonies, 1955	Lange (2004)
Colonial civil servants	Colonial civil servants per capita in African territories, circa 1936	Richens (2009)
IMR 1960	Infant mortality rate in 1960	UN DESA (2009)

Calories per capita	Average available calories per capita per day in 1960	Food and Agriculture Organization. Available at http://faostat.fao.org.
Doctors per 1,000	Doctors per thousand population around 1960 (missing values were replaced by the nearest available year)	World Bank World Development Indicators online. Available at http:// data.worldbank.org/data-catalog/world-development-indicators [accessed 24 August 2013].
D IMR 1960–75	Average annual rate of change in the infant mortality rate between 1960 and 1975	Author calculations based on data from UN DESA (2009)
Food supply (Figure 14.5)	Production and import volume of cereals and starchy roots in tonnes	Food and Agriculture Organization. Available at http://faostat.fao.org.
Food supply (Figure 14.6)	Available tonnes per capita of cereals and starchy roots	Food and Agriculture Organization. Available at http://faostat.fao.org.
Crude death rate (Figure 14.6)	Deaths per thousand population	UN DESA (2009)
Agriculture (% of GDP)	Average of agriculture value-added as a percentage of GDP, as calculated for three 15-year periods: 1960–75, 1975–90 and 1990–2005	World Bank World Development Indicators online. Available at http:// data.worldbank.org/data-catalog/world-development-indicators [accessed 24 August 2013].

Acknowledgements

Funding for this research was provided by the UK's Department for International Development and the Crisis States Research Centre. I thank Jo Beall, Tim Dyson, Jean-Paul Faguet, John Flynn-York, Tom Goodfellow, Elliott Green and Su Lin Lewis for useful comments on earlier drafts.

Notes

1 The theory assumes that higher urban wages reflect rising demand for labour, as well as higher marginal returns to labour, in an expanding modern sector. The wage gap stimulates migration among rational individuals seeking to maximise their incomes until the labour market clears.

2 The lack of comparable data on wages in the informal sector precludes the possibility of accurately determining the influence of wage differentials between rural areas and the urban informal economy.

3 The reclassification of rural areas as urban also contributes to urbanisation in a statistical sense, but reclassification is logically a by-product of natural population increase and migration, so the focus here is on these factors.

4 Dyson (2011) provides evidence that urban natural increase outpaced rural natural increase around the turn of the twentieth century in Sweden and again in the immediate aftermath of World War Two, but these are exceptional cases of relatively brief periods of urbanisation without migration.

5 All population, urban population and GDP estimates used in this article were log transformed to normalise sample distributions. Similarly, all urbanisation estimates were square root transformed. In this model, coastline and waterways data were also log transformed to correct for skewness. For details of all variables and sources see Table A.2.

6 Angus Maddison's historical estimates of world population and GDP indicate that per capita output increased from US$412 in AD 1 to just US$606 in AD 1700 (expressed in 1990 international Geary–Khamis dollars). From this one can infer that factor productivity growth was very limited over this period. In other words, there was very little increase in energy surplus per capita.

7 The bulk of world trade in the pre-industrial era involved relatively light-weight, non-perishable and high-value items such as spices and luxury textiles (see Braudel 1984; Bairoch 1988).

8 Whether growth in surplus energy supplies is a sufficient condition for urbanisation is difficult to answer definitively. History indicates that cities form wherever surplus energy becomes available, suggesting that the very presence of the surplus is sufficient to spur agglomeration. To verify this empirically is virtually impossible.

9 In a cross-country statistical study, Bairoch and Goertz (1986) demonstrated that the pace of urbanisation in nineteenth-century Europe was driven primarily by changes in agricultural productivity, by the pace of industrial growth, and by the expansion of trade. However, they found evidence that the most important factors driving urbanisation varied over time within and between countries. In particular, their results concerning the role of agricultural productivity were ambiguous. In some models the coefficient was positive, suggesting that rising output facilitated urbanisation, while in others the coefficient was negative. They speculate that agricultural success in certain regions resulted in the retention rather than the release of rural labour.

10 Surplus food expansion contributes to mortality decline through improved nutrition, which is an important determinant of variations in disease-related morbidity and mortality rates.

11 Urbanisation is a finite process. As a result, a country's rate of urbanisation naturally decreases as its level of urbanisation increases. By contrast, there is technically no upper limit on urban

growth. This explains continued urban growth in some fully urbanised countries, such as many of the South American countries, which continue to experience fertility rates that exceed the replacement rate of 2.1.

12 The direction of causality assumed in Figure 14.4 could be challenged by the argument that colonial rulers invested more where African populations were larger (and therefore offered a larger pool of labour to exploit). Given that total population and urban population are highly correlated, this is a potentially valid criticism. However, given the paucity of pre-colonial cities in the region, it is unlikely that Europeans invested in areas with existing urban populations, so a causal link between colonial investment and urban population size is reasonable. Moreover, total population and level of urbanisation are not correlated at all. In results not reported here, Frankel's colonial investment figures were also found to be negatively correlated with crude death rates in 1950 and positively correlated with income per capita in 1950, consistent with the hypothesis that colonial investment had the dual effect of reducing mortality and improving access to surplus food supplies.

13 This lag between mortality decline and fertility decline is usually explained as a consequence of historical factors that have made high birth rates culturally desirable in the region (see Iliffe 2007; Clapham 2006).

14 This approach follows the logic (although not the exact form) of a 'Granger causality test' (see Granger 1969; Bloom et al. 2008). A variable X can be said to 'Granger-cause' Y if X at time $t-1$ (X_{t-1}) explains variation in Y at time t (Y_t) when Y at time $t-1$ (Y_{t-1}) is included as a control variable on the right-hand side of the equation.

References

Acemoglu, D., S. Johnson and J. A. Robinson (2001) 'The colonial origins of comparative development: an empiri-cal investigation'. *American Economic Review* 91(5): 1369–401.

Anderson, D. M. and R. Rathbone (2000) *Africa's Urban Past*. Woodbridge: James Currey.

Bairoch, P. (1988) *Cities and Economic Development: From the dawn of history to the present*. Chicago, IL: University of Chicago Press.

— and G. Goertz (1986) 'Factors of urbanization in the nineteenth century developed countries: a descriptive and econometric analysis'. *Urban Studies* 23(4): 285–305.

Barrios, S., L. Bertinelli and E. Strobl (2006) 'Climatic change and rural–urban migration: the case of sub-Saharan Africa'. *Journal of Urban Economics* 60(3): 357–71.

Becker, C. M. and A. R. Morrison (1995) 'The growth of African cities: theory and estimates'. In A. Mafeje and S. Radwan (eds) *Economic and Demographic Change in Africa*. Oxford: Clarendon Press, pp. 109–42.

Bhattacharya, P. C. (1993) 'Rural–urban migration in economic development'. *Journal of Economic Surveys* 7(3): 243–81.

Bloom, D. E. and J. D. Sachs (1999) 'Geography, demography, and economic growth in Africa'. In W. C. Brainard and G. L. Perry (eds) *Brookings Paper on Economic Activity 2: 1998*. Washington, DC: Brookings Institution, pp. 207–95.

— D. Canning and G. Fink (2008) 'Urbanization and the wealth of nations'. *Science* 319(5864): 772–5.

Braudel, F. (1984) *Civilization and Capitalism, 15th–18th Century. Vol. 3: The perspectives of the world*. New York, NY: Harper & Row.

Byerlee, D. (1974) 'Rural–urban migration in Africa: theory, policy and research implications'. *International Migration Review* 8(4): 543–66.

Cameron, R. (1997) *A Concise Economic History of the World: From paleolithic times to the present*. Third edition. Oxford: Oxford University Press.

Childe, V. G. (1950) 'The urban revolution'. *Town Planning Review* 21(1): 3–17.

Clapham, C. (2006) 'The political economy of African population change'. *Population and Development Review* 32(Supp.): 96–114.

Cohen, B. (2003) 'Urban growth in developing countries: a review of current trends and a caution regarding existing forecasts'. *World Development* 32(1): 23–51.

Cooper, F. (2002) *Africa Since 1940: The past of the present*. New York, NY: Cambridge University Press.

Crafts, N. and A. J. Venables (2003) 'Globalization in history: a geographical perspective'. In M. D. Bordo, A. M. Taylor and J. G. Williamson (eds) *Globalization in Historical Perspective*. Chicago, IL: National Bureau of Economic Research, University of Chicago Press, pp. 323–64.

Davis, J. C. and J. V. Henderson (2003) 'Evidence on the political economy of the urbanization process'. *Journal of Urban Economics* 53: 98–125.

Davis, K. (1955) 'The origins and growth of urbanization in the world'. *The American Journal of Sociology* 60(5): 429–37.

— (1965) 'The urbanization of the human population'. *Scientific American* 213 (September): 40–53.

— and H. H. Golden (1954) 'Urbanization and the development of preindustrial areas'. *Economic Development and Cultural Change* 3(1): 6–26.

de Vries, J. (1984) *European Urbanization 1500–1800*. London: Methuen and Co.

Diamond, J. (1997) *Guns, Germs, and Steel: The fates of human societies*. London: Vintage.

Dyson, T. (2003) 'HIV/AIDS and urbanization'. *Population and Development Review* 29(3): 427–42.

— (2010) *Population and Development: The demographic transition*. London: Zed Books.

— (2011) 'The role of the demographic transition in the process of urbanization'. *Population and Development Review* 37(Supp.): 34–54.

Fay, M. and C. Opal (2000) *Urbanization Without Growth: A not so uncommon phenomenon*. Policy Research Working Paper No. 2412. Washington, DC: World Bank.

Fei, J. C. H. and G. Ranis (1964) *Development of the Labor Surplus Economy: Theory and policy*. Homewood, IL: Richard D. Irwin.

Frankel, S. H. (1969) *Capital Investment in Africa: Its course and effects*. New York, NY: Howard Fertig.

Gallup, J. L. and J. D. Sachs, with A. Mellinger (1999) *Geography and Economic Development*. CID Working Paper No. 1. Cambridge, MA: Center for International Development, Harvard University. Available at www.cid.harvard.edu/ciddata/ciddata.html [accessed 24 August 2013].

Galor, O. and D. Weil (1999) 'From Malthusian stagnation to modern growth'. *American Economic Review* 89(2): 150–4.

Garenne, M. and A. E. Gakusi (2006) 'Vulnerability and resilience: determinants of under-five mortality changes in Zambia'. *World Development* 34(10): 1765–87.

Granger, C. W. J. (1969) 'Investigating causal relations by econometric models and cross-spectral methods'. *Econometrica* 37(3): 424–38.

Grauman, J. V. (1977) 'Orders of magnitude of the world's urban population in history'. *Population Bulletin of the United Nations* 1976(8): 16–33. New York, NY: United Nations.

Graunt, J. (1662/1964) 'Natural and political observations made upon the bills of mortality'. *Journal of the Institute of Actuaries* 90: 4–61.

Harris, J. R. and M. P. Todaro (1970) 'Migration, unemployment and development: a two-sector analysis'. *American Economic Review* 60(1): 126–42.

Iliffe, J. (2007) *Africans: The history of a continent*. 2nd edition. Cambridge: Cambridge University Press.

Kelley, A. C. and J. G. Williamson (1984) 'Population growth, industrial revolutions, and the urban transition'. *Population and Development Review* 10(3): 419–41.

Lall, S. V., H. Selod and Z. Shalizi (2006) *Rural–Urban Migration in Developing Countries: A survey of theoretical predictions and empirical findings.* World Bank Policy Research Working Paper 3915. Washington, DC: World Bank.

Lange, M. K. (2004) 'British colonial legacies and political development'. *World Development* 32(6): 905–22.

Lewis, A. (1954) 'Economic development with unlimited supplies of labour'. *The Manchester School* 22(2): 139–91.

Livi-Bacci, M. (2007) *A Concise History of World Population.* Fourth edition. Oxford: Blackwell Publishing.

Lowry, I. S. (1990) 'World urbanization in perspective'. *Population and Development Review* 16: 148–76.

Maddison, A. (2007) *Contours of the World Economy, 1–2030 AD.* Oxford: Oxford University Press.

— (2009) 'Historical statistics: world population, GDP and per capita GDP, 1–2003 AD (March 2009)'. Available at www.ggdc.net/maddison.

Mazumdar, D. (1987) 'Rural–urban migration in developing countries'. In E. S. Mills (ed.) *Handbook of Regional and Urban Economics: Volume I.* Amsterdam: Elsevier, pp. 1097–128.

Miner, H. (1967) 'The city and modernization: an introduction'. In H. Miner (ed.) *The City in Modern Africa.* London: Pall Mall Press, pp. 1–20.

Potts, D. (1995) '"Shall we go home?" Increasing urban poverty in African cities and migration processes'. *Geographical Journal* 161(3): 245–64.

Preston, S. H. (1979) 'Urban growth in developing countries: a demographic reappraisal'. *Population and Development Review* 5(2): 195–215.

Reader, J. (2004) *Cities.* London: Vintage.

Reher, D. S. (2004) 'The demographic transition revisited as a global process'. *Population, Space and Place* 10(1): 19–41.

Richens, P. (2009) *The Economic Legacies of the 'Thin White Line': Indirect rule and the comparative development of sub-Saharan Africa.* Economic History Working Paper No. 131. London: London School of Economics and Political Science. Available at http://eprints.lse.ac.uk/27879 [accessed 24 August 2013].

Stren, R. and M. Halfani (2001) 'The cities of sub-Saharan Africa: from dependency to marginality'. In R. Paddison (ed.) *Handbook of Urban Studies.* London: Sage Publications, pp. 466–85.

Szreter, S. (1997) 'Economic growth, disruption, deprivation, disease, and death: on the importance of the politics of public health for development'. *Population and Development Review* 23(4): 693–728.

UN DESA (2009) *World Population Prospects: The 2008 revision.* New York, NY: Population Division of the Department of Economic and Social Affairs of the United Nations Secretariat (UN DESA).

— (2010) *World Urbanization Prospects: The 2009 revision.* New York, NY: Population Division of the Department of Economic and Social Affairs of the United Nations Secretariat (UN DESA).

Weeks, J. (1995) 'Income distribution and its implications for migration in sub-Saharan Africa'. In A. Mafeje and S. Radwan (eds) *Economic and Demographic Change in Africa.* Oxford: Clarendon Press, pp. 63–83.

Postscript: Building new knowledge and networks to foster sustainable urban development

Thomas Melin

Contrary to common opinion regarding urbanisation in developing countries, cities are not inherently problematic – they are neither the source nor the cause of political, economic, social, cultural or environmental challenges. Although such challenges manifest in the urban arena, the real issues arise from inadequate preparation, lack of proper management, and unsustained and often insensitive responses to rapid urbanisation and related processes. It is often a lack of adequate planning and reactive approaches to development that hinder long-term sustainable growth. That being said, cities provide an opportune platform for applying solutions to the growing number of challenges experienced at local, national and regional levels – cities are engines of economic development, platforms for the efficient use and management of resources, contributors to food security, and counteragents to the growing effects of climate change. However, the necessary conditions must be in place to effectively draw on cities as opportune solutions instead of systemic catalysts. Properly planned cities provide both the economies of scale and the productive population densities that have the potential to reduce per capita demand for resources such as energy and land. Strong demographic growth in a city is neither good nor bad on its own; however, experiences from around the world demonstrate that urbanisation has been strongly associated with improved human development, rising incomes and better living standards – many indicators also agree that urbanisation, if well managed, can encourage positive growth. Nevertheless, these benefits are not always a natural outcome of urbanisation; they require well-devised public policies that can steer demographic growth, turn urban accumulation of activities and resources into healthy economies, and ensure equitable distribution of wealth. When public policies are designed for the benefit of small political or economic elites, urbanisation will almost inevitably result in instability, creating cities that are unliveable for both rich and poor alike.

Over the last four years an intellectual and attitudinal migration has been experienced in global discourse – moving from a limited understanding of and aversion to urbanisation and the growth of cities to a wider acceptance that urbanisation is happening, and happening fast, and can instead provide an entry point for strategic development. This shift in paradigm is already generating the fundamental operational change that is desired in global and regional cities. In order to truly understand the evolution of this global discourse, one must first understand the evolving thought process behind urbanisation.

Past trends: thinking and perspectives in 2008–09

As cities grow in size and population, harmony between the spatial, social and environmental aspects of a city and amongst its inhabitants becomes of paramount importance. This harmony hinges on two key points: equity and sustainability. It is notable that in 2008–09 the majority of interventions in cities were driven by communities or non-governmental organisations (NGOs), resulting in impacts primarily at the neighbourhood level rather than on the scale of the cities and towns themselves. UN-Habitat's *State of the World's Cities 2008/2009* report captured the innovative thinking of this time, which is set out in the following bullet points:

- Central governments play a critical role in determining the prosperity and growth of cities.
- Balanced urban and regional development can be achieved through consistent and targeted investments in transport and communications infrastructure.
- Cities are becoming increasingly unequal.
- High levels of urban inequality are socially destabilising and economically unsustainable.
- Focused and targeted investments and interventions can significantly improve the lives of slum dwellers.
- Cities provide an opportunity to mitigate or even reverse the impact of global climate change as they provide the economies of scale that reduce per capita costs and demand for resources.
- Further commitment to pro-poor, inclusive urban development is needed.
- Compact and well-regulated cities with environmentally friendly public transport systems have a positive environmental impact.
- Coordination and collaboration between national, provincial and local authorities can achieve harmonious regional and urban development, provided they share a common vision and demonstrate sufficient political will and good planning.

The urban development agenda had undergone a drastic transformation in the years following the World Urban Forum (WUF) 5 in 2010 ('The Right to the City – Bridging the Urban Divide') and WUF 6 in 2012 ('The Urban Future'). This transformation reflected a substantial shift in thinking and engagement of urban issues – resulting in evolved perspectives aimed at understanding the city in a more interdisciplinary and participatory manner.

Current trends: thinking and perspectives in 2012–13

There continues to be an earnest need for coordinated, multi-sectoral approaches to dealing with urban issues that place local authorities squarely at the centre of driving, negotiating and monitoring the formulation and execution of the urban development agenda. In what promises to be one of the more remarkable forthcoming developments in the overall pattern of urbanisation in Africa, the region's population is poised to outgrow both Europe's and Latin America's.

At present, UN-Habitat advocates for a new type of city – the city of the twenty-first century – that is, a people-centred, public-oriented city, one that is capable of integrating the tangible and more intangible aspects of prosperity, and in the process shedding the inefficient, unsustainable forms and functionalities of the city of the previous century. It also promotes the notion of urban prosperity that transcends narrow economic success to encompass a socially broad-based, balanced and resilient type of development. Urban prosperity tightens the links between individuals and society with their everyday environment, i.e. the city itself. UN-Habitat suggests a fresh approach to prosperity, one that reaches beyond the sole economic dimension to take in other vital elements such as quality of life, infrastructure, equity and environmental sustainability.

Also advocated is a shift in attention around the world to emphasise a more robust notion of development – one that looks beyond the narrow domain of economic growth that has dominated ill-balanced policy agendas over the previous decade. It encourages a transformative change towards people-centred, sustainable urban development inclusive to all.

Future trends: thinking and projected perspectives for 2030

Today, 40 per cent of Africa is considered urban; by around 2030, Africa's collective population will become 50 per cent urban – and the quality of life in cities in 2030 will be directly connected to the manner in which urban policies and the urban form of cities are planned and managed today. Therefore, we must ask ourselves: who are these people migrating to cities and how do we equip our cities to better accommodate them? As many of these migrants will be coming from rural settings, lack of education and vocational training will be a concern – policies must be able to ensure that all urban dwellers can avoid the so-called 'poverty trap' that stops them from maximising those opportunities that the urban environment is designed to provide. Legislation, research, academia, government, professional associations and the private sector must anticipate and prepare for the needs and expectations of their cities' futures – this requires smart social, economic, infrastructure and environmental planning and investment, guided by strategic national policy frameworks that recognise and operate on regional, national and local levels.

Persisting challenges

UN-Habitat recognises that urbanisation in Africa has not yet brought the economic development and degree of prosperity that might have been anticipated. Inadequate education and lack of infrastructure, combined with poor governance, have constrained the efficient use of productive resources and the industrial development that might have accompanied earlier efforts. At the same time, the ongoing urban economic momentum that is currently driving Africa is a spin-off of a number of characteristic factors of prosperity at work in other regions of the world – this includes agglomeration economies, location advantages and diversification of the economic base, albeit all in nascent form.

In addition, despite growing commitment and laudable efforts, many African cities continue to be plagued by deep-seated corruption at multiple levels of government, inadequate policies and policy implementation, weak governance, ineffective spatial/physical planning, design and management, poor communication between the government and the public, and a lack of clear vision with the required enabling capacity and resources. All of this has strangled the positive by-products of urbanisation, instead leading to dilapidation and systemic strains on an already fragile system.

Now what?

Crucial to advancing and harnessing the rich potential of African cities and responding to the range of urban challenges are the development and strengthening of strategic regional networks and the (re)building of public and other institutions. These interventions require the nurturing of existing structures and the development of quality leadership at multiple levels to spearhead performance at the city scale. Equally important is the tightening of existing local fiscal and accounting processes for greater tax revenues; the creation and enforcement of local legislation and procedures that promote sound spatial/physical planning, design and management; and the creation of enabling environments that foster good urban governance.

UN-Habitat calls for a strengthening of regional and national networks through national urban policy. In order to improve the delicate situation in Africa, UN-Habitat proposes the following:

- Cities must create the conditions (and record accurate data) that will enable them to understand and anticipate trends, including the growth or decline of specific areas or regions, if they are to be in a position to develop expansionary or recovery strategies.

- City regions, urban development corridors and mega-urban regions continue to emerge or to become increasingly visible across Africa. Their spatial and functional features demand new urban management methods to ensure consistent area-wide governance. African cities must connect to regional and global business networks, enhance quality of life, improve basic infrastructure and communication networks, address public transport deficiencies and environmental conditions, and respond to inequality and poverty issues, if they are to turn into real engines of national growth and prosperity.
- Cities must accommodate demographic and spatial expansion, with a concomitant development of well-devised urban structures that reduce transport and service delivery costs, optimise land use and support the deployment and/or protection of open spaces – promoting compact, denser cities with smaller footprints.
- Cities must improve connectivity, mobility and accessibility and develop well-planned integration of land use, density and transport, as this can reduce energy consumption drastically, making cities more sustainable.
- It is in a city's interest to establish links with other neighbouring urban areas in order to facilitate complementary functions and acquire a strong collective regional identity, in the process achieving greater economic momentum than if they remain in isolation.
- New or strengthened, more effective local and regional institutions, new links and alliances across the three tiers of government (national, provincial or state, and local), together with a comprehensive vision with clear plans favouring inclusiveness are all crucial for equitable development and prosperity.
- It is vital for cities to work together – cities within a large urban configuration are in better positions to effectively protect, manage and plan for physical environments that span multiple jurisdictions.
- The economic surpluses that large urban agglomerations derive from productivity gains can be channelled into the protection of natural resources in the region, with the costs of maintaining these indivisible public goods shared equitably among the population.
- Given the rapid urbanisation in Africa, if cities are to meet population needs, municipal finance must be strengthened, with more fiscal freedom and own-source funding. This can be promoted through improved local legislation and collection of revenues.

Critical considerations: looking forward

In an enhanced bid to build new knowledge and strengthen networks around urban development on the continent, there is a need to continue increasing the participation of relevant actors at all levels of urban development

– specifically, the marginalised and disadvantaged, bearing in mind that the city should be inclusive to all. Even as citizen participation is promoted, it is crucial to couple longer-term visionary planning with short-term upgrading of neighbourhoods and to ensure that such processes are adequately anchored in appropriate public institutions, as they are the overall managers and custodians of city development. African cities are known to have been neglected, often leading to dilapidated infrastructure and a lack of social cohesion; there is now an acute need to robustly promote long-term planning that directs and informs African urbanisation, encompassing the present while anticipating the future. This calls for pressure on elected officials to think beyond their political term in office.

Notably, it is understood that the collection of information and further analysis of urban data are imperative to understand and interpret cities; however, the ability and capacity of public and private institutions to translate this knowledge into action through institutional processes, instruments and tools are elements that are needed but are often overlooked. As captured by Gordon Pirie in Chapter 7 on urban transportation, there is a need for practitioners and policy makers to formulate more effective interventions. Comparative studies and data collection can anticipate difficulties, avoid errors and replicate successes, although the volume, scale and comparability of evidence can make this a daunting task; as case studies and surveys multiply, the possibility of absorbing, synthesising and applying more-or-less comparable findings recedes. Institutions need to be strengthened in order to effectively address these concerns.

Further emphasis is required on inadequacies in the built environment professions. This limitation is both in terms of the number of urban planners, architects and surveyors and in terms of the scope and relevance of their education and training to respond to current issues on the continent and at global level. Urban Africa is rapidly developing – its new and growing cities demand to be strategically accounted for and accommodated in this growth trajectory. This is further reflected in Edgar Pieterse's chapter (Chapter 11), in which he recognises the need to build the institutional capability and readiness to advance the local (and regional) case for the urban agenda among core institutions such as national ministries dealing with urban issues (finance, infrastructure, economic development, planning, environment, etc.), local government associations, universities, non-governmental organisations (NGOs), social movements of the urban poor and enlightened businesses. In Chapter 10, James Duminy, Nancy Odendaal and Vanessa Watson agree that, in the midst of a 'policy crisis' facing African urbanisation, a lack of properly trained urban planning and management professionals able to respond to urban complexity from a progressive pro-poor value base is a major contributing factor to urban dysfunction. Reforming the research–education nexus at the heart of the planning profession is key to ensuring that future urban practitioners respond to city challenges in a meaningful way.

Equally important, as set out by AbdouMaliq Simone in the chapter on infrastructure, economies and social transformation (Chapter 12), more comprehensive knowledge is needed about how resources and materials actually flow through cities. Infrastructure largely exists to move water, power, materials and waste from one place to another. Unfortunately, infrastructure inadequacies are conventionally calculated in terms of availability and access; there is often limited understanding of the exact volumes, directionalities, flows, uses and articulations involved. A range of new mapping devices, planning techniques and financial modelling can support strategic decisions as to how to maximise the productive impact of new infrastructure investments.

It is evident that there is a dire need for the collection, interaction and management of actionable data – creating new knowledge and information that is current and periodically updated, born of action-oriented research. Research itself should be the result of the consolidation of networks and collaborative partnerships between and among public and private actors. Access to important knowledge, information and data is critical for determining what is available in the public domain and in what format. This is highlighted in Chapter 3, on sub-Saharan African urbanisation and global environmental change, in which Susan Parnell and Ruwani Walawege acknowledge that 'understanding the future impact of global environmental change on migration presupposes that there is a consensus on the current drivers of human settlement, something that is more than usually difficult to establish for Africa where data are out of date, census figures are not always accurate and the important data are not always in the public domain'. The issue of access to urban data, whether on transport, commerce, planning, fiscal processes or social amenities, becomes important to public and private entities, including local, regional and global investors.

Chapter 3 also identifies that there are no uniform official definitions of 'urban' or 'rural' used across the continent, and many countries do not even have agreed definitions (Potts 2005; 2010), despite the fact that recently there has been a number of high-profile international publications providing a synthesis of urbanisation trends in Africa (UN-Habitat 2009; World Bank 2009). Further, this reflects a real ambiguity among scholars over what is understood by migration and urban life in Africa (see the contrasting accounts in IOM 2009; Myers 2003; Crankshaw et al. 1992; Simone 2004; Montgomery et al. 2003; Potts 2010).

International urbanisation is mainly based in Western European and American thinking that, over time, has proved to be unsustainable. Africa is now faced with a historical opportunity to establish new thinking and critical approaches and to lead as pioneers – this, supported by accurate data and information, can lead to actionable results. In order to know what and where the knowledge gaps are, there needs to be an inventory taken of initiatives, projects, institutions and urban actors that have an interest in or are working in this direction already. Urban or city observatories can be promoted as tools for evaluation and assessment and for updating urban data, and monitoring and evaluation mechanisms can be developed to ensure that this information stays current and anticipates the expectations and future needs of urban Africa. Such information would be useful to direct government policy and to inform investors, planners, architects and urban practitioners on where their cities are going and how to enhance them. In Chapter 12, AbdouMaliq Simone reinforces this by urging consideration of the impetus, practices and movements of Africans across the region to construct new spaces of operation, habitation and transaction. The extensiveness of need and the impact of global economic change and urban social transformations that are currently under way combine in a manner that requires new thinking and expectations, highlighting what is possible and how this can lead to concrete results. Only by identifying more comprehensive ways to map, understand and engage urban real economies will the momentum for infrastructure-led and environmentally sustainable economic growth be maintained.

The importance of ensuring the relevance of any data captured or generated is further emphasised in Edgar Pieterse's chapter (Chapter 11), which highlights that 'over and above the problem of basic data availability, we are also confronted by an intellectual legacy in the urban field that is atheoretical, aspatial and often even ahistorical'. He urges the need to 'appreciate that all data must be interpreted, and interpretation depends on theoretical assumptions'. New knowledge therefore needs to pursue and mature research that is theoretically inquisitive and thorough, spatially astute and cognisant of the past.

Exploration of the ways in which citizens can participate in the collection and management of data and information on issues in their living and working neighbourhoods is notable. Sourcing and gathering information therefore shifts from being the responsibility of government or of government institutions to being an activity of interest, concern and engagement for the users of cities and towns across Africa. In tandem with this thinking is Gordon Pirie's observation that the accumulating words, images and statistics on transport practices in African cities present intertwined intellectual and policy challenges. He notes that the intellectual challenges have to do with what is known about urban transport and how that knowledge is acquired. The policy challenges arise from this knowledge, and are about its application and appropriateness (Chapter 7). Here, the 'how' becomes as important as the 'what'. Pirie further observes that 'massive and expensive transport surveys are conducted rarely, take a long time to analyse, and, in rapidly changing situations, soon become outdated. Routine, low-cost, automated data collection about travel patterns using mobile phones is an alternative and might generate new micro-detail that could be useful for transport planners in particular localities' (Chapter 7).

What is clear is that Africa needs an African 'urbanisation of excellence' that recognises its own drivers of urbanisation, shepherds its urban transitions, and respects its policy imperatives. There is a need to create academic institutions, local authorities and networks that promote and invest in visionary thinking. The Association of African Planning Schools, a peer-to-peer network of mostly Anglophone sub-Saharan African universities that teach urban and regional planning, is a move in this direction, having launched a programme to promote case study research and publication among African planning academics. This 'visionary thinking' in and about Africa can be provoked by factors highlighted by James Duminy, Nancy Odendaal and Vanessa Watson in Chapter 10, on education and research imperatives, and includes promoting planners capable of collaborating with many different actors involved in the development process and introducing teaching methods that encourage the development of these skills and ethical positions through experiential learning. Indeed, the strengthening of new knowledge and education at primary, secondary and tertiary levels plays a critical role; exposing students to new ways of understanding and thinking about urbanisation, cities and human settlements will enhance the quality of those professionals who engage in urban planning, development and management processes. This is further emphasised in Chapter 11, which submits that what is required is investment in long-term capacity to build durable institutions that can respond to the knowledge, policy development, training and implementation challenges associated with the urbanisation question. In addition, far more emphasis needs to be given to building capacity among scholars, researchers in think tanks, effective knowledge networks, forums linking policy analysts and decision makers, and international networks of practice and activism that focus on the general problems and that may be thematically connected.

Integral to moving forward is the development of a national approach with local adaptation to cities, taking account of local climates, economies, cultures and needs. Developing a regional or sub-regional approach with national grounding and relevance will also be important since city regions and economic trading blocs and markets require and demand that countries and cities no longer be looked at in isolation but as part of a greater vision. An African urban legacy that will withstand the test of time hinges on more synergistic action between and within cities, across multiple tiers of government, and, in research, the better integration of the disciplines that study cities.

References

Crankshaw, O., T. Hart and G. Heron (1992) 'The road to Egoli: urbanisation histories from a Johannesburg squatter settlement'. In D. Smith (ed.) *The Apartheid City and Beyond: Urbanization and social change in South Africa*. London: Routledge, pp. 136–46.

IOM (2009) *Migration, Environment and Climate Change: Assessing the evidence*. Geneva: International Organisation for Migration (IOM).

Montgomery, M., R. Stren, B. Cohen and H. Reed (eds) (2003) *Cities Transformed: Demographic change and its implications in the developing world*. Washington, DC: National Academies Press.

Myers, G. (2003) *Verandahs of Power: Colonialism and space in urban Africa*. Syracuse, NY: Syracuse University Press.

Potts, D. (2005) 'Counter-urbanisation on the Zambian copperbelt? Interpretations and implications'. *Urban Studies* 42(4): 583–609.

— (2010) *Circular Migration in Zimbabwe and Contemporary Sub-Saharan Africa*. Woodbridge: James Currey.

Simone, A. (2004) *For the City Yet to Come: Changing African life in four cities*. Durham, NC: Duke University Press.

UN-Habitat (2008) *State of the World's Cities 2008/2009: Harmonious cities*. London: Earthscan and United Nations Human Settlements Programme (UN-Habitat).

— (2009) *Global Report on Human Settlements: Planning sustainable cities*. Nairobi: United Nations Human Settlements Programme (UN-Habitat).

World Bank (2009) *World Development Report 2009: Reshaping economic geography*. Washington, DC: World Bank.

Contributing authors

Jo Beall is currently a director at the British Council charged with higher education. She is the former Deputy Vice Chancellor at the University of Cape Town (UCT). During her tenure at UCT she chaired the executive of the African Centre for Cities (ACC) and was actively involved in ACC activities. The paper in this volume draws from her involvement in the Crisis States programme at the London School of Economics and Political Science, where she led the urban focus of that multi-year, multi-city study.

Stephen Berrisford trained as both a lawyer and a planner, with degrees from the Universities of Cape Town and Cambridge. From 1993 to 2000 he worked in various capacities in the public service in South Africa, for the Cape Town and Johannesburg municipalities as well as with the national Department of Land Affairs, where he was Director: Land Development Facilitation. Since 2000 he has worked as an independent consultant, based in Johannesburg until 2011 and now in Cape Town. His work focuses on the identification of appropriate principles and rules to design legal frameworks for urban planning and development in African cities. He works in a number of countries, with particularly strong experience in South Africa, Zambia, Kenya and Ethiopia. His clients include governments and international agencies such as UN-Habitat, the Cities Alliance and the World Bank. He is an Honorary Adjunct Associate Professor in the African Centre for Cities at the University of Cape Town and a Visiting Professor at the University of the Witwatersrand, and he was a Visiting Scholar at the University of Sheffield in 2010. He has published a number of articles and book chapters in the field of urban planning law reform in an African context.

Jonathan Crush is the CIGI Chair in Global Migration and Development at the Balsillie School of International Affairs in Waterloo, Ontario, and Honorary Professor at the University of Cape Town. He has published extensively on global migration and African food security issues. He is the Principal Investigator of the African Urban Food Security Netork (AFSUN).

James Duminy is a researcher at the African Centre for Cities, and acts as general secretary of the Association of African Planning Schools. He holds an undergraduate degree in biochemistry and microbiology (from Rhodes University), a master's degree in town and regional planning (University of KwaZulu-Natal or UKZN), as well as an MA in urban history (University of Leicester).

His interests include the history and status of planning education in Africa; emerging approaches to analysing and theorising cities in the global South; the historical relationship between urban form and planning; rights-based approaches to development; and the symbolic politics surrounding street re-naming in (South) African cities. He contributed to the 2009 UN-Habitat *Global Report on Human Settlements* (Chapter 8), and has authored several conference papers relating to urban development and planning education in Africa.

Sean Fox is a lecturer in human geography in the Department of Geographical Sciences at the University of Bristol. Prior to joining the Bristol faculty he was a Teaching Fellow in the Department of International Development at the London School of Economics (2007–11) and a Research Associate with the Crisis States Research Centre (2006–11). He is co-author of the book *Cities and Development* (2009) and has published research in journals including *Environment and Planning C: Government and Policy*, *Journal of Peace Research*, *Population and Development Review* and *World Development*. He has also served as an adviser on urban development issues for a range of organisations including the Bill & Melinda Gates Foundation, Care International, Oxfam and UN-Habitat.

Bruce Frayne is Director of the Master of Development Practice (MDP) programme and Associate Professor in the School of Environment, Enterprise and Development (SEED) in the Faculty of Environment at the University of Waterloo, Canada. Bruce is an urban planner and geographer by training, and teaches on the International Development programme at Waterloo. His research interests fall within the broad ambit of sustainable cities, and encompass the three related areas of human migration, urbanisation and food security, with a regional focus on sub-Saharan Africa. Bruce has more than 20 years' experience in international development, during which time he has managed a number of influential research, policy and capacity-building networks, including the Southern African Migration Project (SAMP) for Queen's University, the Regional Network on AIDS, Livelihoods and Food Security (RENEWAL) for the International Food Policy Research Institute (IFPRI), and most recently the African Food Security Urban Network (AFSUN) for Queen's University and the University of Cape Town. Bruce has published widely in the field of international development, and his latest book, *Climate Change, Assets and Food Security in Southern African Cities*, is co-edited with Caroline Moser and Gina Ziervogel (Earthscan, 2012).

Tom Goodfellow is a lecturer in urban planning and international development at the University of Sheffield. Prior to taking up this post in 2013, he was a fellow in international development at the London School of Economics and Political Science (LSE) from 2011 to 2013. During 2008–11 he was a research associate with Oxfam GB as part of a collaborative research studentship, through which he advised Oxfam on the development of their urban and sustainable livelihoods strategies. He was also an associate of the Crisis States Research Centre at LSE from 2007 to 2011, helping develop its work on cities and conflict in fragile states. He has published in journals including *Urban Studies*, *Geoforum*, *Cities* and *Comparative Politics*. He has a master's degree in international relations (LSE) and a degree in social and political sciences (Cambridge).

Thomas Melin is Acting Head, Office of External Relations at the United Nations Human Settlements Programme (UN-Habitat), where he specialises in Inter-Agency Coordination, Institutional Reform and Strategic Partnerships. Thomas Melin is the agency's focal person for the United Nations Advisory Committee of Local Authorities (UNACLA). He is also responsible for the establishment of the global Sustainable Urban Development Network (SUD-Net), which facilitates collaboration between a range of urban knowledge networks, targeting Public Space as a platform to encourage participatory planning and stakeholder engagement. A Swedish national, Thomas is an architect and planner who received his education and training at Lund University, Sweden. He has a long association with the African Centre for Cities, championing stronger academic engagement in African cities.

Nancy Odendaal is currently Senior Lecturer in City and Regional Planning in the University of Cape Town's (UCT) School of Architecture, Planning and Geomatics. Prior to that she was a researcher with the African Centre for Cities at UCT where she was responsible for the coordination of the Association of African Planning Schools, a peer-to-peer network of schools in mostly Anglophone Africa. Following her work as coordinator of the network, Nancy now represents AAPS on the Global Planning Education Association Network (GPEAN) Governing Council. Her research and teaching interests include metropolitan planning, planning theory and infrastructural transitions in cities of the global South. In addition to her academic work, she has conducted commissioned research on planning and transformation, land use management and planning standards.

Gordon Pirie is Deputy Director of the African Centre for Cities. Transport provision and use have been his research preoccupation for several decades. The emphasis of this work has been on transport as a tool of urban, national and international geopolitics, on the lived experience of transport and transport workers, and on transport as a lens though which to view fallible and partial modernity. Gordon's publications include two books on British imperial aviation in the 1920s and 1930s, and a suite of book chapters and papers on transport and travel in British colonial Africa and in postcolonial South Africa during and after apartheid. He has also written more generally about the conceptualisation and measurement of distance, accessibility and mobility for progressive policy making.

Carole Rakodi is an Emeritus Professor and Associate of the International Development Department, School of Government and Society, University of Birmingham. She is a social scientist and town planner who has worked on urban issues in Africa for many years, especially in Zambia, Zimbabwe and Kenya, and also in Tanzania, Ghana and Nigeria. She has published widely on land and housing markets, urban planning and management, household livelihoods, and urban politics and governance. She is author of *Harare: Inheriting a settler-colonial city: change or continuity?* (Wiley, World Cities Series, 1995) and has edited several volumes and journal special issues, including *The Urban Challenge in Africa* (editor, United Nations University Press, 1997), *Urban Livelihoods: A people-centred approach to reducing poverty* (main editor, with Tony Lloyd-Jones, Earthscan, 2002) and 'State–society relations in land delivery processes in African cities' (editor, *International Development Planning Review* 28(2), 2007). From 2005 to 2011, Carole was director of the Department for International Development-funded research programme on religions and development, which worked with partners in India, Pakistan, Nigeria and Tanzania, as well as with other British universities.

David Simon (BA Cape Town; BA Reading; DPhil Oxon) is Professor of Development Geography at Royal Holloway, University of London. His particular research interests include development theory, policy and practice; the development–environment interface; urbanisation and urban–rural interaction; transport and regional and national development planning; and critical approaches to the roles of information and communications technologies in these fields. He is a specialist on sub-Saharan Africa and also has research experience in Sri Lanka, Thailand, the Philippines and the UK. He is a former editor, and now chair, of the editorial board of the *Journal of Southern African Studies*. He serves on the Scientific Steering Committee of the Urbanization and Global Environmental Change core project of the International Human Dimensions Programme on Global Environmental Change (IHDP), and until recently was adviser to UN-Habitat on cities and climate change. His most recent books are *The Peri-Urban Interface: Approaches to sustainable natural and human resource use* (co-editor, Earthscan, 2006), *Fifty Key Thinkers on Development* (editor, Routledge, 2006) and *Aquatic Ecosystems and Development: Comparative Asian perspectives* (co-editor, with F. Schiemer, U. S. Amarasinghe and J. Moreau, Margraf/Backhuys, 2008). He was lead co-editor of a special issue of *Third World Quarterly* in 2009 entitled 'Remapping development studies: contemporary critical perspectives'.

AbdouMaliq Simone is an urbanist with particular interest in emerging forms of social and economic intersection across diverse trajectories of change for cities in the global South. Simone is presently Research Professor at the University of South Australia and Visiting Professor of Urban Studies at the African Centre for Cities, University of Cape Town. Key publications include *In Whose Image: Political Islam and urban practices in Sudan* (University of Chicago Press, 1994), *For the City Yet to Come: Urban change in four African cities* (Duke University Press, 2004) and *City Life from Jakarta to Dakar: Movements at the crossroads* (Routledge, 2009).

Warren Smit is a researcher at the African Centre for Cities, University of Cape Town. He has worked as a researcher on urban issues in South Africa since 1993. His areas of research interest include urban governance, strategic city-wide planning and urban health.

Ivan Turok is Deputy Executive Director at the Human Sciences Research Council in South Africa and Honorary Professor at Cape Town and Glasgow Universities. He is editor-in-chief of the journal *Regional Studies* and an expert adviser on city and regional development to the United Nations, the Organisation for Economic Co-operation and Development (OECD), European Commission, South African Government, UK Government and African Development Bank. He has published over 100 academic papers, chapters and books, including the 2011 *State of South African Cities Report*, *The State of English Cities* (2006), *Changing Cities: Rethinking competitiveness, cohesion and governance* (2005), *The Jobs Gap in Britain's Cities* (1999) and *The Coherence of EU Regional Policy* (1997).

Ruwani Walawege is a researcher working with the Climate Systems Analysis Group based at the University of Cape Town. She has an MSc degree in atmospheric science from the University of Cape Town. Her current focus is on developing training and learning materials to improve the understanding of climate science, and to help develop tailored products and climate services to benefit adaptation research and projects.

Vanessa Watson is professor in the School of Architecture, Planning and Geomatics at the University of Cape Town (UCT) and Deputy Dean of the faculty. She holds degrees from the Universities of Natal, Cape Town and the Architectural Association of London, and a PhD from the University of the Witwatersrand. She is the author or co-author of seven books, 40 journal articles and numerous chapters and published conference papers in the field of planning. Her particular areas of focus are planning theory, the institutional context of planning and large-city planning. She has a particular interest in developing perspectives on planning from the global South. She has undertaken consultancy work for UN-Habitat on the 2009 *Global Report*. She is an editor of the journal *Planning Theory* (UK) and sits on the editorial board of *Planning*

Practice and Research (UK), *The Journal of Planning Education and Research* (USA) and *Progress in Planning* (UK). She is co-chair of the Association of African Planning Schools. Vanessa is also on the executive committee of the African Centre for Cities at UCT.

Index

decentralisation, 175, 203, 207, 212, 234, 235, 240, 243, 246; and institutional reconfiguration, 148; importance of, 12; in 'Anglo-Saxon' tradition, 153; of planning powers, 171; policy and strategy options, 161–3

decolonisation, 241

deindustrialisation, 78

democracy, 149, 151, 188, 203, 212–14, 234; deficit of, 171; enhancement of, 162; in access to data platforms, 158

demographic bulge, 208

demographic change and transition, 1, 25, 53, 85–6, 111, 237, 248, 261, 262; global, 7–8

demographic composition of Africa, 222–3

demolition campaigns, 167, 173, 176

density through compaction, 156

development: relation to urbanisation, 60–81; robust notion of, 286; state-led, 83

Development Bank of Southern Africa, 215

development control, 174; as public good, 175–6

dichotomous urban–rural policies, 253, 254

difference, 88–92

Dili, 26

disasters, risks of, 175–6; risk reduction planning, 248

disease: constraint on urbanisation, 262, 265, 267, 271, 274–5; control of, 267, 275; spread of, 261

displacement of populations, 35

distribution of wealth, 223

diversification, economic, need for, 65–7

doctors, registered, statistics for, 277

Dodoma, 246

Douala, 138

drought, 52; effects of, on cities, 239

Durban, 30, 252; transition from apartheid, 29–30

East African Community (EAC), 226, 251

Economic Commission for Africa (ECA), 13, 64

Economic Community of Central African States (ECCAS), 226

Economic Community of West African States (ECOWAS), 226, 251

economic revival of Africa, 60–81

economic stagnation, 12–13

Economist, The, 63

education, 48, 90, 99, 101, 155, 267, 287; Islamic, 100; non-completion of, 209; private, 99; religious, 99

educational networks, power of, 198

Egypt, 241

El Salvador, 21

elderly, 209

elders, 87, 91 *see also* gerontocracy

elections, local, 162

electricity, supply of, 66, 153, 223; investment in, 222

elites, 190, 202, 210, 228; capture of planning law processes by, 169; mobility privileges of, 143; political, 203, 205

employment: rate of, 69; stable, 13

empowerment, 142; paradigm of, 206–7; promotion of, 111 *see also* Bicycling Empowerment Network

energy systems, grid-based, 160

environmental change, trends in, 36–42 *see also* global environmental change (GEC)

environmental issues of cities, 163, 288, 290

equity, 285

Eritrea, 20

Ernst & Young, 63

ethical dilemmas of planning processes, 192

ethically-based associations, 92

Ethiopia, 20

ethnicity, 85, 86, 95, 97; use of term, 89

evictions, 167, 173, 176, 201, 205

exceptionalism, of African urbanisation, 3

experiential learning, 195–6, 292

externalities of cities, negative, 72

family, changing relations in, 87–8

family planning, need for, 275

fertility rates, 46, 47–8, 85, 269; decline of, 208; reduction of, 101, 275

financial modelling, need for, 290

financial sector, development of, 233

flooding, 37, 52

Flyvbjerg, Bent, 193

food: access to, 2, 112–13, 128 (related to incomes, 121–3); availability of supplies of, 258; informal economies of, 125, 126, 127; security of *see* food security;

through, 221–4; investment in, 14, 64, 66, 159–60, 207, 223, 251, 270; transformation of, 155
infrastructure-led growth, 210–12, 221
innovation, incubation of, 215
Institute for Transportation and Development Policy, 215
institutional capacity, building of, 292
institutional framing of urban development, 240
institutional reconfiguration, 148–66
institutional reform, agenda for, 154–63
institutions, robust, creation of, 214–15
integrated development planning, 186
integrated economies, role of cities in, 71–3
integrated rapid transport systems, 136
internally displaced people (IDP), 48, 52
International Energy Agency, 65
International Finance Corporation, 180
International Monetary Fund (IMF), 63–4, 65, 67
intraregional approaches to infrastructure financing, 233
investment, 243; as indicator of colonial influence, 268; in urban development, 178, 269 see also foreign direct investment (FDI) and infrastructure, investment in
Iraq, 22
Islam, 86, 89–90, 93, 95–6, 96–7; healthcare charities, 100; 'self-governing strangers' quarters, 97
Ismaili religion, 99
Izala movement, 96

Johannesburg, 10–11, 44, 86, 93, 97, 98, 116, 117, 122, 123, 125, 134, 136, 252; informal recyclers in, 195
Juba: as site of violence, 26; flight of population from, 23; growth of, 24
Jubilee 2000 campaign, 246

Kalimase, Vincent Lombume, 200, 218
Kamete, Amin, 189
Kampala, 135, 136, 138; shrinking population of, 23
Kano, 97
Kenya, 91, 138, 243
Keynesianism, 241
Kibera, 100

Kigali, 30; as battleground, 22; as secure space, 28–9; growth of, 25
Kiit, Salya, 27
Kinshasa, 4, 20, 23, 24, 27, 84, 200
kinship relations, 86, 91
Kisumu, 138
Krugman, Paul, 60
Kumasi, 97

labour practices, forms of, 231
labour unions, 90, 91; growth of, 268
labour-intensive public services, 209
Lagos, 4, 44, 52, 84, 134, 135, 136, 138, 142, 225, 246, 252
land, access to, 211 (of poor people, 169); appropriate use of, 212; speculative acquisition of, 70; urban, ownership of, 25
land use: codes of practice for, 12; optimisation of, 288; top-down planning of, 188; traditional, 12 (regulation of, 162)
landlords, extortion by, 205
landslides, 37
Lerise, Fred, 188, 192
Lesotho, 124
life expectancy, increases in, 275
Lilongwe, 225, 246
Lipton, Michael, 246
lived poverty index (LPI), 123
livelihood strategies, diversified, 87
local government, 150, 153, 288; enhancement of, 239
local level of urban production, 231
Lomé, 225
Lord's Resistance Army (LRA), 24
low-carbon economies, 159
Luanda, 20; cost of living in, 70; growth of, 24
Lusaka, 116, 117, 120, 124, 125
luxury property development, 70

Makoko (Lagos), 190
Malawi, 112, 124
Mali, 96; Muslim women's associations in, 98
malnutrition, 110; chronic, 127; 'hungry seasons', 119–20; in South Africa, 113
Malthusianism, 260–1
Managua, 26
Manzini, 116, 117, 120, 125, 126
mapping devices, need for, 290

organisation, new forms of, 91
Orientalism, 83
orphaned children, 209
Ougadougou, 141
outsourcing, of manufacturing and
    farming, 66

paradigm change, need for, 204
Parnell, Susan, 253
participation, 151, 157, 212, 213, 228, 288–9;
    in planning, 142, 176, 178, 191
participatory budgeting, 213–14, 217
patriarchy, 48, 85, 97 *see also* elders
patronage, urban hierarchies of, 227
peace, building of, 101
pedicabs, use of, 139
Pentecostal churches, 95, 98
peri-urban areas, 9, 42, 240, 248, 254;
    incorporation of, 45
phronesis, 196
Pick n Pay company, 124
Pieterse, Edgar, 186–7
planners, with progressive values, 192
planning: definition of, 188; master
    planning, 186; professionals in, 178,
    184–99; urban, state of, 185–7
planning law: avoidance of, 169, 175;
    colonial, 186; complexity of, 169;
    compliance standards, 168; functions
    of, 174; importance of, 173–6;
    improvement of, 176–81; legitimacy of,
    174–5; new models for, 171; principles
    of good regulation, 177; reform of,
    167–83 (design of, 180)
planning practice in Africa, imperatives
    of, 190–2
planning research, pragmatism in, 193
Planning Sustainable Cities, 172
playing draughts on the streets, 190
police, traffic, 142
political movements, 88, 91, 94; relation
    with religious movements, 96–7
political parties, 89, 90, 228; role of, 217–18
politicians, failure of, 177–8
pollution, of the air, 72, 137
poor, the, 90, 175, 189, 214, 228; access
    to land, 169; access to urban
    opportunities, 210; anti-poor bias,
    194; autonomous organisation of,
    208, 213; bargaining position of, 181;
    criminalisation of, 208; housing for,

212; in regulatory norms of planning
    law, 168; pro-poor policies, 289 (in
    transport, 133); recognition of, 205–6;
    representation of, 178; repression
    of, 190; resilience of, 63; self-
    empowerment of, 204–5; suspicion of,
    202; urban, 203, 207
population, growth of, 3, 44–5, 268,
    272; a neutral fact, 284; as driver of
    urbanisation, 47; predictions for,
    62; reduction of, 275; urban, 257
    (determinants of, 261); statistics for, 5
Port Harcourt, 94, 98
positivistic approach to knowledge, 83, 84
post-colonial urbanism, 239
post-war transition, in African cities, 18–34
poverty, 10, 12, 61, 77, 84, 87, 100, 113, 115,
    141, 156, 177, 180, 250, 288; definition
    of, 122–3; intergenerational, 141;
    reduction of, 110, 154, 155, 246
    (relation to urbanisation, 75); urban,
    2; urbanisation of, 62 *see also* lived
    poverty index
poverty trap of cities, 286
primary commodities: exports of, 61,
    65, 69, 77; investment in, 267; non-
    renewable, 210
primate cities, 9
privatisation, 153, 160; of public services,
    154; of transportation, 143
productivity of urban agglomerations, 73
property rights, 70, 167, 265
proportionality, in planning regulation, 179
public discourse, informed, need for,
    217–18
public goods, maintenance of, 288

Quetta, 24

radio and television programming, 230
railways: building of, 221 (Chinese
    involvement in, 66); fuelling of, 265;
    improvement of, 267; operating
    conditions of, 134–5; vandalism of, 134
    see also 'Gautrain'
rainfall, increases in, 37, 42
'real' economies of cities, 224–7
reclassification of settlements, 45
recycling, 209
regional urban development, 221–36, 252,
    292; agenda for, 225

sustainability, 285
Sustainability Institute, 215
sustainable urban development, 154–7, 161, 187, 221, 284–92
Swaziland, 112, 124

Tanzania, 91, 112, 186, 188–9, 192, 215, 240, 243; abolition of local government in, 150
taxation, 211; local, 288; property-based, 176; size of tax base, 9, 15, 205, 210
technological change, effect on urbanisation, 266
technology, diffusion of, 277
tenure: security of, 211; transparency of, 222
time lags in distribution facilities, 232
time-wasting activities in cities, 229
Timor-Leste, 26
Tiyanniya brotherhood, 100
Todaro, M. P., 259
Touba, 96, 98, 100
trade, removed from streets, 229
trade unions see labour unions
traffic congestion, 133–4
transparency: in planning system, 179, 189; in tenure arrangements, 222; in urban management law, 12
transport pressures in urban Africa, 133–47
transportation: costs of, 266; deficiencies of, 288 (data for, 144); energy efficiency of, 160; environmentally friendly, 285; infrastructure, factor in urbanisation, 264; policy challenges of, 291; surveys of, 291
travel, dignified, concept of, 141
travel-to-work times, 73
Turkey, 210
Turok, I., 253

Uganda, 24, 27; riots in, 26
unemployment, 13, 122, 222; of youth, 208–9
United Cities and Local Governments – Africa, 216
United Nations (UN), population predictions for Africa, 62
United Nations Committee on Trade and Development (UNCTAD), 67
United Nations Development Programme (UNDP), 110, 186

United Nations Human Settlements Programme (UN-Habitat), 60, 148, 151, 159, 186, 200–1, 222–3, 286; definition of slum dwellers, 10; Global Report on Human Settlements, 187, 239; proposals for sustainable urbanisation, 287; State of African Cities, 217; State of the World's Cities, 149, 172, 285
United Nations Population Fund, 7
United Nations Urban Management Programme, 186
United States of America (USA), experience of urban warfare, 22
Universal Church of the Kingdom of God, 94
urban, definition of, 42, 290
urban autochthony politics, 92
urban bias, 238, 246; moving beyond, 239
urban cleansing, 27
urban consolidation, 205
urban development strategy, scale of, 235 see also regional urban development
Urban Forum, 186
urban identities, new, 27–30
urban life: diversity of, 85; invisibility of aspects of, 84
urban malaise, 23
urban management, 53, 76
urban observatories, establishment of, 291
urban planning, state of, 188–9
urban planning professionals, education and research imperatives of, 184–99
urban policy, drivers of, 201–4
urban populations, mobility of, 90
urban prosperity, concept of, 286
urban research, relevance reflex of, 216
urban resourcefulness, 222
urban revolution in Africa, context of, 1–17
urban strategy, 237–56; arguments for, 253; failures of, moving beyond, 239–48
urban transition, African, not exceptional, 275
urbanisation: agenda for tackling of, 200–20; and development, 60–81; as factor of economic growth, 284; as global historical process, 257–83; crisis of, 204–5; definition of, 42–52; denial of realities of, 187; driving factors of, 52–3; dynamics of, 2; early, 266–9, 275, 277; global, theory of, 261–6; improving quality of, 61–2, 78; in postcolonial